SOCIAL HEGEMONY AND EDUCATIONAL INEQUALITY

**Problems of Ideology and Knowledge
in Educational History Texts**

JOE A. STORNELLO

JOHN D. CALANDRA ITALIAN AMERICAN INSTITUTE
QUEENS COLLEGE, CITY UNIVERSITY OF NEW YORK

STUDIES IN ITALIAN AMERICANA
VOLUME 13

John D. Calandra Italian American Institute
Queens College, CUNY
25 West 43rd Street, 17th floor
New York, NY 10036

ISBN 978-1-939323-10-1
Library of Congress Control Number: 2020938675

Table of Contents

Foreword

Public Education and the Immigrant Experience

This is the second edition of the book titled *Social Hegemony and Educational Inequality: Problems of Ideology and Knowledge in Historical Texts*, by Dr. Joe A. Stornello. First published in 1998 by the John D. Calandra Italian American Institute, it was a result of Dr. Stornello's dissertation research on the history and limitations of public education in the United States since the early 1800s. The book's first edition has been used extensively in graduate and undergraduate education courses and is now out of print. Although we decided to leave the book's organization unchanged in the preparation of this second edition, feedback from users of the original reported that they found the intellectual journey more direct by reading the preface and the introduction, and then jumping ahead to chapter 4, before returning to chapter 1. In the parlance of educational psychology, this order of reading helped them form a schema.

Dr. Stornello questions the historical interpretations of the education values among Italian immigrants. He demonstrates that the contention that Italian American family culture and customs stood in opposition to public school education and/or academic success in school had no basis in the working-class family or community. He clearly establishes the importance of education for Italian Americans and the social forces that directly influenced their experiences, opportunities, and choices. He calls attention to the positive attitudes and expectations Italian parents had of public school education and "the hope they invested in it as the most important second step (the first being the Church) of their children achieving a life free of backbreaking labor and insecure economic dependence"[1] (see also Stornello p. 262).

Today, society is still confounded by the governance and delivery of public education. Major urban centers like New York City still debate mayoral or district control of public education including the propagation of smaller and more specialized charter schools to compensate for large-scale public education failures.[2] Understanding the historical evolution of public education in the United States and its impact on the immigration waves over time can provide guidance to the continuing debates over public education delivery. For example, the development of Dr. Leonard Covello's community-based education for Italian and Irish immigrants in the early 1900s has now led to the establishment and success of some charter schools with greater community participation.[3] In addition, the growing importance of pre-K public education has evolved from the great interest in the Italian Montessori education of younger children previously available only at costly private education institutions.[4]

Each ethnic group that has immigrated to the United States dreamed of achieving a better life. One central aspect of this dream is the opportunity to improve oneself and increase the quality of life through education. Andrew Greeley's study *Why Can't They Be Like Us? America's White Ethnic Groups* claims that differences in behavior exist among the different white ethnic groups (including Italian Americans) in the United States. He maintains that the knowledge of a group's heritage is necessary to comprehend their behavior.[5] The Italians who settled in the United States form an ethnic group that brought with them a unique cultural experience. As in the case of other ethnic populations, in order to ensure survival in the United States, they had to assimilate into their neighborhoods, schools, and workplaces.[6] Based on such factors as cultural, generational, and financial considerations, each individual group, as well as persons within the groups, had a different view of educational attainment.

In *Melting of the Ethnics: Education of the Immigrants (1880–1914)*, Mark Krug recognizes the importance of educational achievements of Southern Italian immigrants and other new immigrants:

> Education for living in the American democratic society was the goal of schooling, with the clear implication that society was far superior to the mode of living so dear to the hearts of most immigrant parents. Most educators and teachers profoundly believed in the sacred mission of Americanization and had an abiding faith in the ability of the American environment and of American education to transform human nature. The "refuse of Europe" was to be bettered and ennobled by the infusion of American values and ideas.[7]

Even African American sociologist Booker T. Washington, in his studies of the wave of immigrants at the turn of the twentieth century, laid emphasis on the lowly rank of Italians and that the Italians were so ignorant that they were uneducable. He stated in *The Man Farthest Down* that "[t]he Negro is not the man farthest down. The condition of the colored farmer in the most backward parts of the Southern States in America, even where he has the least education and the least encouragement, is incomparably better than the condition and opportunities of the agricultural population in Sicily."[8]

Washington wrote this after his visits to the farm fields near Palermo and the Sulphur mines in the mountainous part of Sicily. He made this trip in 1910, a little more than a year after the tragic earthquake that killed 120,000 people in Messina and Southern Italy.[9] Washington, an educator, author, orator, and adviser to Republican presidents, was a leader in the African American community in the United States from 1890 to 1915. Representative of the last generation of black American leaders born into slavery, he spoke for the large majority of black people who lived in the South but had lost their right to vote through the efforts of southern legislatures. He contended that the wave of Italian immigration to the United States was to supplement the plantation work force in the South. They were generally perceived[10] to have fewer skills than the African American population in the United States. In fact, in Louisiana Italian immigrants (predominantly from Sicily) were paid less than the freed African American slaves.[11]

The majority of Italians who settled across the United States came from Southern Italy, mostly not from Italy's cultural centers, but rather from the rural countryside. Some had the basic educational skills of reading and writing, and others were proficient in manual trades, usually learned through apprenticeships. These Italians emigrated to enrich their lives and families and to provide good education for their children.

Early historians and sociologists believed that Italian immigrants were uneducated and uneducable and therefore did not value education. Thomas Kessner, in *The Golden Door: Italian and Jewish Immigrant Mobility in New York City, 1880–1915*, shows that, whereas both ethnic groups moved up the occupational ladder, the Italians limited their climb mostly to blue-collar work, possibly due to their need for immediate financial security. Kessner states that the Italians considered education an unimportant continuation of one's childhood. He says,

> the maintenance of this Italian attitude had the following effects on the offspring: the second generation's occupational similarity with their elders, especially in unskilled jobs; the persistence of offspring in Italian immigrant neighborhoods; the fact that the second generation did not differ much from the first generation in occupational interests; and the fact that participation in American schools made no great impact on their occupational viewpoint.[12]

These academics did not include in their analysis the fact that most Italian immigrants prior to coming to the United States did not have access to schools or were needed to farm the land to survive. Most towns in Southern Italy had no schools; some selected towns had schooling up to the fifth grade. In order to get further education Italians would have to send their children far away to towns or big cities, a costly proposition without friends or relatives in those locations with whom they could board. One of the immigrant objectives was to take advantage of schooling in the new country. The entire Italian nation was affected by the lack of schools in Southern Italy and educational underdevelopment of rural regions: Southern Italy did not develop until the 1960s and 1970s, after the country's second wave of global mass migration, including to the United States. The evolution of Southern Italian educators in Italy parallels the evolution of Italian American educators in the United States.

At the turn of the twentieth century, scholars of education believed that educating new immigrants would be disruptive to American society. In his book *Changing Conceptions of Education*, Ellwood P. Cubberley wrote:

> About 1882 the character of our immigration changed in a very remarkable manner. Immigration from the north of Europe dropped off rather abruptly and in its place immigration from the south and east of Europe set in and soon developed into a great stream. After1880, southern Italians and Sicilians; people from all parts of that medley of races known as the Austro-Hungarian Empire—Czechs, Moravians, Slovaks, Poles, Jews, Ruthenians, Croatians, Servians [sic], Dalmatians, Slovenians. Magyars, Romanians, Austrians; . . . began to come in great numbers. . . .
>
> These southern and eastern Europeans are a very different type from the north Europeans who preceded them. Illiterate, docile, lacking in self-reliance and initiative and not possessing the Anglo-teutonic conceptions of law, order and government, their coming has served to dilute tremendously our national stock, and to corrupt our civic life. ... Our task is to break up their groups or settlements, to assimilate and amalgamate these people as part of our American race, and to implant in their children, so far as can be done, the Anglo-Saxon conception of righteousness, law and order, and popular government, and to awaken in them a reverence for our democratic institutions and for those things in our national life which we as people hold to be of abiding worth.[13]

Dr. Joe A. Stornello in this book rejects the thesis that upward social mobility in American society happens by individual merit, the system of public school education is an economically and politically neutral institution dedicated to preparing all children for upward social mobility, and the failure of the majority of Southern Italian immigrants and their descendants to prosper educationally and economically parallel to English, Irish, and German, etc., immigrants is a consequence of low intelligence and/or alien and enduring cultural traditions, values, and beliefs.

Dr. Stornello's research has revealed that such claims as these have little or no merit. However, he does not think saying so will change public sentiment "for there is a great body of social and educational literature, which defends and reproduces these claims of a classless society, of meritocracy, of democratic and neutral educational institutions, and of Italian inferiority and/or alien cultural insularity."[14]

Professor Stuart McAninch of the University of Missouri-Kansas City in the introduction of this book supports Dr. Stornello's argument that

> practices on the parts of school and university educators which perpetuate unequal educational opportunity are legitimated by ideological distortions in historical texts which are commonly used in the courses. Stornello shows that claims by Olneck and Lazerson in *The School Achievement of Immigrant Children: 1900–1930* that patterns of retarded educational performance and social mobility by Italo-Americans over a period of several decades and generations result exclusively because of their "ethnic culture" are false and only based on a distortion of the educational institutions towards the immigrant populations.[15]

When Italians settled in the United States, the youngest family members were expected and obliged by law to attend American schools. Attending school was difficult: The immigrant (and second-generation) students confronted a language barrier, harsh peer scrutiny, unrealistic perceptions of America, and, in many cases, little or no career guidance. The early generations of Italian American families lived in poor neighborhoods, crowded into few rooms, and the home was not conducive to formal studies. Students, to help their families, would often hold one or two part-time jobs. In some families, Italian adolescents would be sent to the United States to live with relatives and *paesani*. These students experienced great anxiety about using their hosts' resources and achieving financial independence.

According to Mark Krug, Italian Americans were not so much indifferent to the prospect of being educated as they were concerned about the American education system itself. He writes,

Italian immigrant parents ridiculed the world of the Yankees and often did all they legally could to limit the years of school attendance. Italian boys were encouraged to go to work as early as possible to add to the family's income and the girls were taken out of school at the end of the legally mandated school attendance. Public schools were considered by many Italian immigrant families as breeding grounds of atheism and immorality. (Krug p. 33)

Dr. Stornello goes on to say,

The history of Southern Italian immigrants and their descendants in American society, therefore, may begin with their specific place of origin and all that constitutes the society and culture of that place. But as soon as the immigrants left the villages and towns of their origin they embarked upon a profound journey and experience of transformation. This transformation was not immediate, to be sure, but it was set in motion. It was completed in the cultural, economic and political context of the United States. The identification, establishment and explanation of the particularities of experience by Southern Italian immigrants and their descendants, in other words, must be reconstructed within the context of the social dynamics of American society's class, racial and religious conflicts. (p. xvi)

Many of the first- and second-generation Italian Americans chose to leave school at an age when they were able to make respectable incomes. Others who continued to higher educational levels found the ladder of success lonely. Especially after the postwar immigration wave, second-generation Italian Americans were expected to surpass the educational achievements of their parents. As families became more financially secure in the United States, educational opportunities became available to more individuals.[16]

Krug observes of the Italian immigrant community's employment evolution: "Many of these jobs were in the police, fire, and sanitation departments of large cities, in the post offices, and in the electric and telephone companies. Italians seldom occupied top positions in industry or commerce and many remained in blue-collar jobs particularly in the construction industry." On the other hand, Krug adds "both the Jewish and the Italian immigrations included artisans and intellectuals who provided a ready pool of potential leaders and spokesmen."

Commenting on this Italian immigrant reaction to the American public school system, Professor Rudolph Vecoli of the University of Minnesota (in

his testimony before the 1970 Pucinski Subcommittee on Education and Labor) said,

> It is clear that Cubberley wished not to Americanize, but to Anglo-Sax-
> onize the little immigrants. . . . Cubberley felt that the obligation of the
> public schools in areas of great immigrant concentrations was to assim-
> ilate the children of the newcomers into the superior American race. His
> view was generally accepted by school administrators and teachers. On
> the whole, they shared Cubberley's contempt for the cultures, values, and
> mores of the immigrants. Clearly, these influential Americans who dealt
> directly with the immigrants and their children did not believe in the melt-
> ing pot concept. They favored Americanizing or Anglo-Saxonizing.[17]

Leonard Covello, in *The Heart is the Teacher*, documents his own experience
as such an immigrant child at the turn of the twentieth century, coming from
Southern Italy with a strong educational value and succumbing to the American public education system. He succeeded (in spite of the concerns and obstacles documented by education historians) in becoming an Italian American
educator and earning a master's degree and a doctorate. Early on in 1911 he
questioned whether the Italian immigrant youth failures were a fault of the
teachers or of the system: "Maybe it's not the teacher so much as the system
which is wrong. Apparently the school is set up with only one purpose—termi-
nal goal, college entrance. Everything is cut and dried. The only trouble is that
the student is far from being cut and dried. He is an individual, with individual
needs and abilities."[18]

Dr. Covello, writing in *The Sociological Background of the Italo American School Child*, states that for the Italian parent (that is, the Southern Italian
peasant) the concept of education consisted of the parents imparting to their
children their society's cultural, social, and moral values. The Italian peasant,
Covello says, in order to maintain the Southern Italian way of life, opposed
education from outside the family. He indicated that the Italians' mistrust of
school was developed in Southern Italy and was maintained in America.[19]

Professor Richard Gambino, in *Blood of My Blood*, states that Italian
Americans' general lack of participation in organizations is an outcome of
their family attitudes (that is, a mistrust of organizations other than the family, including educational organizations and the Catholic Church). Because of
their negative attitude toward schooling and their desire to remain close to the
family, Italian Americans have gone into blue-collar rather than white-collar
work.[20]

Dr. Stornello writes:

Leonard Covello and his East Harlem community of mostly immigrant Italian and Irish Americans fought a hard political battle to secure a high school for the children there . . . Once a comprehensive academic high school was won it was quickly transformed into a community center. Covello consciously recognized and rejected the strategy of divide and conquer, and, instead, proceeded to use the school for the education (in its broadest conception) of the community, the families, and the children ... Benjamin Franklin High School did not follow Cubberley's prescription for training children to take their place in the social pyramid as efficient cogs. Both ambitions and social responsibility were fostered through an education which generated the knowledge needed to confront and respond to actual social needs and relations of the young students there and their families, that made students responsible for themselves and their community, and as human beings.

The students of Benjamin Franklin High School who became teachers, dentists, doctors, nurses, lawyers, artists, judges, state and federal representatives, government employees, and contributors to their East Harlem community make up a long list. (p. 271)

Benjamin Franklin High School represented a revolutionary transformation of the state system of public school education, but the change was not immediate. Covello's approach to community-based education is in recent years becoming more adopted by the public education system, especially to educate the newest immigration waves of Asians, Hispanics, and other global populations from Eastern Europe and Africa.

Even as late as the 1970s, many Italian American students were bilingual and had difficulty speaking English. A report titled *A Portrait of the Italian American Community in New York City* conducted by the Congress of Italo American Organizations (led by civil rights leader Mary Sansone) found that "Italian pupils with English language difficulties form the third largest ethnic group with language difficulties, according to the survey figures."[21] Many of those Italian bilingual students went on to become Italian American educators, not having forgotten their experience of feeling isolated and remote inside the U.S. public education system.

Today there are 630,000 Italian American educators from pre-K to post-secondary education. The growth of the percentage of Italian American educators is greater than the percentage growth of the Italian American population.

Italian American educators are also more widely dispersed geographically throughout the country. Research using U.S. Census data from 1980 to 2012 demonstrates how descendants of Italian immigrants prioritized the value of education in order to succeed in the education industry. Since 1980 the number of Italian American educators in the United States has more than doubled, from 275,500 to 643,270 in 2011. Italian Americans represented 5.6 percent of all the educators in 1980, approximately equal to the overall Italian American population, and increased to 7.8 percent in 2011, nearly two percentage points above the distribution of Italian Americans in the country. This growth was seen especially among women throughout the United States being more geographically diverse then the Italian American population geographic distribution. Since 1980 there have been significant education achievements among Italian American educators, especially in graduate studies. Italian American educators also have contributed to a larger proficiency in study of the Italian language.[22]

History demonstrates that Italian Americans are now a fundamental part of educating the United States population: At the turn of the twentieth century, Italian immigrants to the United States sometimes were considered uneducated and uneducable, but as of 2012 these immigrants and their descendants have achieved parity with and in some cases surpassed non-Italians in educational achievements.

Dr. Stornello clearly brings out the historical ruling-class influence on educating the immigrant populations that served efforts by the Anglo Saxon hierarchical population to downplay their abilities and channel them into vocational trades. However, this book stops short of addressing the contemporary social ruling class's imposing equal education by racial identification. Although not the intent of the original civil rights population groups, the result is that racially identifying equality has led to many divisions among public education and private education institutions, especially impacting the more recent immigrant populations.[23] Contemporary student performance analysis has been focused on racial achievements rather than on individual achievements that exist within the racial populations.[24] This is contrary to Greeley's assessment that "the knowledge of a group's heritage is necessary to comprehend their behavior." Racial identification obscures individual achievements.

In the 1980s and 1990s the civil rights regulations of the student population defined as white in New York City was considered to do better in high school graduation rates than student populations of other racial classifications. In a 1990 study by the John D. Calandra Italian American Institute, presented at an education conference chaired by former First Lady of the New York State

Matilda Cuomo, it was shown that Italian Americans in New York City were the third-largest high school dropout student population (21 percent) after Hispanics and blacks respectively.[25]

Following the Italian American high school dropout report, the CUNY Center for Puerto Rican Studies requested the Calandra Institute to conduct an analysis of the Puerto Rican dropout rate compared to overall the Hispanic rate.[26] It was found that the rate for Puerto Rican students was 35 percent, in contrast to that of non-Puerto Rican ethnic groups categorized as Hispanic at 26 percent. The Caribbean Institute requested a high school dropout analysis comparing Caribbean black Americans to other black Americans.[27] Results showed that the rate for Caribbean black students was 19.57 percent compared to 25.8 percent for other black Americans. In both cases, it was not the racial discrepancy that was of interest but the ethnic heritage identification. On the other hand, the Asian student identification studied only the achievements of Asian-heritage students at Harvard University while neglecting Asian ethnic heritage of Filipino, Indonesian, Malaysian, and Vietnamese, etc. achievements.[28]

Assessing student achievement by racial categories neglects ethnic populations within those categories needing special attention, whether in instruction, community, and/or family. After two hundred years of public education in the United States, societal educators are still thinking about the student population in terms of predetermined categories rather than delivering instruction according to individual needs and achievement and their ethnic heritage experience. In many ways, public education through democratic necessity is moving toward more individualization of the educational base via community programs and development of charter schools, but these efforts are still limited by racial identification that restricts individual learning and achievement. At present, student records are maintained by racial identification. This has resulted in limited student achievement analysis and in many cases obscures racially divisive population relationships in the schools.

This second edition of *Social Hegemony and Educational Inequality* is warranted because although the particulars of regulatory social engineering have changed, the objectives of divisive ethnic and racial subjugation and stratification have not. In the name of civil rights, distinct ethnic social groups are sorted, submerged, and categorized as racial groups. Rather than foster greater equality, as was perhaps intended, comparative racial categories tend to encourage competition and conflict between ethnic social groups for recognition, rights, and resources.

Moreover, the practice of inclusive racial categories obscures the actual experiences and struggles of particular groups embedded within one or another racial category. This is as true among ethnic social groups categorized as white (or Caucasian) as it is among ethnic social groups categorized as Hispanic (or Asian, Indian, Native American, or African American).

We live in a society and during an historical period where economic and political competition and distress are used to engender aggressive, often violent antipathy toward all immigrants, but especially toward people of color and non-fundamentalist religious groups. We see as well ethnic groups within the same racial category fighting one another for what they think is a better position from which to compete in U.S. society. It is also a period in which we are encouraged to abandon the struggle for democratic, rigorous public schools and instead pay for elitist private or charter schools that will more effectively separate, segregate, and stratify students by race, ethnicity, color, language, class, sex, religion.

It is a good thing, we hope, that those who are educators, or who will become educators, know well the society to which they work and the kind of society with which they prepare their students to engage.

Vincenzo Milione, Ph.D.
John D. Calandra Italian American Institute
Queens College
The City University of New York

ENDNOTES

1   Louis Gesauldi, *The Italian American Experience* (Lanham, MD: University Press of America, 2012).

2   http://www.centerforpubliceducation.org/research/charter-schools-finding-out-facts-0.

3   News about charter schools, including commentary and archival articles published in the *New York Times*. https://www.nytimes.com/topic/subject/charter-schools.

4   https://amshq.org/Families/Why-Choose-Montessori, American Montessori Society, 2019.

5   Andrew M. Greeley, *Why Can't They Be Like Us? America's White Ethnic Groups* (New York, NY: Dutton, 1971).

6   Thomas Sowell, *Ethnic America: A History* (New York: Basic Books, Inc., 1981).

7   Mark Krug, *The Melting of the Ethnics: Education of the Immigrants, 1880–1914. Perspectives in American Education* (Bloomington, Indiana: Phi Delta Kappa, 1976).

8   Booker T. Washington, *The Man Farthest Down* (New York: Double, Page & Company, 1913).

9   Salvatore LaGumina, *The Great Earthquake: America Comes to Messina's Rescue*(Youngstown, NY: Teneo Press, 2008).

10   Michel Huysseune, *This Country Where Many Things Are Strange and Hard to Understand: Booker T. Washington in Sicily* (*RSA Journal* 25/14).

11   Jerre Mangione and Ben Moreale, *La Storia: Five Centuries of the Italian American Experience* (New York: HarperCollins, 1992).

12   Thomas Kessner, *The Golden Door* (New York, NY: Oxford University, 1977).

13   Elwood P. Cubberley, *Changing Conceptions of Education* (Boston: Houghton Mifflin Co., 1909).

14   Joe Stornello, *Social Hegemony and Educational Inequality* (New York: The John D. Calandra Italian American Institute, 1998).

15   Michael R. Olneck and Marvin Lazerson, "The School Achievement of Immigrant Children:1900–1930," in *The Social History of American Education*, eds. B. Edward McClellan and William J. Reese (Urbana: University of Illinois Press, 1988).

16   Richard D. Alba, *Italian Americans into The Twilight of Ethnicity* (New York: Prentice Hall, Inc., 1985).

17   Rudolph J. Vecoli, "The Significance of Immigration in the Formation of an American Identity," in *The History Teacher*, vol. 30, no. 1 (November 1996).

18   Leonard Covello with Guido D'Agostino, *The Heart is the Teacher* (New York: McGraw-Hill, 1958).

19   Leonard Covello, *The Sociological Background of the Italo American School Child* (Leiden, Netherlands: E. J. Brill, 1967).

[20]   Richard Gambino, *Blood of My Blood: The Dilemma of the Italian-Americans (*Garden City, NY: Anchor Press/Doubleday, 1974).

[21]   Josephine Casalena, *A Portrait of the Italian-American Community in New York City.* Volume I (Congress of Italian-American Organizations, Inc., New York, N.Y. Jan 1975).

[22]   Vincenzo Milione, Itala Pelizzoli, and Carmine Pizzirusso, "Growth of Italian-American Educators in the United States," presented at the Italian American Studies Association Annual Conference, Toronto, Canada, October 19, 2014.

[23]   Civil Rights Act of 1964.

[24]   Executive Order 11246, signed by President Lyndon B. Johnson on September 24, 1965.

[25]   Vincenzo Milione and Joseph V. Scelsa, "Statistical Profile of Educational Attainment Including High School Dropout Rate Indicators for Italian American and other Race/Ethnic Populations: United States, New York State and New York City (1990)," *Italian-American Students in New York City, 1975–2000. A Research Anthology* edited by Nancy L. Ziehler. Studies in Italian Americana 3. John D. Calandra Italian American Institute, The City University of New York, 2011.

[26]   Vincenzo Milione, Joseph V. Scelsa, and Carmine Pizzirusso, "Statistical Profile of Educational Attainment and High School Dropout Rates Among Puerto Ricans and Other Hispanics in New York City," (New York: John D. Calandra Italian American Institute, City University of New York, 1991).

[27]   At the request of and in coordination with Dr. Veronica Udeogalanya of the Caribbean Research Center at CUNY's Medgar Evers College in 1991, the high school dropout rate was calculated compared to the African American high school dropout rate from the respondents in the racial category of black using the same statistical techniques as used in the Italian American analysis.

[28]   Anemona Hartocollis, "The Harvard Bias Suit by Asian-Americans: 5 Key Issues." *New York Times*. December 20, 2018.

Preface

It is reasonable to ask what a text bearing such a title has to do with the study of Italian Americans and their experiences in American society. To identify, establish, and explain the experiences of Italian Americans is not so easy unless we are prepared to embrace and accept as legitimate certain claims about economic and political relations in American society, the state system of public school education, and Southern Italian immigrants and their descendants. That is, upward social mobility in American society happens by individual merit, the system of public school education is an economically and politically neutral institution dedicated to preparing all children for upward social mobility, and the failure of the majority of Southern Italian immigrants and their descendants to prosper educationally and economically parallel to English, Irish, and German, etc., immigrants is a consequence of low intelligence and/or alien and enduring cultural traditions, values, and beliefs. My research has revealed that such claims as these have little or no merit. I do not think it is sufficient to say so however, for there is a great body of social and educational literature which defends and reproduces these claims of a classless society, of meritocracy, of democratic and neutral educational institutions, and of Italian inferiority and/or alien cultural insularity.

This essay does not begin with Southern Italian immigration or the Italian American experience. It does several other things which are a necessary prelude to reconstructing Italian American experiences. Specifically, it reconstructs economic and political relations in nineteenth-century American society before the great Southern Italian immigration; it reconstructs the relation between the dominant economic conditions of production, class, ethnic, religious, cultural and ideological conflict, and the formation of the state system of public school education; and it deconstructs the ideology, historical explanations, and rhetorical constructs of educational and social history texts.

This foundational critical research and critique is necessary if an intelligent and revealing inquiry into the historical particulars of the experiences of Southern Italian immigrants and their descendants in American society is to proceed and is to produce knowledge about their past and their present. Once it is established that the American society confronted by the new immigrants was already stratified by class and race, that it was riven by class, racial, and religious conflicts, and that its social, economic, and political institutions were shaped by this stratification and these conflicts, it is no longer adequate or acceptable to explain the experiences of Italian Americans as the manifestation of traits and tendencies unique to them alone. This essay illuminates revealing historical aspects of nineteenth-century American society, its tradition of antagonistic economic and political relations, and its tradition of democratic radicalism; and the essay illuminates the role of the state system of public school education as an instrument of class and ideological hegemony (and, soon after the great Southern Italian immigration, of economic and political stratification as well). In short, this essay undermines and refutes the social ideology of meritocracy, the educational dogma of achievement ideology, and the myth of public schools as economically and politically neutral institutions of a democratic society.

The history of Southern Italian immigrants and their descendants in American society, therefore, may begin with their specific place of origin and all that constitutes the society and culture of that place. But as soon as the immigrants left the villages and towns of their origin they embarked upon a profound journey and experience of transformation. This transformation was not immediate, to be sure, but it was set in motion. It was completed in the cultural, economic and political context of the United States. The identification, establishment and explanation of the particularities of experience by Southern Italian immigrants and their descendants, in other words, must be reconstructed within the context of the social dynamics of American society's class, racial and religious conflicts. Indeed, even scholars of Italian ancestry are apt to speak of colonies to describe those urban centers where Italian immigrants settled. Such language and description stresses voluntary congregation, and such an explanation of residential settlement depends on sociological explanations of transplanted identity and culture. But in places like Kansas City, Missouri, however, there were enforced covenants which dictated where people belonging to certain ethnic or racial groups could or could not reside.

In America immigrants from the island of Calabria, the island of Sicily, or from a mainland village near Naples were all classified as Italian, even though none of these immigrants were likely to understand the speech or customs of the other. In nineteenth-century and early twentieth-century Italy the marriage of a man from Naples to a young woman from Sicily would be extraordinary, but not so in America. And in America the racial classification and segregation of Italian immigrants in one city generated different sorts of experiences from those experienced by Italian immigrants in another city where class distinctions, instead of race, dominated daily life among all residents. Or, to put it another way, the experience of Italian immigrants in Genoa, Wisconsin, was different from that experienced in St. Louis, Kansas City, Chicago, Flint, New Orleans, or New York City. But, too, the Italian immigrants and their descendants can also be said to have common experiences by virtue of their participation in American society and its culture.

This essay lays the foundation for future explanatory research into the heterogeneous experiences of Italian Americans (or that of other American groups) as generated by their confrontation and interaction with American society. And it does this by demonstrating clearly why historical tendencies of poor educational and social progress of Italian immigrants and their descendants cannot be explained on the basis of claims about a homogeneous culture, a low IQ, or something else said to be unique to this American group. Indeed, by founding subsequent research on the historical continuity of antagonistic economic and political relations and their regulation in American society, it will be made clear that the Italian American experience is a distinctly American experience.

Joe A. Stornello
January, 1999

INTRODUCTION

Beyond Interpretation: Explaining
Social Hegemony and Educational Inequality

In *Social Hegemony and Educational Inequality: Problems of Ideology and Knowledge in Historical Texts*, Joe A. Stornello has provided a particularly important historiographic work in the field of educational history. While it provides a scholarly critique of a number of standard histories of American education, it also theoretically explores the role of historical narrative in ideologically legitimating school organization, cultures, and practices. Dr. Stornello especially stresses the role of historical narrative in legitimating two key functions of twentieth-century American school systems: 1) sorting and preparing students for different social class strata (and different and unequal access to power and opportunity) through such measures as tracking and standardized testing, and 2) inculcating a dominant capitalist and republican (but distinctly non-democratic) ideology. This book serves as an important theoretical underpinning for historical study of the educational (and social) experiences of children from immigrant communities in American school systems since it reveals much about how the education of predominantly working-class immigrant children during the nineteenth and early-twentieth century was conceived and planned by the architects of those systems—and problematizes how such conception and planning have been explained in histories of American education.

Dr. Stornello has written an interdisciplinary evaluation of historical narratives commonly used as texts in history of American education courses. For this study, he draws on Marxist and critical realist theories of social ontology, on critical realist social science methods of research and writing, on tools of textual analysis adapted from hermeneutics and literary criticism, and on study of secondary- and primary-source materials in economic, social, political, legal, and educational history. Using a genuine interdisciplinary method of inquiry that enables a coherent analysis and commensurate integration of the knowledge produced by these disciplinary fields, he critically explores the nature of historical knowledge as well as problems in assessing the correspondence of explanations within historical narratives to actual historical events and underlying social structures which determine those events (historical reality). Focusing his critical textual analysis on accounts of Horace Mann's career and ideas as the leading reformer in the movement during the antebellum period to establish state systems of common schools, he works to differentiate between knowledge which illuminates historical reality and ideological claims which mystify historical reality.

Dr. Stornello grounds his textual critiques in a careful, structural, essentially materialist explanation of American history during the late-eighteenth and nineteenth centuries. He stresses as the defining characteristic of that period the developing and continual class conflict between elites engaged in the construction of the modern capitalist economy and a non-democratic republican State and ideology, on the one hand, and non-elites engaged in the struggle to create viable democratic challenges to elite domination of economic and political institutions and ideological hegemony, on the other. He also addresses the often complex and contradictory relations of middle-class social groups to both the governing and laboring classes, and he identifies the key professional, administrative, and technical roles these social groups played in the formation, legitimation, and maintenance of rudimentary state systems of common schools.

Dr. Stornello posits the formation of rudimentary common-school systems within the class conflicts characteristic of the mid-nineteenth century, and he particularly highlights as a significant factor the failure of elite political, economic, and ideological measures to generate a malleable laboring class. Elite support for formation of state common-school systems was in response to that fundamental failure, as key elements of the governing classes turned to systematization of schools to achieve levels of hegemony and social control which other institutions had failed to achieve.

Dr. Stornello's critical analysis of texts in educational history rests on his comparison and contrast of narrative explanations of the common-school movement and Horace Mann's role within that movement to his structural analysis of late-eighteenth and nineteenth-century American history. Addressing influential texts from Ellwood Cubberley's *Public Education in the United States* to *American Education: A History* by Wayne Urban and Jennings Wagoner, Jr., he works to identify patterns of distortion or exclusion of evidence. He especially focuses on documenting a pronounced tendency among writers of texts commonly used in university history of education courses to deny or obscure the roots of the common-school movement in the class conflicts characterizing mid-nineteenth century American society—and to also deny or obscure the hegemonic nature of emerging school systems.

Dr. Stornello carries his analysis a step further by reflecting on the consequences of failure to accurately represent efforts to establish state systems of common schools and the relationship of those efforts to structural processes shaping the American economy, state, and society during the mid-nineteenth century. In this regard, he considers how ideological claims in educational histories which mystify the origins of American school systems can contribute to the perpetuation of unequal educational opportunity through the legitimation among teachers and administrators of an achievement ideology which does not correspond with the social structures and stratified unequal social relations characteristic of a capitalist republic in the United States. Ideological mystification of the sort commonly found in histories of education promotes the myth that success comes through individual effort and educational achievement rather than understanding of the reality that chances of individual success are contingent on factors correlated with social class which themselves are structurally determined. Such mystification, he cogently argues, also de-legitimates collaborative organization on the part of non-elite social groups to rationally analyze, resist, and seek viable alternatives to non-democratic institutional practice characteristic of the capitalist economy and republican State.

Careful readers may not agree with particular factual claims and critical interpretations made by Dr. Stornello. They may not entirely agree with Dr. Stornello's theoretical approach to establishing correspondence between historical reality and historical explanation. Yet, I suspect that most will find it difficult to argue against his claim that failure to methodically and rigorously seek that correspondence leaves readers vulnerable to ideological mystification. Even more daunting to those of us who teach the historical and social foundations of American education is Dr. Stornello's argument that practices on the parts of school and university educators which perpetuate unequal educational opportunity are legitimated by ideological distortions in historical texts which we commonly use in our courses.

Certainly, Dr. Stornello has theoretically demonstrated that historical explanations have powerful ideological consequences for how organization and cultures of school systems are conceived, placed into social context, and either legitimated or problematized. His work powerfully suggests that in the cases of both the construction of historical explanations and the evaluation of historical explanations, the social stakes are extremely high. He explores the devastating intellectual and social consequences of lack of theoretical rigor in historical research and dialogue—and in the application of that research and dialogue to social and educational analysis.

Consequently, Dr. Stornello has presented careful and critical readers who profess commitment to democratic educational ideals with a formidable and vitally important task: to assess whether he has established the correspondence which he has sought to establish. If he has fundamentally succeeded in identifying the structures which have been determinative in the historical development of capitalism and the republican State in the United States, then his critique of the history of American school systems is damning from the perspective of democratic ideology—and the implications of his analysis for educators in the field of history of education and in schools are sobering. If, however, the reader concludes upon reflection that he has not succeeded either in providing a viable theoretical means for establishing correspondence or in successfully implementing those means in constructing his own historical explanation and his critique of the explanations of others, then it becomes the intellectual (and ultimately social) responsibility of that reader to work to construct a more viable means for defining historical reality and establishing correspondence, and to construct an historical explanation which more closely corresponds with historical reality.

Stuart McAninch, Ph.D., Associate Professor
Urban Leadership and Policies Studies in Education
University of Missouri-Kansas City

CHAPTER ONE

THE PRESENT IS INCOMPREHENSIBLE IF THE PAST IS UNKNOWN: IDENTIFYING THE OBJECT OF STUDY

Introduction

This extended essay is the first stage in a larger critical research project aimed at unravelling the history of social relations in American society in order to identify, establish, and explain the actual intersection between the state system of public school education and the social experiences of Italian-Americans, in particular, and selected other ethnic and racial groups. These American groups have largely remained dependent for generations on wage labor, have largely occupied subjugated and/or subservient social positions, and whose material possessions have seldom extended beyond home ownership and items of necessity. These long standing socio-economic class positions do not correspond to the achievement ideology of public school education. Nor does the social experience of significant numbers of these different American groups correspond to Horace Mann's contention that a public school education "prevents being poor." I am particularly interested in identifying and establishing empirical, actual, and structural explanations for the constitution of these historically enduring social relations and apparent social/educational incongruities as distinct from reductionist, racist, cultural and/or ideological explanations.

The obvious place to look for knowledge about the history of American society and the state system of public school education are educational history texts. The explanations I found in this body of literature and have overheard in public discourse are interesting — not least of all because a thread of consensus, or common ideology, runs through them. Is it true, as Olneck and Lazerson claim in their 1988 essay, that patterns of retarded educational performance and social mobility by Italo-Americans over a period of several decades and generations result exclusively because of their "ethnic culture"?[1] Is it true that Black-American students, regardless of parental economic status, consistently score lower on the SAT test than all other groups except Hispanic-Americans because of their "culture" as Dinesh D'Souza explained at a 5/14/96 forum debate over affirmative action?[2] Or, is it true, as Thomas Sowell argues in *Ethnic America*, that the retarded educational performance and static social mobility of Italo-Americans, and of Black Americans as well, for much of the twentieth century can be attributed to cultural obstacles and intellectual incapabilities?[3] In each case the identification and explanation of incapability and/or inferiority of these American groups depends upon interpretations of the state system of public school education and its relation to society (historically and currently) constructed by educational historians. The consensus among these explanations is in fact consistent and coherent with the dominant ideological paradigm of society and schools.[4] But do discursive consensus and ideological coherence constitute valid explanations? To answer this question I turned to historians and social scientists in other disciplines.

My interdisciplinary research into the history of American society and the state system of public school education, however, uncovered profound contradictions between explanations of social inequality given by numerous educational historians and those of historians in other disciplines. For example, the educational historian Lawrence Cremin claims universal public education was always the humanitarian cause closest to Horace Mann's heart.[5] The historical biographer Jonathan Messerli, on the other hand, establishes a different explanation through a definitive examination of primary documentary evidence. Before Mann was persuaded to exchange his position as President of the State Senate and become Secretary to the Board of Education for the State of Massachusetts, his connection to education had been limited to his strategy of elevating himself in Dedham's local politics — to which end he joined the Masons, and got himself elected Justice of the Peace and to the local school committee. A civic duty he fulfilled by giving one speech.[6] The educational historian Carl Kaestle claims Stephen Simpson was a nineteenth century labor radical whose commitment to protecting private property was representative of the laboring class — a claim supporting his argument against divisive cultural, ideological and material class conflict during the antebellum period.[7] Joseph Dorfman, the economist and historian of American political economy, demonstrates to the contrary that Simpson was a middle-class capitalist and political opportunist.[8]

Thus instead of finding the illumination of the history of social relations, my research has uncovered profound obstacles to the production of authentic knowledge about what American society actually is and its history. The authors of educational history texts tend to construct explanations of the history of public school education based on interpretations rooted in the traditional Liberal philosophy of individualism and its atomistic theory of society. Accordingly, society is not structurally organized around a particular mode of economic production — e.g., capitalism. Such a society is not constituted by social relations of a particular kind. An atomistic conception of society obscures the social power of cultural meanings, ideological constructions and conditioning material relations upon aggregate class behaviors and experiences[9]. Within an atomistic society, in other words, there are no necessary associations between individuals, and such associations as do exist (or that have been observed as existing in the past) come to be through voluntary agreements and/or contracts between individuals. Following the logic of the atomistic conception of society, any observed relation between social experiences and schools must be coincidental and circumstantial rather than structural in origin. In other words, success/failure of individuals in society is determined by the presence/absence of individually endowed abilities.[10]

When we step outside the coherent circle of Liberal philosophy and its conception of atomistic society, glaring problems become apparent, especially in those educational history texts where the author explains society and public school education as if the rhetoric, i.e., ideology, of particular individuals, or groups of individuals, was or is in fact reality. The first and most significant problem is certain educational historians have accepted the ideology of the rul-

ing class as knowledge about the actuality of social relations and social institutions and the relation between them. The second problem emerges when we
acknowledge that an ideology can be coherent and yet wrong. That it is in fact
wrong stems from the ideology's lack of correspondence with reality. A third
problem is the presence of inconsistencies and contradictions between their
operant Liberal philosophy and certain explanations, as when some educational
historians claim that public school education socially mediates class positions.
Inconsistency is again apparent when they claim that public school education is
a mechanism and resource of upward social mobility. In other words, these
authors tend to substitute theories of atomistic society and individualism (i.e.,
the tenets of dominant ideology) with theories of social structures and hierarchically organized class divisions. If schools exist independent from society, then it
is impossible for them to effect the constitution of social relations — which are,
after all, voluntary. If schools are structurally integrated in society, then they
may have some effect on the constitution of social relations — which are what
they are by virtue of existing within society, by being socially organized and
involuntary. Thus many leading educational historians have misunderstood the
constitution of society, the state system of public school education, and social
relations, or they have covered it up. In either case, inconsistencies and contradictions undermine their explanations and render them invalid.

Except by idealism or ideological mystification, explanations about the particularities of one historical moment cannot be constructed out of explanations
of another, nor can knowledge of society be produced out of incongruent knowledge claims about a specific historical social reality. History is the dynamic
record, or remains, of social change and/or transformation that has reached a
more or less identifiable point of completion. The War of Independence, the
formation and institutionalization of the state system of public school education,
and the Civil War mark such points in American history, as does the period of
mass migration from Eastern and Southern Europe to the United States that
roughly began in 1880 and ended about 1924. The particular changes and/or
transformations such events generated in American society represent points of
transition from one state of being and associative living to another. To adequately understand the constitutive social reality of such events (as changing
and/or transformative), it is first necessary to have knowledge of the historical

particularities of society before the actual events affecting cultural, ideological and/or material social relations occurred. It is only through this retrodictive process that social ideologies and material relations which continue, are initiated, or cease to be (and degrees thereof) after such events can be adequately identified, established, and, however tentatively, explained. It is clear from this that events and social experiences in the first half of the twentieth century cannot be adequately identified and explained without first resolving the pervasive inconsistencies and contradictions governing historical explanations of the antebellum period. Historically specific social relations and experiences in twentieth century America cannot be made comprehensible if we have no coherent and corresponding explanation of the historical formation of the state system of public school education as an integral component of nineteenth century American society. This is the case because the explanations of twentieth century social relations by so many educational historians and their social policy allies are premised on their correlative explanations of public schooling and the nature of its socializing function in the nineteenth century. This first stage of the larger research project is thus largely but not exclusively restricted in scope to the antebellum period of American history. I have further restricted the focus of this stage of research to social relations and the formation of the state system of public school education. I focus in particular on those historical explanations of social relations in the antebellum period found in the seminal educational history texts published in the twentieth century — especially as they center around Horace Mann. Indeed, it is in this period that the dominant ideological paradigm of the historical reality of American social relations and the state system of public school education is rooted and from which it emerges. To paraphrase Horace Mann: as the child is father to the grown man, just so is the public school to society and the state.

The objectives of this essay are to exegetically analyze and deconstruct the explanations, distortions, and silences identified in the educational history texts, and, in contra-distinction to the dominant ideological paradigm (which I identify and explicate in the next chapter), to establish a coherent explanation of the state system of public school education within a corresponding historical context of economic and political relations.

Methodology

I will adopt a methodology which resolves these problems of obscured history and theoretical incoherence on one hand, and on the other is also consistent with producing knowledge about actual events and social relations that can be distinguished from strictly interpretive and/or ideological assertions. This methodology is in fact dictated by two distinct objects of study: economic and political relations in history, and educational history textbooks which claim to explain these social relations in history. The first requires an historical reconstruction. The second requires exegetic analysis and deconstruction.

For the task of reconstructing social relations in the historical context in which the state system of public school education emerged, I employ Karl Marx's social theory. More consistently and coherently than the adherents and practitioners of other social science theories, Marx's dialectical critique of capitalist society clarifies the relation between human agency and historical materialism, and the reciprocal interactions of intersubjective cultural meanings, ideology and material conditions. He illuminates the integrating continuities between the economic and the political in the constitution of society. Marx's theory and methodology of social study as science, moreover, enable the identification of historical and human forces manifested in capitalist society, and, beyond this, the identification of the sorts of social structures this particular mode of economic production generated, depended upon, and reproduced. These social structures ground and constitute social relations and also operate on the context within which human beings experience their lives — thus largely conditioning (in the absence of a revolutionary transformation of these structures) the historical course of society and the ideological forms necessary for it to rationalize, legitimate, and reproduce itself.[11]

Such a theory of society entails a realist ontology, which is: society is a structured entity.[12] I make use of a particular aspect from Marx's critique of capitalist society. This derives from his development of the *labor theory of value*, which establishes as the foundational condition of social relations in a capitalist society the premise that capital is itself a social relation rooted in a particular mode of production. This particular mode of production is most clearly evident in the appropriation by one class of the surplus value created through the productive labor of another, structurally subjugated class. In her elaboration of Marx's critique of bourgeois political economy, Ellen Meiksins Wood clarifies the point:

> The Mechanism of surplus value is a particular social relation between appropriator and producer. It operates through a particular organization of production, distribution and exchange; and it is based on a particular class relation maintained by a particular configuration of power.[13]

In other words, the social (economic and political) relations which exist between "appropriator" and "producer" are relations generated by the same structure that sustains the mechanism of surplus value appropriation. It is not a social relation specifically determined or voluntarily entered into by individuals, but is a particular relation constituted by society. And society is the ensemble of economic, political, and juridical social relations that both correspond with and reproduce a particular organization of production. The actual extraction of surplus value, the separation of the producer from his/her product — and hence, labor and its true value — is conditioned by unequal and antagonistic class relations which are reproduced by the capitalist state. It is this ensemble of structured social relations into which men and women are born, live, strive, understand themselves, and attempt to satisfy their diverse needs.

Marx's critique of capitalist society is distinguished first by a social theory rooted in the recognition that these conditions and relations of inequality (economic and political) do not emerge ineluctably from nature but were (and are) constructed and reproduced through socially organized human agency, and thus are changeable. And, secondly, by his life long enterprise in identifying and establishing the structural mechanisms of the capitalist mode of production around which social relations were organized, and that enabled one class to enrich itself through the appropriation of another class's labor value; and the identification and explanation of other structural and/or ideological mechanisms by which this process of appropriation and accumulation was protected, legitimated, and reproduced.[14] His critique of capitalist society emerged in fact out of his research into classical political economy and its lack of correspondence with actual social relations in society, and into the counterproductive and destructive tendencies within capitalism: the movement of capital accumulation that led to periodic expansion and concentration followed by crises of collapse and devastation. And, in an attempt to explicate the silent voids in bourgeois political economy, Marx identified those economic and political structures within the capitalist mode of production that generated a particular organization and condition of social relations: distinct stratification between the capitalist class and the working class and the sorts of conflicts and crises between these classes which, by the early-nineteenth century, had become commonplace in American society.

In capitalist society, incorporating as it does an extensive division of labor, there appear to be a plurality of class fractions and social positions.[15] The capitalist class and the working class are each internally stratified, and it is this condition which accounts for the plurality of fractions and positions. Differentiation between the capitalist class and the working class under conditions of apparent social plurality, therefore, entails mapping out a stratified configuration of assertive powers and/or liabilities along the lines of socially determined unequal property ownership and distribution of resources and rights.

For my purposes in this essay, the two classes, and the fractions within each, and the hierarchical location each occupies in society will be distinguished one from the other by: those positions whose powers include the construction and imposition of policy (laws), that protect and replicate a particular course of institutional, political and economic activity, and determine the distribution of resources and rights in society — and, too, whose powers include ownership of property and/or the means of production as well as the authority to decide the conditions under which production takes place; an ancillary group of positions — principally occupied by lawyers and judges and police — which directly facilitate and support and are aligned with those of the first group; those positions which do not include direct economic and political policy making or ownership of the means of production, but which do entail surrogate powers of authority and control over others in behalf of the interests the capitalist class; those positions which neither include the ownership or control over the means and conditions of production, nor powers of authority over others, but which do

entail the production of surplus value which is appropriated by others; and, finally, those lowest social positions occupied by unskilled laborers, the poor without resources of any kind, and the lowest position of all — that occupied by the
indentured and enslaved. The capitalist class and the working class, and the
different class fractions of each, make up society, are in fact generated by a
particular social organization of economic conditions of production, and, hierarchically, each reflects disproportionate shares of the resources produced by
society. In short, all social positions have attendant powers and/or liabilities
which are structurally determined.[16] Transformation of a particular order of
economic and political relations — which entails particular class and social positions — thus entails the transformation of those structures which make society what it is. As a matter of fact, social relations in both the colonial and
antebellum periods[17] are nearly incomprehensible without a clear understanding
of the integration of the economic and political in the constitution of American
society.

  This theory of society, of economic and political relations (i.e., a realist
social theory, the labor theory of value, stratified classes, and social position)
constitute the critical criteria I have used to historically reconstruct social relations in late colonial and antebellum American society. This historical reconstruction provides the critical context within and against which to exegetically
analyze and deconstruct the educational history texts. First, what do these
particular texts say society is, what do they tell us about Horace Mann and the
formation of the state system of public education in particular, and what do they
tell us about the function of schools in the context of social relations? Second,
and equally important, what do they not tell us about these things? Third, what
kinds of things do they not address at all? Finally, when taken together, what
distinctions can be made between the historical reconstruction of social relations and the explanations of this object of study offered by the educational
historians? The historical reconstruction which provides the critical context for
this exegesis and deconstruction is meant to accomplish three additional objectives: it is meant to be a constant reminder that society exists (or, in this case,
existed) independent of the text and outside the discourse about it; and, secondly, it is meant to provide the basis for a new understanding of the state
system of public school education as a structural component of society. Lastly,

by being rooted in a realist social theory, the historical reconstruction of social relations identifies, establishes and explains relevant socioeconomic circumstances in society which will provide a standard by which to distinguish between ideological constructions and valid knowledge claims.

This last objective is especially important and necessary in view of the fact that individual and groups of texts are often coherent within their own rhetorical construction. And too, the majority of educational history texts more or less cohere with the dominant ideological paradigm of the relation between public school education and society. The continuity and endurance of this ideological paradigm of schools and society extends from Horace Mann to the present day. In addition, powerful groups in society have historically had a vested interest in protecting and replicating this ideology.[18] Thus, as long as one remains within the textual and ideological sphere of educational history one could be and often is overwhelmed by astonishing consistency and coherence. It is, however, a rhetorical, i.e., ideological, coherence.[19] Accepting a rhetorically, an ideologically constructed view of reality, and proceeding as if this idealist ontology were in fact what actually is constitutes an epistemic fallacy of a mystifying kind.[20] This is easily illustrated in the present when we hold up achievement ideology (which posits as real the equation: education = upward mobility) on one hand and the legion of unemployed or severely underemployed Ph.D.s on the other hand. In other words, rhetorical coherence is revealed as mystifying ideology the moment we attempt to establish a measure of correspondence between such an assertion and its actuality in society. Indeed, it is the absence of such a correspondence that makes such assertions ideological.

In addition to exegetic analysis and deconstruction of the educational history texts addressed in this essay, I also endeavor (as indicated above) to establish correspondence, or its absence, between the authors' explanations of society, schools, and social relations, and those given by other researchers into the same historical period and events. I intend through this process to establish a minimal test of correspondence, as a definition of truth rather than a criterion of truth.[21] For example: author-A claims that in spite of historical evidence of material differences and unequal distribution of resources and rights, ideological consensus in fact exists between these different social groups and, in effect, unifies and directs their beliefs and behaviors in institution building; but author-A does not elaborate on the evident differences, nor illuminate the constituted social relations which generate these differences. Authors-B, -C and -D, on the other hand, working in other disciplines, have uncovered and preserved evidence of both consensus (among the ruling elite of society and surrogate allies) and intense cultural, ideological and material conflict (between the consensus class and the laboring classes) in the same historical period of study; in addition, authors -B, -C and -D have identified and established active mechanisms employed by the dominant group to fragment, subvert, and/or pacify segments of other classes with whom it is in conflict. The first author's claim falls apart as an historical explanation when judged in relation to the knowledge claims (supported by corresponding evidence) of the second group of authors; i.e., consensus does not and cannot exist between antagonistic social classes having incommensurate paradigms of society. Thus, even though both classes might call for public education, for instance, the similarity of language cannot be reduced to the same understanding of what "public education" entails for each — particularly when these classes are fighting each other in the countryside, the polling booth, the workplace, on opposite sides of picket lines, in the streets, and in the courts and prisons over constituent structures undergirding unequal social relations. Author-A's explanation is thus incongruent with other explanations of the same object of study, and it fails the test of correspondence — i.e., author-A's explanation does not correspond to the particulars of social reality revealed by the other authors by virtue of being silent about specific empirical events and practices which undermine his/her explanation. Failure on both counts thus raises a critical question: what is author-A's larger *ideological* argument that depends on the consensus claim?

Society is an open system. It has many levels of experience and activity that may or may not be readily apparent or understood: for example, the experiences, interests and understanding of society held by dockworkers are not those of men constructing and imposing transatlantic trade policy — and the connection between one and the other is unlikely to be apparent or understood in the same way by either or both groups. Society has multiple layers of structures which interact: for example, the structured economic and political relation between appropriator and producer; the structured relation between race, ethnicity and/or religion and employment, areas of settlement, and wage rates;

economic structures that generate the concentration of wealth rather than the diffusion of wealth; legal structures which enable and empower and protect the interests of particular groups in society but not others; and so on. The multiple levels of experience and activity and the layers of interacting structures are sometimes consistent and sometimes contradictory. A particular event, e.g., the construction of a trade policy, tax laws, or a particular social institution, emerges out of the interaction of or tensions between several layers and structures of society and human actors occupying structurally specific class and social positions. It is not that such an event has many different explanations (it could have as many explanations as actors), but that an authentic historical explanation of the event entails an interdisciplinary reconstruction of the stratified reality of society out of which the event emerged — and what follows its emergence.

My ultimate interest in this essay is to identify and establish one small but complex piece of the whole. Contrary to those educational historians who adhere to the dominant ideological paradigm and ignore or deny the actual relation between the state system of public school education, unequal property relations and class conflict, and contrary to critics of this paradigm who argue that public school education was primarily and predominately for the preparation of a co-operative trained labor force, *I intend to demonstrate that the state system of public school education was constructed and implemented in the antebellum period as primarily a hegemonic institution.*

Summary of Essay

This first chapter identifies and explains the object of study (explanations of antebellum society and constituent social relations, Horace Mann, and the formation of the state system of public school education popularized in twentieth century educational history texts), and it elaborates the methodology undergirding the study. The second chapter identifies and explicates the dominant ideological paradigm governing the majority of educational history texts. This dominant ideology constructs for us what we are *meant* to know and understand about the relation between what Lawrence Cremin eloquently phrases as "freedom, popular education, and republican government."

Chapter three provides an historical overview of the antebellum period of nineteenth century American society through a strategy which counterposes Marx and Mann, both of whom published critiques of capitalism in 1848. This overview will be largely concerned with the structure of society, socio-economic circumstances, and antagonistic class relations found in and around the northern and northeastern states, which, in turn, will be related to the formation of the state system of public school education. Reference to other states, e.g., North Carolina and Ohio, will be made for purposes of identifying corresponding social relations. Slavery as a foundational condition of social relations in the Southern states makes the issue of universal public education there a mute question during the historical period examined in this essay. However, I want to make clear here that all rhetoric about free men, popular education, upward social mobility, representative government, etc., in antebellum America (and reproduced by a majority of twentieth century educational historians) must be considered against the social reality of slavery, and the systemic political and economic subjugation of women and indentured laborers. Moreover, it should be kept in mind that limited white male suffrage was *granted* to rural and urban laboring white men as a compromising hegemonic response to their vigorous and sometimes violent demands, e.g., their armed insurrection in Rhode Island. In other words, freedom during the historical period under examination herein was a popular ideal but seldom, if ever, a reality extended to or experienced by many persons.

Chapter Four is an interim review of the critical issues relevant to the object of study. Chapter Five is an exegetic analysis and deconstruction of the historical and/or ideological explanations found in the educational history texts selected for critique in this essay. In Chapter Five I recognize the critical event of Jonathan Messerli's biography of Horace Mann, which has proved to be a historical point of change in the writing about American public education history.[22] Chapter Five is organized around those texts published prior to 1968, and those texts published during or after 1968.[23]

Chapter Six concludes the essay. By the end of this essay I will have established several things: *first*, only a second revolution would have enabled the hegemonic triumph of revolutionary democracy and democratic social relations over republican ideology and unequal social relations, i.e., the new nation state inherited the unequal class structure and social positions of the British colonial order, and the ruling class acted quickly to secure its domination of society and the state. *Second*, class conflict was nearly continuous from the 1740s onward, but in the late 1820s and again in the late 1830s the laboring classes, led by radical autodidact laborers, organized themselves and articulated a coherent democratic economic and political program and hegemonic vision in opposition to the dominant ruling class and its ancillaries. *Third*, the lawyers and courts had secured the triumph of republican ideology (by embracing English common law as the law of the land) very early. Indeed, as Christopher L. Tomlins establishes,[24] it was in place before the War of Independence and reproduced after — but the confrontation between democratic culture on one hand and republican ideology on the other had to wait until the laboring classes began to experience the effects (initially through the conspiracy trials, imprisonment, and the repression of labor associations) and understand the source. *Fourth*, with republican ideology in place it had to be protected, extended, and reproduced — because it was necessary to legitimate (i.e., to cover up) the mechanisms of appropriating and accumulating capital, and for securing the power necessary to determine the unequal distribution of property, rights and resources. And given the failure of factional political parties and nativism to squelch democratic culture and insurgency, and the failure to fully establish republican hegemony, a new disciplinary institution was deemed essential: the state system of public school education.

There are four reasons which Horace Mann explicitly articulates (items a - c) or anticipates (item "d") undergirding this decision: (a) The minds of children were believed empty and their behavior plastic, thus all one had to do to secure social control (i.e., hegemony) was to control what constituted consciousness. This would be accomplished, according to Mann, by carefully determining the belief system into which children were inculcated. This inculcation, in turn, would determine what the child as adult would believe about the constitution of society and their place in it, and, as well, their behavior would correspondingly be morally disciplined to make them fit for this society. (b) The critical problems of the existing order of community schools were: they exposed social inequities in the distribution of resources and privileges; for typically only children from well-to-do families were able to take advantage of these schools beyond the lowest grades. And, for the wealthy, a separate system of academies or tuition schools existed. The community schools, moreover, generally lacked systemic structural mechanisms for determining who or what ideas filled the child's mind. And, too many people stayed in these local schools just long enough to learn to cipher and read, resulting, some believed, in an undisciplined tendency to read the "wrong" newspapers, pamphlets, and books and thus "misunderstand" the true nature of economic and political relations. (c) The real problem with the dissemination of literature written by autodidactic labor radicals was their inflammatory ideas about society inspired wrong ideas about the economy and politics in the minds of those who read these texts or heard about them. This tendency thus made it prudent for the ruling class to inculcate the children of laboring classes who would and could attend the new institution. More importantly, however, it was necessary to ideologically insulate the children of the white, Protestant, middling class against the corrosive and destructive ideas of "socialists," "anarchists," "levelers," and "agrarians," and thereby securely absorb them into existing social relations. And (d), by the early 1850s the professional and middling class came to see that the state system of public school education, especially the construction of high schools, would significantly advantage their children over both native and immigrant laboring class children — most of whom seldom had more than a few years of schooling, and even of those who finished grammar school few were able to continue into and graduate from high school. The *fifth* thing I thus establish is the state system of public school education was a disciplinary institution, but more than this it was a mechanism of republican ideology and hegemony. The U.S. Constitution had effectively isolated the location of rule from direct access of the people, and, too, it positioned the federal state in a superseding position over individual states. The courts were empowered by the Constitution and by common law precedent to mediate and intervene between legislative action and private property, and had by the early 1800s secured the employer's ownership of the laborer's physical laboring force (it was bought and sold in the wage exchange). What remained was to inure children to the legitimacy of these unequal social relations, and the state system of public school education was the social institution by which to insure the capture, control and transformation of their minds. Presto (so it was thought): ideological hegemony over every school child, which over time would translate into accommodating, cooperative individuals and social order. It is against and within this historical context that the explanations of social relations and the formation of the state system of public school education will have been critiqued.

And finally, in closing, I will look at what the knowledge produced about the connection between the state system of public school education and social relations in the antebellum period suggests for the larger research project, of which this essay is the first stage.

ENDNOTES

[1]   Michael R. Olneck and Marvin Lazerson, "The School Achievement of Immigrant Children: 1900-1930," in *The Social History of American Education*, eds. B. Edward McClellan and William J. Reese (Urbana: University of Illinois Press, 1988), 257-286.

[2]   "'Resolved: Affirmative Action Should Be Abolished,' *The Nation versus The National Review*," (Washington, D.C.: National Public Radio Broadcast, 14 May 1996).

[3]   Thomas Sowell, *Ethnic America* (New York: Basic Books, 1981), 121.

[4]   See the next chapter of this essay for the identification and explication of this dominant ideology.

[5]   Lawrence A. Cremin, "Horace Mann's Legacy," *The Republic and the School: Horace Mann on the Education of Free Men*, by Horace Mann, ed. Lawrence A. Cremin (New York: Teachers College Press, 1957), 6.

[6]   Jonathan Messerli, *Horace Mann: A Biography* (New York: Knopf, 1971), 88-89, 223-224. While it is true that Mann as a representative in the General Court voted in favor of James Carter's legislative initiatives to promote a cohesive state system of public school education, so did a majority of other representatives. His votes demonstrate support, but from such meager evidence it is extraordinary to infer that public education was the cause closest to Mann's heart.

[7]   Carl F. Kaestle, *Pillars of the Republic: Common Schools and American Society, 1780-1860* (New York: Hill and Wang, 1983), 90-91.

[8]   Joseph Dorfman, *The Economic Mind in American Civilization 1606-1865*, 2 Vols. (New York: The Viking Press, 1946), II: 645-648.

[9]   Karl Marx, in his "Preface" to *A Contribution to the Critique of Political Economy*, trans. S.W. Ryazanskaya, ed. Maurice Dobb (New York: International Publishers, 1970), uses ideology in a specific sense. Laws, politics, arts, philosophy, religion — i.e., social institutions and practices — are ideological forms of the economic conditions of production. Ideology, used in this sense, is

distinguished from what is actual and knowable about society, and tends, therefore, to rationalize and legitimate actual social relations by mystifying their relation to the economic conditions of production. There is another sense or meaning which has become attached to ideology: that is a belief system of a group/groups — as in a cultural system.

Antonio Gramsci, elaborating on Marx, argues that class conflict organizes itself around opposing ideologies, that is opposing paradigms of what society actually is. These opposing ideologies arise out of actual material conditions and social relations. The decisive element in this ideological conflict, he argues, ultimately falls on the side with the superior power to propagandize not only its ideology but also its hegemonic vision of the organization of society. And hegemony constitutes the imposition of a corresponding or linking relationship of the ideological to the material organization of society. In the absence of a truly democratic and egalitarian classless society, hegemony in capitalist societies is by definition the ideological and material domination of one class over others, which have become through various mechanisms of coercion and compromise more or less cooperative in the social organization of their domination. Ideological conflict as a component of class conflict does not become threatening to the dominant ruling class until the insurgent class's ideology is joined to a hegemonic vision which is successfully propagandized, wins increasing numbers of adherents, and thus directly challenges the dominant class's power of social control. See: Antonio Gramsci, An Antonio Gramsci Reader, ed. David Forgacs (New York: Schocken Books, 1988), 189-221.

I have chosen to distinguish between these two senses of ideology by retaining "ideology" to convey the first meaning, and I have substituted "culture" to express the second meaning. Culture, as expressed here, is the extensive and embracing collective of meanings, traditions, customs, values, norms, and language of society. All classes exist within the culture emergent from capitalist society (i.e., unequal economic and political relations, unequal distribution of resources and rights, and the commodification of all aspects of one's social existence), and different ideologies signify opposing subjectivities conditioned by material differences between classes.

[10]   See Michael Olneck and Marvin Lazerson, passim. Their's is an interesting embellishment of the Liberal thesis. Instead of individual peculiarities, they find that ethnically specific culture is the determining mechanism explaining different rates of academic performance and upward social mobility between distinct immigrant groups.

[11]   See: Karl Marx, "*The Communist Manifesto*," In *Karl Marx: Selected Writings*, ed. David McLellan (New York: Oxford University Press, 1977), 221-247. And, Karl Marx, *Marxist Social Thought*, ed. Robert Freedman (New York: Harcourt, Brace and Co./Harvest Books, 1968), 188-89, passim.

Marx's real contribution to the study of society as it actually is stems from his determined critical effort to identify, establish, and explicate the all important distinction between ideology and reality. Marx did not invent an ideology of property and class relations specific to capitalism and the social order which it generated. More comprehensively and accurately than others, he identified and explained economic and political relations of production and the structures undergirding them which distinguished capitalist society from other types of social organization of production. As a matter of fact, as chapter three of this essay will illustrate, socially organizing structures, along lines of unequal ownership of property and rights, were constructed, imposed, protected, and reproduced in America (before and after the War of Independence) by human actors occupying elite social positions who understood what they were about — even if they did not always anticipate or appreciate the long term consequences. These northern European Protestant aristocrats and capitalists did not need Marx's knowledge to construct an unequal and undemocratic society, but we need Marx's knowledge of capitalistic society as it actually was historically (and tends to be still) to help us make sense of what they did, how they did it, and of the social and historical consequences which obtained through their actions.

12   Marx, "Preface," *Critique.*

13   Ellen Meiksins Wood, *Democracy Against Capitalism: Renewing Historical Materialism* (Cambridge, U.K.: Cambridge University Press, 1995), 23.

14   See: Marx, *Value, Price and Profit*, trans. and eds. Eleanor Marx Aveling and Edward Aveling (Chicago: Charles H. Kerr & Company Co-operative, n.d.); Marx, *Grundrisse*, foreword and trans. Martin Nicolaus (London: Penguin Books, 1973); and, Marx, *Marx on Economics*, ed. Robert Freedman (New York: Harvest Books, 1961).

15   Both the capitalist class and the working class, as considered in this essay, are internally stratified into fractions; thus my references to socioeconomic groups, governing classes, working classes, etc., are all informed by the notion of class fractions.

16   The notion of social positions is drawn from the ontological relation between society and the individual conceptualized by Roy Bhaskar. To adequately apprehend the constitution of this ontological relation,

> we need a system of mediating concepts, encompassing both aspects of the duality of praxis, designating the 'slots', as it were, in the social structure into which active subjects must slip in order to reproduce it; that is, a system of concepts designating the 'point of contact' between human agency and social structures. Such a point, linking action to structure, must both endure and be immediately occupied by individuals. It is clear that the mediating system we need is that of the positions (places, functions, rules, tasks, duties, rights, etc.) occupied (filled, assumed, enacted, etc.) by individuals, and of the practices (activities, etc.) in which, in virtue of their occupancy of these positions (and vice versa), they engage. I shall call this mediating system the position-practice system. Now such positions and practices, if they are to be individuated at all, can only be done so relationally.

Roy Bhaskar, *The Possibility of Naturalism* (Brighton, Sussex, UK: The Harvester Press Ltd., 1979), 40-1; quoted in Andrew Collier, *Critical Realism: An Introduction to Roy Bhaskar's Philosophy* (London/New York: Verso, 1994), 149.

17   The separation between these two periods is a disciplinary convention. They are demarcated by the War of Independence which establishes the United States of America as a nation state. The war for independence from Great Britain does generate a structural social change — the elimination of the crown's domination of internal power relations. It did not, however, constitute a structural transformation of society. This distinction is critical, as I will establish and explain in chapter three, for it marks the meaningful divide between revolutionary democratic culture and ideology, and reactionary or conservative republican ideology about the constitution of social relations.

My adoption of culture, as explained in footnote 9 above, is specifically to convey the idea of shared beliefs about the constitution of social reality held by a particular group and expressed as a different articulation of a common meaning. These beliefs may or may not be ideological, but the point is they are held in opposition to those articulated by another group. Obviously, the ruling elite and its allies share cultural meanings. In the context of this essay, however, my use of culture is reserved for those groups in opposition to the dominant ideology of the ruling elite. Democracy, for example, is an emergent culture and complex of meaning which tends to be articulated (beginning in 1765 and continuing into the twentieth century) by agrarian yeoman, artisans, and laborers in ways distinctly different from Whig republicanism (and Federalist, Republican, Democrat, Nativist republicanism); and, too, life, liberty, the pursuit of happiness, equality, education, and freedom are a common language but whose meanings are bitterly contested between the governing classes and the laboring classes. A common language and culture thus exists for both groups as a social reference, but the meaning and understanding of one is incommensurate with the other. This difference is expressed empirically as economic and political class conflict.

[18]   See: Jean Anyon, "Workers, Labor and Economic History, and Textbook Content," *Ideology and Practice In Schooling*, eds. Michael W. Apple and Lois Weis (Philadelphia: Temple University Press, 1983), 37-60; Ruth Miller Elson, *Guardians of Tradition: American Schoolbooks of the Nineteenth Century* (Lincoln: University of Nebraska Press, 1964); Frances Fitzgerald, *America Revised* (Boston: Little, Brown and Company, 1979).

See as well: Diane Ravitch, T*he Revisionists Revised: A Critique of the Radical Attack on the Schools* (New York: Basic Books, 1978). And, Michael B. Katz's response: "The Politics of Educational History," in *Reconstructing American Education* (Cambridge, Ma.: Harvard University Press, 1987), 136-159.

[19]   "Rhetorical schemes differ in the way each element [of reality, writer or speaker, audience, and language] is defined, as well as in the conception of the relation of the elements to each other. Every rhetoric, as a result, has at its base a conception of reality, of human nature, and of language. In other terms, it is grounded in a noetic field: a closed system defining what can, and cannot, be known; the nature of the knower; the nature of the relationship between the knower, the known, and the audience; and the nature of language. Rhetoric is thus ultimately implicated in all a society attempts. It is at the center of a culture's activities." James Berlin, *Writing Instruction in Nineteenth-Century American Colleges* (Carbondale, Il: Southern Illinois University Press, 1984), 1-2.

[20]   ". . . **epistemic fallacy** - that ontological questions can always be reparsed in epistemological form: that is, that statements about being can always be analysed in terms of statements about our knowledge (of being), that it is sufficient for philosophy to 'treat only the network, and not what the network describes'." Roy Bhaskar, *Reclaiming Reality* (London, UK: Verso, 1989), 13.

When looked at in this way, then, and taking account of Berlin's definition in the note above, all rhetorical constructs of reality are, by definition, fallacies. Textual coherence, therefore, must not be mistaken as the determining criterion of what is real. Ultimately, the statement about its object must be distinguishable from the object itself; thus, the validity of a statement depends on both coherence and correspondence.

[21]   Andrew Collier, *Critical Realism*, 238-242.

[22]   Messerli's biography of Horace Mann first appeared as a Ph.D. dissertation in 1963 (Harvard). It was subsequently published in expanded form in 1971 by Alfred A. Knopf, New York.

[23]   This division roughly reflects when scholars began to reference Messerli's dissertation, and when a dramatic shift in Horace Mann's prominence in the reproduction of the dominant ideologi-

cal paradigm can be observed.

[24]   Christopher L. Tomlins, *Law, Labor, and Ideology in the Early American Republic* (Cambridge, U.K.: Cambridge University Press, 1993), passim.

CHAPTER TWO

HORACE MANN, FREEDOM, POPULAR EDUCATION, AND
REPUBLICAN GOVERNMENT: THE DOMINANT
IDEOLOGICAL PARADIGM

With the following four sentences the widely respected educational historian Lawrence A. Cremin introduced the acclaimed and influential Teachers College/Columbia University "Classics In Education" publication series in 1957:

> This series presents the sources of the American educational heritage. There could be no more appropriate beginning than a volume of selections from Horace Mann's reports (1837-1848) to the Massachusetts Board of Education. As the commanding figure of the early public school movement, Mann more than anyone articulated the nineteenth-century American faith in education. His work still stands as the classic statement of the relation between freedom, popular education, and republican government.[1]

It is important that Cremin's introduction for the entire series be understood as distinct from his introduction to Mann's writings, which comes several pages later in the same volume. The series' introduction is not simply reducible, for it is not preparatory to the elaborated explanation of Mann and his works found in the second, and it requires a different kind of reading and understanding. It is what it appears: The formal announcement of the "Classics in Education" series. It is also more than what it appears. The first of the four sentences is the key to unveiling the meaning conveyed by the next three sentences . . . and to alerting us that all four must be understood simultaneously. The series presents the "sources" of the American educational heritage, the whole edifice of which is built on and mediated through Horace Mann's work and his vision of American society and its system of public school education. It is, perhaps, the most concise statement embodying the dominant ideological paradigm about what constitutes the historical reality of the American system of public school education and its essential contribution to social relations after 1837 as constructed and reproduced in a great many educational history texts.[2] The embedded paradigm becomes visible when Cremin's declaration is restated as: The heritage of American public schools, for which we are largely indebted to Horace Mann and his work, is "freedom, popular education, and republican government."

My reading of Cremin is not arbitrary: the rhetoric has changed in thirty-nine years, and the emphasis is no longer specifically focused on Horace Mann,[3] but the ideological paradigm I have identified in Cremin's statement is recognizable in this passage from Urban and Wagoner's 1996 educational history text:

> While Katz sees the public school as an institution imposed by the establishment on the lower classes, his critics tend to see the common school, and public schools in the twentieth century, as imperfect institutions that nevertheless attempted to overcome, or mitigate, social divisions in American society and to help the members of the lower orders of that society to better themselves.[4]

Here, too, we find that the heritage of the state system of public school education extends from the common schools (i.e., Mann's work) to the present, and it is the social institution mediating the relation between individuals, society, and the state. This social institution is characterized as homogeneous — i.e., its socializing function is undistinguished by geographical location, historical time, or student population — and as the primary means of upward social mobility as well as the primary mechanism of creating social equality. Implicit in Cremin's statement but explicitly evident here is the claim that the state system of public school education was originated to uplift the "lower orders," thereby transform social relations, and, however imperfect, it has not deviated from this social purpose. The dominant ideological paradigm of the public school system education thus stresses "individualism," "freedom," "achievement," "upward social mobility," and "republican government." But the internal contradictions need to be recognized.

While our attention is directed toward the horizon of individual achievement and promised betterment, it is also directed away from actual conditions of unfreedom and stagnant or downward social mobility. And, too, we are not meant to see that the so-called transformative movement of public school education is to adapt the individual student(s) to society as it actually exists — rather than toward the transformation of society. The transformation of social relations, in other words, is ultimately illusory, for mitigation entails transforming the individual to accommodate existing social relations. If the dominant ideological paradigm were an historically accurate explanation of actual social relations, it would be unnecessary to argue the purpose and outcomes of the state system of public school education in society. We'd have freedom. We'd have relatively equal and democratic social relations. We certainly would not have whole classes ("lower orders") of Americans whose actual social conditions required institutional mitigation and betterment.

The construct of the dominant ideological paradigm stresses freedom and equality through upward social mobility which is mediated and enabled by public school education. For an ideology (any ideology) to have effective meaning, some degree of *correspondence* must exist between its constructive rhetoric of social reality and the empirical and actual conditions in society which the audience experiences. For the ideology of social betterment through the system of public school education to have meaning, a social reality of unfreedom, unequal social relations, and unequal distribution of resources and rights must be empirical and actual, and it must be acknowledged as a precondition to the transformation of the individual student and society generally. This social reality must exist if the rhetorically constructed relation between "freedom, popular education, and republican government" is to make sense. Moreover, this social reality must exist if "achievement ideology" is to have any meaning whatsoever. In circular fashion this brings us back to the state system of public school education as the means to upward social mobility, freedom, republican government, etc. The dominant ideological paradigm thus posits two social realities: the first is one of unequal social relations and unequal distribution of resources, and it is characterized by class conflict that often boils over into class warfare; the second is a construction of a stable, orderly society characterized by achievement and upward social mobility accomplished through the mediating institution of the state system of public school education. The first social reality is necessary — that it may be ideologically exploited — to give meaning to the second social reality. The first is the product of uneducated individuals, and the second emerges through the education of individuals. Embedded in this formulation is another construction: because the state system of public school education transforms unequal social relations and mindless class violence generated by lack of education into stable "same class" social relations and upward social mobility through education, then empirical evidence of continued inequality and class conflict must be explained by causes other than public school education and the society which it is claimed to generate.

Acknowledging actual social conditions on the way to focusing the discourse on achievement ideology, therefore, serves to obscure the institution's failure (inability, as a matter of fact) to alter unequal social relations throughout its one-hundred-fifty years history. And, to obscure this history is to also mystify the structural (as in real rather than ideological) function of the system of public school education in American society.

In other words, the dominant ideological paradigm does not negate the existence of unequal distribution of resources and rights; indeed, it needs the latter to use to its own advantage (i.e., to reproduce the false consciousness of achievement ideology inculcated in students.) But the way in which the dominant ideology presents these inequalities is both interesting and coherent. What the dominant ideology covers up is the fact that the existing inequalities are both the products and consequences of the unequally *structured* social (economic and political) relations. This cover up or mystification is the key objective of the dominant ideology. To accomplish this objective it (based upon and grounded in the historical Liberal ideology which dates from the 17th and 18th centuries) presents a conception of society within which there are absolutely no *necessary* relations among individuals. Specifically, this dominant ideology negates the fact that associative relations constitute the precondition for the very exist-ence of any society. Thus, premised on this view, society consists of "uncon-nected" (i.e., atomistic) individuals *and* any empirical relations among individu-als are constituted by each individual voluntarily — through agreements and contracts.

This illustrates why "individualism" is one of the most vital pillars of the dominant ideology. Thus the state does not have to create equality. All it has to do is preserve that which has already been posited ideologically (i.e., the natural existence of equality.) Therefore, if there are empirical inequalities in society they are the effects of particular individuals — lack of ability, motivation, etc. — and not structural. It is precisely within this ideological context that the domi-nant ideology can introduce such concepts as "achievement" and "upward mo-bility" without apparent contradiction. Basing upward mobility on individual achievement, and this upon individualist ideology, the dominant ideology simulta-neously precludes the portentous realizations that every society is inherently a structured entity and that the individual's access to life chances is determined by his/her social position within the constraining class structure.

It is precisely this dominant ideology which the educational historians cri-tiqued in this essay have accepted as the foundation of their "scholarship"! And, too, it is this ideology that constitutes the social *ontology* of these au-thors.[5]

It is not surprising, therefore, that in spite of a growing number of historians, economists, social scientists and cultural critics[6] whose research challenges the mystifying ideology of a free, democratic and open society accessible to all by virtue of the universality of American public school education, the dominant ideological paradigm remains enormously potent, and has no shortage of ardent and influentially positioned defenders among the socially recognized profes-sional and intellectual academic elite.[7] Indeed, Michael B. Katz's 1968 argu-ment that the system of public school education institutionally embodies and reproduces class conflict is still being singled out for attack three decades after its publication.[8]

Using Horace Mann as the fountain head of American "freedom, popular education and republican government" makes sense within the context of the dominant ideological paradigm and is, in fact, a rhetorical invention which has had long standing utility. Horace Mann was the commanding social architect of the ideological construction and the institutionalization and imposition of the state system of public school education in the nineteenth century. During the years between 1837 and 1848 Mann did secure a state system of public school education in Massachusetts and he did propagandize its necessary and pressing economic and political adoption throughout the nation and its territories. His writings on the subject of public schools and their relation to society are the "classic statement" in as much as they have been and are still reproduced in many parts of the world and continue to be used in the education and training of American public school teachers. And, the social objective of the school system as constructed and elaborated by Mann remains an undergirding, foundational principle of curriculum, subject content, pedagogy, and social organization in late twentieth century American public schools.

These points are generally accepted as true by most if not all educational historians. To recognize these details about Horace Mann and his abiding influence, however, does not explain them. The explanation of the school system's social objective as constructed by Mann is, according to the version embodied in and propagandized by the dominant ideological paradigm, to raise-up individuals of the common orders of American society that they may exist in social harmony as free, equal, educated, moral, industrious, and productive Americans. According to Mann's own writings, however, the schools' positive objective was not the redistribution of resources but to exercise its singular and superior capacity for capturing and inculcating the *consciousness* of every school child.

> It is an experiment which . . . offers the highest authority for its ultimate success. [. . .] "Train up a child in the way he should go, and when he is old he will not depart from it." This declaration is positive. If the conditions are complied with it makes no provision for a failure. Though pertaining to morals, yet, if the terms of the direction are observed, there is no more reason to doubt the result, than there would be in an optical or a chemical experiment.[9]

The direction the children were to go as determined by the state system of public school education would inure them to the legitimacy of republican ideology and stratified unequal social relations. Mann did not separate the public school from society, indeed one was the origin of the other:

> . . . the true business of the schoolroom connects itself, and becomes identical, with the great interests of society. [. . .] As 'the child is father to the man,' so may the training of the schoolroom expand into the institutions and fortunes of the State.[10]

Mann was also clear about the pressing necessity for adopting his program of social objectives to undergird the system of public school education:

> [Education] does better than to disarm the poor of their hostility towards the rich; it prevents being poor. Agrarianism is the revenge of poverty against wealth. The wanton destruction of the property of others,— the burning of hay-ricks and corn-ricks, the demolition of machinery, because it supersedes hand-labor, the sprinkling of vitriol on rich dresses,—is only agrarianism run mad. Education prevents both the revenge and the madness. . . . a fellow-feeling for one's class or caste is the common instinct of hearts not wholly sunk in selfish regards for person, or for family. The spread of education, by enlarging the cultivated class or caste, will open a wider area over which the social feelings will expand; and, if this education should be universal and complete, it would do more than all things else to obliterate factitious distinctions in society.[11]

And, just as he lists the on-going events of direct class conflict, he is just as blunt about the sort of social conflict on the horizon should his construction of public schools and education be ignored:

> . . . a republican form of government, without intelligence in the people, must be, on a vast scale, what a mad-house, without superintendent or keepers, would be, on a small one; the despotism of a few succeeded by universal anarchy, and anarchy by despotism, with no change but from bad to worse.[12]

Mann is equally explicit in outlining the positive method to be employed to insure the knowledge to be inculcated and the beneficial social outcome which would follow:

> Hence, the Constitution of the United States, and of our own State, should be made a study in our Public Schools. . . . and, especially, the duty of every citizen, in a government of laws, to appeal to the courts for redress, in all cases of alleged wrong, instead of undertaking to vindicate his own rights by his own arm; and, in a government where the people are the acknowledged sources of power, the duty of changing laws and rulers by an appeal to the ballot, and not by rebellion, would be taught to all the children until they are fully understood.
>
> Had the obligations of the future citizen been sedulously inculcated upon all the children of this Republic, would the patriot have had to mourn over so many instances, where the voter, not being able to accomplish his purpose by voting, has proceeded to accomplish it by violence. . . .[13]

My immediate purpose here is to illustrate that Mann's construction of the state system of public school education, and his argument for its social function and the instructional methods (*no* critical examination of dissenting economic and political views) to be employed do not lead so directly to a free, popular, and democratic order of social relations as numerous educational historians, and Cremin in particular, would have us believe. Secondly, it has been necessary to cite Mann at some length in order to raise critical issues about the social context in which he was recruited to lead the campaign for a state system of public school education, issues which Cremin and other adherents of the dominant ideological paradigm have mystified. Mann was not addressing the common ranks of the people in his Twelfth Annual Report, from which these quotes are taken; rather, he was directly addressing the economic and political elite about the middle and laboring classes. And as a lawyer and one of the most powerful Whig politicians in Massachusetts aligned with the elite and their economic and political agenda,[14] he was telling them how to establish ideological and cultural hegemony to protect their already established material and legal dominion over these lower classes.[15]

We can detect in Mann's writing something of the actual social relations making the enterprise of public school education immediately pressing: the elite's and its allies' domination and control of social resources and rights, and their control and self-serving exploitation of such civic institutions as the courts and government were under direct and occasionally violent attacks by the laboring classes and increasingly by members of the lower-middle rank. As long as these attacks had been manifested as isolated events, these social eruptions were susceptible to quick repression. They were widely commented on in the mainstream and party newspapers, on the floor of the legislature, and in the clubhouses — in much the same language as used by Mann — but as sporadic and isolated events they were not perceived as a serious threat requiring unified class action. This all changed in the 1820s and 1830s. The problem of class conflict and the intense struggle over property and the unequal distribution of resources and rights became urgently pressing for Mann and his generation of elite when the rebellious laboring classes, led by radical autodidacts in league with radical printers, organized into popular movements crossing both trades and state lines. It was not simply that working men (and, significantly, women) were organizing strikes and their own political movements in opposition to elite domination, but they were simultaneously constructing and propagating their own critique of society: unequal economic and political relations determined by property and land ownership, by elite dominated courts and government, and by the artificial and arbitrary undemocratic organization of production and distribution of resources. In addition, they were promoting their own alternatives to these unequal social relations and the structures undergirding them, and advocating revolutionary democratic action to transform society and the state.[16] And, too, the elite was especially motivated because attempts at co-opting the working men's movement and suppressing their leadership through bribery, arrest and imprisonment, and partisan representative politics had proved only partially effective in diffusing their forces and revolutionary energy.[17]

Drawing directly on Mann's words, then, it is clear the state system of public school education was not for the redistribution of resources, nor specifically for improving the material conditions of the lower classes. The state system of public school education was created for the primary purpose of stabilizing and perpetuating the existing order of social relations by establishing hegemonic social domination and control. And the way to this end was to mold the consciousness of children, to inure them to a "legitimate" republican ideology. Inculcated to believe themselves members of the same "class" ideologically and culturally, they would be unlikely to attack the material relations of the "class." Achievement ideology undergirding the empirical Protestant/Capitalist social order was Mann's reformist prescription for the social objective of the state system of public school education. Moveover, it was a prescription easily adapted to schools as vehicles of upward social mobility — for those in a position to exploit its resources, and thus providing an essential element of correspondence that would reinforce achievement ideology — and to schools as a disciplinary institution (defining for lower class children who attended what is real, what constitutes knowledge, what is socially possible, permissible and proper; regulating their behavior, and keeping them off the street until they could go to work). And lastly, the significant social fact to be recognized is the state system of public school education was not generated by various working men's organizations that demanded an *equal, public supported, general education for all children* (as distinct from publicly subsidized education for children of the better off and rich),[18] rather the movement for a state system of public school education, as led and ultimately secured by Horace Mann and his allies, was energized by members of the economic and political elite. It was an institution approved by them that was embraced by the middle class and imposed upon the lower classes.[19] The practical challenge faced by Mann in promoting "the common school" was disguising its ideological and class origins and objectives in order to persuade the laboring classes to tolerate the system long enough for it to take hold and accomplish its social purpose.[20]

Horace Mann's words by themselves, however, do not prove anything one way or another. I have relied on them here to raise the arguments that (1) Mann was himself engaged in the construction of ideological mystification — for example, Christopher L. Tomlins' study of law and social relations prior to the Civil War confirms that ". . . the duty of every citizen, in a government of laws, to appeal to the courts for redress, in all cases of alleged wrong. . . ." was to accept and submit to a social order based on undemocratic and unequal social relations,[21] and (2) that the dominant ideological paradigm of the origins and development of the state system of public school education in fact mystifies

Horace Mann, his social position and practices, his ideas, and his objectives, and, by extension, the actual relation between "freedom, popular education, and republican government."

To better establish and explain the connection between actual social relations and the formation of the institution it is necessary to look beyond Horace Mann, for ultimately his role was structurally generated, and the responsibility for singling him out and setting him in motion as the social architect of the state system of public school education belongs to others in the elite echelon.[22]

And, it is necessary to look beyond Mann's historical moment to identify and establish the roots of the social crisis Mann refers to. Finally, it is necessary to trace the development of this social crisis through 1837 - 1848, specifically. It is necessary as well to see what impact the Declaration of Independence and the War had on the common people and their understanding of society and their rights as citizens which undergirded their assault against existing social relations and the structures they identified as supporting these particular relations.

ENDNOTES

[1]   Lawrence A. Cremin, "Series Preface," in Horace Mann, *The Republic and the School*, iii.

[2]   I obviously reference Cremin in relation to the cited passage written by him, but, too, I will frequently reference him as representative of others who also hold to and reproduce the dominant ideological paradigm rather than repeatedly list them.

[3]   The use of Horace Mann as the foundation for the ideological explanation of the relation between the system of public school education and American society was submerged after the publication of Messerli's critically definitive biography of Mann in 1971. Messerli's research clearly exposes and refutes much of the ideological mystification constructed around Mann, and what it does not refute outright, its problematizes. In short, mystification of the relation between the state system of public school education, social relations, and the ideological and material organization of society could no longer use Horace Mann without being exposed.

[4]   Wayne Urban and Jennings Wagoner, Jr., *American Education: A History* (New York: McGraw-Hill, 1996), 113.

[5]   I am indebted to Professor Morteza Ardebili, of the University of Missouri-Kansas City, for the critical clarification of my explication of the dominant ideological paradigm as embedded, communicated, and reproduced in the educational history texts.

6   E.g., W.E.B. DuBois, Carter G. Woodson, Ruth Miller Elson, Ellen W. Schrecker, Jean Anyon, Jerome Karabel and A.J. Halsey, Samuel Bowles and Herbert Gintis, Michael B. Katz, David Nasaw, Colin Greer, James D. Anderson, Paulo Freire, Henry Giroux, Paul Violas, and Jay MacLeod. See bibliography for full citations.

7   E.g., Adolph Meyer, Diane Ravich, Carl Kastle, Maris Vinovskis, William Reese, Warren Button and Eugene Provenzo, Wayne Urban and Jennings Wagoner, William Bennett, and Chester Finn. See bibliography for full citations.

8   Michael B. Katz, *The Irony of Early School Reform: Educational Innovation in Mid-Nineteenth Century Massachusetts* (Cambridge, MA: Harvard University Press, 1968); attacked by Ravich, 1978; Vinovskis, 1980; Kastle, 1983; and relativized by Urban and Waggoner, 1996.

9   Horace Mann, *"Twelfth Annual Report* (1848)," in *The Republic and the School: Horace Mann on the Education of Free Men*, edited by Lawrence A. Cremin (New York: Teachers College/ Columbia University Press, 1957) 100-101.
        Readers are directed to: Horace Mann, *Annual Reports*. 12 vols. Washington, D.C.: NEA/ Horace Mann League, 1947.
        The entire series of Mann's twelve reports was readily available through the 1950s, and it is the 1947 edition that I have relied on most heavily in my research. The publication, however, of Cremin's convenient, heavily edited, slender volume became the standard textbook edition of Mann's Reports and remains the only representative in print. For this reason and whenever possible, I quote Mann's text from this edition and identify it hereafter as: Mann\Cremin.
        The reader will not find the whole or portions of Mann's 1841 Report in Cremin. For a useful abbreviation see: Horace Mann, "From Report for 1841 'Pecuniary Value of Education,'" in *The American Mind*, 2 vols., edited by Harry R. Warfel, Ralph H. Gabriel, and Stanley T. Williams (New York: American Book Company, 1937) I: 430-31.

10   Mann/Cremin, 80.

11   Mann/Cremin, 87.
        Mann's claim that education prevents poverty is usually and frequently quoted to mean education leads to a material increase. Mann's meaning is metaphorical, however, as the balance of the passage attests. If you think your poverty is not artificially created, imposed and permanent, but a matter of chance and therefore transitory, then you really aren't poor; hence, you harbor no resentment toward the wealthy. Education is an ideological resource, not a material one. See: Thomas Skidmore's comments in *Rights of Man to Property* (1829), in *Socialism In America From the Shakers to the Third International: A Documentary History*, ed. Albert Fried (Garden City, NY: Doubleday Anchor, 1970) : 124-132; and, in: Joseph Blau, ed., *Social Theories of Jacksonian Democracy* (Indianapolis: Bobbs-Merrill, 1954) : 355-364, on the relation between education and hunger and unequal rights. See: Herbert Gutman, "Joseph P. McDonnell and the Workers' Struggle in Paterson, New Jersey," *Power and Culture*, ed. Ira Berlin (New York: The New Press, 1987), 107-110. Gutman quotes from the official reports of Lawrence Fell, who found uneducated native born and educated immigrant working class young in factories suffering conditions in the 1890s which were identical to those conditions of exploitation and oppression reported by Seth Luther in his "An Address To The Working-Men Of New-England (1832)," *Religion, Reform, and Revolution: Labor Panaceas in the Nineteenth Century*, eds. Leon Stein and Philip Taft (New York: Arno Press, 1969), np.

[12]   Mann/Cremin, 90.

[13]   Mann/Cremin, 93.

[14]   It could be argued, as Merle Curti does in *The Social Ideas of American Education* (reprint Totowa, NJ: Littlefield - Adams, 1974), 115-117, that after taking John Quincy Adams' House of Representative seat in Washington, D.C. in 1848, Mann's criticisms of Capitalists and his statements against slavery, especially where he attacked Daniel Webster's stance on the issue, put him at some distance from the elite; but the fact remains that as a lawyer and politician in Massachusetts government Mann's activities and voting record were indistinguishable from those of the Suffolk County leadership, and as Secretary to the Board he opposed racial integration of schools, and abolitionist activities or statements by teachers. See: Messerli, 369-70, passim.

[15]   See: Sean Wilentz, *Chants Democratic: New York City and the Rise of the American Working Class, 1788-1850* (New York: Oxford University Press, 1984), passim; Tomlins, passim.

[16]   Thomas Skidmore, passim; Seth Luther, passim.

[17]   Wilentz, *Chants Democratic*, passim.

[18]   Sol Cohen, ed., *Education in the United States: A Documentary History,* 5 vols. (New York: Random House, 1974), II:1051-1054. See: Thomas Skidmore, passim; and, Seth Luther, passim.

[19]   "The Winchendon committee argued that the availability of foreigners to perform the 'least desirable' sorts of work enabled 'our sons to rise to other employments.' To seize the new opportunities for its children a town required an advanced educational system, especially a high school; there was no other alternative if parents desired their children to rise on the economic and social scale. 'Shall we,' asked the committee, 'stand still, and see our children outstripped in the race of life, by the children of those who are willing to pursue a liberal and far-sighted policy?'" *Winchendon*, 1852-53, p. 15; quoted by Katz, *The Irony*, 30.

[20]   In order to fortify and build support for the "common schools" among the middle and laboring classes, Mann latched onto and publicly over-exaggerated any objection that hinted of elite obstruction. See: Messerli, 412-23, passim.

[21]   Tomlins, 99-219, 331-384, passim.

[22]   We cannot explain why Horace Mann was selected to construct a state school system by treating him as a specie apart from the social relations of his particular historical moment. He was raised on a middling successful farm; he had some benefit of village school education and, later, sufficient tutoring; he attended and graduated from Brown University, stayed on as a tutor for two years and married the President's daughter; was a lawyer, trained at Litchfield, the preeminent law school in the nation at that time, which is to say he was fully inculcated into the ideology of English Common Law with its embedded categorizations of masters and servants, and their respective powers and liabilities; he was a capitalist and employer who understood and practiced disciplinary management (although he understood this as "moral") in his mills (which failed in the market depression of 1832); he legislatively supported other manufacturers who did likewise; he was a debt

collector for merchants and manufacturers; he was a money lender; he was a Whig politician made extremely uncomfortable by the idea of popular democracy, which was the seed of doom and destruction of the social order he embraced; his social reforms were aimed at rationalizing disciplinary institutions (asylums and prisons); he was a committed and energetic advocate of temperance; and, not least of all, he was allied with and trusted by the elite. By early 1837 Horace Mann was one of Massachusetts' most powerful Whigs and President of the Senate of the General Court. He was a hardworking, talented, adept lawyer and politician having much in common with other prominent lawyers, capitalists, and Whigs in and out of government office; and, as a matter of fact, his voting record in the General Court was indistinguishable from those of the Protestant/Capitalist Whigs from Suffolk County. There is little on the surface of Mann's economic, legal, and political record, in other words, to explain his agreement to step down from his powerful position in state government and take up the promotion and development of a state system of public school education in mid-1837. He did not, moreover, advance himself, or volunteer himself, or express an interest in the position of Secretary to the School Board. Indeed, except for a small circle of elite capitalist politicians with whom Mann was closely allied, his action was baffling and inexplicable to friends, party regulars and political opponents alike.

Edward Everett, Governor, and Edward Loring and Edmund Dwight, both State Senators and wealthy capitalists — the former a lawyer and Litchfield classmate of Mann's, and member of a prominent Bostonian family, and the latter a wealthy manufacturer — decided amongst themselves to place Mann on the School Board Committee and then persuade him to take the position of Secretary to the Board. The salary for the Secretary had been set at $1500 annually — more than twice the annual salary of a continuously employed master tailor in good economic times (perhaps the highest paying journeyman position at the time, $6-12 weekly according to Sean Wilentz in Chants Democratic, 50), but something less than he obtained from his law practice and as President of the State Senate — a sum that Dwight promised to increase by $500 per annum for as long as Mann would serve in the position, a promise he guaranteed by rewriting his will. It is also worth recalling that in 1837 the nation was in the depths of a crippling economic depression, such that Mann's salary (little though it may seem to us now) must be understood as substantial.

In short, up to the moment he became Secretary to the Board of Education for the State of Massachusetts, Horace Mann's background, career, and ideology were archetypal of a particular group of ambitious, socially conservative republican men who propelled their fortunes through the practice of law, commerce, manufacturing, land speculation and politics. When looked at in this way, there is nothing obvious or simple about Everett's, Dwight's and Loring's identification of Mann as the specific person they wanted for Secretary. See: Messerli, passim.

CHAPTER THREE

POLITICS, ECONOMICS, PUBLIC SCHOOLS, AND
AMERICAN SOCIETY IN THE NINETEENTH CENTURY:
HORACE MANN AND KARL MARX IN OPPOSITION

This chapter is a partial reconstruction of economic and political relations in American society before the Civil War. My purpose here is to identify antagonistic class relations, some of the structural and cultural forces energizing these relations, and to illuminate some of the mechanisms employed by the governing classes[1] to secure and protect social positions of privilege and power within the developing capitalist state. And secondly, my purpose is to demonstrate that one of the primary institutional mechanisms thus employed was the state system of public school education, which was constructed, invested with particular ideological and hegemonic functions, and imposed within the juncture of these historical social and structural conflicts.

I begin with an incidental event in the middle of the nineteenth century. In 1848, *The Communist Manifesto* by Marx was published in London, and *The Twelfth Annual Report* by Horace Mann was published in Boston.[2] Neither document has been out-of-print since publication; and this little fact in the history of ideas about society is enormously significant, for one prescribes the transformation of the bourgeois state by the proletariat, and the other prescribes the transformation of the proletariat by the bourgeois state. If, as John Dewey and Andrew Collier (Bhaskar) each claim, ideas or beliefs can constitute the motivating cause of behavior, that ideas are immaterial qualities with the power of undergirding actual events,[3] then the question arises by what sorts of mechanisms and/or circumstances do some ideas become actual while others remain dormant potentialities? This question seems all the more provocative because the arguments of Marx and Mann are simultaneously propaganda and prescription to confront, explain, and resolve a pervasive social crisis that challenged the legitimacy and authority of the capitalist state. As the progress of history has demonstrated, of the two economic-political programs, Horace Mann's ideas for capitalist hegemony became structurally integrated into the state, while Marx's ideas of a transcendent democracy were and remain unrealized.[4]

Two Confront Society

Mann, in the *Twelfth*, and Marx, in the *Manifesto*, are similarly unsparing in their harsh criticism of the social consequences of class inequities generated by capitalism; and, both promote visions of a future state free of class conflict. But for Marx the realization of a "true democracy" required a conjunction of emancipatory action by the oppressed laboring classes and a structural transformation of the state, whereas Mann located the causes and the correctives of social inequities and crises in individual behavior. In spite of the critical differences between Marx's view that experience is historical and social, and Mann's that experience is ahistorical and individual, both similarly stress the fact that consciousness is the product of social conditioning. Marx posits in the *Communist Manifesto* the notion that laborers will be educated through their material development and conditions, and through their experience of alienation and exploitation under capitalism, and will then act in common accord to correct social, economic, political injustices and inequities which are the causes of their oppression. Mann, on the other hand, acknowledges antagonistic class relations and the threat of agrarianism (a code for a revolution of the poor and working class against the rich) in his *Twelfth Annual Report*; but, he argues that by controlling the learning environment and ideas into which young children are inculcated, they will develop a pro-capitalist consciousness and corresponding behaviors. Thus Marx prescribes a proletarian capture and transformation of state as the primary means toward achieving a truly classless and democratic society. And, Mann prescribes ameliorative social reforms by the capitalists, and, through public education, the capture and transformation of the middle class child's consciousness (and, the mind of the proletariat child as s/he comes briefly into the system), as the means by which to assure the reproduction of a stable capitalist republican state. Thus one proposes structural transformation of society as the means to realize just and equitable democratic social relations, and the other proposes the transformation of individuals as the means of ameliorating social relations and preserving the state.

Society and Consciousness

In his 1856 *"Preface"* to *Critique of Political Economy*, Marx writes:

> In the social production of their existence, men inevitably enter into definite relations, which are independent of their will, namely relations of production appropriate to a given stage in the development of their material forces of production. The totality of these relations of production constitutes the economic structure of society, the real foundation, on which correspond definite forms of social consciousness. The mode of production of material life conditions the general process of social, political and intellectual life. It is not the consciousness of men that determines their existence, but their social existence that determines their consciousness.[5]

He argues that an historically particular material base of society generates the kinds of economic and political relations possible within it, corresponding ideological institutions, and the state, which regulates these relations and institutions. Human beings born into this complex network of economic and political relations understand their society, the productive relations which constitute it, and themselves culturally, i.e., through the social ideas, beliefs, traditions, customs and associative relations by which their experiences are conditioned and through which their actions acquire meaning. This is the case whether the state is a communal tribe in a South American jungle, or is aristocratic, where the Right of Kings is the dominant ideology, or capitalist, where competitive individualism undergirds the dominant achievement ideology.

In the capitalist, or "bourgeois" State, Marx tells us, ideology serves to mystify or hide the true mechanisms which generate the "antagonism that emanates from the individuals' social conditions of existence."[6] The consciousness engendered by social experience in a capitalist state must be distorted and made false through a mystifying ideology. Were it otherwise, wage laborers believing that something is wrong with the employer deciding what their wages will be in a free trade market might not be satisfied with higher wages, they might want a new organization of social relations of production based upon equal rights and a just distribution of the profits generated by their labor.[7] Before a true democratic state can be realized, therefore, before antagonistic and exploitative bourgeois economic and political relations can be overthrown, false consciousness must itself be transformed. But this transformation depends on there first being a real change in "the material productive forces of society." According to Marx, then,

> No social order is ever destroyed before all the productive forces for which it is sufficient have been developed, and new superior relations of production never replace older ones before the material conditions for their existence have matured within the framework of the old society. Mankind thus inevitably sets itself only such tasks as it is able to solve, since closer examination will always show that the problem itself arises only when the material conditions for its solution are already present or at least in the course of formation.[8]

In 1848, the capitalist forces of production in the United States were still in the process of development. Indeed, in the United States, between 1776 and 1865, there was more than one center of ideological and material struggle for control of the mode of production and of productive forces: there was, especially in the North, an increasingly intense capitalist class struggle between merchants, factory owners, middle class managers and the professional classes on one side, and subsistence farmers, tenant farmers, artisans and journeymen, craftsmen and women, wage-laborers, poor, and indentured laborers and slaves on the other.[9] There was also a bitter economic and political contest between remnants of the older agrarian aristocracy—found in some Northern areas but largely centered in the slave states of the South—and merchant and industrial capitalism. There was in the North, certainly and predominantly, and in the South on-going contention between mercantilists and industrial capitalists. And, too, there was on-going conflict between slave-owners and slaves, and in the North between Black freedmen and white artisans, journeymen and unskilled laborers, and between all of these groups and the masters. But in 1848, industrial capitalism was largely centered in the North and would not have control of the state until after the Civil War.

Marx, in *The Communist Manifesto*, properly identifies the particular historical social antagonisms and their cause, but, for the reasons he explicates above, the revolutionary clarion call in the *Manifesto* was anticipatory. Although Marx is enthusiastically optimistic in propagandizing the second revolution (the first being the revolution of capital and the bourgeoisie), Mann took the revolutionary potential of the energized laboring classes (white and black) seriously. As Secretary to the Board of Education for the State of Massachusetts, Mann shouldered the task of constructing an institutional preventive to render a renewed democratic revolution *unthinkable* if not impossible. And there is this essential and critical difference between these two social theorists: Marx was a critic of the capitalist state; Mann was its willing agent.

American Society and Antagonistic
Social Relations

At a certain stage of development, the material productive forces of society come into conflict with the existing relations of production or—this merely expresses the same thing in legal terms—with the property relations within the framework of which they have operated hitherto. From forms of development of the productive forces these relations turn into their fetters. Then begins an era of social revolution. The changes in the economic foundation lead sooner or later to the transformation of the whole immense superstructure. In studying such transformations it is always necessary to distinguish between the material transformation of the economic conditions of production, which can be determined with the precision of natural science, and the legal, political, religious, artistic or philosophic—in short, ideological forms in which men become conscious of this conflict and fight it out.[10]

The War of Independence on one level was not a revolution, but a bloody battle between British and American mercantile capitalists for economic power. Quite simply the colonial Whig leadership and merchants found the British and Tory yoke on their economic and political activities too restrictive. It is one thing, however, to want to enlarge your trading opportunities and put off burdensome competition, taxation and disciplinary regulations, and quite another to convince ordinary people with little or no property to take up arms and die for your cause. The cause must be made their own. Public opposition against riches, kings and aristocracy, and popularization of revolutionary democratic ideology for equality under God and among men, and for life, liberty, and happiness, as ultimately and officially sanctioned by the *Declaration of Independence*, persuaded enough independent Yankees, resident aliens, various tribes of Amerindians, Southerners, laborers, tenants, slaves, and freed ex-slaves to join the fight, to economically and politically support the colonial army, and see that the English King's colonial allies and his soldiers were defeated and sent packing.[11] This revolutionary democratic ideology and radical vision of society was highly successful in mobilizing the colonial laboring classes against the English and wealthy Tories. But their mobilization and commitment to the cause of democratic ideology and social vision was also a manifested opposition to the reorganization of economic and political relations along the lines of unequal property ownership which had become increasingly extreme in the decades before the War. The fervent embrace of democratic ideology by the laboring classes threatened to undo what the War had accomplished for the Whig leadership, merchants, and landlords.[12] In fact, the tension between these radical ideas about what should constitute the New State and the common law constitution of the actual state based on traditionally stratified social classes — which was formalized in Philadelphia in 1787, ratified by all thirteen states by 1790, and legally sanctified under Marshall's tenure as Chief Justice — would continue to threaten the state's legitimacy in times of economic distress and social displacement.

On another level, however, the War of Independence was a revolution (which we now know was not successful). Historians Gary B. Nash, Dirk Hoerder, Joseph Ernst, Edward Countryman, Marvin L. Michael Kay, and Eric Foner, among others, convincingly reconstruct the cultural context and economic and political relations between crown, merchant and landed elite, and common people in the decades leading up to the War of Independence. Their research establishes that what began as a strategy by the Whig leadership, merchants and landlords to intimidate the crown's imperial administration and its allies, the Tories, and thus win beneficial economic and political accommodations, became for the commoners in the towns and back-country an opportunity and a cover for revolutionary insurgency against existing unequal economic and political circumstances. To retain some semblance of leadership of the people after 1760 — and thereby remain with the people rather than stand with the Tory elite as targets of their antagonism after 1765 — the Whigs found themselves pushed hard from below into increasingly belligerent public opposition to the British and their colonial allies, for which they were penalized by the retaliatory policies of the British. The Whigs began by wanting a beneficial accommodation; but the common people wanted a radical transformation of society. For the common people then, the war against British rule of colonial society was a Revolutionary War.[13]

Just as a tension between ideas about the proper constitution of the state would persist in dividing ordinary people against the Whig leadership and merchants, so too would antagonistic class and race relations repeatedly challenge the ruling elite's appropriation and monopolization of the state and its powers. Indeed, as Christopher L. Tomlins documents, the reorganization of the state and government through the Constitution and centralization of powers, an action coupled to a carefully constructed independent judiciary which was to insure the security of the state, was inspired by the elite's fear of and reaction against popular sovereignty, democratic fervor, and antagonistic social relations.[14] Between the powers of the state and the democratic aspirations and energies of the people, in other words, the elite had interposed law as a mediating, regulatory, and disciplinary structural layer.[15]

In the *Federalist No. 10*, James Madison argues that

> The diversity in the faculties of men, from which the rights of property originate, is not less an insuperable obstacle to a uniformity of interests. The protection of these faculties is the first object of government. From the protection of different and unequal faculties of acquiring property, the possession of different degrees and kinds of property immediately results; and from the influence of these on the sentiments and views of the respective proprietors ensures a division of the society into different interests and parties.
>
> The latent causes of faction are thus sown in the nature of man. . . .[16]

Madison's argument is a reproduction of that popular ideology propagandized by the economic and political elite to obscure the true causes of inequity between the property owners and those owning little or none. The facts of the matter, however, refute Madison's contention. The possession of property in America had always depended upon the privileged distribution of resources and rights from the first years of Dutch and British incursion. Indeed, one of the underlying forces propelling the Colonies into war against England was the antagonism of the common people against arbitrary social structures of privilege and wealth. They sought to transform society through an egalitarian transformation of the rules governing the distribution of resources and rights. Madison understood this motive, and his argument is reactionary. It is a rhetorical attempt to undermine the critical position of the working classes by shifting the argument from social structures and their construction to human nature. Based on his argument in *Federalist No. 10*, the existing social hierarchy, with all of its inequities, is a product of human nature, and, given the diversity and unchanging constitution of human nature, the object of the state is to protect those possessing greater faculties from those having less. By framing social and political inequality within the logical fallacy of human nature, Madison avoids a direct confrontation over the construction and further development of those social structures which generate unequal social positions and material circumstances.

The state which Madison conceptualizes and which is ultimately realized, in short, would both protect and foster those social structures the commoners want transformed. The unequal social relations of the capitalist state did not materialize out of thin air without historical precedence, and the reality of unequal social positions was not determined by a neutral and benign human nature. The state and social inequality were constructed. The wealthy and the working class did not exist in their distinct spheres of social life by virtue of some innate human nature, but these classes and the divisions between them were also socially constructed.[17] Indeed, this is quite clear in New England, where largely independent yeomen farmers (and/or their wives and children) were in significant numbers separated from the land and transformed into wage dependent laborers through mechanisms of the state under the control of the economic and political elite.

At the conclusion of the Colonies' War of Independence approximately 70% of the New England agrarian population were yeomen, largely independent subsistence farmers.[18] The situation in the Southern colonies was more complex, for while it is true that it was an agrarian population and culture, its economy was based not on independent farmers, but on indentured and slave labor. In either case, however, mercantile capitalism was well established in the form of commercial trading in the sea ports along the Atlantic sea coast, in trading centers along the many rivers and waterways, in the major towns and cities of the period, and between the colonies and foreign nations. Before the War, the typical pattern of commercial trade called for the colonial merchants to ship raw materials to the West Indies and England, and bring manufactured commodities, and indentured and slave labor back. More often then not, ships from the colonies transported goods to the British West Indies, where they would exchange one load for another bound for the colonies or for England. If they made the journey to England, once unloaded they would contract for manufactured commodities destined for the colonial market.[19]

By way of retaliation for the War, the British closed off the British West Indies to American Trading ships. Although this seriously hampered American shippers, American wholesale merchants blinked and then plunged right back into trading directly with and through their traditional trading partners—the British merchant houses. "England supplied America with manufactured commodities such as glass, iron, and medicine on credit. In exchange, American merchants seasonally exported foodstuffs, lumber, and fish to Britain. [. . .] During the last month of 1783 they bought L199,558 worth of British commodities; during the next year, the first full year of peace, wholesalers purchased almost triple that amount. The total roughly equaled the average yearly importation of British wares in the decade before the Revolution. [. . .] By importing vast quantities of goods into postwar New England, merchants glutted the market as they had done in 1745 and 1763."[20] The British then demanded payment in species to satisfy all accounts and debts.

The individual American states of the new national confederation already faced an economic crisis. They had financed the war with borrowed money, and, as Alexander Hamilton—first Secretary of the Treasury—and some others argued, these debts had to be settled for reasons of establishing the state of the union internally and externally. Hamilton's plan, which included the formation of the Bank of the United States, was vigorously opposed by the Jeffersonians and anti-Federalists, but not defeated. In 1781, Hamilton had written to Robert Morris,

> A national debt, if it is not excessive, will be to us a national blessing; it will be a powerful cement of our union. It will also create a necessity for keeping up taxation to a degree which without being oppressive, will be a spur to industry.[21]

But the taxation was oppressive, because payment was demanded in species, not paper money, goods, or exchanged labor as had been the custom; and, due to the shipment of species abroad for payment on commercial accounts, there was very little hard money in the colonies. Moreover, in Massachusetts, for example, the General Court (i.e., the state legislature—made up mostly of Boston Merchants) proportioned the tax levy to fall heaviest on land rather than capital and moveable property. According to Van Beck Hall, "In 1784 the ten leading shipowning towns contained only 12 percent of the total taxpaying males who held two-thirds of the state's inventory, 72 percent of her vessel tonnage, and 87 percent of her wharfage facilities, but were assessed for only 14 percent of the state's total tax bill."[22] Thus, the Merchants, whose assets were largely in stock, paid hardly any tax at all.[23]

The yeoman farmers of Massachusetts were thus forced to bear the brunt of taxation. Their situation, in short, was untenable. On one side was a new and, from their perspective, harsh system of taxation—worse, in fact, than what had existed before the War. Moreover, the burden of taxation had forced many yeomen war veterans to sell their Continental and state certificates at greatly reduced value in exchange for specie. More often than not the speculators who purchased the certificates were merchants, lawyers, and government men. Massachusetts governor James Bowdoin, for example, had bought up L1,000 in certificates at a fraction of their face value.[24]   At the same time, the yeomen were being hard pressed to settle their accounts (again in species) with the country retailers, who were themselves being hard pressed for specie payment of their accounts by the wholesale merchants in the shipping centers, who were in turn being held up for specie payment of their accounts by the British.

The familiar world and culture of the New England yeoman was being changed, and changed in ways that enraged them, not least of all because these changes contradicted the revolutionary ideology and anticipated democratic society they had just fought a war for and had mistakenly believed to be the blue print for the state. In short, "deprived of specie for payment of state taxes and personal debts, New England farmers faced the tough realities of the marketplace. Creditors tore some yeomen from their land and movable property. 'The constables are daily venduing our property both real and personal, our land after it is appraised by the best judges under oath is sold for about one-third of the value of it, our cattle about one-half the value,' angrily petitioned the townsmen of Greenwich, Massachusetts, in January 1786."[25] Similar protests were raised in Rhode Island, Vermont, and Connecticut. Only in New Hampshire were taxes actually lowered.

Their protests and their plight, however, did not receive much sympathy from the men in the legislatures.[26] In Massachusetts, where the legislature was located in Boston, the new State Constitution of 1780 had increased the property qualifications for voting sufficiently to exclude the majority of the male population (and, of course, all women and blacks were excluded regardless).[27]

The yeomen concluded the worst, that one aristocracy had replaced another, and the "revolution" had been betrayed. Said Plough Jogger,

> I have been greatly abused, have been obliged to do more than my part in the war; been loaded with class rates, town rates, province rates, Continental rates and all rates . . . been pulled and hauled by sheriffs, constables and collectors, and had my cattle sold for less than they were worth. . . .
>
> . . . The great men are going to get all we have and I think it is time for us to rise and put a stop to it, and have no more courts, nor sheriffs, nor collectors nor lawyers. . . .[28]

Plough Jogger was not alone in thinking the "great men" and "lawyers" were conspiring to deny representation and take control of the state. The great men and their lawyers were in fact taking farmers' property. Yeomen farmers in the western and northern counties of Massachusetts, many of them veterans of the War, rose up to "regulate" the courts and prevent further foreclosures until they could have their grievances heard in the General Court and obtain a redress. In Rhode Island, however, the debtors had taken control of the legislature and were issuing paper money. In New Hampshire, Howard Zinn reports, several hundred men surrounded the legislature, which was meeting in Exeter, in September 1786, and only dispersed before the threat of military action.[29] But in Massachusetts, the militia refused to engage the farmers. Sam Adams helped write up a Riot Act under Governor James Bowdoin's order, and, financed largely by Boston Merchants[30] and aided by a number of more secure but ambivalent yeomen,[31] General Benjamin Lincoln led a private army into the field against the protesting farmers. Shays' Rebellion was thus forcefully put down — for the moment.[32] Several were killed in the field, and several more were later hanged for sedition.[33]

The government's action against the protesting farmers had the positive effect of spurring eligible voters across Massachusetts to test their voting power in the election of 1787. Bowdoin was turned out of office, as were most of the pro-government men in the out-county areas. The change in government, however, did not abolish the tax, or shift its burden.[34]

The South had its own problems. Slave revolts were not unknown in the Southern States before the War of Independence, but with the spread of revolutionary democratic ideology the slaves were contained only through armed

suppression.[35] Indeed, South Carolina was hardly represented in the War, because its militia had been needed at home to repress revolutionary stirring among
both the yeoman farmer and the slave population.[36] And, in addition to violent
coercion and repression, laws proliferated throughout the South forbidding the
teaching of slaves to read and write.[37]

The revolutionary democratic ideology and social vision necessary to arouse
the population had accomplished its objective too well. If achieving a strong
federal state had seemed remote before 1787, it was no longer so; a centralized
government was necessary to protect the state against the "mobbish" revolutionary zeal of the population (as evidenced in Shays' Rebellion, among its sym-
pathizers, between landlords and tenants, and the rumbling among the slaves),
encourage and protect manufacturing, establish a national economy and bank,
and regulate potentially disastrous trading competition between the states, and
between the American state and other nations. Not least of all, a strong centralized federal state was a prerequisite to capturing resources and their distribution. Thus, when the states' constitutional representatives met in Philadelphia to
fine tune the Articles of Confederation in late 1787, the agenda was changed,
the doors closed, and a new Constitution was drafted. Significantly absent in
the new document was a recognition of God given inalienable rights, among
which were life, liberty, and the pursuit of happiness. "Blessings of Liberty"
was all that remained suggestive of the generative revolutionary democratic
ideology — and under the regulation of the courts and their imposition of common law, these blessings would prove to be few indeed for the laboring classes.[38]
The new Constitution represented a new form of state, but clearly it was largely
shaped by the economic interests and prejudice of the ruling class, and it was
certainly meant to strengthen these prejudices and protect these interests:

All communities divide themselves into the few and the many. The first
are the rich and well-born, the other the mass of the people. The voice of
the people has been said to be the voice of God; and however generally this
maxim has been quoted and believed, it is not true in fact. The people are
turbulent and changing; they seldom judge or determine right. Give therefore to the first class a distinct permanent share in the government. . . . Can
a democratic assembly who annually revolve in the mass of the people be

supposed steadily to pursue the public good? Nothing but a permanent body can check the imprudent of democracy. . . .[39]

If Hamilton's conception was not already exclusive enough, "slaves, indentured servants, women, and men without property" were not represented at all.[40] On the other hand, the State as framed in the Constitution found favor among all but a few of the representatives: "the manufacturers needed protective tariffs; the moneylenders wanted to stop the use of paper money to pay off debts; the land speculators wanted protection as they invaded Indian lands; slaveowners needed federal security against slave revolts and runaways; bondholders wanted a government able to raise money by nationwide taxation, to pay off those bonds."[41] Little, it would seem, had changed since the decades leading up to the War of Independence.

But not all of the political leadership agreed with the Constitution or the conception of state it represented. Thomas Jefferson was in France, and though he is credited with exerting some influence on Madison, he could do little of account from the other side of the Atlantic to direct the Convention. Among those present, Elbridge Gerry of Massachusetts and Luther Martin of Maryland both opposed ratification; and Patrick Henry had stayed away in protest.

It was Jefferson, acting through Madison, who secured the nine state approval before the Constitution could be ratified; but it was Madison in the *10th Federalist* paper who concisely distinguished between the theory of state popularized in the *Declaration of Independence*, and the actual state carried forward by the Constitution:

> The most common and durable source of actions has been the various and unequal distribution of property. Those who hold and those who are without property have ever formed distinct interests in society. Those who are creditors, and those who are debtors, fall under a like discrimination. A landed interest, a manufacturing interest, a mercantile interest, a moneyed interest, with many lesser interests, grow up of necessity in civilized nations and divide them into different classes, actuated by different sentiments and views. The regulation of these various and interfering interests forms the

principal task of modern legislation, and involves the spirit of party and
faction in the necessary and ordinary operations of the government.[42]

Madison's construct of the state is clearly rooted in and emerges out of
particular foundational economic conditions of production, and it embraces unequal economic and political relations; but, more than this, Madison also recognized the state could not be fixed to one elite group or another else its fate be too
closely linked with the group's. The principal task of government must be the
regulation of tensions between those with property, and between those with
property and those without. The state, while dependent on the nation's aggregate productivity and wealth, must be insulated from the clutches of one or
another fraction of the elite, and especially so from direct democratic governance by the common people. Political parties are conceptualized as necessary
organizations through which competing factions fight it out for privileged access
to and control over the distribution of resources. Competitive energies and
actions of different factions would thus be more or less safely channelled through
party and government institutions — a process which will prove especially important in the late 1820s and after. Such elaborate measures to insulate the
state were necessary because the known competing interests were not superfi-
cial in nature; indeed, Madison articulates a whole strata of economic, social,
and political cleavages. The Whig federalists, as well, did not want a repeat of
colonial circumstances where one party dominated economic and political policy
regulation to the disadvantage or exclusion of all others. But more than this
concern, however, they were reminded almost daily of the people's democratic
aspirations and social objectives. The growing sentiment among ordinary people
that the revolution had been betrayed by the Whig leadership and its merchant
and lawyer allies, and that, perhaps, the revolution had been called off too soon,
represented the one cleavage which could threaten the development and progress
of the new state.

Madison's conception of social relations and of an effective structural organization to contain opposing cultures of government and class conflict was
eminently practical. In the decades before the War of Independence, the merchant and landed elite had divided between the Tories and the Whigs. In the
heat of their competition the Tories strengthened their relations to British rule
and the Whigs, seeking to counter this advantage, enlisted the common people.

The consequences of this strategy were soon apparent: organized groups of common people attacked the structural constitution of colonial society and British rule. Under Madison's plan political parties, government and legislation were both the field of struggle and the goal. Thus whatever might take place between factions of the elite or between the different social classes, the structures of the state would remain strong and in place — safe from revolutionary democratic insurgency from below and reactionary monopolization from above by virtue of a greatly empowered judiciary. Indeed, although Madison does not say so in the passage quoted above, the constitutional invention of an independent judiciary as a safeguard of freedom and *property* would effectively block threats against the state from particular factions or social classes should either gain control of the legislature. Madison and some other framers of the Constitution had another reason for fearing democracy — they were in fact doing precisely what they warned would happen under popular governance: an organized *junto* having the trust of the people could capture the state and turn it to selfish ends. Madison's federalist construct of government and its division of separate powers would stand against another group's or class's replicating the federalist triumph. Legislative action under Madison's plan could well result in reforms, but not in wholesale structural transformations.[43]

The Federal State came into being with the ratification of its Constitution by 1790. But only the ratifying convention of North Carolina gave the Constitution its unambiguous vote for ratification. In every one of the other states, however, ratification passed on a mere majority of two to ten votes.[44] The adoption of the Bill of Rights in 1791 helped to placate some of the opposition to the new Constitution of the United States, but, as the narrow margin of its ratification indicates, a sizable proportion of the citizenry saw it as the product of a conspiracy between the rich and lawyers to protect privilege and property at the expense of democracy, and to institutionalize economic and social inequities by excluding the majority of the people from direct determination of their governance.[45]

In the decades between 1791 and 1848 the opposing conceptions of state would be expressed through the revolutionary democratic ideology of the laboring classes, and through the increased agitation for freedom among the slaves; through the capitalist (i.e., republican) ideology of Northern merchants and industrialists, and the states' rights ideology of agrarian New Englanders and

Southern slave-owners. The compromise combination between the Northern capitalists and Southern plantation aristocrats lasted as long as it did because in the early decades of the nineteenth century the mercantile and industrial capitalists were not unified nor strong enough to assert their economic and political dominance, and both factions had a common interest in repressing the democratic demands and socio-economic protests of the laboring classes and slaves.

The material progress of industrial capitalism in the North and the agricultural industry in the South depended principally on plentiful cheap labor, but, too, the material social conditions generated by both modes of production were such that neither free-laborer nor slave-laborer willingly lent themselves to either productive enterprise.[46] Whether free or slave, laborers understood the socioeconomic circumstances imposed upon them and expressed their opposition through revolutionary democratic ideology and covert as well as overt acts of resistance. Protest, resistance, and democratic agitation confirmed for the governing classes that the laboring classes (free or slave) were dangerous and unreasoning.[47] However, denied the vote by mechanisms of property qualifications and/or race, sex, indentured servitude, or slavery, and hampered by poor transportation, communications, and general poverty, laborers and slaves were largely isolated and constrained from mounting a unified and cohesive threat to the modes of production which oppressed them or the institutional structures of the state which promoted and protected these economic and political relations. Controlling isolated demonstrations of opposition and antagonism by the laboring population, therefore, was a relatively direct matter for the ruling elite. Violent coercion against slaves and sympathetic whites and the enforced segregation of the races — coupled with the withholding of literacy education — were generally effective means of control in the South (and in the North as well). Limited suffrage and economic dependence were highly effective means of social control in the North, and when these conditions proved insufficient, as they did with increasing frequency, police violence served. In both parts of the country violence was an instrument of the state, rationalized as necessary for the protection of property — thus protection of the "republic" — and so instituted by law. In addition to these strictures, political and economic domination of the people in both the North and South was sustained by the opposition to and/or neglect of universal public education.[48]

Social Relations, Social Crisis,
and Public Instruction

In 1778, Thomas Jefferson submitted to the Virginia State Legislature his *Bill for the More General Diffusion of Knowledge*. Although his proposal for public funding of a school in each of Virginia's county districts, the provision of three years education for white girls and boys, extended grammar school education for a limited number of capable boys, and, finally, scholarship support for the university education of one in approximately seventy-one boys a year was rather modest and would ultimately most benefit the property owning classes,[49] the Bill was ignored.[50] In the North, Benjamin Rush, in 1786, and Noah Webster, in 1790, advocated forms of public education that, like Jefferson's, were not directly taken up a matters of social policy. On one level, all three proposals had the potential of extending the economic and political franchise of the white, Protestant Anglo-American middle class. Jefferson's proposal, different from the other two, also envisioned an independent (i.e., self-sufficient) agrarian class which would constitute a counter-balancing political power against Whig/Federalist domination.[51] Rush's proposals for greatly enlarged higher education, if implemented, would have created additional competition among the Anglo-American capitalist elite. His proposals for the education of the masses, on the other hand, were actually quite modest: tax supported "free schools" for children (free and white) through the age of 12 years. But for such a privilege they would be required to pay the schoolmaster 1s6 to 2s6 in tuition as an incentive for him to cultivate as many students as possible. Webster's proposals (while remarkably advanced in educational/learning psychology) were not immediately attractive for being nakedly utilitarian: "Artificial wants multiply the number of occupations, and these require a great diversity in the mode of education. Every youth must be instructed in the business by which he is to procure subsistence."[52]

On another level all three proposals were visionary in the sense of implicitly acknowledging actual antagonistic social relations and harsh socioeconomic circumstances, and explicitly articulating social programs of public education which they believed would generate the necessary correctives. Jefferson, Rush, and

Webster were to different degrees political and ideological antagonists, but historically they were in the social vanguard among the governing classes in conceptualizing a state system of public school education as a state mechanism for reconstructing culture, consciousness, and economic and political relations. That none of their proposals were immediately adopted must be understood in the context of a few realities: notably a society conditioned by the buying and selling of human beings or their labor contracts, but also the continued aristocratic culture of social deference, or, in other words, the blind arrogance of the ruling class and their presumption of the subjugation and supplication of all the other classes.[53] Jefferson's rhetoric of political idealism, that the (free) common people should be educated and enfranchised and thus be made economically and politically independent, was not so persuasive as to be embraced by the governing classes — although it may have acted as a starting point for more radical democratic critics of society such as Thomas Skidmore or David Walker. The more alert among governing classes would begin to realize by the late 1820s, however, that ignoring the conservative, social control, hegemonic arguments and programs of Rush and Webster had been an astonishing political blunder.[54]

The reasons for the neglect of a general and equal public education in the first decades of the republic, therefore, are not difficult to identify. Embedded in the Whig culture of the early nation, in the Constitution, and embodied in the subsequent organization of the state and its institution of law was the widely held belief among the elite in the legitimacy of social inequities between the superior classes of educated, intelligent property owners and the inferior classes of poor and laborers who owned little or no property — or who were property. This belief, expressed eloquently by Hamilton and Madison in the above quotes, was neither unique nor exceptional.[55] The material division between classes was substantiated as well in the religious teachings of the period which held the intelligent, morally righteous and industrious were amply rewarded with property and riches (one of Horace Mann's archetypal arguments), and the degenerate, ignorant, lazy and idle were properly marked by poverty, skin color, and/or their subservient, dependent social status. And though these precepts were roundly attacked beginning in the 1730s by the itinerant preachers of first Great Awakening, the elite were hardly inclined to abandon them. Indeed, the rationalized conceptualization of the basis (i.e., individual morality and worthiness or its lack) for the unequal division of property and privilege was nothing less than a social zeitgeist among the wealthy (and want-to-be-wealthy), which legitimated the economic and political institutionalization and the ideological mystification of this social division.[56]

In addition, this achievement ideology had short and long term practical value. It appeared to explain and thus legitimate the institution of slavery and the social positions of black slaves and freedmen (women), and indentured laborers or tenant farmers. And, increasingly, it legitimated the inequities of wage labor. It also served to undergird arguments of the period to abolish hold-over poor and debtor relief laws. Because poverty and/or debts were brought on by individual improvidence, slough, or idleness, public relief was an obstacle to moral regeneration, the influential political economist John McVickar argued. The removal of relief thus forced the poor to be industrious.[57] In other words, the poor had a choice between the poor house, which was increasingly a factory, or the factory proper.[58]

The truth of the matter, however, was the development of manufactures required laborers, lots of them. Hamilton, in his paper promoting manufactures, stressed that the labor necessary to operate their labor saving machinery could be supplied by women and children;[59] e.g., the wives, daughters, sisters and children of the New England yeomen hard pressed for money to pay their land taxes and small debts to retail merchants. Even though this source of labor was numerous, it was insufficient on two counts: first, the proliferation of manufactures required a concentrated and increasing population of laborers, otherwise a essential force for its growth was unavailable—hence the need to increase the labor force by drawing in as much of the mass as possible; and second, a limited labor population meant a market imbalance of supply and demand, or, in other words, relatively high wages.[60] An increasing and concentrated population was also an increase in consumers for manufactured goods.

Abolition of poor laws and congenial forms of public relief coupled with an active campaign to lure immigrants from Europe were necessary policy measures to increase the laboring class population, decrease wages, and thus further enhance the growth of manufactures. And, too, throughout this period of development, the buying and selling of contract human labor and/or human beings constituted a thriving and profitable enterprise in its own right. Other measures to foster investment and the proliferation of manufactures were government grants of exclusive charters for various internal improvement ventures (e.g., roads, bridges, canals, and railroads), the Bank of the United States and the public debt, state charter banks and the issues of paper money, and the protectionist measures promoted by northern manufacturing capitalists and enacted first by Jefferson, and again in 1816.[61]

Women, children, immigrants, indentured laborers, and slaves were required, too, because able-bodied men either required higher wages, or, if they were sensible and ambitious, they left New England (and the South as well) to try for better in the West.[62] In fact, only those who did not expect to stay for long, or those without alternatives, or those newly arrived and anxious for a start were willing to endure the 72-hour work week and the dangerous and oppressive conditions in the factories.[63] In short, the dominant political and economic leaders of the state commonly held that the nation's prosperity and survival depended on a sound political economy: a stable social order, a differentiated and regulated laboring population, capital for investment, internal development of transportation and communication, the rapid development of manufactures and commerce, protection against liability, and the necessary security of these interests and investments internally and externally. It must be acknowledged, however, that the nature of this protection was perceived in opposing ways by the North and the South, and eventually by the West.[64]

Public education was thus neglected or actively blocked for pragmatic reasons as well as elitist reasons. In the absence of adequate and available adult labor, child labor was necessary. Pressing material circumstances — it was no longer a matter of saving money, one had to earn money — and the on-going transformation of the trades also propelled children of the laboring classes into the mills, factories, and "bastard workshops".[65] And, too, children could not work in a factory 12 to 14 hours a day and also attend day schools. Moreover, it was believed that material necessity (i.e., poverty, or near-poverty), severe work discipline, and popularized achievement ideology (e.g., Benjamin Franklin's *Poor Richard's Almanac*) were sufficient to motivate or coerce industriousness among the women and children.[66] Because, too, property flowed from superior intelligence, and was the primary qualification for voting, the lack of property was characterized as a mark of ignorance or moral degeneracy and was considered sufficient evidence for denying universal suffrage. The principal reasons for denying public education, perhaps, can also be explained by the fact that education had been the traditional resource and culture capital of the economic and political elite, and it was one of their prerogatives to decide that somebody else had to be sacrificed to do the real labor of production. Dorfman reports, that

> Francis Walker Gilmer, graduate of William and Mary, a lawyer, and later Jefferson's agent in selecting the original faculty of the University of Virginia and himself its professor of law, argued that both in enacting usury laws and in repressing combinations to raise wages the state justly overrides natural rights for the social welfare. Men, he said in his *A Vindication of the Laws, Limiting the Rate of Interest on Loans* (1820), have a natural right to do collectively what each is admitted to have a right to do separately, but the restraint on journeymen must be borne, for otherwise the great manufacturers could not exist and society would consequently be deprived of many useful and necessary fabrics.[67]

Note that for Gilmer the good of the laboring classes (their "natural rights") is excluded from what constitutes society and the "social welfare." In fact, we do not have to read far along in Dorfman's study of the theoretical architects and policy makers of the American economy and state to realize that these men were typically college graduates who established themselves in the upper echelons of society as lawyers and/or chaired academics, merchants and manufacturers, stock and land speculators, judges, bankers, and appointed or elected officers in state or federal government.[68] These social classes of men — the elite and their surrogate professional and middle class allies — understood that education was the means by which one entered the domain of power, and power was the means to increase personal and aggregate wealth. Education was thus a valuable, exclusive class resource to be protected — not distributed. It was not only expedient to deny to journeymen and unskilled laborers the same right of combination freely exercised by merchant, corporate and manufacturing capitalists,[69] but it was equally expedient and self-serving to deny their children an education — an education, in other words, such as they understood education: privileged culture capital and an economic and political commodity.[70]

Achievement Ideology As Mystification

Throughout the first decades of the nineteenth century achievement ideology had been widely circulated in speeches and writings to propagandize the belief among the laboring classes that the unequal division of property was a natural consequence of proper morality, merit, and industriousness (i.e., individual faculties). To fully appreciate Horace Mann's contribution to the state and capitalist society, therefore, it must be first established that achievement ideology was deliberately constructed to be mystifying, and those who promoted it understood the real economic and social consequences of industrial capitalism.[71]

Having won the bitterly contested election against the Federalist candidate, John Adams, Jefferson was immediately faced with intense pressures to simultaneously promote and protect manufacturing. The concentration of the population into centers of manufacturing where they would be subjugated under the burdens of wage dependency was obviously antithetical to Jefferson's vision of an independent yeomen republic. He turned for advice to his close friend Thomas Cooper, whom he thought among the wisest of men in the States.

> It may be said, [Cooper] wrote Jefferson, that if manufacture is introduced, "you introduce capitalists who live by the life blood of the starving poor whom they employ," and that the mass are "systematically kept in abject poverty and to all real purposes and interests enslaved." But the great increase in national power and wealth might overbalance the evils. For instance, how can armies be obtained for defending the country, when by a kind of idle labor a man in four or five days a week can earn enough for subsistence and in addition enough whisky for intoxication?[72]

Taking Great Britain as the model to copy, the aggregate power and wealth of the United States depended, capitalists argued, on following a similar path of domestic manufacturing. Embracing the model, however, entailed more than determining the requirements for constructing an economically independent state. It also included embracing as belief and policy the English political economy of master and servant. Many of the elite, like Hamilton, Madison, Cooper and Franklin Dexter, spurned the masses and saw democracy and universal suffrage as great evils, and, therefore, accepted unequal divisions of property and rights as normal or beneficial, and permanent. Jefferson on the other hand, Joseph Dorfman contends, persuaded himself (following Cooper's counsel) that while manufacturing might generate immediate social hardship and turmoil, the overall growth of markets, commerce, national wealth and expansion of national borders would lead to an increase in opportunity for advancement by the laboring population.[73] But, as Dorfman also makes clear in this same context, the Jeffersonians did little while in office to curtail Hamilton's economic programs and policies.[74] Regardless which of these views about the permanency of economic and political oppression was held by policy makers, or the extent and nature of their rhetorical bickering, which was usually spirited by being in or out of political office, their public policies were very nearly interchangeable: in the North, manufactures and commercial ventures were encouraged and supported (with public funds) at the expense of other classes; and, in the South, the institution of slavery would continue for decades—although, government policies enacted to protect northern manufacturing had the increasing effect of circumscribing southern commerce. The decision to suppress political and economic resources and rights among the laboring classes was not determined by metaphysical notions or the best of intentions; it was hard nosed, clear sighted, and practical; unfortunate for the majority but necessary for capitalist expansion and the power of the state.[75]

Opposition Turns to Promotion
of Public School Education

The obvious questions then are: what social events generated a changed attitude among significant numbers of the capitalist elite, professionals, and middle class toward a state system of public school education, and why Horace Mann?

The explanation to the first question involves the historical development and transformation of the laboring classes. The development and protection of manufactures accomplished in great measure what its proponents in the academies, business, and government predicted: increased population, especially an increased laboring class through steady immigration; the growth of cities; increased commerce; increased markets; increased development of transportation in the forms of canals, roads, and railroads; increased machine technology and production; increased military capability and might; increased investment banking — and speculation; increased flow of capital (domestically and internationally); increased aggregate national wealth — although concentrated in the upper stratum of society; and, increasingly, a strengthened federal state. It must also be remarked, as Marx argued, that the material development of capitalism leads inevitably to the material development of labor. The periodic economic crises precipitated by out-of-control speculation, bank issues of paper money, monopolies, overstocking in retail and wholesale commerce, and overproduction by manufactures and agriculture (cotton and wool especially) generated extreme hardships in the countryside and towns. But extreme hardship was especially true in the merchant and manufacturing centers where concentrated populations, the breakdown of the trades, the proliferation of bastard workshops, and the intensification of wage dependency made obtaining necessities during these crises a matter of life and death. Under such socioeconomic circumstances, people were driven by resentment, desperation, and visions of a society founded on the precepts of independence, equality and "the common good" to organize mass protests to demand economic and political reforms, work and food.[76] At all times the physical and psychological tyranny over Black-Americans generated extreme hardship that inspired periodic attempts to wrest their freedom from the brutality of white society.[77]

As local events these outbursts of public protest and demand for redress might have been (and in the first decades of the nation often were) squelched at the local level without much concern for widespread consequences. But improved transportation and communications did more than benefit merchants and manufacturers, and did more than tie the nation together as a large marketplace — protest and democratic insurgency no longer remained a local affair. News of intensifying and widespread agitation for suffrage and equal rights was carried by word of mouth and newspapers over new roads and canals between states, cities, towns and back-country villages.[78] News of worker actions in New York City became the topic of agitated conversation in Providence, in Lowell, in Philadelphia, and in Cincinnati. Protests against the tyranny of racism in the North and slavery in the South and West were no longer lone voices in the wilderness but were increasingly clarion calls trumpeted from Boston to Charlestown to New Orleans.[79] News of crises and protest, in other words, travelled with new speed and made it apparent that grievances in one place in fact reflected pressing national problems which most severely beset the laboring classes regardless of race or locality.

In the late 1820s the Working Men's Associations formed, first in Philadelphia, then New York, and soon thereafter with chapters organized in New Jersey, Rhode Island, Connecticut, New Hampshire, and Massachusetts. Thomas Skidmore, a descendent of Irish immigrants, was a self-educated mechanic, and one of the principal organizers and leaders of the New York Working Men's movement. Skidmore argued at organizing rallies, in the Association's party circulares, and in his 1829 treatise, *The Rights of Man to Property!*, that the grim economic and social conditions of the laboring classes were structurally determined by the arbitrary and unequal distribution of property and by a government and courts constructed to protect and perpetuate this inequity.

> Whoever looks at the world as it now is will see it divided into two distinct classes; proprietors, and non-proprietors; those who own the world, and those who own no part of it. [. . .] The truth is, all governments in the world have begun wrong: in the *first appropriation* they have made or suffered to be made of the domain over which they have exercised their power and in the *transmission* of this domain to their posterity. Here are the two great and radical evils that have caused all the misfortunes of man. [. . .] If still there be those who shall say that these unjust and unequal governments ought not to be destroyed, although they may not give to man in society the same equality of property as he would enjoy in a state of nature; then I say that *those are the persons* who, in society, *if anybody*, should be deprived of all their possessions, inasmuch as it is manifestly as proper for them to be destitute of property as it is for any one else.[80]

The only remedy, Skidmore declared, is a new government and a new constitution which abolishes the corrupt system of inheritance, and guarantees equal allotments of property to every citizen (upon reaching the age of maturity at 18) and limited to the life time of the holder. In addition to this critique of the state, was Skidmore's radical democratic insistence that no persons (i.e., Blacks, Indians, immigrants—who declared residency, women) be excluded from citizenship or voting rights. Skidmore, insisting that child labor was an abomination as great as the institution of slavery, and likewise an evil means by which capitalists forced wages down, charged that children were not property, but young citizens, and they should be educated at public expense until they reached the age of maturity.[81] And, too, higher education should be provided for every citizen who wanted it.[82]

The formation and spread of the Working Men's movement in the late 1820s is a benchmark in the relations between the laboring class, capitalists, and the state. Indeed, Andrew Jackson's election as President in 1828, and Van Buren's succession in the election of 1836, were a consequence of the Democratic party's flagrant pandering to the issues (except for universal public education and the equal distribution of property) raised by the Working Men. Touting these issues in conjunction with a reformist platform was also effective in appealing to large numbers of middle class of clerks, managers, self-employed artisans and small shopowners who were distressed by laborers' militancy, and blamed it on the proliferation of commercial and manufacturing monopolies, and the cycles of economic crises — which hurt them as well. The Democrats had no real intention of restructuring the state in line with the revolutionary democratic Working Men's platform authored by Skidmore, nor was it particularly responsive to the demands of the trades union movement which followed. But by addressing outstanding issues of (white male) suffrage, untenable banking practices, and by appearing to attack monopolies, the Democrats effectively exploited the laborers' revolutionary energy at the same time they diffused it by drawing a good many into factional party politics.[83]

Taking advantage of the democratic organization of the New York Working Men's Association, National Republican (Whig) political opportunists Noah Cook and Henry Guyon, among others, infiltrated the movement.[84] They formed a secret alliance with Robert Dale Owen and other middle class reformers who found the culture and platform of the Working Men too distastefully rowdy, too independent, and too radically democratic. Together, the opportunists and the reformers conspired to capture the leadership of the movement. Their "coup de main" on 29 December 1829 caught Skidmore and the Committee of Fifty by surprise at a sub-committee meeting. Few members of the Working Men were in the hall, which had been packed with Cookites and Owenites specially for the occasion.[85] Following the coup, the membership was splintered between Skidmore and the Committee of Fifty on one side, and the combination of Cookites and Owenite reformers on the other side prior to the 1830 elections. The struggle for control of the Working Men's Party did not end with the ouster of Skidmore and the democratic workmen however. Owen imagined that with Skidmore out of the way, he and his allies would take over and successfully promote the state guardianship educational program; but the reformers were thoroughly outmaneuvered. Within three short months of the coup, the Owenites found themselves shut-out as well.[86] Thus the Working Men's Associations' attempt to constitute a revolutionary democratic challenge to the dominant political parties was effectively undermined.[87]

Cook, Guyon, and a group of Clay Supporters directed the newly constituted Working Men's Party in support of more moderate reform politics which appeared to challenge unequal economic and political relations but, in fact, would have left them intact. The main political thrust of the Party in any case was to fragment voter support for Tammany Hall Jacksonians. The radical holdouts bravely following Skidmore's leadership, on the other hand, became increasingly isolated along with Skidmore under attacks from both middle class reform socialists and capitalists.[88] Their position was also undermined through the use of much of their critique of the state and their party platform issues by the Tammany Democrats as political fodder in electioneering rhetoric against Republicans and Whigs.[89]

Skidmore died in 1832 in the Cholera epidemic which swept New York that year. Francis Wright, the most famous of the middle class socialists, returned to Great Britain for a five-year visit, and Robert Dale Owen, her frequent collaborator, returned to Indiana where he increased his wealth through land speculation, was active in blocking freed blacks from settling there, and became a power in the state's Democratic party.[90] This might have been the end of the

Working Men's Party, but the political utility of the laboring classes (as scape-goat or champion) made them a necessary faction to the competing political parties throughout this period. To the extent that the more radical elements of labor had been effectively silenced or drawn into the normalizing channels of party politics, as Madison had envisaged, the state was secure—or so it seemed for the moment, for out of the ashes of the Working Men's movement organized and militant labor unions would soon emerge.[91]

The first organized wage labor strike I am aware of was led not by radicals or the Working Men's Associations, but by women and children in 1825 in New York City.[92] Again, in 1828, women and children went out in strike at the mills in Dover, New Hampshire.[93] In 1834 women and children turned out against the Lowell factories of the Boston Associates.[94] "In 1835," Zinn reports, labor-ers in "twenty mills went on strike to reduce the workday from thirteen and a half hours to eleven hours, to get cash wages instead of company scrip, and to end fines for lateness." By his count there were 140 strikes in the manufactur-ing states during 1835 and 1836.[95] The economic distress, which began in 1827, intensified in 1829, and became a catastrophic crisis in 1837 and wouldn't let up until 1844.

According to Zinn, "fewer than a million Americans lived in cities" in 1790; "in 1840 the figure was 11 million. New York had 130,000 people in 1820, a million by 1860." In New York, Boston, and Philadelphia working class families lived packed into single rooms in tenements with little ventilation, and no water, heat, or toilets. Raw sewage fouled the streets which were without sewers. Cholera broke out in 1832, typhoid in 1837, and typhus in 1842.[96] Many immi-grants crowding into the tenements of the manufacturing towns and cities dur-ing this period were from Germany, England[97] and other northern European countries. The great majority of unskilled immigrants arriving during this period, however, were Irish Catholics — some of whom had been radicalized in the failed Irish revolution and the years of strife which followed, but many others were awakened through their participation in the labor agitation in the mines and factories of England.[98]

The English immigrants and many of the Germans at least were Protestant, many were skilled workmen or shop keepers, and were thus gladly welcomed — even to the extent of accommodating the Germans' insistence on keeping their own language. The Irish, on the other hand, posed a new sort of social problem which alarmed the Anglo-American native stock.[99] The manufacturers were initially delighted, for the poor Irish were often willing to take on the dirtiest and most dangerous tasks, and they worked for substantially lower wages than native-born workmen, women and children. Thus as Irish wage laborers increasingly populated the mills and factories, and the "bastard shops," native-born men, women and children were put out — circumstances which marked the Irish as enemies of the native white laboring class. And, as might be expected, this animosity was exploited economically in the factories, and exploited politically in electioneering by Federalists, Whigs, Republicans, Loco Focos, Know-Nothings, and Democrats.

The Irish Catholics might have been the perfect immigrant group of scape goats, and they were used as such, except for a number of striking characteristics. They had a long history of resistance and survival under English genocide and oppression.[100] In addition, a strong communal identity and habit of struggle was nurtured by their hostile reception and segregation in American society on one hand, and, on the other hand, by Catholic religion which inculcated them into a community of faith radically different from the individualist tenets of Protestantism.[101] Perhaps, of greater distinguishing importance, poverty was not a sin, indeed, Catholicism taught poverty brought one nearer to Christ; but enriching oneself by robbing another combined two of the deadly sins. While the Irish were relatively few in number, their willingness to dig canals, build dams, and accept low wages made it worthwhile for manufacturers to tolerate them. But when they came by the hundreds of thousands in the 1830s through the 1840s they displaced the native poor as the great dangerous class threatening the "American" state.[102]

Bolstered by their historical and social background, fleeing starvation and economic and political oppression, inspired by American propaganda of freedom and economic opportunity, and enriched by revolutionary ideology, the Irish Catholics were not easily intimidated or denied. To the chagrin of the Anglo-American capitalists and political leaders, the Irish had made a quick study of radical working class labor politics under English capitalist domination, and like their American-born kinsman Skidmore, they had few illusions about the causes of unequal division and legal protection of property.[103] Wherever there were

mill strikes or, increasingly, general strikes in the main manufacturing cities, the
Irish swelled the ranks of the most militant strikers. And, too, again like their
famous kinsman, many of the Irish leaders were self-educated autodidacts.[104]

The economic and political elite in America had long believed education
was their private domain. They so considered education their exclusive privilege that they enacted measures to insure it would remain exclusive. Although
the local community schools were basically good for teaching primary literacy,
they were not intended for higher learning. The elite, in any case, provided
tutors or sent their children to tuition schools and academies. But many young
men from middling level families (e.g., Horace Mann) were able to obtain the
necessary tutoring from local clergy and/or itinerant scholars to help prepare
them for college or clerking in a business. In 1820, it was still possible for an
ambitious white, middle class boy with modest means from the country or town
to acquire an education at Brown, Yale or Harvard by taking a job in town to
earn money for his fees. As increasing numbers of these middle class boys
joined the student population, however, the elite alumni pressured the universi-
ties to increase tuition. When initial increases only slowed the influx, the next
measure enacted was an increase in the academic entrance requirements. Tuition
and entrance criteria were steadily increased until only the sons of the wealthy
could secure the requisite academic preparation and money for admission. As
the academic criteria and fees for admission increased at Harvard, for example,
tuition and academic rigor increased at all of the feeder prep schools as well.[105]
Other established and exclusive colleges in the North East (and the South, specifically in Virginia and Georgia) followed a similar pattern. The capitalist middling classes reacted to the shut-out by creating their own colleges or reforming
existing ones, e.g. Amherst in Massachusetts, the University of the City of New
York, and Antioch and Kenyon Colleges in Ohio. Frederick Rudolph reports,
however, that nearly as soon as utilitarian reforms were attempted or instituted
a backlash of the elite set in to reestablish, stabilize, or impose the classic and
exclusive norm.[106]

Education was thus safely in the hands of the "rich and well-born." Clearly,
however, this comfortable arrangement was inadequate. The spread of radical
literature among the autodidacts of the white laboring classes (and among Free
Blacks and slaves, as well, but for them the Bible was the first great revolution-

ary text followed closely by Walker's *Appeal*) was seen as a greater threat to the state than the British navy had been in 1812.[107] The mainstream popular press delighted in stories warning against labor unions being organized in every quarter and populated variously by Irish, Scottish, Welsh, English, Dutch, nor German radicals, wild women, savage children, and Catholics who would not be happy until they destroyed the American System and the Republic. Whole sections of cities and towns were solidly populated by proliferating Irish Catholics and their priests and nuns. Catholic schools and Working Men's mechanics schools were being organized. Hardly a week seemed to pass without a strike or protest march for work and/or food. With bad manners they refused lower wages during a market crisis, they protested the "high" price of flour and bread dictated by the immutable law of the market, they demanded shorter hours, and they read dangerous propaganda distributed by foreign agents who sought to destroy American law and government.[108]

The laboring classes were neither as blind nor dumb as it may have pleased the governing classes to think. They observed the privileged governing classes, and they observed the passing of power and wealth from educated father to educated son. Genius was not required to profit from such inheritance, nor was genius required to conclude on the basis of appearances that having or not having an education had economic and political consequences. Nor was it altogether a closely guarded secret that the artificial and arbitrary means by which education was distributed or hoarded had a direct bearing on the differentiation of labor, life opportunities, and one's social position. Indeed, Benjamin Tabart's *The Book of Trades, or Library of the Useful Arts* in three volumes, first published in London, and reprinted in the United States in 1807, made this point quite clearly. In his *Book* Tabart lists different crafts and trades under their own heading, and includes in his description of each mention of the wages earned and the necessary education required. Under "The Printer," he writes,

> Journeymen printers, compositors and pressmen, will easily earn from thirty shillings to two guineas a week. The business of the pressmen requires little genius, but a considerable portion of strength. A youth designed for a compositor ought to have been well educated in his own language; and

he will find it of great advantage in the course of his business, if he understand something of the modern and the ancient languages.[109]

Under the heading of "The Merchant," however, Tabart makes no mention of mean wages, and his description of the education required by the merchant takes not a sentence, but four pages. Just as there were obvious distinctions of wealth in American society, there were equally obvious distinctions of education and knowledge.[110]   By the 1820s the laboring classes (and some self-interested middle class reformers) were characterizing the control of education and its unequal distribution as one of the foundational mechanisms of social domination by the governing classes to protect their economic and political privileges. Securing an equal education went hand in hand with securing equal rights and a democratic society, but for democratic radical autodidacts like Skidmore one's rights did not depend on education. As Wilentz explains:

> . . . maldistribution of wealth, [Skidmore] charged, was not an effect of mental superstition, but its cause. At best, the educational reformers were misguided; at worst, they were tricksters: while Skidmore planned for state-funded equal education after the General Division [of property], he thought [Robert Dale] Owen's "sing-song essays" a hoax, that denied the poor were ready to exercise natural rights. At present, he charged, the only lesson the poor needed to learn was that they were entitled to what was theirs. . . . the freethinkers wanted to bestow Right Reason upon the workingmen and lead them to equality; Skidmore sought a political movement in which the dispossessed fought for themselves.[111]

Education, like rights to property, had been unequally distributed by the governing classes. Middle class reformers Robert Dale Owen and Franny Wright argued (much as Horace Mann will later) that education was necessary before one could acquire the full measure of rights and life opportunities, and before economic and political inequalities could be corrected. Contrary to such arguments, Skidmore countered that education was not a prerequisite to rights, justice, and property, but rather, like these, it was a prerogative of democratic citizenship. The fact that the great mass of citizens were denied an education was another means to obscure the undemocratic processes by which they were denied property.

The Working Men rejected the Owenites' state guardianship educational program and, instead, embraced Skidmore's argument and program for rights *and* education. Beginning with the New York Working Men's platform in 1829, which Skidmore had composed, demands by the laboring classes to state legislatures for publicly supported general and equal education for *all* children steadily increased.[112] In addition to demanding a general and equal education, laborers also demanded a termination of the practice of extracting taxes from wage-laborers to publicly subsidize academies and colleges that especially benefited the rich and well-to-do.[113] These demands for a general and equal education acquired force by being linked to an egalitarian democratic vision of society.[114] Such an education entailed a redistribution of civil rights and economic resources, thus directly challenging the exclusive privileges of the elite and well-to-do, and their monopoly of economic and political power.[115]

It is difficult to know absolutely what would have become of these demands for education if they were not along with the other economic and political demands and written petitions evidence of literacy and the power of knowledge — dangerous knowledge as far as the governing classes were concerned — gained largely through self-education. Indeed, although factional party politics and co-optation had dampened the energies of a labor revolution, Skidmore's revolutionary democratic critique of the state continued to resurface, sometimes unexpectedly in the vote seeking propaganda of party scribes, e.g. Orestes Brownson's article "The Laboring Classes," published in July, 1840, and in George Henry Evans' attacks on credit and the banking system and his campaign for land reform.[116] And, too, as Wilentz makes clear, Walker's *Appeal* quickly became the intellectual bedrock of the Black liberation movement.[117]

Thus confronted by organizing, angry, rebellious labor unions, radical immigrant working class politicians, and Black emancipators armed with dangerous revolutionary knowledge of the structures and mechanisms of the state, some members of the Anglo-American capitalist elite began to take seriously Daniel Webster's prescient pronouncement on public education in 1820:

We regard it as a wise and liberal system of police, by which property, and life, and the peace of society are secured. We seek to prevent in some measure the extension of the penal code, by inspiring a salutary and conservative principle of virtue and of knowledge in an early age. We strive to excite a feeling of respectability, and a sense of character, by enlarging the capacity and increasing the sphere of intellectual enjoyment. By general instruction, we seek, as far as possible, to purify the whole moral atmosphere; to keep good sentiments uppermost, and to turn the strong current of feeling and opinion, as well as the censures of the law and the denunciations of religion, against immorality and crime. We hope for a security beyond the law, and above the law, in the prevalence of an enlightened and well-principled moral sentiment. We hope to continue and prolong the time, when, in the villages and farm-houses of New England, there may be undisturbed sleep within unbarred doors. *And knowing that our government rests directly on the public will, in order that we may preserve it we endeavor to give a safe and proper direction to that public will. We do not, indeed, expect all men to be philosophers or statesmen; but we confidently trust . . . that, by the diffusion of general knowledge and good and virtuous sentiments, the political fabric may be secure, as well against open violence and overthrow, as against the slow, but sure, undermining of licentiousness.*[emphasis added][118]

The pushing motivation for investment in a state system of public school education was not limited to establishing a policing institution for the laboring class and immigrants. The capitalists — merchant, agricultural, and industrial alike — were speculating heavily in western lands in addition to their corporate investment ventures in factories, canals, roads, and railroads. Two conditions seemed pressing on their immediate self-interest: 1) the middle class entrepreneurs were smarting from their exclusion from the elite colleges, because it meant an immediate obstacle to avenues of power and wealth, and a lowered social position in the hierarchy; and 2) the heavy investments and properties of the elite and professional middle class required protection as well as able management. With these two conditions uppermost in mind, in addition to the pressures created by revolutionary democratic laborers, Whig party leader and

Massachusetts' Governor Edward Everett made the point very clear to Boston capitalists in 1833:

> We can from our surplus, contribute toward the establishment and endowment of those seminaries, where the mind of the West shall be trained and enlightened. Yes, sir, we can do this; and it is so far optional with us, whether the power, to which we have subjected ourself [the West] shall be a power of intelligence or of ignorance; . . . a reign of darkness, or of light. . . . Let no Bostonian capitalist, then, let no man, who has a large stake in New England, and who is called upon to aid this Institution in the center of Ohio, think that he is called upon to exercise his liberality at a distance, toward those in whom he has no concern. . . . They ask you to contribute to give security to your own property, by diffusing the means of light and thought throughout the region, where so much of the power to preserve or to shake it resides.[119]

The matter of "security to property" became pressing for the nation's capitalists during the depression of 1837 when hungry workmen invited themselves to the New York Mayor's annual banquet for the Democratic party elite, and when, soon after, a protest march of thousands of poor and laborers turned into an orchestrated assault against New York merchants hoarding flour in their warehouses because buyers wouldn't meet their market price.[120] The message seemed clear: no capitalist, his property, or the social order could be considered safe if the laboring classes were left to their own devices and ignorance of political economy.

This then is a partial explanation to our inquiry into what generated the push for a state system of public school education. As we have seen it was not part of a democratic project, nor a beneficent civic response to the requests by working parents for a general and equal education for their children. Schools were to be policing institutions, they were to condition proper public manners and morality, they were to inculcate the proper understanding of political economy, and they were to foster respect within the laboring classes for their social superiors and the sanctity of property which was not theirs. This property included not only commodities and buildings, but laboring time and wages as well; for contrary to what the laborers thought, wages were the owner's property to dispose of as he deemed just and proper, and the laboring time purchased though the wage-labor contract belonged entirely to the employer as well to do with as he would. Labor strikes against decreased wages or for increased wages were thus violent, unrepublican actions against the owner's property and his use of it.[121] The same held true for strikes demanding the same wage for a shorter work day. Schools for the laboring classes, therefore, as explained by both Websters, Rush, Clinton, and Owen and Wright (among others), were understood by the Anglo-American capitalist elite and its surrogate allies as an institutional means to properly enlighten the children of the lower classes about their proper place in the social order and to suit them for what was expected of them as adult laborers. In other words, such public schools were intended to improve them.[122] This was the "school as disciplinary policing institution" motive.

Another motive regarding the middle class and the state system of public school education is considerably more complex and difficult to establish — in part because of the ambiguities within the middle class itself. During the first three decades of the nineteenth century, as already indicated above, white middle class young men were gamely doing their best to climb the social ladder through a college education and the professions (law in particular), politics, and/or small capital ventures. Beginning in the early 1830s, however, small New England textile manufacturers with marginal economic resources were squeezed out of business by the combined forces of larger corporate competitors and a glutted market. In New York City, small masters, shop keepers, mechanics, artisans, and journeymen were squeezed by better financed and larger competitors from above, and by the proliferation of bastard workshops that employed unskilled or semi-skilled workers and an invasion of low-wage taking immigrants from below. And, too, these conditions were greatly complicated by cultural, economic and political antagonisms between skilled and unskilled labor on one hand[123] and masters, merchants, lawyers, and manufacturers on the other; and, too, all social conflicts during this period were conditioned by slavery.[124] The 1837 economic collapse brought on by a great shortage of species (gold and silver) was made dreadfully worse by Nicholas Biddle's punishing constriction of credit — a ploy in his struggle with the President and Democratic Party over the charter of the Bank of the United States — hit the middle class almost as hard as it hit the laboring classes.[125] There was a significant difference, however, in the way the crisis was experienced. While it is true many in the middle class continued to believe in the system, such as Horace Mann, others who experienced the humiliation and sudden desperation of bankruptcy or the loss of their farms suffered a crisis of faith. And in this state of mind, the revolutionary democratic critique of labor against the insulated privileges and arbitrary mechanisms of the Anglo-American capitalist elite took on a resonant meaning — resulting in a growing political militancy against the established economic and political order. Orestes Brownson's 1840 publication of his politically opportunistic rewrite of Skidmore's critique of the capitalist state in the otherwise staid *Boston Quarterly Review* reflected rather than engendered the militant mood of the economically hurting middle class.[126]

Three Movements of the Middle Class

It is against the background of these socioeconomic circumstances that it is possible to detect three simultaneous movements around and through the middle class. The first is put in motion by members of the Anglo-Capitalist elite to energize the movement for a state system of public school education to insulate the children of the middle class from the groundswell of revolutionary democratic ideology and pockets of insurgency.[127] This "school as insulating institution" idea was not new, but the increasing intensity of laborers' rights struggles between 1828 and 1836, the emerging Black liberation movement coupled with an abolition movement among sympathetic (if less radical) whites, and the growth of Irish Catholic immigration gave new meaning and importance to the idea. Insulation was not necessarily an attempt to reproduce the existing social custom of keeping the children of the elite separate from the middle class, and both groups separate from the bad sorts of working class children. Parental occupation, place of residence, cultural customs, and/or the working class child's occupation all served to restrict close relations between the children of different classes and religions. Insulation, rather, was insuring that middle class, white, Protestant children were embraced and inculcated in a learning environment which reproduced a culture, values, and ideology familiar to their social position and as prescribed for them. James Carter, of Massachusetts, had in 1826 pro-

posed an educational model which would bring children from the wealthy and
poor classes together through a common education.[128] Robert Dale Owen, in
1828, together with his allies, promoted an extreme version of Carter's proposal. Owen advocated state guardianship of all children regardless of class at
an isolated location where children would be raised independent of and insulated from the influences of their parents.[129] Neither proposal enjoyed much
popularity: the elite found little to applaud in Carter's plan of social equalization,
and neither the elite nor the laboring classes approved Owen's. Their idea,
however, that education could and would produce the desired type of citizen
(and thus society) was not unique to either gentleman, but had been proselytized
for a considerable time. It was central in Rush's notion of the "Republican
Machine," it undergirded Noah Webster's promotions and publications, and it
was the essence of Daniel Webster's argument for schools as a social policing
institution.[130] More than Rush's, and more than Noah Webster's, it was the
unequivocal class conception of education and its proper social function that
conditioned the "school as insulating institution" motive. In particular, it seems
most likely that it was Daniel Webster's conception of public schools which
persuaded Edmund Dwight and Edward Everett that the task of constructing a
state system of public school education was too important to place in the hands
of an educator and school reformer. They did not want to encourage democratic aspirations, nor did they want their objectives made so obvious as to
generate opposition. They needed one of their own, but one who would pass
scrutiny as a social reformer. In 1837 few fulfilled their criteria better than the
lawyer and powerful Whig politician, Horace Mann.[131]

The "school as insulating institution" motive was not in the least idealistic.
The socioeconomic circumstances of the period (and for duration of the nineteenth century) dictated that the great majority of poor and working class immigrant children would likely attend any school for only a short period — if they
attended at all — before joining their parents in the workshop or factory.[132] And
children of free Black-Americans in the North were already segregated by law,
and in the South, freed or enslaved Black-Americans were denied an education
by law.[133] And too, children of the elite and the greater majority of children of
professionals already attended private academies (or elite public schools like
the exclusive Boston Latin) and would continue to do so. Thus any system of

public school education that could be established would be for all practical purposes an institution of and for the middle class. Any influence such an institution
had on children of the laboring classes would be an added benefit.[134]

The second movement is energized by middle class reformers with indirect
as well as direct linkages to the Anglo-American capitalist elite.[135] The motives
of this group are complex and contradictory: they seem to sincerely want to
effect a harmonious society through the diffusion or Protestant morality, achievement ideology, and capitalist ideology as inculcated by a system of public school
education, but squeezed between the elite from above and the new immigrant
working class from below, and fragmented within by sectarian religious strife
and competition, they promoted a system which attempted several things. The
reformers attempted to heal sectarian divisiveness by promising the inclusion of
the Protestant Bible as the primary teaching text in the new system of public
schools while simultaneously foreswearing partisan interpretation. This was
enormously attractive, because it meant the different sects would be saved the
burdensome expense of supporting their own individual schools. And, too, it
was made more attractive by enabling a unified Protestantism to stand against
the in-rush of Catholic immigrants. So attractive was the proposition that the
different Protestant churches and the businessmen, lawyers, and bankers among
their congregants became the most animated, committed and organized promoters for Mann's proposed state system of public school education and for moving
their state legislatures into line.[136] These middle class reformers addressed
antagonistic class relations by promoting public common schools enshrouded in
achievement ideology, which was aimed specifically at the laboring classes as a
means of obscuring the structured class biases inherent in the system.[137] They
perpetuated social division and fragmentation by the simple means of excluding
Black American children altogether from their schools. As a social institution,
however, the common school did not fully address the economic and political
dilemma faced by the middle class. Appearing to embrace the immigrant working class through the mechanism of the common school might reduce outright
antagonisms, but without something else in place, these social reformers feared
an unwanted equalization would surely follow. At the same time, this something
else ought not to threaten the prerogatives of the Anglo-American capitalist
elite. The "free" high school, as an intermediate level of education between the

common schools and the elite dominated colleges — and distinct from the "union schools" sharply attacked by Mann in 1841 — was the additional component. It gave an educational and training advantage to middle class children over their working class counterparts, but it did not specifically compete with the academies and colleges of the elite.[138]

But Mann, understanding the economic and political relations in the industrializing east, steered clear of promoting high schools.[139] To do so at any time during his tenure as Secretary to the Board of Education would have been to expose the class dynamics inherent in his program to implement a state system of public school education. As long as he could contain and focus the reform movements' energies on realizing common schools, there was a good chance he could diffuse, negate, or lull working class suspicions — and thus their overt and energetic opposition. Once the common schools were structurally in position, local communities could engage in the inevitable political struggle to secure the added taxation to support a high school.[140]

The third movement in the middle class posed the greatest threat to the economic and political campaign for a state system of public school education. Those of the middle class disillusioned with the Anglo-American capitalist elite and their domination of the economy and government, together with those of an independent democratic "old republican" view of society vigorously opposed a state system of public school education. It was an unwanted intervention, a usurpation of their rights, their autonomy, and their freedoms. It was an unwanted intrusion into their families and their communities and their culture. It was undemocratic. It was nothing short of an attempt by the elite to completely dominate — to dictate what people should think and believe.[141] This third movement of middle class opposition would be overcome at different times in different states, but it would continue to be a source of agitation (and it remains so).

With these views in mind of the state system of public school education as a white Protestant institution, as a social disciplinary and policing institution, as an insulating social institution, as a resource in marginal upward social mobility, and, finally, as a hegemonic institution, we come to the critical question: Why was Horace Mann delegated to lead the school movement in the state of Massachusetts (and from there throughout the nation)?

Horace Mann Is Set into Motion As
the Social Engineer of the State
System of Public School Education

We learn from Merle Curti that the "common school" reform movement did not begin with Horace Mann, but with James Carter, a Massachusetts educator, social reformer, and member of the state legislature. Indeed, "it was largely due to his energy and persistence that the bill drafted by his pen for the establishment of the State Board of Education was finally passed by the legislature in 1837."[142] Given Carter's leadership in the matter of public education, it would seem logical and appropriate that he be appointed Secretary to the Board; and too, this was the usual course in politics: advancing the interests of one's superior associates was a typical means of advancing oneself. It was in just this way that Thomas Cooper was rewarded by the Republicans, first with a social position as a Pennsylvania judge, and later with a position at Dickinson College, in Carlisle, Penn., teaching chemistry, and eventually as President of the University of South Carolina.[143] Carter, on the other hand, may have been passed over because of his early insistence that bringing children of the wealthy, the farming country, the poor, the laboring classes, and immigrants together in one congenial learning environment of free schools taught by eminently qualified men would equalize and unify the population.[144] Carter was not without his supporters, but, obviously, he failed to understand the cultural, ideological, economic, and political dynamics resulting from his legislative success. He had acted on the demand and enthusiasm of the laboring classes for free schools for general and equal education, but in so doing he had forced the issue, and he had forced the dominant economic and political powers to take command of the issue in order to protect their interests.

Before the bill's passage, Edmund Dwight, a powerful Whig and one of Boston's wealthiest manufacturing capitalists, and Edward Everett, capitalist investor and land speculator, and Whig governor of Massachusetts, met to consider an effective course of action. Defeating the bill could prove exceedingly dangerous given the existing social crisis generated by economic depression, widespread unemployment, and militant labor unrest. Passing the bill was no less problematic, for they had no intention of losing their labor force or their position in the social hierarchy by turning child laborers into their economic competitors and social, political equals. And it was in this pressurized political context that Dwight and Everett persuaded Horace Mann to take charge of the Secretary's post, because the position and the task were too important to be placed in the hands of a "mere educator."[145]

Mann was industrious. He was respected by his own middle class constituency and by the wealthy merchants and manufacturers of Boston. He was a lawyer who had proved adept at making money through interest on loans to debtors and by serving as a collector for creditors. He had owned two textile mills with his brother and understood the political economy of ownership and wage-labor management. He was an active and respected temperance reformer. He was instrumental in the promotion of railroads and industry. He was a Whig loyalist who had worked his way up through the ranks to hold the powerful seat of President of the State Senate. When all of his attributes were added together, there was no other in the commonwealth who could be more or better trusted to promote a state system of public schools while simultaneously protecting the interests of capital.[146]

Mann at first refused. What did he know about schools or education? Little or nothing. Dwight persisted, he even promised to supplement the Secretary's $1500 salary by $500 yearly if Mann would take the position. Messerli, Mann's biographer, describes this time as one of intense introspection during which Mann meditated on the social and economic crisis engulfing the Republic, and upon his own personal crisis. He still suffered from the shock of his wife's death. He was deeply alarmed by the increasing population, especially the waves of Irish Catholic immigrants, and the increasing numbers of violent religious and labor confrontations. He believed, too, that the increasing militancy of the laboring classes might soon burst into open revolution. And he found the unlicensed greed and self-serving manipulation of government, banking, and judicial power by a growing number of Anglo-American capitalists repugnant.

Mann ultimately persuaded himself to step down from his powerful position as President of the State Senate and accept that of Secretary to the Board, an action which appeared to many of his friends and contemporaries as a great step down. They failed to see , however, that the battle for social control and political domination of the state was shifting: armies of the poor were concentrated in the cities; the burgeoning population of immigrants, especially Germans and Irish Catholics, who challenged the customs and traditions of the native Protestant culture; increasing numbers of organized and united labor unions; the development of interstate communication, transportation, and cooperation among and between militant strikers leading to work and food riots, and city-wide general strikes; the spread of literature propagating revolutionary ideology; the Black-American liberation and abolition movements; and universal suffrage movements, such as the "Dorr Rebellion" that would erupt in Rhode Island in the early 1840s; and so forth.[147] What Daniel Webster, Everett, Dwight, and Mann understood was the simple reality of numbers. As early as 1765 the economic and political elite in American society were aware of, feared, and sought out mechanisms to contain and suppress the common people's independence and aspirations for a democratic society.[148] By 1837 the Anglo-American capitalist elite and native born middle class were significantly and increasingly outnumbered, and their social position of domination depended more than ever before upon an effective social program for establishing hegemony over the masses. The elite and their surrogates feared, however, that in as much as self-education had created a dangerous laboring class, an equal education (such as they themselves enjoyed) would only strengthen the laboring classes' democratic militancy against the capitalists and the state. An *effective* public education, therefore, must lead both the middle and laboring classes away from revolutionary democratic opposition to capital, and, as had been demonstrated by the Democrats, draw their productive energies into a cooperative relation with the capitalists. This is precisely what Mann and other capitalist social reformers set about to accomplish.

Mann had no sooner accepted the position of Secretary to the Board of Education then he embarked upon learning everything he could about education, school architecture, curriculum, organization and administration, funding, teacher training, supervision, and psychology (in the form of Phrenology). He read everything he could find on the theory of education, he visited nearly every school in the state of Massachusetts, and he corresponded with men in the colleges and in the school movements in other states, as well as with interna-

tionally known figures.[149] On the basis of his own experiences, his reading of
Noah Webster,[150] perhaps Benjamin Rush, and everything else on the political
economy of education and society that he could lay his hands on, Mann believed
he could bring about the necessary social transformation. The laboring classes
were not, in fact, the immediate obstacle, for they (white and Black) had been
agitating and petitioning for a general and equal public education, and where
nothing of the sort had been available they had proceeded to teach themselves
and each other — their desire, therefore, would be the mechanism through
which they would be drawn into the system. The real obstacle to public education were factions within the Anglo-American capitalist elite and the middle
class.[151]

Beyond any doubt, Horace Mann was the best choice to be architect of
public schools for the capitalist state. Mann's immediate challenge would be to
convince the propertied elite and middle classes of the possibility of such a
reform institution as he had in mind, and that it was in their long-term self-
interest to provide the monies to make it a reality.[152]

Horace Mann In Motion (As Critic and
Savior of the Capitalist State)

At this point in time, 1837, Marx was still a university student in Germany,
and Mann was 41 years of age. Still a relatively young man, he had been a
beneficiary of, participant in, and witness to the economic and political changes
of the world into which he had been born. In a way which is difficult for us in
the late twentieth century to understand, Mann felt the social crisis swirling
around him as a personal and a universal reality. His whole adult life, his philosophical world view, and his position in the social hierarchy had to this point
been linked to and determined by the capitalist society and state; so it is not
surprising that Mann perceived the revolutionary democratic tendencies among
the poor and laboring classes a personal threat as well as a threat to the state. It
would be a mistake, however, to reduce Mann to a two-dimensional nineteenth
century capitalist.

In many ways, it is true, Mann followed a stereotypical pattern of the middle-class capitalist: from country to city, from private tutor to university, from farm and home industry to manufacturing, from small town lawyer to state and national political figure, from modest means to comfortable wealth, etc., and he was consistently conservative in his politics and elitist in his social views. But, in his own way he was also an intellectual, rejecting Calvinism early in life for Lord Brougham's Natural [Science] Religion, and, about the same time, embracing Combe's version of Phrenology — an advanced science of the mind and behavioral psychology during this historical period.[153] Moreover, Mann was personally opposed to slavery, and, by turns, opposed to states' rights ideology and political practices which sustained the institution. And, too, unlike many of his capitalist brethren, Mann's unwavering support of industries, machines, and technology had less to do with personal monetary gain (although this motive was not absent) than with a firm belief that in machines lay man's ultimate emancipation from nature's bondage. He refused to see, however, as Marx would not, that before machines under the control of the capitalist could lead to human emancipation, it would first be the cause of great destitution and suffering among the laboring classes.

By most historical accounts, Horace Mann was a self-made man and a national saint.[154] Neither characterization, however, is true. Nor was he a surrogate demon masquerading as a social do-gooder. Messerli's biography of Mann is by far the most balanced account of Mann's remarkable accomplishments, and his genuine commitment to social reform. And, too, although Messerli is often enamored with his subject, he is unembarrassed by revelations of Mann's contradictions, his loyalties to the "rich and well-born," his antipathy to universal suffrage and democracy, his elitism and his disdain for the poor, immigrant, and laboring classes.

Horace Mann embodied individual characteristics as well as a particular social position well suited to the task Everett and Dwight wanted him to accomplish. Mann was solidly middle-class in background and was closely linked to the wealthiest and most powerful of the Boston merchant and industrial capitalist families; his career path through university education, law, speculation and industry, and political office was typical of ambitious Anglo-American middle class Protestant/capitalist men who actively sought elite positions among the

governing classes; although an intellectual, he was more importantly a pragmatic lawyer; and, his values, attitudes, voting record, and public behavior were
hardly distinguishable from that of the typical aristocratic Whig capitalist of
Boston. All of these qualities were undoubtedly what Dwight and Everett had
in mind when they set Mann in motion by thrusting him into the Secretary's
position. What distinguishes Mann, I think, and singled him out as *the* best
person for the job, had to be his perceived character of honesty and morality,
coupled with his fixed idea that capitalism was the only possible foundation upon
which the state could stand. In other words, by virtue of his internal contradictions, his holding firmly to two interrelated beliefs (i.e., social reform and social
reproduction,) he would prove to be equally persuasive with the capitalist elite,
the middle class, and the laboring classes. This point cannot be overstressed,
for Mann clearly understood that the success of his state system of public school
education depended ultimately on the willing cooperation of these groups of
antagonists.[155]

Horace Mann: Constructing Social Hegemony

As we have seen, education had served the dominant classes as an exclusive culture capital. It was also a route exploited by ambitious young men from
the middle class to get close to and sometimes obtain social positions of property, wealth, and power; and, self-education by the laboring classes had served
as the means to knowledge of the structures and mechanisms of the state, the
critique of these entities, a reiteration of revolutionary democratic ideology and
culture, and organized resistance. What Mann set out to do, therefore, was
profoundly complex. He had to preserve the exclusivity of elite education, at
least in appearances, while he worked to foster alternative institutions of common learning; and he had to disarm self-education and alternative private elite
institutions of learning—without appearing to do so from a position of power
and privilege—while substituting a hegemonic *common school* education. And,
finally, he had to educate the capitalist elite and middle class that they might
develop an historical perspective of their affairs and those of the state, which,
ultimately and in the long run, were inseparable.

By all accounts Mann travelled extensively criss-crossing the state of Massachusetts; working fifteen hour days, seven days a week, for months on end without pause, Mann gave hundreds of speeches promoting the necessity of universal education in the form of the Common Schools. By means of effective rhetorical argument, his speeches (reinforced by his annual reports) embraced achievement ideology at one pole and the pecuniary value of *common school* education to capital at the other pole; thus the laboring class heard "achievement" and the capitalists heard "morality, respect for property, and cooperative, productive laborers." And both classes heard the Achievement ideology of "increased wealth, productivity, opportunity, and property," all of which would follow from *common school* education and lead inevitably to the expansive growth and strength of the Republic.

Mann published his *Fifth Annual Report* in 1842. In it he sets out to empirically prove that educated laborers are more cooperative, more productive, and significantly increase the factory owner's wealth. He tells his readers that his findings are not based on simple, short term observation, for such a test is decidedly inadequate for being subject to all sorts of errors of judgement. Instead he has visited with and corresponded with manufacturers employing a good many laborers, such as are able to speak to the issues of individual *and* aggregate productivity of their labor force, and are thus in a position to distinguish and measure the productivity of their educated and uneducated employees both in the short-term and over the long-term.

> No observing man can have failed to notice the difference between two workmen, one of whom—to use a proverbial expression—always hits the nail on the head, while the other loses half his strength, and destroys half his nails, by the awkwardness of his blows; but perhaps few men have thought of the difference in the results of two such men's labor at the end of twenty years.
>
> But when hundreds of men or women work side by side, in the same factory, at the same machinery, in making the same fabrics, and, by a fixed rule of the establishment, labor the same number of hours each day; and when, also, the products of each operative can be counted in number, weighed by the pound, or measured by the yard or cubic foot, —then it is

perfectly practicable to determine with arithmetical exactness the production of one individual and another class.

So where there are different kinds of labor, some simple, others complicated, and, of course, requiring different degrees of intelligence and skill, it
is easy to observe what class of persons rise from a lower to a higher grade
of employment.[156]

Based, thus, on his scientific survey and the authority of experienced observation in the factories, Mann has concluded that educated laborers are the most
efficient and productive employees. The possibility that this report might also
be read by the laboring classes was also considered:

> The capitalist and his agents are looking for the greatest amount of
> labor, or the largest income in money from their investments; and they do
> not promote a dunce to a station where he will destroy raw material, or
> slacken industry, because of his name or birth or family connections. The
> obscurest and humblest person has an open and fair field for competition.
> That he proves himself capable of earning more money for his employer is
> a testimonial better than a diploma from all the colleges.[157]

By turns then, first one appeal, then the other, each directed to opposing
audiences. During a period of extensive unemployment and intense competition
for work . . . the message to the laboring classes is clear: get a common school
education, for it will distinguish you from the "dunce" or the gentleman next to
you and make you more desirable to the capitalist. During this same period of
economic distress when every means of production is dear and nothing can be
wasted, the message to the capitalist is no less clear: support common school
education for the laboring classes to insure the protection and productivity of
your property, and thereby the increase of your wealth.[158] The message to the
native born Anglo-American middle class is much more subtle and oblique. It is
revealed in the reproduced letters: the better educated rise to better positions
and better wages, while the majority of uneducated or poorly educated (typically, but not exclusively, immigrants) are regulated to the most menial tasks and
receive the lowest wages.[159]

We should not make the mistake, though, of thinking Mann's message and conception of an effective public school education had no relation to reality or to wide-spread and enduring influence. According to Curti,

> Circulated to the number of 18,000 copies by the New York legislature, translated into German, and cited again and again in school periodicals and in the addresses of educational leaders, this report enlisted from an imposing number of prominent and well-to-do citizens in Massachusetts the testimonial that Mann was to be regarded as a benefactor to humanity for having demonstrated so convincingly that 'the aim of industry is served, and the wealth of the country is augmented, in proportion to the diffusion of knowledge.'[160]

Through his astute mixture of rhetoric and ideology Mann bridged the antagonistic forces of capital and labor in support of the common school system to the extent both classes might perceive the system as the primary means of achieving their distinctly different objectives. Although a monumental accomplishment, it was ultimately inadequate. Laborers may have perceived the common school system as the means to a competitive edge in securing employment, but this in itself did little to alter their experience and understanding of capitalism, the real division between owning the means of production and being the means of production, and the vast inequities embodied in these diametrically opposed positions. Nor, in fact, did it satisfy their aspirations for a democratic society.

What remained to be discovered, and the problem which captured Mann's intellectual energy, was how to transcend the common school system as an educational institution and transform it into a social reproductive and hegemonic institution which would directly affect economic and political relations. This was the problem, Mann believed, whose solution would reinforce and sustain the state; or, if he failed, would ultimately be the cause of the state's undoing.

Throughout this period, in spite of accruing wide-spread support from capitalists and substantial middle class commitment for the *common school system*, tensions between laborers and the capitalist class remained intensely antagonistic and frequently turned violent. Feeling that the situation was fast approaching cataclysmic proportions, Mann seized upon his 1843 honeymoon with second wife Mary Peabody to study the educational systems of Europe, particularly those in England, France, and Germany. Mann and Mary spent five months in Europe, much of that time in the company of George Combe and wife. Mann had the opportunity of meeting Thomas Carlyle when delivering to him a journal sent by Emerson, and Charles Dickens escorted Mann through London's prisons and laboring districts. Rather than close his mind, Mann made a study of the social consequences of full blown free market industrial capitalism upon the laboring classes and the poor. He was stunned by the extreme social divisions between extravagant wealth and the most desperate poverty and degradation.[161] His observations led him to two conclusions: 1) capitalism without moral checks was an abomination, and, 2) the lower classes were a decidedly inferior bunch quite unfit to participate in republican government. The capitalists thus needed social and moral enlightenment for their own long-term interests, if not for the sake of the laboring classes; and the laboring classes, the mass of people in society, were, in their unreformed state, a monstrous threat to the social order and the state.

The English, clearly, had not solved the problem upper-most in Mann's mind. He would, however, discover the solution to the problem, not in an industrial State, or within the domain of a representative system of government, but in Prussia. Drawing on Mann's recorded perceptions and reaction to Prussian society and political economy, and the manner in which the Prussian schools were integrated into the whole, Messerli writes:

That the destiny of Germany should hang on Prussia was remarkable. Compared with other parts of Europe, it had few of the obvious resources from which national eminence was constructed. Lacking cities bustling with manufacturing and mercantile activities, it had based its rise on the agrarian mineral wealth. By diligence, sacrifice, and a Spartan commitment to national goals, Prussia had arrived on the scene as the leading power in the European heartland. Ruled by an absolute monarch whose will was carried out by a ruthlessly disciplined army and narrow-minded and highly efficient bureaucracy, in an age of incipient nationalism, Prussia was admired as a model by other aspiring nation-states. Its citizens were well fed and clothed, literate and absolutely loyal, even if this meant they were also cogs in a national machine whose lives took on meaning largely in terms of some manifestation of national purpose. Work, sacrifice, and patriotism were Prussian ideals, all synthesized into an unquestioning obedience to the state. Such was the envied and admired achievement of the Prussian rulers, and the credit for their accomplishment rested with the most organized system of education on the continent. No creation of some fickle village or town board, the schools were an instrument of the state and their curricula were first and foremost a matter of national political policy. Through them, schoolmasters carried out a program of instruction which systematically, efficiently, and unswervingly aimed at achieving national rather than individual, familial, or local goals.[162]

Mann and Mary departed Europe by way of Liverpool. The journey back was difficult, their ship being tossed about by stormy seas. This was not all that troubled Mann during the return trip, however, for the solution to the problem of reconciling the laboring classes with capitalism seemed as great a difficulty as was the actual antagonism between the two classes. All that he had observed and studied in Europe had completely shaken Mann's sense of the rightness of republican representative government, but such was the government of the United States. How then, did one construct an integrated, efficient, productive, stable Prussian system under conditions of the politically turbulent government of America where the masses nursed on degenerate revolutionary democratic ideology?

Mann might have been paralyzed by this dilemma but for a letter he received shortly after his return from George Combe,

The enlightened Germans who know your country have again and again made this remark to me. "You," said they, "teach that national happiness can be reached only thro' national education, intelligence, and morality. The United States are trying to experiment whether this condition can be reached by placing power in the hands of the ignorant masses. In Germany, especially in Prussia, we are trying the experiment whether we cannot reach it sooner and with less intermediate evil by placing power in the hands of the moral and enlightened, and employing it for the enlightenment and civilization of the masses, with the view of giving them political power in proportion to their attainments in knowledge and morality! "Time," they say, "will show which plan will succeed best; but in the interim, so far as America has gone, we prefer the steady peaceful morality of our own system, to the turmoil, dishonesty and mobbish tyranny of the Americans."[163]

The way seemed clear. In 1844, and with greater emphasis in 1845, Mann's reports stressed the overwhelming necessity of teacher training institutes. He pointed to such models as the Troy Institute, in Troy, New York; and, he returned to the advantages of hiring such eminently trained female teachers — a course of action he had first promoted in 1841 and which he now promoted with frenetic energy in conjunction with his plans for normal schools. Mann also multiplied his efforts to open more common schools, to secure financial support from Dwight and other capitalists for the teacher training institutes, and for increased vigilant supervision of the common school teachers. He redoubled his attention to the design and content of textbooks. All the while he was actively fighting off political and religious sectarian attacks against the *common school* system — much of this opposition Mann actually encouraged by publicly attacking the emergent high school movement (union schools) and private academies.[164] And if this were not already an over-full agenda, Mann closed ranks with the Protestant sects against the Catholic schools as a source of dangerous teachings against American culture, institutions, and government. And, too, from his point of view, the Catholic schools were a real obstacle to his program to inculcate the Irish through the *common school* system.

The *Twelfth Annual Report*, presented in 1848, would be Mann's last before taking John Quincy Adams's seat in the federal House of Representatives as a Whig representative from Massachusetts. No longer promoting the common school system piece by necessary piece, the *Twelfth* is the penultimate synthesis of his learning, and his blue-print for a national state system of public school education modeled on the Prussian State school system, and adapted to the peculiar conditions of the American state.

Had Mann read Marx by this time? Did he even know of Marx's existence? His critique of unbridled capitalism, his understanding of the social decay which it generated, did not depend on a familiarity of Marx's writings. It is hard to imagine that he was not familiar with the Working Men's Associations, their platforms and manifestos. And considering his personal opposition to slavery, he may have read David Walker's *Appeal*. As an owner of textile mills, an employer, and a political backer of industrial enterprises, Mann would surely have attended to Seth Luther's 1832 attack (published in Boston, and citing Mann's mill by name) on the actual conditions of children in the mills and the impossibility of furthering education under such an oppressive capitalist regime.[165] And, Orestes Brownson published the *Boston Quarterly Review* in Mann's back yard, so to speak, and being an astute Whig politician he may well have read Brownson's article on the laboring classes which appeared in 1840 as part of the campaign to attract votes for the Democratic Party.[166] In other words, Marx's writings might well have been redundant, for the American laboring class, and the plebeian class before them, had already established a rich literature of critique and invective against the capitalist state. And, too, Mann's walks through Boston and his sojourn in London had revealed to him in ample evidence the dark side of capitalism.

Mann was opposed to the evils of capitalism, not to capitalism itself. This is an important distinction, for unlike Marx, Mann did not see that the socioeconomic circumstances of despair and destitution necessarily followed from the capitalist mode of production or its "ideological forms," nor that an unequal division of property was inherently permanent or necessarily evil. Most certainly, he agreed with the Prussian view expressed in Combe's 1843 letter: that the masses would be given "political power in proportion to their attainments in knowledge and morality." Until such time, however, anything which suppressed their revolutionary democratic ideology, their culture, and their insurgent radicalism was justified.

Mann's critique of capitalism in his 1848 report must be interpreted in this context. He is not advocating the overthrow or transformation of the capitalist state or mode of production. Not at all. His *Twelfth* is in many respects a morality sermon aimed at individual capitalists, and his delineation of the social conditions and bitter strife wrought by capitalism in England stands as his allegory, his story of what is and what's to come if American capitalists do not check their greed, and ameliorate the social hardships they have pressed upon the laboring classes.

To emphasize his point, Mann gives his audience a small lesson in political economy: a healthy, productive laborer generates wealth for his employer. The tenements which this same employer has erected for his labor force, however, and from which he extracts additional wealth in the form of rent, are so unhealthy a habitation that his productive worker soon falls ill. The laborer's productivity in the factory thus decreases or stops altogether. The employer may think nothing of this and replace the workman, woman, or child from the excess of unemployed. But notice, Mann instructs his audience, instead of extracting wealth from the laborer, the employer must now pay — for now, not having the means of remaining in the tenement, the laborer and family must seek community relief. The employer has thus lost the laborer's productivity and his rent. And, too, the employer has contributed to the poor relief fund through the taxes he has paid, so when the laborer receives aid, it is as if it came directly from the employer's pocket as well as from the aggregate wealth of the community. It is in the capitalist's self-interest, therefore, to protect his profits and the wealth of society by providing healthier living conditions for the laboring classes in exchange for their rent.[167] Mann's critique of capitalism and its social obscenities comes to no more than this attempt to enlighten the Anglo-American capitalist elite as to where their best interests and those of the state lay.

Were this all of the blue-print for the future order of the state, Mann would be largely forgotten by now. The true significance of his *Twelfth Annual Report*, however, resides not his revelation of the laboring class monster engendered by unchecked capitalist greed, but in his scientific argument about the pliability of the child's mind and the social development of consciousness and behavior. In Mann's own words, and echoing those of Noah Webster, "the inflexibility and ruggedness of the oak, when compared with the lithe sapling or the tender germ, are but feeble emblems to typify the docility of childhood, when contrasted with the obduracy and intractableness of man." And the state system of public school education, as he had designed it, "shall be trained to wield its mighty energies for the protection of society."

> . . . the true business of the schoolroom connects itself, and becomes identical, with the great interests of society. The former is the infant, immature state of those interests; the latter, their developed, adult state. As 'the

child is father to the man,' so may the training of the schoolroom expand into the institutions and fortunes of the State.[168]

The balance of the *Report* is a detailed plan of how and why the schools will accomplish this phenomenal feat. It is the Prussian program of inculcation and indoctrination of poor, immigrant, laboring, and middle class children into a rigidly controlled social and behavioral learning environment, staffed by technically trained and carefully monitored female teachers, whose texts and methods of instruction will also be carefully controlled to insure the faithful reproduction of the dominant beliefs, culture, language, and morality of the Protestant, Anglo-American capitalist state. The body of knowledge into which the child is to be inculcated is Protestant capitalism: individual achievement, industry, productiveness, strict morality (temperance and respect for property and authority), and competition (as well as acceptance of an unequal socioeconomic hierarchy). In addition to this achievement ideology, the child will be inculcated in the primary documents of the state, the federal and state constitutions, the Bible, and the righteous justice of the law; however, Mann stipulates, these documents will not be subject to interpretation and debate. Moreover, the children will be fully versed in a citizen's responsibilities under a republican government, and the necessity of respecting the intelligent leadership of their government representatives. Again, except for explaining the process of republican government, debate over policy issues, the mechanisms governing the distribution of resources, and factional politics will be excluded.

Mann's blue-print for the state system of public school education is a design for a hegemonic, normalizing system of Whig, Protestant, capitalist indoctrination.[169] The institution of English Common Law, re-baptized as American law, secured property and the economic and material division of the social classes. Mann conceptualized and helped establish an institution of public education to protect the social order by securing the consciousness of the nation's white Protestant middle class children — who would become, if not actual members of the Anglo-American capitalist elite, members of the governing classes and protectors of the state through their exercise of surrogate managerial powers over the working class. As for the consciousness of the growing numbers of immigrant working class children, it would be disciplined by either a few years in the common schools or by the pressing actualities of necessity and wage-labor — and if this proved inadequate, there were reform schools and prisons. And whatever Mann's statements about evils of slavery, he made no provision within his system for the education of slave or child of freed Blacks.

Mann is, in the final analysis, a middle class capitalist reformer of the type Marx has described as a bourgeois socialist: One who wants "all the advantages of modern social conditions without the struggles and dangers necessarily resulting from them. [One who desires] the existing state of society minus its revolutionary and disintegrating elements. . . . [One who seeks] reforms, therefore, that in no respect affect the relations between capital and labour, but, at the best, lessen the cost, and simplify the administrative work, of bourgeois government."[170] Mann believes these reforms can be accomplished through the causal system of indoctrination he has constructed.

His undeniable achievement results in large measure, however, from the dominant economic and political elite of the state seizing upon and advancing the state system of public school education and shaping this institution to serve their vision of the social order. It is an education meant to dominate the child's consciousness through a capitalist achievement ideology of competitive individualism and meritocracy; through the cultivated belief in the illusion, if not reality, of socioeconomic advancement through education; and through the suppression of individual identity, critical thinking, and scientific inquiry by means of inculcating children in a narrowly constructed rhetoric of a socially homogeneous culture and undisputed history.[171] It is also a form of education designed to separate the native born middle class from the immigrant working class, and white workers from their black counterparts.[172]

And finally, the social insulating motive, the social disciplinary motive, white Protestant supremacy, and the legitimacy of capitalist economic and political relations undergirding the state system of public school education are expressed in differentiated forms after the Civil War and well into the twentieth century under the banners of juvenile justice, reform schools, industrial education and manual training (in the South) and vocational education (in the North), and aimed specifically at poor, ethnic and racial minority children.[173] From the perspective of the late twentieth century it must be admitted that Mann's blue-print of the state system of public school education as normalizing social reproduction, as played out (however imperfectly) over the past 130 years, has proven reliable as an effective brake against the forces of class revolution and democratic social transformation.

Mann, History, and the Public School:
Reflections

Mann occupied a particular social position on the side of republican capitalism against democratic ideology and insurgency. His successes in bringing about the task for which he had been set in motion depended not especially on his individual agency but on the neat fit between his own ambitions and ideology and the social position into which he had been installed. Moreover, Mann inhabited a class position which conditioned his identification, culture, politics, experiences and understanding of American society. Perhaps the clearest illumination of the linkage between individual action and social and class position is the fact that Mann was not unique in embracing the Prussian model of social indoctrination and hegemony through public education. John Pierce, famous for his educational reforms in Michigan, came from New England, also graduated from Brown, and, like Mann, also embraced the Prussian model of social control and hegemony through universal public education.[174] Different geographical localities and particular conditions may call for apparently different responses, but at the structural level congruent social positions tend to dictate corresponding economic and political events and ideas/actions between localities and individual actors. And finally, as demonstrated in the cases of Jefferson, Rush, and Carter, when *individuals* act independently of class position, their actions or proposals are unlikely to have lasting social consequence. Mann's achievements, in other words, were those of a surrogate endowed with specific social powers and tasks by those whose interests he embraced and represented, and who possessed the economic and political resources and cohesive will to transform ideas into institutions. The state system of public school education was made manifest in American society not through individual agency, but through collective class cohesion and action.

The state system of public school education which Mann helped to conceptualize and bring about developed parallel to the development of the material conditions and economic and political relations of the capitalist nation state. Child labor and not child education was the norm for the majority of children in the United States until there was plentiful and cheap adult immigrant labor in the late 1800s and early 1900s. When the adult labor force exceeded the demand, compulsory school attendance laws, which had long been ignored, were enforced. These laws were a disciplinary police action by the dominant social classes. Truancy, or even the use of bad language in school, was often cause for a sentenced term in a reform school.[175] Nor were teachers exempt from repressive screening and scrutiny; political activity, marriage, dialectical pedagogy, use of texts not approved or prescribed by the curriculum were just a few of the things which would prevent certification (which in itself is a mechanism to screen and control prospective teachers) and hiring, or were cause for a teacher's dismissal.[176] The added layer of the high school to that of the common schools followed shortly after Mann's return to legislative politics as a middle class mechanism to advance their children over those of the immigrant working class. In the absence of true consciousness, full intellectual and material development, and unified, cohesive emancipatory action the democratic revolution begun by the laboring classes in the late 18th century remains unfulfilled.

Finally, the efficiency and durability of Mann's blue-print for what Hans Magnus-Enzensberger has termed "the industrialization of the mind," can be seen in Jay MacLeod's Ain't No Makin' It, an extended eight-year ethnographic study of two groups of young men in a New Haven, Connecticut, housing project.[177] One of these groups, the Hallway Hangers, consistently identifies the real gulf between school, its embedded achievement ideology, and the absence of gainful or meaningful employment opportunities. Although they can name the gulf between promise and social reality, they have no critical language or counter-ideology by which to transform their social and material conditions into emancipatory economic and political actions. Their opposite, the Brothers, buy into the achievement ideology and the school. A number of them go on to college. But when structural currents negatively affect the local economy, and

thereby render them unemployed, they internalize the socioeconomic circumstances and believe that their unemployment results from their own inadequacies. Their education, whatever positive content it may have contributed to
their store of knowledge, significantly and deliberately deprived them of a dialectical understanding of the capitalist state in which they live. It rendered them
politically impotent.

This loss of critical social language, understanding and consciousness necessary to the formation of class cohesion and for emancipatory economic and
political action is precisely the product of public school education Horace Mann
intended. And, too, it is for this reason that training teachers spend the bulk of
their time in the study of methods and classroom behavior control, and why they
study Horace Mann in their "foundations" courses and not Marx: to help make
secure the capitalist state, and positively participate in the reproduction of its
hegemony over the tumultuous masses.

ENDNOTES

[1]   Recall my breakdown of the class structure in American society in Chapter One above. I use
the plural form "governing classes" here, because while the elite capitalist social group began
moving out of direct commerce and manufacturing in the 1820s according to Jaher, their wealth
was tied to and dependent on the prosperity and stability of those to whom they extended credit
and in whose interests they participated, the merchant and manufacturer new comers, and the
rising industrialists. In addition to this internally stratified class, the professionals (especially
lawyers, accountants, and public administrators — to eventually include school superintendents
and principals, etc.) and the middle level industrial, merchant, banking, and insurance managers
and clerks were also tied to the dominant capitalist class, by culture, race, and/or ambition; and,
too, their position within the hierarchy of economic and political relations required that they
oversee the lower classes of poor, laborers, immigrants, and so on. The professional and middle
classes, as I have described them, are not defined by income or state of mind, although these
factors are relevant and indicative, but by their dependent and subservient class position within
the hierarchy of capitalist social relations; i.e., they do not own the means of production, instead
they serve the owners; and although they may grow wealthy as a consequence of the services they
perform through their positions, the fact is they are typically the ones who communicate and
impose the capitalist's will on the workers, and who manage the daily affairs of economic
production. There are, in other words, a multiplicity of class fractions that comprise the governing classes. In actual economic and political practice, however, they tend to act in consort to
protect capital/property against the democratic impulses of the laboring classes and their demands for the equitable distribution of resources and rights.

See: Frederic Cople Jaher, *The Urban Establishment* (Urbana: University of Illinois
Press, 1982), 15-316.

2   Horace Mann, *"Twelfth Annual Report* (1848)," The Republic and the School, 79-112; Karl Marx, *"The Communist Manifesto,"* 221-247.

3   John Dewey, *How We Think* (Indianapolis, IN: D.C. Heath, 1910; reprint Buffalo, NY: Prometheus Books, 1991); Collier, *Critical Realism*, 151-155.

4   The classical theories of political economy authored by Smith, Ricardo, Say, and the Physiocrats (combined with American home-grown variants, e.g., Alonzo Potter, Jacob Cardozo, Francis Wayland, John McVickar, and Horace Mann, who held the chair in political economy — as well as the office of the President — at Antioch College after leaving federal and state politics) dominated theory and debate during the historical period investigated here. But in actual practice — by individuals of the merchant and industrial elite, corporations, and by the governing classes as a collective — pragmatic self-interest was determining; i.e., whatever lent itself to the appropriation and acquisition of profit, and/or that which contributed to the security of the state (i.e., the protection of property and the continued economic and political domination of society by the governing classes) determined policy.

The theory of state I am working with holds that the American state is intimately wedded to the foundational conditions of economic production; and its governmental institutions (administrative branch, legislative branches, courts, schools, tax collecting bodies, and police forces, etc.) and political parties are mechanisms through which the capitalist elite exercise and reproduce their domination of society. The state is, for all practical purposes, the primary entity utilized by the class which dominates or controls it to both advance its interests and protect these interests from internal and external threat.

5   Marx, *The Critique of Political Economy*, 20-21.

6   Marx, *Critique*, 21.

7   See: Bryant, quoted in: Avery Craven, Walter Johnson, and F. Roger Dunn, eds., *A Documentary History of the American People* (Boston: Ginn & Co., 1951), 312-313. Bryant reports on twenty tailors arrested and jailed in 1836 for refusing to sell their labor for the wage rates offered.

To the extent significant numbers of the working class hold to a culture and consciousness incongruent with the foundational economic conditions of production and the dominant political organization of society, the state itself will be destabilized by antagonistic social relations. Production will be disrupted and/or crippled, and the preservation of the state and elite dominion will depend increasingly on violent coercion and suppression. Violent coercion is temporarily effective, at best. But the long term stability of a society which is constituted by inherently unequal economic and political relations depends ultimately on finding a mechanism which engenders false consciousness, which obscures and mystifies the structural causes of inequality, and which constructs (or which profoundly contributes to the construction of) the appearance of cultural congruity between society as it is said to be and individual experiences of economic and political relations. This mechanism(s) must, finally, produce the internalization of coercive policing of behavior. Individual resistance or revolt, or that of isolated groups, can be and is successfully suppressed as deviant social behavior; but when the same revolt is enacted by an entire class, their behavior is revolutionary. An effective mechanism of social control, therefore, must attack the formation of "class consciousness" at the level of the individual — hence the crucial importance of liberalism's atomistic theory of society and individualism as the foundation of achievement ideology — and, too, it must propagandize this ideology throughout society.

8   Marx, *Critique*, 21.

9   My research has not uncovered evidence of a legal proscription against indentured servitude in the United States. Indeed, Gino Speranza, an Italo-American and officer of the Society for the Protection of Italian Immigrants of New York, presented evidence of Italian workers held in contract bondage by employers enforcing indentured contracts with armed guards in West Virginia, in 1903, in an attempt to outlaw the practice. Gino C. Speranza, "Forced Labor in West Virginia," in *A Documentary History of the Italian Americans*, eds. Wayne Moquin and Charles Van Doren (New York: Praeger, 1974), 117-121.

10   Marx, *Critique*, 21.

11   This summary holds in outline, but at the level of specifics socio-economic circumstances and class relations in the decade before the War of Independence and during the War were extraordinarily complex. By the conclusion of the Seven Years War wealth holding in Boston, Philadelphia, and New York City was heavily concentrated among the upper five percent of the colonial ruling class. There was a corresponding concentration of the majority of the population among the propertyless. From New York to North Carolina both Tory and Whig leadership, merchants, and landlords had repeatedly called upon the British army and cheered its bloody suppression of popular insurgency movements. The violent tensions between the ordinary people and the Whig elite were not lost on the British who pardoned William Prendergast after the Whigs had sentenced him to a grisly death for daring to represent the demands of the tenant and small farmer insurgents in the Hudson Valley; they refused Cadwallader Colden's panicked petition for military intervention in 1773 and 1774; and, at the on-set of the War, they promised the back-country insurgents land reform against the Whig landlords, freedom to indentured laborers and slaves, and protection to the Amerindians in exchange for their loyalty to the crown. See: Gary B. Nash, "Social Change and the Growth of Prerevolutionary Urban Radicalism;" and Marvin L. Michael Kay, "The North Carolina Regulation, 1766-1776: A Class Conflict," in T*he American Revolution: Explorations in the History of American Radicalism*, ed. Alfred F. Young (DeKalb, IL: Northern Illinois University Press, 1976), 3-36, 71-124; and Billy G. Smith, *The "Lower Sort": Philadelphia's Laboring People, 1750-1800* (Ithaca: Cornell University Press, 1990).
       Antagonistic class struggle lay at the heart of the strained alliance between the Whig leadership and merchants and the mass of commoners against the British:

> The Boston Mob, raised first by the Instigation of Many of the Principal Inhabitants, Allured by Plunder, rose shortly after of their own Accord, attacked, robbed, and destroyed, several Houses, and amongst other, that of the Lieutenant Governor; and only spared the Governor's, because his Effects had been removed. People then began to be terrified at the Spirit they had raised, to perceive that popular Fury was not to be guided, and each individual feared he might be the next Victim to their Rapacity. The same Fears spread thro' the other Provinces, and there has been as much pains taken since, to prevent Insurrections, of the People, as before to excite them.

General Thomas Gage to Conway, 23 September 1765, quoted by Dirk Hoerder, "Boston Leaders and Boston Crowds, 1765-1776," in <u>The American Revolution</u>, ed. Alfred F. Young, 235.

[12]   The Whig leadership and merchants in their arrogance all too frequently made the political error of assuming their interests were those of the common people. That the interests between these two classes were not the same but were in fact in opposition and conflict — as the people independently demonstrated in the Stamp Act attacks against the economic and political elite, the second dumping of a shipment of tea a few weeks after the Boston Tea Party, the march of back-countrymen on Lexington, and in the closures of courts and raids on jails and armed confrontations of sitting legislatures before and after the War of Independence — meant the Whigs had to repeatedly relearn the political lesson that the people wanted a democratic revolution and transformation of economic and political relations instead of the Whig program of unincumbered acquisition of wealth in complete disregard of the old traditions of *policing* (i.e., a harmony of interests and a corresponding duty to the welfare of the whole community). See: Tomlins, 35-59, 81-97, passim.

[13]   See: Edward Countryman, "'Out of the Bounds of the Law': Northern Land Rioters in the Eighteenth Century;" Joseph Ernst, "'Ideology' and an Economic Interpretation of the Revolution;" Eric Foner, "Tom Paine's Republic: Radical Ideology and Social Change;" Dirk Hoerder, "Boston Leaders and Boston Crowds, 1765-1776;" Marvin L. Michael Kay, "The North Carolina Regulation, 1766-1776: A Class Conflict;" and Gary B. Nash, "Social Change and the Growth of Prerevolutionary Urban Radicalism," in *The American Revolution: Explorations in the History of American Radicalism*, ed. Alfred F. Young (DeKalb, IL: Northern Illinois University Press, 1976).

[14]   Tomlins, 1-106, passim.

[15]   Tomlins, 97.

[16]   James Madison, "Federalist No. 10," *Political Thought In America: An Anthology*, ed. Michael B. Levy (Prospect Heights, IL: Waveland Press, 1982), 111.

[17]   See: Howard Zinn, *A People's History Of The United States* (New York: Perennial Library/ Harper & Row, 1980), 83; Ronald Hoffman, "The 'Disaffected' in the Revolutionary South," *The American Revolution*, ed. Young, 279-280, passim.

[18]   David P. Szatmary, *Shays' Rebellion: The Making of an Agrarian Insurrection* (Amherst, MA: The University of Massachusetts Press, 1980), 1.

[19]   Szatmary, 20-21.

[20]   Szatmary, 21-22.

[21]   George Brown Tindall and David E. Shi, *America: A Narrative History*, 4th ed. (New York: W.W. Norton, 1996), 329.

[22]   Van Beck Hall, *Politics without Parties: Massachusetts, 1780-1791* (Pittsburgh: University of Pittsburgh Press, 1972), p.29; quoted in Szatmary, 32.

[23]   Szatmary, 32.

[24]   Szatmary, 45.

[25]   Szatmary, 33.

[26]   Tomlins indicates to the contrary that in some states, Pennsylvania in particular, popular governments were established that began numerous actions to transform property relations in the new nation. He argues that these popular legislative acts as much as anything else excited the economic and political elite to develop a superseding legal organization to limit the powers of individual state governments. No sooner were "'agrarian' designs" initiated, however, than a unified and cohesive elite reaction was fired up to put an end to levelling democracy. See Tomlins, 60-97.

[27]   Howard Zinn, *People's History*, 90.

[28]   Plough Jogger, quoted by Zinn, 91.

[29]   Zinn, 92.

[30]   Zinn, 93.

[31]   Michael Merrill and Sean Wilentz, "William Manning and the Invention of American Politics," in *The Key of Liberty; The life and Democratic Writings of William Manning, "A Laborer,"* 1747-1814, by William Manning, eds. Merrill and Wilentz (Cambridge, MA: Harvard University Press, 1993), 19-21, 25.

[32]   Szatmary argues, however, that the energy of the rebellion was diffused not so much by military force as by a turn-about of British sympathies, the emigration of key rebels, and by political co-optation. Those of the Shayites who remained behind in Massachusetts were momentarily quieted by compromises made by the General Court and the liberalization of credit — and, too, they were soon distracted by the political fight against ratification of the new Federalist Constitution. See: Szatmary, 119.

[33]   Zinn, 91-94. The response of the ruling class to popular protest was historically consistent with pre-War of Independence actions. The elite took-up arms against the people in Boston in 1765, and again in 1771 in the Hudson Valley. In 1761 in North Carolina and again in 1766 in the Hudson Valley, the ruling class resorted to the British Army to put down popular insurgency. See Gary B. Nash, ibid., passim; Edward Countryman, ibid., passim; and, Marvin L. Michael Kay, ibid., passim.
    Of the utmost significance, however, is the fact of widespread protest by yeoman farmers, tenant farmers, and working class townsmen against unresponsive and unrepresentative legislatures and oppressive courts. The burden of taxation without representation, and the confiscation of their farms (or imprisonment) for debts — socioeconomic circumstances caused by politicians, merchants and lawyers — convinced the insurgents that the Revolution had been betrayed. See: Szatmary, passim.

[34]   Merrill and Wilentz, 24.

[35]   See: Winthrop D. Jordan, *White Over Black: American Attitudes toward the Negro,* 1550-1812 (Chapel Hill: University of North Carolina Press, 1968), 110-115, 393-399, passim; Benjamin Quarles, *The Negro in the American Revolution* (Chapel Hill: University of North Carolina Press, 1961, 1991), 38-40, 42-48, 61-67; Sean Wilentz, "Introduction," in *Appeal to the Coloured Citizens of the World, but in particular, and very expressly, to those of the United States of America,* by David

Walker (Boston: by the author, 1829, 1830; reprint New York: Hill and Wang, 1995), ix-xi, xx-xxi (page references are to this reprint edition).

[36]   See Zinn, 76; Jordan, 302-303. See, too, Hoffman, passim.

[37]   See: David Walker, passim; Frederick Douglass, Narrative of the Life of Frederick Douglass, An American Slave [1845] (reprint New York: Penguin, 1986). See, too: James D. Anderson, The Education of Blacks in the South, 1860-1935 (Chapel Hill: University of North Carolina, 1988), chapter one, passim. Although each of these sources (two direct, primary accounts, and one excellent interdisciplinary historical explanation) touch on white antagonism toward education and literacy of Black-Americans in the South, they also illuminate the prevalence of similar antagonisms in the North — where, in spite of singular exceptions, the education of Black-Americans was more often an idea than reality.

[38]   See: Tomlins, passim.

[39]   Alexander Hamilton, 1787, quoted by Zinn, 95.

[40]   Zinn, 90.

[41]   Zinn, paraphrasing Charles Beard, 90.

[42]   James Madison, *"Federalist, Number 10,"* quoted by Charles A. Beard, *The Economic Interpretation of The Constitution of the United States* (New York: The Free Press, 1986), 14-15.

[43]   See: Marshall, *Dartmouth College v. Woodward, 1819, Documents of American History,* ed. Henry Steele Commager (New York: Appleton-Century-Crofts, 1958), 220-223; and Tomlins, part I, passim. See, too: Herbert G. Gutman, "Joseph P. McDonnell," *Power and Culture,* 93-116. In this essay Gutman illuminates the profound structural limits of legislative power as a vehicle for transforming socioeconomic circumstances.

[44]   Tindall and Shi, 314-317.

[45]   See: Manning, *The Key of Liberty.* It must be acknowledged that there were also hold-overs of the old aristocracy, as well as members of the new capitalist aristocracy sympathetic with Hamilton's views who thought the new Constitution, and the Bill of Rights in particular, went too far toward enfranchising the lower classes. Some portion of the opposition to the ratification of the Constitution must be attributed to conservative and reactionary factions within the elite. Likewise, significant numbers of the laboring classes supported the Constitution and celebrated its ratification because they imagined that it created a popular government which would protect them from exploitation at home and from oppressive competition from foreign merchants and manufacturers.

[46]   Herbert G. Gutman, "The Black Family In Slavery and Freedom," *Power and Culture,* 357-379; John Ashworth, *Slavery, Capitalism and Politics in the Antebellum Republic,* Vol. I (New York: Cambridge Univ. Press, 1995), 1-12.

[47] See: Tomlins, 61; Ashworth, passim; Wilentz, *Chants Democratic*, passim; and J.T. Headley, *Pen and Pencil Sketches of the Great Riots* (New York: E. B. Treat, 1882; reprint New York: Arno Press, 1969), 1-288.

[48] Universal public education was out of the question in the South. Landlords in the northern states had no interest in educating the children of their tenants. In northern cities of Boston, New York, and Philadelphia, the elite were experimenting with Lancasterian and Charity schools — which a substantial number of laboring classes boycotted because of the pauper stigma attached to such schools. And, scattered about in New England and the western territories autonomous community district or religious sectarian schools were the norm. Education, as a cultural and class privilege, was a resource of the elite. It was a resource necessary for the acquisition of wealth and the power to protect it in a society stratified by economic and political inequalities. And, too, such a resource was also an expensive commodity — made deliberately so to insure its exclusivity. Thus an "educated" mass of laborers posed a real threat to elite social domination, which they could imagine but as yet had no notion of how to contain except by denial and withholding.

[49] Under existing forms of education in the South at this time, the Planter class and professional elite hired private tutors for their children or sent them to private academies in the U.S. and Europe. Under Jefferson's plan each organization of 100 freeholder families would be taxed to support a primary school, and a combination of counties would each support a common grammar school. Although the children of the lower class of freeholders would receive three years of schooling, with a few selected for scholarship support, the primary and grammar schools and the teachers would continue to be publicly supported. Any boy whose parents could afford a modest tuition could complete the entire course of education whatever his intellectual faculties. In effect, then, the cost to the upper classes for the education of their children was substantially reduced.

[50] Thomas Jefferson, "A Bill For The More General Diffusion Of Knowledge," *Public and Private Papers* (New York: Vintage Books/The Library of America, 1990); 39-47. Computing the number of potential scholarship boys of Jefferson's proposed 1778 bill is an estimate. He names 71 counties, and each is divided into 100s — I am guessing he means families — for the purpose of establishing a primary school. The 71 counties are combined to form 20 groupings, and a grammar school is proposed for each one of the twenty. Each county will promote one boy after three years of study to the grammar school (71 boys total). After the first year one-third of this group will be cut (say 23, leaving a balance of 48 boys). After the second year of grammar school all but one is cut. In the revised version of the bill, reproduced by Gordon C. Lee in his Columbia/Teachers College edition, Jefferson proposes to rake from the "rubbish" twenty scholars to continue for six years additional study in the grammar schools, after which time the ten best scholars of the twenty are advanced to William and Mary College for three years of study — with the second ten best perhaps employed as masters in the primary schools. Thomas Jefferson, *Crusade Against Ignorance*, ed. Gordon C. Lee (New York: Teachers College, 1961).

[51] So Jefferson argued before economic and political power was decisively concentrated in the federal state. Actual socioeconomic circumstances in the South and the North, however, nullified the limited democratic potential of Jefferson's vision. Indeed, the popular insurgencies of Regulators of North Carolina before the War of Independence and Shays' Rebels in Massachusetts after the War illustrate the social reality confronting the self-sufficient yeomen in a capitalist society. By small commercial debt or by excessive taxation the yeomen were pried from their land by lawyers representing merchants, or acting as government agents. In either case land speculators and the

planter class benefited. Without a transformation of debtor laws, terms of repayment, the determination and levying of taxes on a sliding scale based on capital wealth, or the possession of a surplus of species, a modest education was and would prove to be an inadequate foundation for yeoman self-sufficiency. And, as a final observation, Jefferson's system could and would do nothing to alter the fact that the elite did already and would continue to dominate the capital economy, the government and the development of the State.

[52]   Benjamin Rush, "A Plan for the Establishment of Public Schools . . ." (1786); and Noah Webster, "On the Education of Youth in America" (1790), in *Essays On Education In The Early Republic*, ed. Frederick Rudolph (Cambridge, MA: Harvard University Press, 1965), 1-23, 41-77.

When recast in terms of capitalist self-interest a few decades later (and against the background of social unrest) by Massachusetts State Governor Edward Everett, however, Rush's plan for investing in state colleges as a direct means to promote commercial finance and industry would be given a warmer reception. See: Edward Everett, "At a Public Meeting, Held at St. Paul's Church, Boston, 21st May, 1833, on Behalf of Kenyon College, Ohio," *Orations and Speeches On Various Occasions* (New York: Arno Press, 1972), 329-330.

Webster's arguments in 1790 for public education may not have been embraced as he laid them out, but they were carried forward influentially by his entrepreneurial ventures, notably his *American Spelling Book* (1831) and his *American Dictionary of the English Language* (1828). Webster's contention that instructing children in American language — its pronunciation, its connotative and denotative meanings, and a standardized spelling (frequently distinguished from British spellings) — and American literature was fundamental to shaping an American consciousness would, however, find a powerful convert in Horace Mann. Webster's argument for the relation between language, consciousness, and a homogeneous national identity together with the example of Prussian education and its relation to social order would gel in Mann's mind as key idea structures undergirding his theoretical and policy construction of a state system of public school education.

[53]   See: Alfred F. Young, "George Robert Twelves Hewes (1742-1840): A Boston Shoemaker and the Memory of the American Revolution," *The New England Working Class and the New Labor History*, eds. Herbert G. Gutman and Donald H. Bell (Urbana: University of Illinois Press, 1987), 3-4, 34-35, passim.

[54]   Education of one sort or another was a perennial topic of debate as well as a social activity during the early national period among the Protestant religious sects, the elite and professional social strata, and different sorts of social reform movements. There were church schools, church dominated public village schools, private academies, as well as Lancasterian schools and charity schools. By and large these were local and autonomous enterprises. In addition, there were educational societies such as those directed by Robert Dale Owen, or Horace Mann's friends and social reformers, Samuel Gridley Howe and Catherine Beecher. It can be argued that all of these individuals, groups, and their activities established a climate conducive to the formation of a state system of public school education. Several points of distinction must be made however: 1) the lack of morality attributed to the laboring classes and poor was the dominant rationale undergirding these early education movements; 2) many of these educational reform movements had overlapping leadership with the temperance societies; 3) these activities did not constitute a state system; 4) none of these embraced an integrated or an equivalent education for Black-American children; 5) although promoted in large measure by members of the professional and intellectual elite, it was only the most far sighted among the economic and political elite (e.g., Edward Everett and Edmund Dwight in Massachusetts) who were prodded by these early initiatives and the availability of federal money for the

promotion of public education on one hand, and the strident insurgency of the laboring classes on the other to take the step of instigating a state system of public school education. Their initiative was meant to strategically undermine and usurp that of the Working Mens' and the trades union movement and the Free Black anti-slavery insurgency rather than as a democratic response to the popular constituency and its demands for a general and equal public education for all. There is also evidence which indicates the linkage between education as an ideological agency, workers, and a stable social order was not a new idea or program. The New England manufacturer Samuel Slater initiated Sabbath schools as early as 1796 in an attempt to inculcate his employees. See: Steve Dunwell, *The Run Of The Mill* (Boston: David R. Godine, 1978), 23.

But Slater and others who viewed education as a mechanism for shaping values and beliefs, and thereby directing behavior, seem to have been a decided minority. The dominant consensus among the elite before 1835 appears to be that too much education, like too much democracy, was a dangerous thing — it would lead to economic and political levelling. The Southern elite outlawed all forms of education of Blacks. The movement of the Northern economic and political elite as a class behind a state system of public school education developed gradually. Horace Mann was instrumental in gaining the support of many of the elite for a Prussian model system of education which was hegemonic rather than socially transformative, but not even his best efforts were wholly successful. Some among the Northern elite, like Franklin Dexter of Massachusetts, may never have come over. And, the Southern planter elite obstructed public education for the white and black laboring classes into the twentieth century.

55   See: Messerli, 271: "one portion of mankind are to be refined and cultivated, the other to suffer, toil, and live and die in vulgarity." — Quoting Mann's report of his meeting in 1837 with Franklin Dexter, "a prominent attorney and one of the leading men of Massachusetts."

56   See: Jaher, passim; Francis Wayland, *The Elements of Political Economy*, reprint edition (Boston: Gould and Lincoln, 1860), 106-107, 121.

57   Dorfman, II:520, 571.

58   See: Hoerder, 254-255. Pre-War of Independence Boston committeemen make liberal use of the poor relief fund to erect and operate privately owned textile factories for the forced employment of the poor. See: Dunwell, 15, 24, 97; poverty will generate mill workers. For explication and documentation of struggle over the contract use of convict labor see: Wilentz, *Chants Democratic*, 133, 233.

59   Dorfman, I:291.

60   Steven Ross documents higher wages for skilled workmen and laborers generally during the early years of settlement, but by the 1820s, following the increase and surplus in the laboring population, socioeconomic circumstances for Cincinnati workers increasingly resembled those in New York City and the factory regions of New England. Steven J. Ross, *Workers On the Edge: Work, Leisure, and Politics In Industrializing Cincinnati*, 1788-1890 (New York: Columbia University Press, 1985), 10-17.

61   The struggle over tariffs would remain one of many heated political issues between the North and South up to the Civil War. See: Wilentz, *Chants Democratic*, 152, passim. See: John C. Calhoun, "Speech on the Tariff Bill" (1816), and, "Exposition and Protest" (1828), *Union and*

Liberty: The Political Philosophy of John C. Calhoun, ed. Ross M. Lence (Indianapolis: Liberty Fund, 1992), 299-309, 311-365.

[62]   Sean Wilentz, "Society, Politics, And The Market Revolution, 1815-1848," *The New American History*, ed. Eric Foner (Philadelphia: Temple University Press, 1997), 65.

[63]   For a contemporary historical account, see: Seth Luther, passim.

[64]   Joseph Dorfman, I:255, passim.

[65]   See: Seth Luther, passim; and, "The Working Man's Party Of Philadelphia Calls For Free, Equal Education For All" (1831), *Education In The United States*, ed. Sol Cohen, II:1054-1056; see as well, Dunwell, 15; and, Wilentz, *Chants Democratic*, 107-142.

[66]   See: Dunwell, 23-24, 46.

Some time between the late 1820s and early 1840s, New England manufacturers, less secure of their domination of the women and children in their employ, sent agents ("slavers") to recruit young women from areas at great distances from the factories. What paternalism, discipline, contracts and rhetoric failed to secure in the way of compliance and conformity, dependence and isolation might. If nothing else, bringing in young women from afar made them an effective wedge against resistant women and children from the surrounding countryside. M.B. Schnapper, *American Labor* (Washington, D.C.: Public Affairs Press, 1972), 41; and, Dunwell, 97.

[67]   Dorfman, I:394.

[68]   See: Dorfman, passim; and Jaher, passim.

[69]   Tomlins, 101-219; Wilentz, *Chants Democratic*, 38, 98, 151-52, passim.

[70]   As a matter of fact, opposition of the elite and its surrogate allies to the extension of education to the working classes (white and free Black) during this period of American history predates similar opposition to the education of Black-Americans among the Planter class and its allies in the South after the Civil War and continuing into the twentieth century. As a practical matter of commerce and the exploitation of laborers, the less literacy among workers the better. In the North, workers were required to sign (or make their mark) on contracts as a condition of employment which gave the employer absolute power while simultaneously exempting him from responsibility for injuries. (See: M.B. Schnapper, 41-54; and, Tomlins, 331-384.) In the South: before the Civil War, literacy was viewed as the foundation of revolution among Freed Blacks and slaves; and, after the Civil War wholesale produce buyers and employers exploited illiteracy to cheat and impose oppressive, exploitive labor and purchasing contracts.

For an explanation of law, contracts and social relations in the North, see: Tomlins, 223-297; for a general overview of the textile industry, its development and relations of production in New England, see Steve Dunwell, 2-101. For an explanation of law, contracts and economic and political relations in the South, see: James D. Anderson, 18, 25-27, 186-237, passim.

The resistance to the extension of education to the white and immigrant working classes or Blacks as understood by the elite in the North, before 1837, and in the South had an ideological basis as well. Achievement ideology and its basis in individual faculties and character — as an explanation of economic and political inequality — would crumble in a moment if the children of the working class should prove equal or superior to the children of the elite in the same classroom. And, in the South, the ideology of white supremacy would crumble should Black-Americans demonstrate their intellectual equality or superiority over uneducated working class whites or the educated elite.

And, too, in the North prior to 1837, and in the South (for much of its history) autodidacticism among the working classes and Blacks provided the foundation for promoting economic and political self-determination and a revolutionary democratic assault on the existing organization and structured inequities of society. A laboring class autodidact such as a Thomas Skidmore or David Walker was perceived as enormously dangerous to the social order. An entire population of white and Black educated, literate workingmen and women was an idea too terrible to actualize willingly. In the South, the white governing classes passed laws forbidding the teaching of Blacks, and imposed violent penalties upon any caught violating the law and especially upon Blacks found in possession of Walker's Appeal or other reading materials. After the Civil War, and with the stimulus of Northern philanthropists, whites would undertake a protracted campaign to deprive, subvert, suppress, manipulate and otherwise limit the education sought by or made available to Black-Americans. In the North, the elite and its allies spared little energy or expense in exploiting the literacy of workingmen and women through books purporting to explain political economy to the workers (e.g., Stephen Simpson's), the popular press, handbills and journals to discredit Skidmore, Walker, and others like them. See: Wilentz, *Chants Democratic*, 182-216, passim; David Walker, passim; James D. Anderson, passim. On Stephen Simpson, see: Edward Pessen, *Most Uncommon Jacksonians* (Albany, NY: State University of New York Press, 1967), 75-78.

In both historical and geographical locations, it was fear generated by the self-education of laborers and resulting democratic insurgencies (and visionary programs), and the dependence of capital upon a cooperative, hegemonically dominated labor force that proved to be the motivation undergirding the governing classes' instigation of a state system of public school education — an education they could dictate and manipulate to serve their interests, and antithetical to the ideas and social vision popularized by radical, revolutionary democratic autodidacts.

[71]   See: Dunwell, 14-49; Edward Pessen, *Riches, Class, and Power* (New Brunswick, NJ: Transaction, 1990), 84-89; and Dorfman, II:541. In particular, closely read *The Twelfth Annual Report*, by Horace Mann, in which he articulates the unconscionable socioeconomic circumstances of laborers found in an industrial capitalist society on the one hand, and, on the other hand, promises that his system of public school education will so inculcate the child as to prevent his being poor. The implication clearly is one's hard circumstances derive from ignorance. However, in his discussion of physical education, which is a brief lecture in political economy, Mann is quite clear about the fact that poor, unhealthy housing is not a matter of the workers' ignorance, but is instead a condition created by the capitalist and landlord who owns these dwellings and extracts rent from the inhabitants forced to live there. In this connection, as well, see Dunwell, cited here, for a description of the treatment of the Irish laborers employed in dredging the canals and constructing the textile mills in Lowell, Massachusetts.
See, too: Seth Luther. His address is a direct critique and detailed rebuttal of the practice of popularizing achievement ideology to the hilt while simultaneously promoting and protecting a society and system of production which is grinding the working people down and makes achievement and upward social mobility impossible for all but a rare few.

[72]   Letter from Copper to Jefferson, quoted Dorfman, II:532.

[73]   Dorfman, I:440. Leonard W. Levy is not so generous in his appraisal of Jefferson's practices and policy decisions. Contrary to the democratic political idealist that Jefferson projects in much of

his rhetoric, in practice he was a harsh, elitist autocrat no more inclined toward the democratic aspirations and movements of the common people or tolerant of his political rivals than others of his class and social position. See: Leonard W. Levy, *Jefferson and Civil Liberties: The Darker Side* (Chicago: Ivan R. Dee, 1989).

⁷⁴   Dorfman, I:417. Although historians debate the particulars of Jefferson's presidency, Dorfman's argument regarding the continuity of Hamilton's programs under Jefferson appears to hold in general. According to Sean Wilentz:

> Jefferson's election, although it doomed the Hamiltonians' finance system, did nothing to halt the early industrialization of the crafts and the spread of capitalist wage labor. However genuine Jefferson's more radical speculations on property and democracy may have been, neither his nor his successors' policies attacked locally based efforts to improve manufacturing, finance, and transportation. [...] Many manufacturing entrepreneurs found the Jeffersonians' laissez-faire instincts more congenial than Hamiltonian centralism. Jeffersonian leaders, meanwhile, displayed little enthusiasm (and sometimes outright hostility) toward the infant craft Unions.

Sean Wilentz, "The Rise of the American Working Class, 1776-1877," *Perspectives On American Labor History,* eds. J. Carroll Moody and Alice Kessler-Harris (DeKalb, IL: Northern Illinois University Press, 1990), 89.

⁷⁵   In 1820, the lawyer Daniel Raymond wrote in his *Thoughts on Political Economy*:

> It does not . . . depend upon the will of the man who has no property, whether he will have any portion of the product of labour; but upon the man who has property. If those to whom the whole surface of the earth belongs, choose to say that those . . . who have no property, shall not labour; or, in other words if they do not choose to employ them, they will, by the established laws of property, have no legal right to any portion of the product of labour; and must starve, unless supported by the bounty of others — they must become paupers.

Quoted by Franklin Folsom, *Impatient Armies of the Poor* (Niwot, CO: University Press of Colorado, 1991), 26.

⁷⁶   See: Zinn, 59-246; Wilentz, *Chants Democratic*, passim; and Folsom, 4-107.

⁷⁷   See: Winthrop Jordan, passim.

⁷⁸   See: Folsom, 32.

⁷⁹   See: Tomlins, 99-179; and Wilentz, *Chants Democratic*, 145-296, passim. See, too: William Cullen Bryant, "The Right of Workingmen To Strike" (June 13, 1836), *A Documentary History of the American People*, eds. Avery Craven, Walter Jonson, and F. Roger Dunn (Boston: Ginn and Company, 1951), 312-313. On the matter of Black liberation see: Wilentz, "Introduction," in David Walker's Appeal, vii-xxiii. Slavery was not officially abolished in New York until 1827.

⁸⁰   Thomas Skidmore, *The Rights of Man to Property! being a Proposition to make it equal among the adults of the present generation: and to provide for its equal transmission to every individual of*

each succeeding generation, on arriving at the age of maturity (New York, 1829), Chapter IV, pp.125-144; abridged in *Social Theories of Jacksonian Democracy,* ed. Joseph Blau (Indianapolis, IN: Bobbs-Merrill, 1954), 355-357.

[81]   See: Wilentz, *Chants Democratic,* 187-188.

[82]   See: Skidmore, passim. For commentary on Skidmore's political economy see: Dorfman, II:641-645. For historical context and critique see: Wilentz, *Chants Democratic,* 172-216; and, Herbert G. Gutman, et al., *Who Built America?: Working People and the Nation's Economy, Politics, Culture, And Society,* 2 vols. (New York: Pantheon Books, 1989), I:326-7. For a historiographic study see: Pessen, Riches, 58-66.

[83]   Wilentz, *Chants Democratic,* passim.

[84]   Mark A. Lause, "Introduction: The Hard-Earned Obscurity of Thomas Skidmore," *The Life Of Thomas Skidmore* (1834), by Amos Gilbert (Chicago: Charles H. Kerr, 1984), 9.

[85]   Wilentz, *Chants Democratic,* 202-208. On the class and occupational composition of the three groups see: Ibid., 206.

[86]   Wilentz, *Chants Democratic,* 204-05, passim.

[87]   Wilentz, *Chants Democratic,* 204-216.

[88]   The use of the press as an ideological weapon in the struggle for the consciousness of the working class was especially intense in response to Skidmore. The heavily financed press opposition to Skidmore and his program to transform society and property relations was a deliberate campaign of those engaged in the ideological struggle for the minds of the working classes. See: Wilentz, 191-207.
In his 1834 biographical sketch of Skidmore, Amos Gilbert observes:

> . . . when it is considered what a thorough and continued conviction pervaded his mind of the overbearing assumptions of the rich, and the oppression, degradation and sufferings of the poor, and by how many devices the former had attempted, and partially succeeded in reconciling the latter to their condition, it is not strange that he should look on the possession of wealth with an eye of distrust when he came forward as the advocate of universal, equal rights: — The game had often been played with success, — so often that the privileged classes were entitled to no confidence; — but that they should now come forward at a time, when a generous and general impulse was given, and soothe it into quietness and peace — that they should divert attention away and induce an awakened generation of producers to withdraw attention from the steady pursuit of their own rights, and evaporate it, as it were, in their admiration of the talents, and the boldness of a few individuals, — was with him a subject of the deepest regret.
> . . .

Amos Gilbert, *The Life Of Thomas Skidmore* (1834), ed. Mark A. Lause (Chicago: Charles H. Kerr, 1984), 36-37.
Literacy in the early decades of the United States appears to have been more widespread than promoters (and numerous educational historians) of the state system of public school education

would have us believe. Before Skidmore published his *Rights of Man to Property!*, his critique of American capitalist society had been preceded by critical writings of Dr. Cornelius Blatchly (1817), and by Langdon Byllesby (1826), and followed by Seth Luther (1832). Perhaps the most famous of radical attacks on the social order before Skidmore's was Thomas Paine's *Common Sense*, published in 1776. According to Eric Foner, it went through 25 editions and "reached literally hundreds of thousands of readers" in its first year to reach "'all ranks' of Americans." (Eric Foner, "Tom Paine's Republic: Radical Ideology and Social Change," in *The American Revolution*, ed. Alfred F. Young (DeKalb, IL: Northern Illinois University Press, 1976), 199.) We are told by Amos Gilbert, that Paine's *Common Sense* and the Philadelphia newspaper, *The Aurora*, were significantly identified by Skidmore as among his primary early influences. Given the fact of the intensity of the attack against Skidmore's ideas in the press on one hand, and the speed with which the same opposing economic and political groups sought to co-opt the milder aspects of his and the Working Men's movement's platform on the other, suggests that Skidmore was not the only autodidact workingman to have been so influenced.

Before there was a state system of public school education in which reading texts could be censored to insure the inculcation of right ideas, the fight for the consciousness of the people was fought out in the popular press — where history and ideas were distorted to serve the economic and political interests of those who financed, published and distributed the newspapers. The popular press of the period was clearly not a homogeneous medium, but, importantly, the newspaper publishing efforts of Skidmore and other working class leaders (or groups) were poorly financed and lacked adequate distribution. The surprise is not that Skidmore was overwhelmed in this contest; rather, the surprise is that with so few economic resources at his disposal, his ideas inspired a revolutionary democratic movement. It is, finally, in this contest between Skidmore, his working-men allies and the dominant forces of the economic and political elite on one hand and middle class reformers on the other that the relation between literacy and the struggle for ideological hegemony can be identified and established with unobstructed clarity. (Much the same thing can be said about David Walker's *Appeal* (1829).)

[89]   Wilentz, *Chants Democratic*, 208-213. See, too, the critique of Orestes Brownson in Dorfman, II:644-5, 662-5.

[90]   Dorfman, II:645.

[91]   See: Dorfman, II:645.

It is important to note that David Walker published the first edition of his *Appeal* in 1829 while he was in Boston. The Appeal is every bit as remarkable as Skidmore's treatise, and it is no less a statement of revolutionary democratic ideology. Rather than being rooted in economic critique, however, it is rooted in a comprehensive critique of human rights and culture in American society inspired by revolutionary Christianity and the *Declaration of Independence*. By calling all of white Americans to account for their brutality and hypocrisies, and for Black-Americans (free and slave) to prove their humanity in the only way recognized by white slavers and their allies, Walker's *Appeal* was perceived by some as more dangerous than Skidmore's *Rights*. Where Skidmore advocated a revolution by democratic process, Walker suggested that the realization of an equal and democratic society might need come through armed revolution or God's obliteration of white infidels. The Black liberation movement, often intertwined with (and thus obscured by) the history of the Abolition movement, requires more comprehensive research and explication than I can give it here. But its importance to understanding the processes of hegemony and domination in American society cannot be overestimated. The constructed ideology and culture of race and white supremacy are central to the historical development of American society and economic and political relations. In particular the extension of suffrage to white males drove a political wedge between white laborers and Black; ethnicity and race as employment criteria (or pitting one group against the other during labor disputes) drove an economic wedge between white laborers and Blacks; punitive laws against white and black to prevent association and communion enforced racial separation; and, the construction of a state system of public school education which embraced white children while excluding Black children was a means of inculcating and reproducing a racist as well as a class biased consciousness. Indeed, Walker is passionately blunt about the hegemonic processes employed by dominant white Americans to separate working class ethnic groups such as the Irish from Black-Americans. The effectiveness of these processes can be seen in the progression from Skidmore's demand for equal rights for all to Michael Walsh's opposition to emancipation until the rights of wage laborers were secured. The vision of one is inclusive, whereas the other is divisively fragmented. See, too: David R. Roediger, *The Wages of Whiteness: Race and the Making of the American Working Class* (London/New York: Verso, 1991, 1993); Noel Ignatiev, *How The Irish Became White* (New York/London: Routledge, 1995).

[92]   Isolated strikes are recorded as early as the 1786 Philadelphia printers' strike to secure a wage of $1 per day. See: M.B. Schnapper, 24.

[93]   Zinn, 223.

[94]   Tindall and Shi, 492.

[95]   Zinn, 224.

[95]   Zinn, 213.

[97]   See the letter from J.K. Mills, Esq., Boston, Dec. 29, 1841, addressed to Horace Mann, and reproduced by Mann in his *Fifth Annual Report* (1842). Mills makes the claim several times that overseers and those skilled in business have risen from the ranks of common laborers by virtue of an education. Mills gives the impression that in his firm, which employs "about three thousand persons," common laborers are uneducated immigrants:

> . . . does not include an importation of 63 persons from Manchester, in England, in 1839. Among these persons, there was scarcely one who could read or write, and although a part of them had been accustomed to work in cotton mills, yet, either from incapacity or idleness, they were unable to earn sufficient to pay for their subsistence, and at the expiration of a few weeks, not more than half a dozen remained in our employment. —Horace Mann, *Fifth Annual Report* (1842) (Washington, D.C.: NEA/The Horace Mann League Edition, 1948), 90-92.

Although not intended to especially enlighten us regarding socioeconomic circumstances in the mills, it is illuminating that 57 of the recruited immigrant workers were unable to "earn sufficient to pay for their subsistence." And the cause: the workers' incapacity or idleness.

[98]   See: E.P. Thompson, *The Making of the English Working Class* (New York: Vintage Press, 1966), 167-171, 433-444, passim; and, Michael Durey, *Transatlantic Radicals and the Early American Republic* (Lawrence, Ks: University of Kansas Press, 1997).

[99]   The Irish who came to America were not a homogeneous group. According to Edward Condon's 1887 history, *The Irish Race In America*, half of the Continental Army were Irishmen who had come to America after the 1771-3 English land evictions. Ann K. Bradley claims approximately 30,000 Ulster Irish emigrated to the U.S. in the five years before the War of Independence, and another 150,000 arrived between 1783 and 1814. Condon contends that those who emigrated before 1783 were predominately dispossessed tenant farmers. Those coming between 1783 and 1814, according to Bradley, were predominantly wealthy and middle-class protestants.

     The reaction of Anglo-Americans to these immigrants, especially those fleeing English imprisonment, prosecution and execution after the failed 1798 Irish rebellion, helps to illustrate the distinction between professed political ideals and actual practice in American society: Bradley writes,
"Fearing the spread of extremist ideas, which might abet the domestic republicanism of radical representatives such as County Wicklow-born Matthew Lyon of Vermont, The American Federalist Party passed laws that extended the required residence period for citizenship from five to fourteen years and gave the President the right to expel 'dangerous' aliens by executive decree. 'If some means are not adopted,' insisted Massachusetts Congressman Harrison Gray Otis in 1797, 'to prevent the indiscriminant admission of wild Irishmen and others to the right of suffrage, there will . . . be an end to liberty and property.' A third such law, called the Sedition Act, declared it a misdemeanor to make statements 'with the intent to defame' Congress and the President, or statements that might bring them into 'contempt or disrepute'. Lyon, an ardent admirer of Jefferson and the French Revolution, was the first to be prosecuted." And, William Duane, editor of the Philadelphia *Aurora*, was another prosecuted under the anti-sedition laws.

     Nor did the Irish endear themselves to Anglo-American Protestant conservatives by their enthusiastic support of first Jefferson, and later Andrew Jackson. In short, nativist fear that American "liberty and property" were being trammelled by wild Irishmen (and their women) was entrenched in American republican ideology and public sentiment well before immigrant Irish Catholics swelled the ranks of wage-laborers and strikers.

See: Edward O'Meagher Condon, *The Irish Race In America* (1887) (rpt. Spring Valley, NY: Ogham House, 1976), 39, 43, 68; Ann Kathleen Bradley, *History of the Irish In America* (Secaucus, NJ: Chartwell Books, 1986), 36; William D. Griffin, *The Book Of Irish Americans* (New York: Random House, 1990), 4-50; and Thomas H. O'Connor, *The Boston Irish: A Political History* (Boston: Northeastern University Press, 1995), 10-94.

[100]   I am broadly generalizing the Irish Catholic experience in Ireland, England, and in the United States — because economic, political, and educational oppression conditioned the lives of nearly all Irish Catholics. (See: George M. Fredrickson, *White Supremacy* (Oxford, U.K.: Oxford University Press, 1982); Wilentz, *Chants Democratic*, passim.) The reaction of the Irish to their circumstances, however, was not all of a similar kind. Margaret Haley (1861-1939), in her autobiography *Battleground* — written between 1910 and 1936 — draws attention to a critically important distinction among the American Irish from the 1834 anti-Catholic burning of the Ursuline Convent in Charlestown, Massachusetts, to the period of her father's radical democratic activism in Illinois during the closing decades of the nineteenth century:

          . . . I was to come into understanding of the reasons for the sharp differentiation between the two types of Irish in American politics. I was to learn that the same cause — the oppression of their race in Ireland — had reacted differently on two divisions of the Irish people. Persecution had crushed one group of Irish into submission to an established authority and a

correlative intention of getting from it, by fair means or foul, whatever might be grasped. It had
roused the other group to continuing struggle against any and all injustice. The fighting Irish.
The Tones and the Emmetts and the Parnells. In spirit my father was one of them. On the
American midlands he thrilled to the war-pipes of Home Rule and Land League; but he also
hearkened to the trumpets of the awakening political causes in our own United States.

Margaret Haley, *Battleground,* ed. Robert L. Reid (Urbana: University of Illinois Press, 1982), 8.
Note: Haley is thinking of Robert Emmett, who was executed by the English in 1803 for his part in
the Irish Rebellion, and not Thomas Adis Emmett, Robert's brother, who prosecuted the New York
cordwainers in 1809 for conspiracy against their employers.

[101]   O'Connor, 53-54.

[102]   "In 1835, for example, Calvin Stowe admonished the Western Literary Institute and College of
Professional Teachers that 'unless we educate our immigrants, they will be our ruin. It is no longer
a mere question of benevolence, of duty, or of enlightened self-interest, but the intellectual and
religious training of our foreign population has become essential to our own safety; we are prompted
to it by the instinct of self-preservation.'" —Rush Welter, *The Mind of America 1820-1860* (New
York: Columbia University Press, 1975), 278.
    In his letter to Horace Mann, J. K. Mill reveals that the movement of the native born Anglo-
American laboring class into positions of overseers and management in business and manufacturing
was already well underway by 1841. — Mann, *Fifth Annual Report* (1842), 90-91.
    Indeed, Herbert G. Gutman and Ira Berlin found that between 1840 and 1890 the composition
of the American working class was completely transformed. This transformation paralleled the
transformation of the nature of work — from the relative equality and harmony of interests that
governed the small workshops to the master-servant wage relation of large and small factories.
Native born small masters, artisans, mechanics, and journeymen — the main and most visible
opposition to capitalist social relations between 1765 and 1840 — were increasingly displaced by
lower paid immigrants. By 1890 the numbers of native born laborers directly engaged as industrial
wage-laborers were so few as to be invisible. See: Gutman and Berlin, "Class Composition and the
Development of the American Working Class, 1840-1890," *Power and Culture*, 380-394.
    See, too: O'Connor, 38-55, passim.

[103]   The actual conditions confronting Irish laborers, as well as others, in America also acted to
radicalize and mobilize them. An 1850 report, for example, warns that wages are frequently paid
partly in cash and partly in script honored only in the company store — paid, that is, when the
workman is actually paid at all. Under English law, the writer tells us, the master would be forced
to pay the just wages owed, "but in the United States it is not so, as the defendant is allowed the
means of such tedious procrastination in coming to a settlement as tires out the complainant, so
much so that it is generally considered preferable to relinquish a just demand." See: Edith Abbott,
Historical Aspects of the Immigration Problem (Chicago: University of Chicago Press, 1926; reprint
New York: Arno Press, 1969), 284 (page reference is to the reprint edition).

[104]   One of the most famous was Mike Walsh, who established himself as a journalist with the New
York *Aurora*, in 1839, and soon after became a radical democratic politician powering his way into
the inner sanctum of Tammany Hall. See: Wilentz, *Chants Democratic*, 327-335.
    The political mobilization of the Irish was spurred on as well by the prevalence of an active
Irish press — the *Aurora* of Philadelphia and of New York are perhaps the best known Irish

newspapers, but Griffin and Bradley each document a burgeoning Irish press in America during this historical period.

[105]   David F. Allmendinger, Jr., "New England Students and the Revolution in Higher Education, 1800-1900;" and, Ronald Story, "Harvard Students, the Boston Elite, and the New England Preparatory System," in *The Social History Of American Education*, eds. McClellan and Reese (Urbana: University of Illinois Press, 1988), 65-72, 73-90.

[106]   Frederick Rudolph, *The American College & University: A History* (Athens, GA: University of Georgia Press, 1962), 130.

[107]   Horace Mann went to considerable lengths to censor books and to influence authors as a deliberate strategy to control the moral and civic literature and lessons children would be exposed to. See: Messerli, 345-346.
        Mann apparently made a considerable study of Noah Webster's 1790 essay explaining the relation between reading, consciousness, and social behavior. In his 1842 Report Mann writes: ". . . that the teacher, in forming his pupils' habits of reading, encircles their heads with a bright and radiating light, or wraps around them a cloudy medium, which they will carry through life, to enlighten or obscure every object about them, wherever they may go. . . . But a pupil will naturally follow the analogies of his native tongue, unless he is directed by another standard. What a misfortune to a child to be bred up in the imitation of an outlandish brogue-like or barbarous pronunciation, which like some visible offensive deformity of a person, he will display wherever he goes. . . ." (pp.44-45) Mann, in the context from which this quote is taken, is delineating the necessary traits in a teacher and the reasons for training and testing to insure competency in bringing about the desired transformation of the child.
        It is important to note, as well, the nativist and class bias embedded in Mann's argument. The Irish, English, and Scots might adapt to the set standard of English language studies, but the implications for non-English immigrants (and Black children as well) are far reaching. If an immigrant child does not learn in an English only school, this failure must surely be explained by the child's incapacity or idleness. This is the implicit conclusion corresponding to that of James K. Mills regarding the Welsh laborers who could not earn sufficient wages in his employ to obtain the necessities to stay alive.(p.91) Of course the problem these incapables or idlers pose to society is their tendency to unite in attacks against the social order.

[108]   See: Gutman, et al., *Who Built America*, 333-335; Tomlins, 180-194; and, Wilentz, *Chants Democratic*, 284-286, 315-325.

[109]   Benjamin Tabart, "The Printer," *The Book of Trades*, or *Library of the Useful Arts*, 3 vols. (Whitehall (Philadelphia) and Richmond: Jacob Johnson, 1807), reprinted as *Early American Crafts and Trades*, Vol.I, *Old-Time Crafts and Trades*, Vol.II, and *Early Nineteenth-Century Crafts And Trades*, Vol.III, ed. Peter Stockham (New York: Dover Publications, 1992), III:73.

[110]   Ibid., "The Merchant," II:129-132.

[111]   Wilentz, *Chants Democratic*, 188.

[112]   David Walker was, if anything, more strident in his demands for an authentic public education. He rages against the forms of education perpetuated on free Black children in the North which

stressed mastery of hand writing but left their minds in darkness and ignorance. And, in the most certain terms, he condemns Southerners and Westerners for their brutally violent opposition to any kind of learning by Blacks. See Walker's *Appeal*, passim.

[113]   See: Sol Cohen, II:1052-1061.

[114]   See: Wilentz, *Chants Democratic*, 219-248.

[115]   Wilentz, 177-79.

[116]   Regarding Brownson, see: Dorfman, II:662-665. For Evans, see: Wilentz, *Chants Democratic*, 240, 335-336.

[117]   Wilentz, "Introduction," Walker's *Appeal*.

[118]   Webster, 1820, quoted Sol Cohen, II:1062.

[119]   Edward Everett, "At a Public Meeting, Held at St. Paul's Church, Boston, 21st May, 1833, on Behalf of Kenyon College, Ohio," *Orations and Speeches On Various Occasions* (New York: Arno Press, 1972), 329-330. And, quoted in Merle Curti, *The Social Ideas of American Educators* (New York: Scribners & Sons, 1935; reprint and 2d ed., Totowa, NJ.: Littlefield, Adams, 1959), 69 (page references are to the reprint second edition).
What Everett did not communicate to his audience, interestingly, is he had sent one of his sons off to Ohio to purchase land. A speculative venture which a new college would surely enhance.

[120]   Headley, 97-110; Wilentz, *Chants Democratic*, 294-95; and Folsom, 29-42.

[121]   See: Tomlins, 223-330.

[122]   See: Stephen Simpson's remarks on the disciplinary and improving utility of education reported in Dorfman, II:647.

[123]   Wilentz documents a hierarchy within the laboring classes that differentiated journeymen from common laborers, and workmen from workwomen. This hierarchy was a pattern of social ranking carried over from the artisan trade customs of the colonial period. The hierarchy of tradesmen began to breakdown early in the 1800s, and took a hard pounding by Skidmore, but it wasn't until the formation of the General Trades Union in the mid-1830s, that old barriers between skilled and unskilled workers, and between the traditional tradesmen and the new group of working-women were breached in favor of cooperation and common interests in the struggle against the inequalities of capital and the emerging factory system. See: Wilentz, *Chants Democratic*, 248-254.

[124]   For the white laboring classes in the North there was wage-slavery, and for free Black laborers in the North there was wage-slavery, the threat of being kidnapped and sold into slavery, and for white and Black laborers alike there was the spectre of Southern slavery. Democratic radicals like the Irishman Mike Walsh protested the emancipation of Black-slaves because (1) white laborers were oppressed wage-slaves without rights and whose freedom consisted in the freedom to starve, and thus did not even enjoy the limited protections of food, clothing, and shelter allotted to Black-slaves, (2) emancipation of the Black-slaves would thus intensify the suffering and hardships of all,

and, (3) the capitalists would use the freed Blacks to drive wages down and generally increase unemployment to intolerable levels. See: Wilentz, *Chants Democratic*, 332-333.

It is not clear that Walsh, for instance, protested the emancipation of Black-slaves for racist reasons. The significance of Walsh's opposition, however, is not to be found in itself, but as an indicator of what will come after the Civil War. For as Walsh imagines, the shared economic and political interests of white workers and Black workers will be lost through the hegemonic process of pitting white labor against Black labor in a life and death struggle for scarce resources — and the cause for laborers' democratic rights will be seriously damaged by white workers being embraced in the capitalist economic and political establishment. In other words, Walsh's argument appears to be that emancipation and the abolition of Black-slavery is a strategy by capitalists to win the struggle between democracy and capitalism.

Marx identifies the dilemma succinctly: The "organization of the proletarians into a class, and consequently into a political party, is continually being upset again by the competition between the workers themselves." Marx, "*The Communist Manifesto,*" 228.

[125]   See: Messerli, 236, for a brief account of the impact of the 1837 economic crisis on Henry Lee, a close friend and benefactor of Horace Mann.

[126]   Orestes Brownson, "The Laboring Classes," *Boston Quarterly Review* (1840); reprinted in *Religion, Reform, and Revolution: Labor Panaceas in the Nineteenth Century,* eds. Leon Stein and Philip Taft (New York: Arno Press, 1969), no.

[127]   Merle Curti, 19, 50-100, 139-168; Messerli, 241-42, 245-46, 299-300.

[128]   See: Carter, in Sol Cohen, III:1063.

[129]   See: Wilentz, *Chants Democratic*, 179.

[130]   The race and class ideology which undergirded the projection of categories of stupidity, degradation and criminality upon immigrant, Black, working class and poor children was not unique to the governing classes in the eighteenth and nineteenth centuries; indeed, as an ideology driving middle class educational reformers and a great many practitioners it undergirded this group's beliefs and actions into the twentieth century as well. See: Paul Violas, *The Training Of The Urban Working Class: A History Of Twentieth Century American Education* (Chicago: Rand McNally College Publishing Co., 1978), 120, passim.

[131]   Messerli, 241-42.

[132]   The General Court of the State of Massachusetts did not pass a bill limiting labor time for Women and children 18 years or younger to ten hours a day or sixty hours per week until 1874. And it isn't until 1876 that a child labor law prohibiting the employment of children younger than 10 years is passed. See: Henry F. Bedford, ed., *Their Lives and Numbers: The Condition of Working People in Massachusetts, 1870-1900* (Ithaca, NY: Cornell University Press, 1995), 141-43.

Seth Luther (ibid.) reports the presence of thousands of children laboring in the mills in 1832. Horace Mann, however, makes no mention in his *Fifth Annual Report* (1842) of seeing children laboring in the many mills and manufactories that he inspected prior to its writing. Mann's oversight aside, however, Luther's report in 1832, and testimony before the Massachusetts General Court and subsequent legislation, 1874-1876, establishes the prevailing practice of extensive child labor throughout the antebellum period. Thus the possibility that working class children (native born or immigrant) would benefit from a Common School education appears slight indeed, for all indications suggest that even those who might have attended would have done so for only two or three years at best.

[133]   See: Sol Cohen, III:1619-1624; and, see: III:1624-1631, for autobiographical accounts of Black-American self-determination and agency during the 1830s.

[134]   Selwyn K. Troen, *The Public and the Schools: Shaping the St. Louis System,* 1838-1920 (Columbia: University of Missouri Press, 1975). See, too: Gutman, *Power and Culture,* 108-110.

[135]   David Tyack and Elisabeth Hansot, *Managers of Virtue: Public School Leadership in America, 1820-1980* (New York: Basic Books, 1982); 45, passim.

[136]   See: David Tyack and Elisabeth Hansot, Managers of Virtue: Public School Leadership in America, 1820-1980 (New York: Basic Books, 1982), 15-63.

[137]   Calling these schools "common schools" is quite interesting. On one hand it suggests common, as in "common good" and "common to all." And, too, it implicitly recalls the Working Men's declaration for publicly supported universal or general and equal education — without explicitly addressing the egalitarian democratic vision the Working Men's conception entailed. But the adjective "common" conveys altogether different connotative and denotative meanings to the Anglo-American capitalist elite: commoners, common classes, and uncivilized ignorant immigrants — as in the phrase, "common as dirt."

[138]   See: Michael B. Katz, *Irony of Early School Reform: Educational Innovation In Mid-Nineteenth Century Massachusetts* (Cambridge, MA: Harvard University Press, 1968), 30:

> "The Winchendon committee argued that the availability of foreigners to perform the 'least desirable' sorts of work enabled 'our sons to rise to other employments.' To seize the new opportunities for its children a town required an advanced educational system, especially a high school; there was no other alternative if parents desired their children to rise on the economic and social scale. 'Shall we,' asked the committee, 'stand still, and see our children outstripped in the race of life, by the children of those who are willing to pursue a liberal and far-sighted policy?'"

[139]   There was no pressure on Mann for a high school from the Boston merchants and professionals in any case, because the exclusive public high school, Boston Latin, had opened in 1821 as a preparatory school for Harvard or business.

[140]   See: Michael B. Katz, "Reform by Imposition: Social Origins of Educational Controversy," *Irony,* 19-114.

[141]   David Nasaw, Schooled To Order: A Social History of Public Schooling in the United States (New York: Oxford University Press, 1979), 53-65.

[142]   Curti, 107.

[143]   See: Dorfman, II:527-538.

[144]   See: Sol Cohen, II:1063.

[145]   Messerli, 241.

[146]   Messerli, 242.

[147]   See: Zinn, 209-211.

[148]   See: Hoerder, 235: quoting the letter from General Thomas Gage to Secretary of State Conway, 23 Sept. 1765, cited above.

[149]   Messerli, 25l-252.

[150]   Note Mann's use in the *Twelfth Annual Report* of the same analogy of the sapling/oak used by Noah Webster in 1790.

[151]   Opposition by Catholics to all forms of public school education infused with Protestantism was pronounced throughout the nineteenth century. The conflict and sentiments became more bitter after the Catholic schools were excluded from receipt of school tax funds, and Catholics found themselves forced to financially support a system of schools antithetical to their religion.

[152]   Messerli, ibid., passim.

[153]   Messerli, 243-244, 350.

[154]   See, for example: Robert C. Whittemore, *Makers Of The American Mind* (New York: William Morrow & Co., 1964), 197-215; Curti, 131-33; and Lawrence Cremin, "Horace Mann's Legacy."

[155]   Messerli, passim.

[156]   *"From* Report for 1841{sic} 'Pecuniary Value of Education," *The American Mind*, 2 vols., eds. Harry R. Warfel, Ralph H. Gabriel, and Stanley T. Williams (New York: American Book Company, 1937), I:430-31. Curti and Messerli, however, cite the correct date of 1842 for this report.

[157]   Ibid. Messerli also informs us that prior to a promotional speaking engagement in New York, 18,000 copies of this report were printed and distributed there. ". . . part of them a German translation so that they would also reach 'thousands of immigrants who are equally with ourselves interested in the only means of preserving the institutions of our common country'. . . ." Messerli, 372. See the confirming quote by Curti below.

[158]   Certainly, in addition to Mann's own remarks on the subject, those of H. Barlett, written in 1841 to Mann from Lowell, were every bit as promising:

I have uniformly found the better educated as a class possessing a higher and better state of morals, more orderly and respectful in their deportment, and more ready to comply with the wholesome and necessary regulations of an establishment. And in times of agitation, on account of some change in regulations or wages, I have always looked to the more intelligent, best educated and the most moral for support, and have seldom been disappointed. For, while they are the last to submit to imposition, they reason, and if your requirements are reasonable, they will generally acquiesce, and exert a salutary influence upon their associates. But the ignorant and uneducated I have generally found the most turbulent and troublesome, acting under the impulse of excited passion and jealousy. . . . if you had reference to merit and qualifications, very seldom indeed would an uneducated young man rise to "*a better place and better pay.*" — H. Bartlett, Esq., to Horace Mann, *Fifth Annual Report* (1842), (Washington, D.C.), 94-95.

[159]   Mann, *Fifth Annual Report* (1842), (Washington, D.C.), 90-100.

[160]   Curti, 113. Curti's treatment of Mann's *Fifth Anual Report* follows Ellwood Cubberley's interpretation that Mann's great success was overcoming the opposition of a conservative capitalist elite. Significantly absent in Curti's explanation, however, is Mann's adroit handling of class antagonisms. Mann's supposed success in winning over elite opposition (which Messerli documents was minimal in any case) was due not to rhetorical persuasion, but to his promise and demonstration that the state system of public school education which he was constructing would reproduce the social hierarchy — not disrupt it. It would benefit the already privileged, and secure social order. And, it was for this purpose, and to bring into being just such an institution, that Everett and Dwight set Mann in motion.

In addition, Mann's 1842 *Report*, and his artful formulation of Achievement Ideology, would be resurrected countless times before and after the Civil War, and well into the twentieth century as the fundamental argument undergirding the development of industrial and manual education for black, immigrant, and poor children. And too, his ideas would be refined in the late nineteenth century and early twentieth on the shop floor by Frederick W. Taylor through his scientific efficiency movement, and in the greatly enlarged and stratified state system of public school education by Ellwood Cubberley through his advocacy of centralized bureaucratic administration and class based forms of curriculum and school organization. The tension between the two appeals of Mann's rhetorical argument would prove the test of time, for industrial capitalists and merchants would continue to seek the best trained and most productive workers, and workers, by virtue of their structured social position, would seek an educational edge in a highly competitive job market.

[161]   Messerli, 390.

[162]   Messerli, 392-93. According to Ellwood Cubberley Mann was far from alone in seeing the Prussian model of society and public education as the system to emulate. In particular, see his comments on the Michigan reformer, John Pierce, in Cubberley's *Public Education in the United States*, 2d ed. (Boston: Houghton-Mifflin, 1934), 216.

[163]   George Combe to Mann, July 16, 1843, Mann MSS : MHS, quoted by Messerli, 399.

[164]   See: Mann, *Fourth Annual Report* (1841) (Washington, D.C.: NEA/Horace Mann League, 1948).

[165]   Gutman, et al., *Who Built America?*, 306-310.

[166]   See: Dorfman, II:661-67.

[167]   Mann/Cremin, 81.

[168]   Mann/Cremin, 80.

[169]   See: Ruth Miller Elson, *Guardians*, passim.

[170]   Marx, "*Communist Manifesto*," 242-43.

[171]   See: Tyack and Hansot, 15-104; and, Ruth Miller Elson, passim. Nor has the passage of time brought with it a transformation of these circumstances. For a contemporary analysis of the mechanism of ideological mystification and hegemony through public school education and the textbooks upon which this education is based, see: Jean Anyon, "Workers, Labor and Economic History, and Textbook Content," *Ideology and Practice In Schooling*, eds. Michael W. Apple and Lois Weis (Philadelphia: Temple University Press, 1983), 37-60.

[172]   Michael B. Katz, *Irony*, 30; James D. Anderson, 21-23, 25, 27. Selwyn K. Troen, "Popular Education in Nineteenth-Century St. Louis," in *The Social History of American Education*, eds. B. Edward McClellan and William J. Reese (Urbana: University of Illinois Press, 1988), 119-136.

[173]   For detailed explanations and documentation see: James D. Anderson, passim; and Paul Violas, passim.

[174]   Cubberley, *Public Education*, 230, 357-358.

[175]   See: Katz, *Irony*, 178; David Nasaw, 11, 90-98; and, Paul Violas, 32-36.

[176]   See: Howard K. Beale, *Are American Teachers Free?* (New York: Scribners, 1936; reprint New York: Octagon Books, 1972); Ruth Jacknow Markowitz, *My Daughter, the Teacher: Jewish Teachers In The New York City Schools* (New Brunswick, NJ: Rutgers University Press, 1993); Marjorie Murphy, *Blackboard Unions: The AFT & The NEA, 1900-1980* (Ithaca, NY: Cornell University Press, 1992); and Richard J. Altenbaugh, ed., *The Teacher's Voice: A Social History of Teaching In Twentieth Century America* (Washington D.C.: The Falmer Press, 1992).

[177]   Hans Magnus Enzensberger, "The Industrialization of the Mind," *The Consciousness Industry*, ed. Michael Roloff (New York: Seabury Press, 1974), 3-15; Jay MacLeod, *Ain't No Makin' It: Aspirations & Attainment in a Low-Income Neighborhood*, Second Edition (Boulder, CO: Westview Press, 1995).

CHAPTER FOUR

REVIEWING THE ISSUES

> Just as one does not judge an individual by what he thinks about himself,
> so one cannot judge . . . a period of transformation by its consciousness, but,
> on the contrary, this consciousness must be explained from the contradic-
> tions of material life, from the conflict existing between the social forces of
> production and the relations of production.[1]

Over one hundred and fifty years have passed in which to settle ontological
questions about the historical conjunction between capitalism and the American
system of public school education, and democratic government. Progress by
educational historians toward congruent explanations of the relations between
public school education and economic and political relations, however, is incon-
clusive.[2] For example, to return to the passage quoted in Chapter II by Urban
and Wagoner:

> While Katz sees the public school as an institution imposed by the es-
> tablishment on the lower classes, his critics tend to see the common school,
> and the public schools in the twentieth century, as imperfect institutions that
> nevertheless attempted to overcome, or mitigate, social divisions in Ameri-

can society and to help the members of the lower orders of that society to better themselves.[3]

As Urban and Wagoner present them, these opposing historical explanations of the role of public school education in American society are subjective *interpretations*. The issue between one and the other is rhetorical, i.e., which is the more persuasive text. What must decide the issue between one interpretation and the other is now a question of internal textual coherence, coherence with other texts established within the discipline, and, perhaps, coherence with the reader's *understanding*. A historical social reality independent of the texts and interpretive arguments is absent, and what remains is a collection of more or less inscrutable *texts* of which the historian and/or teacher candidate endeavors to make sense. This is relativist and constructivist history. Readers and teacher candidates are left to form their own *opinion* about the merits of one or the other argument in the *discussion*, because what cannot be done under these terms of *discourse* is say this or that argument is *true*. Indeed, although Katz's excavation of the history of public schools in society is surely not the same as that of his critics, Urban and Wagoner reduce these very different ontological explanations of history to equivalents. In other words, what should be a matter of identified and established empirical socio-economic circumstances is, instead, is a matter of what one thinks.

The effect of relativism is to make educational history a genre of fiction.[4] My contention is relativist history on one hand and interpretive constructions of history on the other are deliberate political acts of ideological mystification dressed up as historical scholarship. And as the textual product of deliberate authorship these acts are meant to shape our beliefs about what constitutes the reality of public school education and economic and political relations through the manipulation of knowledge about the past.

Whenever a historian presents as explanation what is in fact an interpretation dependent for its coherence and persuasiveness upon the exclusion or diminution of knowledge about social reality and congruent evidence which would undermine his/her argument, then we have either ideological mystification, sloppy scholarship, or ignorance. Distinguishing one from the other is sometimes difficult unless we have sufficient interdisciplinary knowledge of the object of study ourselves.

The determination of validity (or defensibility) for an historical explanation and knowledge claim depends in every case on established coherence *and* congruence. Thus ignorance as a cause of misrepresentations is most easily recognized, for the errors are many, often contradictory, and tend to be haphazard — explanations lack both coherence and congruence. Sloppy scholarship can usually be recognized through a close reading of the argument, which is largely a matter of assertions and coherent interpretation without much attempt at establishing a degree of congruence. Ideological mystification is the most difficult process to recognize and critique, for the author appears to have provided adequate documentation of his/her arguments, assertions may be many or few, but the undergirding assumptions and/or social agenda are hidden. Certainly the rhetorical strategy of presenting polemic as historical explanation is one of the conditions which makes ideological mystification difficult to recognize, but it is also one of its defining characteristics. Most often the argument promotes a hegemonic perspective which obscures or misrepresents the historical particularities of actual economic and political relations within the context of specific socioeconomic circumstances, and presents as "knowledge" explanations or claims which contradict and/or mystify these conditions. One educational historian argues, for example, that capitalism benefited all citizens by engendering a society characterized by equal economic opportunities and shared political power; and, more subtly, he emphasizes only the benefits of capitalism — such as increased literacy or improved transportation — while the negative consequences — such as stratified economic and political relations, exploitation of the laboring class, and the concentration of wealth and power among a few — are given only passing mention, if mentioned at all.[5] An ideological account posits as reality the assumption that increased literacy or improved transportation or the development of water treatment systems, for example, happen only because of a specific economic system; that, in fact, there are no viable alternatives that would have generated these benefits for individuals or to society generally. Moreover, an ideological account is one that insists — usually implicitly — that whatever the costs in social inequities and human misery, desperation, poverty, or loss, they were and are necessary to achieve industrial and capital progress and national supremacy.

My argument that the writing and publication of relativist or ideological historiographic texts are deliberate political acts will be developed and supported through my critique of the different texts, which follows. I emphasize here, though, that the underlying purpose of the sort of political act I have described above is to obscure the congruent relation between capitalist economic and political relations, which are inherently unequal and exploitative, and the state system of public school education. By obscuring this relation, the author contributes to the mechanisms of social hegemony. And, of greater importance, the mystification of the particulars of this relation distorts and/or obstructs the production of knowledge about the actual educational and social experiences of different racial or ethnic groups of children.

In all our talk about the *education* of children, for instance, it is easy to ignore or overlook the fact that the educational establishment is itself a multibillion dollar business, which in turn is linked to local and national business interests. There are, in addition to the business of public school education, enormous economic and political forces which depend on a particular organization and ideology of public schooling. The stratification of society and the unequal distribution of resources and rights depend on the reproduction of certain kinds of unequal economic and political relations, and these relations depend for their legitimation upon the manipulation and control of what counts as knowledge about the constitution of society — and its history. Efficient hegemony depends especially on the ideological mystification of historical economic and political relations in society which would — were they and the social structures which generated them known — reveal the processes and reasons undergirding the construction of particular types of state institutions, their development and change over time, and the positions and practices embodied within these institutions.

This program of social construction and engineering is one reason why teachers, as carefully screened and trained social agents, are, by necessity, inculcated in society's dominant and hegemonic ideology.[6] By fostering the internalization of this ideology as a system of beliefs, it is imagined (by Horace Mann and Ellwood Cubberley, among others) that teachers will uncritically (even enthusiastically) reproduce the ideology of individual achievement and self-determination (or the rationalization of social inequities as rooted in individual failings) through the inculcation of their students. This is a *political process* that perpetuates unequal social relations and protects those fundamental conditions of economic production which depend for their continuance on the unequal distribution of resources and rights.

Moreover, this political practice of ideological mystification to obscure the congruent relation between public schools and capitalist society dates back to Horace Mann's invented mythic tradition of public *education* extending back in time to the Puritan settlements, and to his claims for social mobility through education.[7] As will soon become apparent, however, turning to less relativist historians than Urban and Wagoner does not necessarily help our progress toward identification of real social structures, historical events and economic and political relations, or provide explanations which increase our knowledge of the past, or our understanding of the present.

First, I want to establish a categorical separation of the educational history authors/texts to be examined in Chapter Five into two groups, those published before and those published after 1968. This point of separation is established because it is the year in which citation's of Jonathan Messerli's 1963 Harvard doctoral dissertation on Mann began appearing.[8] With the 1971 publication by Knopf of Messerli's definitive biography of Mann, however, the particular historical details of Mann's life and career became accessible to all.[9] In addition to concrete details, Messerli's established congruence, critical analysis and explanation of these details calls into question all explanations of Horace Mann and/ or the common schools which rely uncritically on Mann's own statements and accounts of his character and the purpose of the common schools. In the first group to be considered, therefore, I include Ellwood P. Cubberley, Merle Curti and Lawrence Cremin. The second group, which is substantially larger, includes Michael B. Katz; Carl Kaestle; David Tyack and Elizabeth Hansot; Joel Spring; Wayne Urban and Jennings Wagoner, Jr.; David Nasaw; and, H. Warren Button and Eugene F. Provenzo, Jr.[10]

And, secondly, it is not practical or possible in this particular essay to provide elaborate critiques of the complete texts and arguments belonging to each of the historians I have identified.[11] Nor do I want to reduce their works to sweeping summaries and paraphrases. My plan for all except Cubberley is to select crucial passages which explain some aspect of Horace Mann and/or the common school system and then proceed with a critique.

Endnotes

[1]   Marx, *Critique*, 21.

[2]   Congruence is used throughout this essay to mean a correspondence between an explanation and the object of the explanation. For example, Cubberley's claims in *Public Education* in the United States about Samuel Armstrong, the Hampton Institute and the education of Black-Americans are not congruent with what was known at the time, or what has been established since.

[3]   Urban and Wagoner, 113.

[4]   Barbara Finkelstein, "Education Historians as Mythmakers," *Review of Research In Education 18*, edited by Gerald Grant (Washington, DC: American Educational Research Association, 1992), 255-297.

[5]   The educational historian and text referenced here is unidentified in particular because it is my intent to keep the example generic. My purpose is to illustrate in the abstract how an embedded ideology operates within a text. By keeping the reference generic I hope to avoid creating the impression that this or that particular educational historian and text is singularly cupable.

[6]   See: Beale, passim; Markowitz, passim; and Murphy, passim.

[7]   Lawrence Cremin writes:

"Like any other crusader, Mann saw history on his side. The obligation to build common schools, he maintained, had been laid upon the people of the state by the founding fathers of the colony. 'We can never fully estimate the debt of gratitude we owe to our ancestors for establishing our system of Common Schools. . . . Can there be a man amongst us so recreant to duty, that he does not think it encumbent upon him to transmit that system, in an improved condition, to posterity, which his ancestors originated for him?' Building on the fact that the Puritan fathers, deeply committed to the preservation of learning, had at great sacrifice established schools in the wilderness, Mann conceived a historic tradition of education for freedom, a tradition which his own generation was duty-bound to perpetuate and strengthen." (Cremin, *The Republic and The School*, 18.)

Mann did it. Cremin is doing it: constructing useful myths, folklore, rituals, customs, and duties; "building on the fact," "*preservation of learning*," and "schools in the wilderness," are phrases used to shape our historical understanding of the Puritans and their experiences in a land quite unlike the one they left behind.

See also: Rush Welter, *The Mind of America*, 282-283; and, Messerli, 262-264, 332-339.

[8]   Jonathan C. Messerli, "*Horace Mann: The Early Years, 1796-1837*," unpub. diss., Harvard University, 1963.

9   Jonathan Messerli, *Horace Mann: a Biography* (New York: Knopf, 1971.)

10   There is a third category as well which I have already mentioned: collections of historical documents, American history texts, and American intellectual history. Representative examples of this third category are Henry Steele Commager; Avery Craven, et al.; Warfel, Gabriel, and Williams; Rush Welter; Robert C. Whittemore; and George Brown Tindall and David E. Shi. Although I would not venture to claim these different historians are identical, each identifies and explains the formation of the state system of public school education with Horace Mann and his writings. See bibliography for complete citations.

11   The distinctive nature of Ellwood Cubberley's *Public Education in the United States* dictates that it be critiqued differently from the others.   As I will make clear, his explanation of the past is but ideological preparation and legitimation for what he has to say about socioeconomic circumstances and appropriate social and educational policy in the first three decades of the twentieth century. And, too, the critique of Cubberley's history is substantially longer than the others. This is unavoidable given its position as the ideological foundation from which emerges the great bulk of educational history written after 1909.

CHAPTER FIVE

THE STATE SYSTEM OF PUBLIC SCHOOL EDUCATION AND ITS HISTORIANS

Ellwood P. Cubberley

The history of the state system of public school education as it has been written in the twentieth century owes much to Ellwood Cubberley and his *Public Education in the United States*[1]. It is an indication of Cubberley's continued stature in the educational establishment, in the field of educational history, and in teacher training that he is still cited, quoted and relied upon by numerous educators as the leading interpreter and/or authority on the development of the public school, its administrative organization, and its relation to American society.[2]

In addition, no individual has had greater influence in shaping the twentieth century state system of public school education, its physical and bureaucratic organization, its ideological and social aims, and what constitutes its reality and knowledge of it than Cubberley. He is the twentieth century educational establishment's first and most important master of ideological smoke and mirrors.

Between 1919 when first published and 1934 when the revised second edition was issued, 80,000 copies of *Public Education in the United States*

had been sold.[3] By 1960 Ellwood Cubberley's interpretive history of public
school education in American society from colonial times through the early
1930s had sold 100,000 copies,[4] and in 1965 Lawrence Cremin confirmed its
importance and influence by claiming that it continued to be used as a textbook
in teacher education and had yet to be "superseded."[5] The sales figures, however, reflect only new sales; they do not tell us how many of the 100,000 volumes were resold and sold again to successive classes and generations of teachers, American historians, or the curious. Bernard Bailyn's claim that *Public
Education* was "exceedingly influential" is at best a conservative estimation.[6]
Cremin is not so reserved or circumspect about its importance:

> Indeed, its formulations have become so pervasive that we are largely
> unaware of them; yet they profoundly affect private practice, professional
> pronouncement, and public policy. In short, Cubberley's treatise remains
> contemporary, and almost a half-century after its appearance, it continues
> to define the nature and meaning of the American educational experience.[7]

Cubberley would be pleased, for he wanted nothing less.

At the time *Public Education in the United States* was published, Cubberley
belonged to the educational establishment's select inner circle which developed
and directed public educational policy, and which dominated the training and
placement of those men who were to become state and city school superintendents, and school principals — the men who would directly implement the policies and programs.[8] Other professional schoolmen, educational entrepreneurs,
and religious clerics before Cubberley had written accounts telling their story of
public education's evolutionary progress. Cubberley gives passing notice to
some (such as Small, Martin and Graves), but in fact concentrates on Henry
Barnard as his most distinguished predecessor in educational scholarship and
history.[9] With the possible exception of Barnard, none were positioned such as
Cubberley in the upper echelon of a national organization economically and
politically engaged in a complete reorganization of the public school system in
American society and in defining how the reality of this relation was to be
known, understood, and communicated.[10] Cubberley tells us in his preface to
the revised second edition that his text "represented a method of treatment of
the history of education that was new." And, "[t]hroughout, an effort was

made . . . to set forth our educational history as an evolving series of events from which the recent advances in educational practice and procedure have had their origin. . . ."[11]

Cubberley's position in the educational establishment as engaged propagandist for industrial efficiency and scientific management, as social engineer, as educational entrepreneur, as Dean of the School of Education at Stanford, and as the designated historian among the leaders of the educational establishment make *Public Education in the United States* a most peculiar text. It is stuffed with information about the legal, financial and administrative development of the system of public school education and its integration into the State. *Public Education* is equally impressive in its near total silence about historically specific socioeconomic circumstances which generated economic and political relations prior to the Civil War and after — unless one considers Cubberley's claims valid and fully explanatory that the War of Independence reduced the entire white population to poverty, or that the First World War caused the Great Depression in the United States. But if his claim about the War of Independence, for instance, is valid, there is no explanation for grammar schools and academies for the wealthy, and charity or Lancasterian schools specifically for the working class poor. If "the people" and the "nation" were so equally poor, where did the wealthy come from, and who organized and paid for these schools, and why the distinct class differentiations between them? It is not until Chapter XIV, where he shifts his discussion to the period between 1865 and 1930, that Cubberley has something substantial to say about society and what it had become by 1900, and what this signified for the state system of public school education. But even so he sheds little illumination on how particular socioeconomic circumstances came to be as they are, nor does he explain why they must remain as they are or become progressively more so. His discussion of society and problems generated by economic and political relations after the Civil War focuses almost exclusively on Eastern and Southern European immigrants, their biological inferiority and their corruption of American society, and upon the economic, political, cultural, and educational crises resulting from the emancipation of Black slaves. His discussion, however, depends on assertions, misrepresentations, and sweeping generalizations rather than detailed inquiry, established congruences, and explanation.

It is because of his peculiar rhetorical method of treating the whole of American history up to 1880 that his critics, and Bernard Bailyn in particular, have charged Cubberley and his cohort of presentism, i.e., writing about and explaining the past through the categories, ideas, and values of the present. Objecting to presentism, however, may be a polite scholar's way of branding the text of another practitioner an ideological tract rather than a sincere explanatory effort to reconstruct the historical particulars of society in an earlier time. Or perhaps not. Labeling *Public Education* isolationist, as presentist, as consensus history, while in large measure true, is in fact to gloss over and obscure Cubberley's momentous, complex, labyrinthine rhetorical construction of American social history and the emergence of the state system of public school education.

To fully appreciate Cubberley's concoction of historical details and interpretation it is necessary to read *Public Education* twice, and from opposite directions. This is necessarily the case because Cubberley's narrative is wrapped around two contradictory explanations of the development of the state system of public school education. From front to back it is a 765 page rhetorical construct which Cubberley authoritatively claims is the new history of American education, of the progressive democratic public school system as it has evolved since the days of the first Puritan settlements to the present moment in 1919 (and extended to the 1930s in the second edition).[12] The second and contrary explanation, when reconstructed from back to front, so to speak, is a radically different and less benevolent, less democratic history of the public school as social institution embedded in Cubberley's text. In other words, the forward movement of *Public Education in the United States* is an interpretive reconstruction of American social and institutional history intended to legitimate and obscure under the mystifying rhetorical cover of *democratic progress* Cubberley and company's energized bureaucratic reorganization of the state system of public school education to secure the centralization and concentration of authority and policy making for the purpose of more efficient social control and differentiation of labor. From back to front, however, it is obvious that Cubberley has had to peel away some of his ideological mystification of the nineteenth century.[13] To make twentieth century reorganization initiatives, which his "history" propagandizes and legitimates, appear to be evidence of both democratic progress and scientific efficiency, Cubberley reveals the nineteenth century state system of public school education as a central mechanism of privilege and social control in the struggle between economic classes — to prevent class war,[14] in the struggle of those in economic and political positions of governance against revolutionary democratic insurgents,[15] in the struggle of elite and middle class Protestant sects against working class Protestant sects, and of Protestants collectively against Catholics and Jews,[16] and in the struggle of Anglo-Americans with select allied groups from Western and Northern Europe against Black-Americans, Eastern and Southern European immigrants, and Asian immigrants.[17]

Cubberley's two opposing explanations of the public school's position in society can be visualized using Cubberley's own symbols: Cubberley's progressive movement is the story of the American democratic ladder of opportunity;[18] but, because such a story cannot adequately rationalize the proposed system of reorganizing reforms, Cubberley reveals the American economic and political pyramid of hierarchically organized and differentiated classes and powers.[19] In the first instance, the state system of public school education is a democratic vehicle carrying each American citizen socially upward as far as innate ability and economic means will permit.[20] In the second instance, the state system of public school education is an ideological and institutional hegemonic mechanism for securing and maintaining the stability of the American social pyramid in which economic acquisition and political power are concentrated at the top.[21]

Something of Cubberley's conceptual organization was revealed in his preface, quoted above, and reappears as the first sentence of the last and shortest chapter of his history text:

> In the chapters preceding this one we have traced . . . the evolution of our American public schools from the days of their infancy . . . and have shown the connection between our more pressing present-day problems and our evolution during the past.[22]

The past and the present are inextricably bound together. In Cubberley's history present-day problems are rooted in a past that only makes sense in the context of the present. This is the present-perspective construction of history that Bailyn protests with vigor, and rightly so, but it actually matters only if Cubberley is deliberately intent on writing ***history***. But Cubberley is not writing history, he is writing propaganda to legitimate a particular social/educational ideology and a corresponding program of social determinism.

His rhetorical argument reconstructs the evolutionary development of a progressively "democratic"[23] system of public school instruction — one that overcomes the class-bias and rate-bills of early district schools,[24] that overcomes the incompetence of elected lay administrators of district schools,[25] that overcomes sectarian opposition to secular public schooling,[26] and that by 1861 ultimately establishes on top of the elementary common schools a high school and, shortly after, a college education for all.[27] This story is buttressed by a great many words and pages devoted to the needs and conditions required by children for healthy physical, mental and social development.[28] This is his construction of the democratic ladder. What he in fact identifies, establishes and legitimates, however, is the progressive historical movement away from locally constituted district "public schools" which tended to reflect objective conditions and antagonistic class relations, and which were more often than not only partially inclusive, to a system of State imposed compulsory inclusion constituted by segregated and stratified schools organized along descending lines of race, ethnicity and class,[29] as established by law and State policy, and under non-democratic, hierarchical bureaucratic administration directed by non-elected experts (i.e., technocrats).[30] Undergirding all else (and a more coherent way to read his history in short) is Cubberley's account of a progressive institutional and social movement away from the inefficiency of democracy in an industrial capitalist society toward ever greater rule, order, and efficiency under the direction of the centralized State and administered by a strata of government bureaucrats and school superintendents — from the federal level to the state to the county to the city.[31] This is his pyramid construct of the evolving system of public school education in its relation to society, and, too, this is the ideological conception around which his narrative is organized.[32]

Cubberley's massing of historical details and his rhetorical strategy of describing the State's every advance over popular opposition as "democratic" progress act to obscure his ideology, just as his ideology is meant to mystify the processes and social reality of his program of radical public school reorganization. By abstracting his construction from its cloak of selective historical details and rhetoric, however, it is possible to see his undergirding ideology for what it actually is, and, too, to see how it informs the social construction of twentieth century public school education.

Cubberley is quite clever in the way he ideologically prepares for the "democratic" reorganization of the state system of public school education which he explains in the latter third of *Public Education*. All along he follows what appears to be a standard historical chronology. Occasionally he steps out of strict historical narrative to tell his reader that present circumstances or ideas or practices owe their origin to this or that. To the New Englanders we owe the democratic ideal and the spread of public school education "open to all."[33] We can thank James G. Carter and Horace Mann, for example, for establishing the precedent of the non-elective position of public school superintendence and the more efficient administration of the public school system.[34] We can thank Mann in particular for helping the public school system break free from the strangle hold of the church and clerics.[35] For educational history and scholarship we are deeply indebted to Henry Barnard.[36] William T. Harris, Superintendent of St. Louis schools 1867-1880, was our first great educational philosopher.[37] And so on. To the uncritical eye these asides do not distract from what otherwise appears to be a narrative of historical events and individual leaders important to the *evolution* of the state system of public school education. But, allowing that some things happened when he says they did,[38] his pretense of historical explanation is smoke and mirrors to cover-up the simple fact that *Public Education in the United States* is an ideological polemic. And, as ideological polemic his text has an internal logic of its own, even if it does not follow the disciplinary logic of historiography.

Cubberley's construction of this embedded polemic follows the historical chronology of his sources, but, too, it is stratified. Thus, Emanuel Fellenberg appears first in his narrative, followed by Johann Friedrich, and then Herbert Spencer. These three Europeans have their American counterparts in Horace Mann, Henry Barnard, and Frederick W. Taylor. The ideas and practices of the first group establish for Cubberley the defining stratification of public instruction along the lines of socioeconomic class, derived from Fellenberg, the proper relation of public instruction to the social and industrial needs of society, derived from Herbart, and the necessary and overarching reasons why the schools must be reorganized according to his explanations of society, derived from

Spencer. The second group exemplify how the ideas and practices promoted by the first group were and are insinuated in and made over as the American system of public school education. Cubberley, to obscure what he is about, in fact goes to extremes to keep the two groups separate in his narrative. For example, there is no explicit connection between the Prussian System of social inculcation through teacher education, public instruction and State centralized administration, and Horace Mann. Barnard is an educational scholar and historian, not a capitalist seeking to generate a system of public school education dedicated to the secure production and reproduction of capitalist society. Taylor's systemic program of scientific management is poorly disguised as intelligent, scientific efficiency, and thus is not revealed as a social mechanism for establishing and reproducing unequal economic and political relations — without the danger of class consciousness.

Cubberley has also identified the three Americans as role models for himself: as scholar and historian of the state system of public school education he identifies Henry Bernard; as propagandist and social engineer for the reorganization of a secular (i.e., non-sectarian) public school education and its administration as a social institution dedicated to meeting the industrial and social needs of the State he identifies Horace Mann; as strategic efficiency and management expert he does not identify any one, but in fact presents as his own program the hierarchical and systemic organization of management explicated by Frederick W. Taylor in *Principles of Scientific Management*.[39] The Americans are used, too, to obscure the ideological and social sources, and the historical socioeconomic circumstances which undergird the American system of public instruction.[40] Before he gets to Taylor's scientific reconstitution of social relations however, he first lays down a firm ideological foundation for the proper relation of the public school system, society, and the State — a relation which must be congruent with the undergirding social ontology for *Public Education in the United States* which he does not make explicit until page 496 of his text.

Emanuel Fellenberg, Johann Friedrich Herbart, and Herbert Spencer are, according to Cubberley, European theorists whose educational and social ideas registered on American educational consciousness. In their historical roles Fellenberg, Herbart, and Spencer are significant enough to warrant Cubberley's mention and his readers' attention. But more importantly they have been given critical rhetorical and ideological roles to play in *Public Education* which are central to Cubberley's larger project of explaining and legitimating the twentieth century reorganization of the state system of public school education. In the language of literary criticism, Cubberley uses these historical figures to foreshadow the historical future. Fellenberg is used in particular to foreshadow the modern disciplinary institution, i.e., the reform school, but, too, his educational program as explained by Cubberley serves as the precursor for the stratification of schools and differentiated curriculum along lines of class and race which Cubberley will eventually introduce as the new democratic public school system. Herbart is used to establish the argument for using the educational history textbook as instrumental to the proper inculcation of teacher candidates, and Spencer contributes to the development of the new curricula with his claims for the necessity of universal science education. Cubberley uses Herbart and Spencer as well to establish the ideological legitimation for the class and racial stratification of public school education, of which Fellenberg's program serves as the model. Cubberley's use of Fellenberg, Herbart, and Spencer to serve his argument and the needs of his project also poses problems; thus his treatment of each is seldom straightforward. He is often at pains to focus on the content of their programs and/or ideas while simultaneously obscuring the substance and implications for society. Indeed, Cubberley's efforts to keep content and substance separate, to obscure actual social consequences of these ideas and programs when implemented, will lead him to make substantial omissions, especially in the case of his explication of Fellenberg.

Fellenberg

Fellenberg's Manual-Labor system of education was introduced to the United States in 1829 through a series of published articles written by William Woodbridge.[41] Cubberley tells the reader that "Fellenberg's work was widely copied in Switzerland, Germany, England, and the United States, and contained the germ-idea of our modern agricultural, manual, and reformatory education."[42] Several pages later he is more emphatic about Fellenberg's influence on the development of the American public school:

The one European idea which we did adopt almost bodily . . . because we found it so well suited to early democratic conditions among a people of little wealth, was . . . worked out by Fellenberg and his followers at Hofwyl, in Switzerland, of combining manual labor with schooling. [. . .] The advantages, both pecuniary and educational, of combining schooling and farming made a strong appeal in the days when money was scarce and opportunities limited, and such schools . . . were founded first in Connecticut in 1819, Maine in 1821, Massachusetts in 1824, Kentucky in 1826, New York in 1827, Pennsylvania in 1829, New Jersey in 1830, Virginia in 1831, Georgia and Tennessee in 1832, and North Carolina in 1834.[43]

Cubberley identifies six structural characteristics of Fellenberg's school that are meant to explain why American state public school promoters found it so well suited to socioeconomic circumstances:

1. A farm of about six hundred acres.
2. Workshops for manufacturing clothing and tools.
3. A printing and lithographing establishment.
4. A literary institution for the education of the well-to-do.
5. A lower school which trained for handicrafts and middle-class occupations.
6. An agricultural school for the education of the poor as farm laborers, and as teachers for the rural schools.[44]

Although he does not elaborate, Cubberley at least points out that aspects of Fellenberg's conception served as the model for the American reform school. And elsewhere he will explicitly identify the manual-industrial schools as reform schools.[45] His fragmentary candor on these points, however, is counterbalanced by his studied omission of other social events and movements that might explain the attraction of the Fellenberg program of socialization and class-differentiated content and instruction better than his absurd claim that America was a poor country. In 1827 New York's law abolishing slavery in the state took effect. Andrew Jackson's election as President in 1828 was carried over venomous Whig opposition by the energized support of newly enfranchised working class white males. And, too, in 1829 the New York Working Men's Association under the guiding influence of Thomas Skidmore, the democratic revolutionary, issued its manifesto demanding structural reforms of the social order. Within weeks of their stunning declaration, they announced the formation of the Working Men's Party, which was specifically intended to lead in the organization of workingmen and their friends against the economic and political domination of the rich. 1829 was also the year in which Thomas Skidmore and David Walker each published their revolutionary democratic treatises. About this same time, too, Robert Dale Owen and Franny Wright had been actively promoting a caretaker system of public education which would remove all children, rich and poor, and place them in secluded State run residential institutions where they would be housed, dressed and educated alike.[46]

Cubberley's silence on historical events and social movements has been noted by some of his critics, most often though without the accompaniment of specifics, but no one to my knowledge has identified and established his engaged practice of ideological mystification or constructivism. His purpose in identifying Fellenberg is to leave a favorable impression of residential manual-labor education in his reader's mind, and to connect it in a positive way to the development of the agricultural state college system — where it will have lost all relation to the poor and to reform schools. Cubberley makes the Fellenberg program and its adoption in the United States appear innocent, a positive idea whose popularity crested too soon.

> It was at its height about 1830, but the movement soon collapsed. The rise of cities and wealth and social classes was against the idea, and the opening up of cheap and rich farms to the westward, with the change of the East from agriculture to manufacturing, turned the agricultural aspect of the movement aside for a generation. When it reappeared again in the Central West it came in the form of new demand for colleges to teach agriculture and mechanic arts, but with the manual-labor idea omitted.[47]

Cubberley's use of Fellenberg, though, is more than what it appears. He has told his readers that Fellenberg's ideas and program were introduced in the United States in 1829 through a series of articles, but within a year it was collapsing. There is no common sense explanation to explain why a program of such tentative presence should be allotted the importance it receives in Cubberley's text, and he does not provide one. On the surface of his statement, above, what he does establish by linking the Fellenberg idea to state colleges is it was not merely turned aside for a generation, but done away with entirely for the mass of working class whites who would not attend these state colleges in significant numbers until after the Second World War. Through this tidy bit of rhetoric he has effectively directed attention away from reform schools, their parallel development with the system of public school education, and the increasing numbers of working class children who came to occupy them.[48] He has in effect covered-up Fellenberg's program as it was adapted for use in America.

Nearly 300 pages later, stripped of all Cubberley's mystifying rhetoric, Fellenberg's program of a stratified education, divided along lines of economic social positions, will reappear as democratic schools differentiated for students having different capabilities: academic high schools for the capable and bright top 30% of students, and vocational and/or manual-industrial schools for the lower 70%.[49] Cubberley is doing more than covering-up Fellenberg's significant relation to American social education in this statement.

His explanation of the demise of the Manual-Labor school movement is an obscuring rhetorical maneuver. On page 364, preceding the above quote, Cubberley claims Fellenberg's Manual-Labor idea was enormously popular in the cities for the education of machine workers. Logically, then, the westward movement of agriculture ought not to have had any negative effect on the continued popularity of the Manual-Labor schools in the cities. The only plausible explanation for their demise is suggested in his brief statement: "the rise of . . . social classes"! In other words, the working class for whom Manual-Labor education was intended rejected it, and Cubberley is doing his best to misdirect the reader's attention.

An important part of the consensus he is drawing from and also promoting is the story of the common bond between humanitarian public men as educational leaders and the supporting fellowship of enlightened working men — antagonistic class relations do not fit in this picture of social reality, nor does class conflict over equal general education. Yet Cubberley needs to acknowledge the early emergence of "social classes" to validate his claim of the "evolutionary development" of American society. By 1900 these social classes will have evolved in Cubberley's explanation into permanent social divisions. So here he rhetorically plants what appears to be a seed of the American society to come. The fact that he is obviously aware of class stratification and antagonistic class relations in the nineteenth century[50] but does not explicate and elaborate these socioeconomic circumstances indicates the high degree of authorial intentionality guiding what Cubberley chooses to explain, how he explains it, and where he places the explanation in his narrative. In short, Cubberley is constructing rather than explaining a particular historical reality.

To preserve the psychological impact of an invading immigrant and ex-slave Black laboring class, of emergent class and racial crises, which constitute his rhetorical emotional appeals substantiating the necessary reorganization of the state system of public school education at the turn of the century, Cubberley does not reveal that class divisions were in fact already well developed and the source of considerable antagonism and repeated eruptions of revolutionary democratic insurgency in the nineteenth century. His rhetorical tactic in constructing nineteenth century history is to maintain silence or to minimize the realities of class and antagonistic economic and political relations so that he can pose such conditions as unique to the decades following Reconstruction. At which point in his narrative he will stress the necessity of deliberately reorganizing the state system as the central "democratic" mechanism for responding to the social problems generated by class conflict — as if class conflict only emerged after the slaves were freed and certain immigrant groups settled in the United States.

It is no less interesting that the upstart and demise of the Fellenberg Manual-Labor school took place before Horace Mann was set to work energizing and reorganizing the Common School Reform Movement. Indeed, as Mann makes particularly explicit in his 1841 and 1848 *Reports*, the political expectation of the state system of public school education is it will specifically address the problem of class consciousness and antagonistic class relations in society that emerged in unison with the advance of industrial capitalism. But Cubberley does not acknowledge Mann's (or Barnard's) position, or the fact that Mann's efforts to secure a state system followed the general failure of charity schools, Lancasterian schools, and Fellenberg Manual-Labor schools to attract and inculcate the poor and the working-class on one hand, or, on the other hand, to answer the recognized need for an educational mechanism to distinguish and elevate the middle class from the lower classes. According to Cubberley's construct of antebellum history, therefore, there is the indication of social class development, but typically antagonistic class relations go unexplored and unrecognized except for casual asides such as that evidenced above.

In addition to his silence on Mann's clear historical role in the context of nineteenth century economic and political relations, Cubberley is also silent about the obvious application of Fellenberg's Manual-Labor idea to the education of Black-Americans (Hampton/Tuskegee) and Amerindians (Carlisle). For example, if provision number 4 (literary education for the well-to-do) of Fellenberg's program is deleted, and provision number 5 is modified to delete instruction for the middle-class, one has Samuel Armstrong's Hampton Institute for the education of Black-Americans[51] and Pratt's Carlisle Institute which followed for the education of Amerindians.[52] In particular, provision 6, which equates manual labor with teacher training, is precisely the Hampton Institute's program of training Black-American teachers for the task of inculcating Black-American children into a manual-labor work ethic.[53]

Cubberley's silence is not oversight but deliberate ideological mystification. First, he places the entire responsibility for the South's slow economic, political, and public educational development on the backs of Black-Americans, who were according to Cubberley slaves until the end of the Civil War, and who constituted two-fifths of the total population of illiterates in the United States as late as 1900.[54] Secondly, he racially and ideologically mystifies the actual practices at Hampton and Tuskegee,[55] and the economic and political machinations of the Southern Educational Board, the General Education Board, and of Southern planters and capitalists generally to perpetuate illiteracy (or a delimited form of literacy) among Blacks (and poor whites). Their direct purpose through public policy development and action was to combat independent educational efforts and universal egalitarian democratic political aspirations by Black-Americans and thus protect existing unequal social and economic relations, reestablish white political domination, and to sustain and reproduce a large Black agricultural laboring class.[56] Cubberley won't mention Hampton and Tuskegee again for another 100 pages:

The shop work, based on the "Russian system," included wood-turning, joinery, pattern-making, forging, foundry and machine work. Hampton Institute, after 1870, and Tuskegee Institute, after 1881, developed and applied the same type of technique for teaching trades to Negroes.[57]

This passage specifically relates to Cubberley's elaborated discussion of the generative influence of the "Russian system" on certain American educators and industrialists intent on turning the public schools and colleges toward industrial skills and the applied sciences.[58] He attributes the rise and character of industrial education to the "Russian system" — not to Fallenberg's school and curricular differentiation for a stratified class system. This passage demonstrates in a small way the multiple levels of mystification on which Cubberley's text operates. First, by linking industrial education to the "Russian system" and thus both to technical schools and colleges he is redefining what vocational/industrial education is: training in skilled trades and applied sciences. Secondly, this looks forward to his explication of vocational/industrial education for immigrant working class children in the early twentieth century, and will make the entire institutional socialization process appear to be benevolent and democratic — something it is not. But finally, the passage helps to expose the specific racist and ideological mystification which dominates these pages.

In his discussion of the retarded evolutionary development of the state system of public school education in the South after the Civil War, Cubberley references W.E.B. DuBois's study of the Freeman's Bureau.[59] But, significantly, he does not mention what DuBois had to say about Black-Americans' energized educational, economic and political self-determination, and he does not cite DuBois in his index, nor include DuBois's work in his companion text of *Readings*.[60] Clearly, Cubberley is aware of the actual socioeconomic circumstances in the South, and textual evidence strongly indicates he is also aware of the work of Black historians that refute racist mystifications of these circumstances.[61] There can be no doubt that Cubberley is thus deliberately covering up the fact that Hampton and Tuskegee were an insidious form of the Fellenberg Manual-Labor idea, where learning industriousness through long hours of arduous manual labor for scant wages which must be turned over to the institution in payment for the privilege of learning to work constituted enlightened educational practice.[62] Very little academic/intellectual education took place, and, for that matter, very little in the way of real craft skills were imparted to student-laborers.[63] When his linkage between the "Russian system" and Hampton/Tuskegee is unpacked, the Manual-Labor/Industrial schools are revealed to be little more than work-to-prepare-for-work schools. This is a revelation, however, which is not anticipated in his text, nor is it addressed in any detail by any but a few educational historians who followed Cubberley.[64] As a matter of fact, by relying on Cubberley's explanation of the social and educational history of the South, teacher candidates would be no wiser about the actual relation between Fellenberg's program of education and the actual program at Hampton. Indeed, another two hundred pages later, Cubberley returns us to Hampton Institute, which "The superintendent of public instruction of Virginia, Dr. Ruffner, declared it to be 'the most valuable of all schools opened on this continent for the colored people.'"[65]

> Its founder, General Samuel Chapin Armstrong, had headed a colored regiment during the war, and in 1866 had been appointed superintendent of education for the colored people of Virginia under the Freedmen's Bureau. His training and experience had equipped him well to understand the needs of the Negro race, and during the twenty-five years he directed Hampton, until his death in 1893, he shaped the policy for the education of the Negroes and the Indians (included in 1878) of America, while the men and women he trained went out and became the leaders of their people throughout the South and West. The object of the institution was to train teachers and industrial leaders for the two races, particular emphasis being placed on character building, the missionary spirit, agricultural instruction, vocational course, and the home-making arts.[66]

Cubberley's footnotes for Armstrong and Booker T. Washington, a graduate of Hampton, and famous for founding the Tuskegee Institute, and infamous as the white's Black spokesman for the Hampton idea, are also illuminating. About Armstrong, Cubberley writes:

> General Armstrong was born in the Hawaiian Islands, of missionary parents, and educated there and at Williams College. *For some years he was connected with the department of public instruction of Hawaii,*

where he obtained that knowledge of the education of backward peoples which proved of much use to him in his work for the Negroes of the South. Realizing the need of the colored people for industrial training, he founded Hampton on the shores of Hampton Roads and began his great life-work.[emphasis added][67]

James D. Anderson is more forthcoming about the specifics of Armstrong's knowledge of "backward peoples" and his Hampton idea:

> In his view, the "Colored people" could "afford to let politics severely alone." He maintained, for instance, that black participation in politics in South Carolina resulted in a "shameless legislature" that had "ruined the credit of a great state." Armstrong instructed black leaders to stay out of politics in South Carolina because they were "not capable of self-government," and he blamed the black voters for creating situations which "no white race on this earth ought to endure or will endure." [. . .] His idealized student was a hard worker with elementary education and industrial training. He did not believe that highly educated blacks would remain as "civilizers" among the rural masses. "There is such a thing as over-education," he warned. "A highly educated Negro is as little likely as a highly educated white man to do a work against which his tastes and sensibilities would every day rebel." The highly educated could not serve as models for the masses, who, according to Armstrong, were destined to plow, hoe, ditch, and grub. Therefore, manual labor rather than scholarship became Hampton's chief criterion for educational excellence. "One who shirks labor may be a fine mathematician," noted Armstrong, but "the blockhead at the black board may be a shining example in the cornfield." The idealized "blockhead" or "plodders," as they were called, became the standard by which all students were evaluated. [. . .] "The plodding ones make good teachers."[68]

Armstrong's arguments found a sympathetic audience in Cubberley, who writes about Booker T. Washington:

Washington was born a slave . . . in 1858. [. . .] When fourteen years old, he walked five hundred miles to Hampton and asked for admission. His entrance examination was to clean out a dirty room. So well did he do the job that he not only was admitted, but paid all his expenses there for three years by janitor work. After some teaching experience, he studied further at Wayland Seminary at Washington, D.C., then became an instructor at Hampton, and, in 1881, he became principal of the new Institute chartered by the Alabama legislature at Tuskegee, where he remained the rest of his life. [. . .] He died in 1915.[69]

What Anglo-American white protestant male anywhere in the United States ever gained admission to college by passing an entrance examination consisting of cleaning out a dirty room? While pretending praise, Cubberley is in fact declaring the backwardness of Black-Americans. Clearly the reader is meant to understand that for Black-Americans the most appropriate test for school admission was (and, by implication, is) a set task at unskilled, tedious manual labor to determine the docility and obedience of the applicant. Cubberley's passage illuminates in the best possible way, however, what actually constituted education at Hampton Institute. Such education and training as perpetuated there was not in the skilled industrial trades or applied sciences. And, too, the passage illuminates the manner in which Fellenberg's ideas were incorporated in the United States. But it is precisely this direct relationship between Fellenberg's program and the manner in which it has been adapted, promoted and imposed in the United States for socially constructed class and racial division and subjugation that Cubberley covers up.

Central to Cubberley's legitimation of State control of public school education, to centralized bureaucratic administration, and to a system of hierarchically stratified schools and differentiated curricula is his argument that (1) Eastern and Southern European Immigrants, and the great mass of Black-Americans are backward, illiterate, and pose a dangerous obstacle to the State;[70] (2) 70 percent of all young are incapable or unwilling to benefit from an academic education;[71] and (3) Fellenberg's Manual-Labor idea provides the foundational model for the Industrial/Vocational school which is the "democratic" answer to the social reality of the first two socioeconomic circumstances.

Cubberley writes with at least two audiences in mind: (1) college educated men of the inner circle of superintendency, among whom Cubberley proudly includes himself,[272] and school principals who, to efficiently fulfill the duties of their social positions and scientifically direct the manufacturing processes of the national school system and individual schools must understand the aim, content, methods of instruction and the undergirding reasons of public instruction. And given the high level of organized collaboration and coordination amongst these men in reorganizing and redefining the state system of public school education it certainly appears that Cubberley expected this audience to make the connection between Fellenberg as explained in his text and its manifestation as vocational and industrial education, and to properly interpret its meaning.[73] Thus, for this audience Cubberley can be said to be revealing. (2) Cubberley's second audience are teacher candidates and practicing teachers, who, by virtue of their particularly delimited education and training, might not be expected to recognize the significant relation between Fellenberg and Vocational/Industrial public instruction.[74]   As a matter of fact, by not making the relation and its meaning explicit, Cubberley is mystifying the program of a socially engineered laboring force which is correspondingly subjugated politically and exploited economically. Were the reality of Hampton and its direct relation to Fellenberg's idea of stratified education explicitly illuminated in his text, training and practicing teachers might not be especially enthusiastic about their socially prescribed role as "blockheads" and "plodders," as agents for the reproduction of a socially constructed laboring force. Cubberley's explanation of the "democratic" vocational high school would be exposed for what it is. The exposure of Fellenberg/Hampton would reveal a social reality of antagonistic class and socially constructed race relations on one hand, and on the other hand reveal the anti-democratic ideology and processes undergirding the reorganization of the state system of public school education which his text is meant to advance. But, more importantly, were the truth known, Cubberley and company's program could easily have met the same fate as the Fellenberg Manual-Labor schools of the 1830s.

Herbart

Cubberley prepares the way for Herbart in much the same way he prepared for Fellenberg, by writing at length about Johann H. Pestalozzi.[75] Where Pestalozzi sought to transform the structures of society by giving poor children an academic education on one hand and teaching them skills for self-sufficiency on the other — and thus be prepared to take on the task of social transformation — Fellenberg is held up as a superior model, for he sought the transformation of the poor child without seeking the transformation of existing class relations. When he is ready for Herbart, Cubberley again uses Pestalozzi as his foil. Where Pestalozzi was a country farmer turned educator, "an impractical enthusiast" who defined teaching as spiritual, as an "act of love," Herbart was the son of "a well educated public official," "a well-trained scholarly thinker," and "professor of philosophy in a German University," who defined teaching as both an art and a "science."[76] Cubberley clearly wants it understood that teaching as love for the child, teaching as dedicated to the healthy individual and social development of the child is no good as the foundation for teacher training or as something upon which to erect an efficient system of public instruction. For this, science is required. But not just any science will do, a science of teacher training and a science of instruction which correspond to a science of society is needed. And Herbart establishes this science according to Cubberley.

Among the few things about which Cubberley is consistent is his attack against the "district schools." Scattered throughout his text he gives various reasons against it, but his foremost reasons are local community orientation and governance, unsystematic criterion for teacher hiring, unsystematic selection of textbooks, and individualized instruction. Herbart provides Cubberley with both a theory and practice by which to promote an entirely different conception of the relation between society, public school education and teacher training.

Herbart rejected alike the conventional-social education of Locke, the natural and unsocial education of Rousseau, and the "faculty-psychology" conception of education of Pestalozzi. Instead he conceived of the mind as a unity, rather than divided into "faculties," and the aim of education as broadly social rather than personal. The purpose of education, he said, was to prepare men to live properly in organized society, and hence the chief aim in education was not conventional fitness, natural development, mere knowledge, nor personal mental power, but personal character and social morality. This being the case, the educator should analyze the interests and occupations and social responsibilities of men as they are grouped in organized society, and, from such analyses, deduce the means and the method of instruction.[77]

Certain social conditions and labor forces are necessary to fulfill the needs of capitalist society. Sustaining and reproducing these conditions and the necessary labor forces thus constitutes the legitimate aim of education. The educator's task is to inculcate the child into this society through a particular curricular content and method of instruction.[78] The state system of public school education, therefore, exists not for the healthy development of the individual child, nor is it necessarily to reform, improve, or transform society. Rather, its aim is directed toward meeting the social and industrial reproduction needs of capitalist society. Content and method of instruction are sufficiently and efficiently to prepare each and every child for their place, role, and function in meeting the social and industrial needs of the State.[79] Given the social aim of public instruction the content and methods cannot be otherwise, for the individual's "social responsibilities and duties are determined by the nature of the social organization of which he forms a part."[80] In other words, the purpose of education is to reproduce the organization of economic and political relations as they actually and already exist.

But as the twentieth-century state system of public school education is reorganized to meet the social and industrial needs of the State through its differentiated content and courses of study, and through its stratified levels of schools, it is essential that every subject of study at every level be commensurate with particular methods of instruction meant to establish and extend hegemony over all classes. Indeed, as Cubberley warns, the real danger to society comes not from unequal economic and political relations, which constitute society as it actually is, but from the potential development of critical knowledge and class consciousness.[81] Thus in differentiated content and administrative organization the school must be made consistent with actual economic and political relations of society, and this society must be made to appear normal and the best possible. The state system of public school education thus has two aims: first, to meet the social and industrial needs of the State, and, second, to prevent the emergence of class consciousness.[82]

Both of these aims, to be met efficiently, must be ideologically mystified. Cubberley explains that the 70 percent of all children channelled into the vocational schools, into the Manual-Industrial schools are so directed because they are incapable or unwilling to learn from books.[83] And if questioned by individual parents or students, administrators can point to Lewis Terman's scientific IQ studies, to his ethnically and racially differentiated statistical findings to show that Italian children, Polish children, or Black-American children, etc., typically score so low on the IQ scale of intelligence measurement that if such a child were placed in an academic school they would certainly fail.[84] The teacher, parent and child are meant to understand that placement in a vocational or industrial school is in fact a humanitarian act, a marvelous educational and training opportunity, and the children will now be able to contribute to the progress of society and of themselves.[85] Providing for so many formerly excluded and academically incapable children is, Cubberley claims, evidence of the progressive features of our democratic society.[86] That these same children are identified, sorted, and sent into differentiated educational tracks before or shortly after beginning school, that their educational opportunities, that the content and methods of instruction they encounter, that the organization of social relations into which they are acculturated are all socially determined and constructed for them by a socially dominant class and race constitutes a reality which must be ideologically hidden if economic and political hegemony is to be successfully established — if a stratified, fragmented and differentiated laboring force is to be produced to meet the social and industrial needs of the State — if critical intelligence and class consciousness are to be suppressed.

For such a program as this to take root and prosper, it is essential that teachers in particular be properly inculcated in the dominant ideology and that their training be carefully constructed and properly delimited. Having studied the Prussian system and having travelled there to observe it first hand, Horace Mann clearly understood the necessary importance of State regulated teacher training, and in short order after returning he set about implementing normal schools for this purpose. Child psychology (i.e., understanding how different groups of children learn most thoroughly and effectively), content (i.e., mastery of prescribed textbooks or building materials), and efficient methods of instruction (i.e., appropriate to age, capability, subject, and predetermined aims) soon came to dominate teacher training. But these areas of study and practice alone were and are insufficient to transform the teacher into a reliable and efficient agent of the State. Thus it was necessary that the teacher's training include a correct history of society and the relation of public education to it.

In the middle 1800s it was, perhaps, enough for Horace Mann to dwell upon the Puritans and to tell of their dedication to schooling all children, of their commitment to bringing light into the darkness. By the early twentieth century, however, the Puritan beginning provided a suitable point from which to start, but it was obviously insufficient. Hence Cubberley's teachers' education history for the proper explanation of what constitutes the reality of society, of economic and political relations, of different groups of children and races, and of the public school and its relation to this complex society.

Cubberley relies on Herbart to justify the sort of history he is writing and its aims:

> . . . Herbart now added the two important studies of literature and history, and history with the emphasis on the social rather than the political side. [. . .] History in particular Herbart conceived to be a study of the first importance for revealing proper human relationships, and leading men to social and national "good-will."[87]

Against the background of the Russian Revolution, of the recently concluded First World War, of Black-Americans struggling for integration and equality or revolution or independent self-determination, of organized laborers' campaigns for democracy and their bloody confrontations with goons, Pinkertons, police, and military sent in to crush them, of populist farmers fighting bankers and politicians and the railroads, of increasingly popular socialists and Marxists, of decades of steady immigration from Eastern and Southern Europe, and of cycles of economic crisis, Cubberley's choice of words and his purposeful vagueness appear richly connotative. The separation of "social" from "political" is most interesting; for how can one exist without the other? Without civic political behavior, without contested ideology, rule and culture, one is confronted by the totalitarian State. To jettison the political dimensions of such a state is to posit the State's sanctity and supremacy as an unquestionable fact. And society within a totalitarian State must be rigidly organized, it must be ideologically and culturally homogeneous if the State is to survive, or the State, representing the interest of those for whom it is energized, must rely on the uncertain and costly means of violent coercion to sustain and reproduce itself. In the context of the United States, therefore, to jettison the political is to jettison democracy (at least such notions as the people are supreme) and precepts of self-government. Thus one of Cubberley's circle could read the above passage and understand him to mean an ideologically constructed history to indoctrinate, and to instill a narrowly conceived nativist nationalism . . . to mean the inculcation of the teacher and student into the existing social order and for the production of conformism and social reproduction.

Cubberley, making his point explicit, writes:

> The chief purpose of education Herbart held to be to develop personal character and to prepare for social usefulness. These virtues, he held, proceeded from enough of the right kind of knowledge, properly interpreted to the pupil so that clear ideas as to relationships might be formed.[88]

Horace Mann also made this argument of the role of public school education in preventing class consciousness in a number of his Reports, but most pointedly in his *Twelfth Annual Report*.[89] But for Cubberley to reveal this interesting correspondence between Mann's arguments and his interpretation of Herbart in this context and to his audience of teacher candidates would be to reveal too much. It would expose his manipulative use of Pestalozzi by making a clear connection between Mann, Herbart, and the Prussian system (one that is rather different from that which he has constructed) — a connection Cubberley has studiously ignored. And, too, that Mann and Herbart were actively engaged in devising a form of public education and its proper implementation to secure social control and order might lead to the revelation that both men and their cohorts were responding to antagonistic class relations and social crises. And this in turn might raise questions about the historical socioeconomic circumstances which generated these particular relations, conflicts and crises. It is too soon in his argument to make such a revelation in any case, for he needs Herbart to be relevant to the present moment and transformed into an American presence.

Cubberley's use of Herbart serves a number of his project's needs. Where Fellenberg has been used to delineate the class stratification of public school education, Herbart is used to define the essential pedagogy: aim, content, method of instruction. Herbart is also Cubberley's compelling scientific authority legitimating the dismissal of child development as the aim of public education and shift its aim to shaping social behavior, i.e., "character," compatible with existing social relations and their organization in society. Cubberley also uses Herbart to validate the ideological centrality of the educational history textbook as the mechanism for the inculcation of both the training teacher and the school child into "the right kind of knowledge" which has been "properly interpreted . . . so that clear ideas as to relationships [in society] might be formed." If society is determining, then "proper human relations" are those which already exist. What must follow is making the child understand these relations and his/her place among them as correct, and that these relations could not be better otherwise. According to Cubberley, therefore,

> From full knowledge, and with proper instruction by the teacher, clear ideas or concepts might be formed, and clear ideas ought to lead to right action. . . .[90]

Finally, Cubberley uses Herbart to speak directly to educators responsible for training teachers regarding what constitutes the appropriate learning environment, the proper relation between the teacher and students, and the methods to be employed.

> Interest he held to be of first importance as a prerequisite to good instruction. If given spontaneously, well and good; but, if necessary, forced interest must be resorted to. Skill in instruction is in part to be determined by the ability of the teacher to secure interest without resorting to force on the one hand or sugar-coating of the subject on the other. [. . .] Herbart elaborated the process by which new knowledge is assimilated in terms of what one already knows, and from his elaboration of this principle the doctrine of apperception — that is, the apperceiving or comprehending of new

knowledge in terms of the old — has been fixed as an important principle in educational psychology. Good instruction, then, involves first putting the child into a proper frame of mind to apperceive the new knowledge, and hence this becomes a cornerstone of all good teaching method.[91]

The immediate aim of course is to follow a "methodical organization of the facts" directed by "some definite purpose" "to secure certain predetermined ends in child development. . . ."[92] And, he might have said, to secure certain predetermined ends in teacher development. But he has said enough; he has established Herbart's theory of public instruction and its aims, he has validated the utility and centrality of an inculcating "history," and with these functional pieces in place it is time to bring Herbart to America.

Herbart died in 1841 Cubberley tells us, and his works waited until 1865 to be resurrected and popularized by Tuiskon Ziller in Leipzig.[93] American teacher educators studying in Jena, Germany, in the late 1800s became involved with the German Herbartian "scientific society" and returned to the States full of enthusiasm. Three of these American gentlemen proceeded to publish text-books based on Herbart/Ziller: in 1889 Charles DeGarmo published *Essentials of Methods*, followed in 1892 by Charles A. McMurray's *General Method*, and in 1897 by Frank McMurray's *Method in Recitation*.[94] Herbart's theory and practice of a socializing education is now ever so contemporary and American. Indeed, in 1892 the National Herbart Society was founded in the United States, which in turn became the National Society For The Study of Education in 1909, and was still active at the time Cubberley published his second edition.

Cubberley has now posited a model of his organization of stratified schools for differentiated groups of American children. He has set forth the socializing aims of these schools, and the ideological importance of the right historical knowledge to be interpreted for and to teacher candidates that they will become efficient agents of a prescribed socialization. What remains is a theory of society and State action which legitimates his program. For this he turns to his interpretation of Herbert Spencer's social darwinism.

Spencer

Cubberley constructs his theory of the relation between the state system of public school education and society on his understanding of Herbert Spencer:

> In his essay he declared . . . that the only way to judge of an educational program was first to classify, in the order of their importance, the leading activities and needs of life, and then measure the instructional program by how fully it offers such a preparation.[95]

This is a variation of Herbart's Aim, Content, and Method of Instruction. Cubberley tells us the worth of education is to be determined by "the leading activities and needs of life." And if this is industrial manufacturing and commerce? Whomever owns the means of production, the bank, the insurance company, and/or the ships and railroads certainly has different "activities and needs of life" than the puddler, porter or brick layer, than the seamstress, laundress or housekeeper. Cubberley implicitly acknowledges these divisions and differences, and suggestively posits the idea that a scientific and efficient public school education must be organized accordingly.[96] By way of an elaborated footnote Cubberley reinforces his idea:

Spencer's classification of life activities and needs, in the order of their importance, was:

1. Those ministering directly to self-preservation.
2. Those which secure for one the necessities of life.
3. Those which help in the rearing and disciplining of offspring.
4. Those involved in maintaining one's political and social relations.
5. Those which fill up the leisure part of life, and gratify taste and feelings.[97]

This enumeration constitutes a rationalization of a class based hierarchy and its status quo. The prescription of this program, as a matter of fact, calls for social domination through hegemony. But, embedded in this program is also the rationalization for and reproduction of antagonistic class relations.[98] In the competition for limited resources, the economic and political elite want to preserve their position, #1, and their privileged necessities of life, #2, which depends on the proper rearing and disciplining of lower class children, #3, and sustaining unequal social relations, #4, which thus enables leisure, luxury, and refined (i.e., expensive high culture) tastes, #5. But from the position of the working class and the poor, securing one's self-preservation, #1, depends on getting back some of what has been appropriated and acquired by the elite in order that their necessities, #2, might be partially satisfied. The working class is thus pitted against the elite in a struggle for survival and basic necessities which excludes them from over concern about #3 — for they are working and such rearing and discipline is actually taken care of by the State (i.e., by schools, courts, and reform schools or prisons) — and they are confronted with the seeming permanence of # 4, and thus excluded from experiencing such things as leisure time and gratified tastes. But Cubberley does not want anyone to think the working class do not have leisure time. Quoting William Russell, Dean of Teachers College, educators and policy makers are asked "when does unemployment become a vacation."[99] And Cubberley, reinforcing this perverse idea, proceeds hereafter to substitute *excess leisure time* for unemployment;[100] thus one is not so much unemployed as living life at one's leisure. Late in the nineteenth century and well into the twentieth, however, society addressed leisure time and activity for the working class through the mechanism of advertising, the ideology of abundance, and materialism fostered by time-payments and credit for commodity purchases,[101] and through the provision of amusement parks, company picnics and team sports, and organized spectator sports,[102] while keeping up a steady attack against taverns, speakeasies, and unions. Preserving the social order of political and social relations was and remains the item of greatest concern to the privileged in American capitalist society. Securing this order has depended largely on the State's policing powers and on the propagation of nativism and race ideology.[103]

In short, through his explication of Spencer, Cubberley promotes a capitalist social system organized around the unequal distribution of social positions, rights, and resources; it is clearly not a democratic program. It is a program which elevates acquisitive and appropriating behaviors to the status of natural law.

While the rich man's children ride their ponies or enjoy their European tour, the working man's children sweat in the mills and factories to generate wealth to satisfy the taste and feelings of their "social betters" — or they stand in unemployment and/or food lines.[104] And the preservation of elite privileges depends upon the consumption of the fruits of labor's life force and production. While the children of the wealthy enjoy small school classes of intimate to modest sizes, the children of other groups are sandwiched into classrooms of 25 to 50 students (or to 300 and more in the nineteenth century monitorial schools) — if they attend school at all. And these social and educational inequities are precisely what item #4 of Spencer's evolutionary theory of social law legitimizes. In Cubberley's program of centralization and consolidation of administrative authority, of social stratification and hegemony, sustaining and reproducing unequal economic and political relations are the undergirding motivations, and it is an essential social condition for the realization of the society he advocates. For such a reason, like Horace Mann before him, Cubberley rails against the small town and rural district system where far too many children enjoyed the benefit of small class sizes and individualized instruction.[105] The district system was too localized and too independent to insure the program of systemic ideological and cultural indoctrination.

The problem for the state system of public school education is thus extraordinarily complex as Cubberley will make explicit in his next chapter, XIV. To solve the problem, the state system of public education must be organized around these different and opposing social classes, activities and life needs, and it must be done in ways that prevent the emergence of class consciousness and open antagonisms. A reorganized system of stratified schools and differentiated students according to predetermined aims, as set by the industrial and social needs of the State, can accomplish the first goal but not the second. To achieve the second goal, and make it coherent with the first, requires properly trained teachers using a scientifically adjusted content interpreted by efficient methods of instruction which are fitted to each particular group of children. But here Cubberley is laying down his ideological foundation, the undergirding theories and rationalization for the program of socially differentiated classes and educational reorganization. More importantly, he does not want these ideas or his program to appear as they are actually. So he is silent about social darwinism, about survival of the fittest class, and about class conflict over the unequal distribution of life's necessities, and he endeavors to make Spencer over into a humanitarian:

> . . . instead of a few being educated for a life of learning and leisure, he urged general instruction in science that all might receive training and help for the daily duties of life.[106]

"Science" has become a code word for efficient regulation and reproduction of economic and political relations in society. On one side of the equation, a few are educated for a life of learning and leisure, but on the other side the "all" are to be scientifically educated for their "daily duties of life." Some have leisure, and all the rest have duties. Leisure cannot exist without the performance of duties. The equation is based on a stratification of fixed classes.

Through his rhetorical exploitation of Fellenberg, Herbart, and Spencer, Cubberley has effectively established the what, how, and why of the reorganization of the state system of public school education which he will elaborate over the next three hundred pages of his "history." Up to this point, however, he has been constructing the undergirding ideology and models which are essential to making sense of the present social reality, which he will soon make explicit, and an alternative society which he will propose as one toward which his reorganized public instruction leads. Indeed, the first 479 pages of his interpretive reconstruction of educational history are a preparation for his explanation of the present, the specific nature of its social crisis, and his solution to this crisis.

Cubberley addresses the present in two stages: the first is laid out in Chapter XIV, and the second in Chapter XX. The former identifies new immigrants from Eastern and Southern Europe as foremost among the threats to democratic life, institutions and government in America, and a dangerous obstacle to meeting the social and industrial needs of the State. The second identifies Black-Americans, freed at the conclusion of the Civil War, as the primary cause for the economic and educational backwardness of the Southern States. Thus a dangerous mass of poor, illiterate and subnormal racial ethnics in the North and West, and a dangerous mass of illiterate, disease spreading Black-Americans in the South[107] are jointly responsible for the economic and political problems plaguing American society in the first three decades of the twentieth century. As a consequence of these pressing circumstances, Cubberley informs his readers, the state system of public school education has for the first time had to shoulder the burden of educating and socializing the children of these alien and dangerous classes for their place in modern society. This is made extraordinarily difficult by the popular but false and dangerous notions of democracy and equality[108] and the inefficiency of representative government.[109] Cubberley writes, that

> Compared with a highly organized and centralized nation, such as France, Germany, Italy, or Japan, we seem feeble in our ability to organize and push forward a constructive program for national development. Many of the tools and methods they have used so effectively are entirely lacking with us.[110]

Although we lack the fascist tools and methods to meet the alien and racial challenges to our national development, Cubberley explains, the educational establishment has developed vocational education for white ethnics and segregated industrial education for Blacks in the South to provide for the particular capabilities and needs of these groups of children. Indeed, the entire system has been reorganized along scientific lines to meet the social and industrial needs of the State as it actually is.

According to Cubberley,

> The modern city is essentially a center of trade and industry, and home life and home conditions must inevitably be determined and conditioned by this fact. The increasing specialization in all fields of labor has divided the people into dozens of more or less clearly defined classes, and the increasing centralization of trade and industry has concentrated business in the hands of a relatively small number of people. All standards of business efficiency indicate that this should be the case, but as a result of it the small merchant and employer are fast giving way to large mercantile and commercial concerns. No longer can a man save up a few thousand dollars and start in business for himself with much chance of success. The employee tends to remain an employee; the wage-earner tends to remain a wage-earner. New discoveries and improved machinery and methods have greatly

increased the complexity of the industrial process in all lines of work, and the worker in every field of trade and industry tends more and more to become a cog in the machine, and to lose sight of his part in the industrial processes and his place in our industrial and civic and national life.[111]

However appropriate and rational this organization of society may be, there are inherent dangers:

> With the ever-increasing subdivision and specialization of labor, the danger from class subdivision has been constantly increasing, and *more and more has been thrown upon the school the task of instilling into all a social and political consciousness* that will lead to unity amid our great diversity, and to united action for the preservation and improvement of our democratic institutions.[emphasis added.][112]

Cubberley's concerns are not with class stratification, which he readily accepts as permanent, but with the DANGER that emergent antagonistic class consciousness poses to the social order.[113]

Those in positions of authority in the educational establishment are meant to recall Fellenberg, Herbart, and Spencer: A stratified system of public instruction which corresponds with differentiated social positions and classes; a socializing public instruction adapted to different capabilities and social classes/races; and all of which is scientifically designed to insure the survival and reproduction of the capitalist social order as it is actually constituted and thus meet the social and industrial needs of the State. Of course, Cubberley does not explicitly remind his audience of teachers of these three social theorists and/or educational practitioners, nor does he explicitly claim that fascism is a more efficient government by which to organize society. He merely asks his readers to compare a more efficient and ordered society with our own troubled one:

> Contrasted with a highly organized Nation, such as Germany was before the World War, we seem feeble in our ability to organize and push forward a constructive national program for development and progress. The State was highly organized; the people homogeneous; *the officials well educated, and selected by careful service tests; national policies*

were painstakingly thought out and promulgated; the schools were *effectively organized into uniformly good institutions for the advance-* *ment of the national interests; the teachers were carefully trained in* *state institutions, and made into parts of a national army expected to* *follow the flag loyally*; the Church was nationalized, and in part supported by the Government; religion was taught in all schools, and the weight of religion and the backing of the priesthood were used to support the State; and *a great national army was maintained and used as an educative* *force for nationalizing all elements and training the people in obedi-* *ence and respect for law and order*.[emphasis added][114]

Through restrictive immigration laws, through an expanded police/military force, through the abolition of democratic elective processes for selecting school superintendents, and through the systemic adoption of scientific administration and scientifically reorganized public instruction American society can effectively control racial heterogeneity on one hand and on the other hand can effectively "nationalize all elements and training [of] the people in obedience and respect for law and order." The systemic adoption of the prescribed program for reorganizing the state system of public education will, according to Cubberley, simultaneously meet the social and industrial needs of the State and prevent the emergence of dangerous class consciousness, and thus the potential of socialist or Marxist revolution. This is the lesson of Cubberley's *Public Education in* *the United States*.[115]

Cubberley's *Public Education* was last reprinted in 1947. Perhaps because of post-WW II college educated working class ethnic and Black American veterans and women who chose teaching as a career, perhaps because of the demise of Joseph McCarthy and the 1954 Brown V. Topeka Supreme Court Decision, or perhaps due to a combination of many other factors, Cubberley's text as material artifact, as textbook, could no longer be persuasively reconciled by the educational establishment and its practitioners with the changes occurring in American society. Cubberley's blatant nativism and racism, his textual contradictions, the fallacy of much of his interpretive history, and its datedness, if not his thinly veiled enthusiasm for fascism, made the use of his textbook increasingly problematic: *Public Education* raised too many critical questions about the structural social stratification of public school education and the causal sources of educational inequality. The challenge for establishment educational historians became how to preserve Cubberley's myth of humanitarian, intelligent public men leading an enlightened working class in the progressive establishment and development of a democratic-ladder educational institution, and to preserve his ideological mystification of stratified schools and differentiated curricula — and the undergirding anti-democratic ideology and social structures of the state system.

Much of the criticism of Cubberley's educational history, therefore, has been peculiar for its tendency to focus on particular historiographic interpretations and some of his errors of historical fact while leaving his undergirding ideology untouched. In 1960, for example, Bernard Bailyn took aim at Cubberley, as well as at educational historians generally, for constructing a presentist consensus history of the American public school, and for treating it in isolation from other forms of cultural education and generally ignoring the contributions of American historians. The blunt end of Bailyn's criticism is Cubberley was drawing on an interpretative consensus of the evolutionary development of the public school system already established by the end of the nineteenth century.[116] Although Bailyn focuses his aim on Cubberley's history in particular because it had been quickly taken up by the educational establishment after its publication in 1919 as the primary vehicle for disseminating this consensus tradition — he largely ignores Cubberley's social ideology.[117] In 1965 Lawrence Cremin responded to Bailyn's assessment and agreed with him that the history of the state system of public school education ought to be located within the broader historical context of cultural production.[118] The primary purpose of his essay, however, is to identify and then downplay the importance of Cubberley's blatant historical errors, to contextualize his institutional history of public education within the field of educators and historians, to protect the overall text (as it pertains to the legal and administrative development of public school education) and interpretation (specifically the relation between the public school and social progress), and to redeem Cubberley's reputation as preeminent among educational historians.[119] Indeed, despite Bailyn's specific criticism of Cubberley's treatment of the colonial period and his historiographic methods generally, Cremin asserts that even when the flaws of Cubberley's history are acknowledged, *Public Education in the United States* remained unsurpassed in educational historiography.[120]

A decade later, in *The Revisionists Revised*, Diane Ravitch recapitulates the Bailyn/Cremin criticism of Cubberley, but puts her emphasis on his failure to explicate the particulars of actual classrooms and the ways in which "education related to broad social and political currents, and how changes came about."[121] Ravitch's explicit criticism of Cubberley, however, is neither original or perceptive, but her obvious silences are illuminating. She says nothing about Cremin's particular points of rebuttal to Bailyn's criticism or his zealous effort to redeem Cubberley's reputation. By studiously ignoring Cremin's marshalled defense at the same time she rehashes those critical points he shares with Bailyn, she appears to distance herself from Cubberley, his narrow perspective historicism, and his so-called promotionalism. But appearances aside, Ravitch's rhetorical ploy is not a critique of Cubberley's history of the public school system or of his undergirding ideology. Ravitch's desire to appear critical of Cubberley and thus of a different camp or higher order of historians is calculated, and is understandable. Cubberley's nativism, racism and fascist tendencies are everywhere explicit or exposed in *Public Education*, and in 1975 one could not explicitly champion him without coming away befouled and stinking; but Ravitch in fact gets away with it through the rhetorical means of summarizing and quoting a paper by R. Freeman Butts in which he attacks the "culture" premise of Cremin/Bailyn's criticism.[122]   The effect of her strategy is to implicityly legitimate Cubberley.

The sum total of these criticisms is: Cubberley's focus was artificially narrow; his writing was flawed by interpretive inaccuracies and over-all by promotionalism; he subsumed actual instructional practice under legal, financial, administrative, organizational and structural categories of study; and he failed to adequately explain the complex relation between the public school and society.[123] As a matter of fact, however, Bailyn, Cremin and Ravitch go easy on Cubberley — he may have got the parts wrong, his historiographic methods may be wanting, but he got the whole correctly. They may chide him, they may prefer a different sort of historiography, they may have wanted more of this and less of that, but these are trivial matters compared to their fundamental agreement with Cubberley's ideological mystification of the actual relation between public school education, the expansion of the American State under capitalism, and achievement ideology.[124] Thus, once the fight is over and the critics have returned to their desks, Cubberley, his history of the state system of public school education, and his ideology are seen to be very much intact and little the worse for the show of rough handling.

Subsequent assaults on *Public Education*, however, have been less kind, but have generally limited their criticism to Cubberley's racist characterization of Black-Americans and the end of chattel slavery, and of all the immigrant groups from Eastern and Southern Europe and their participation in the American political system. A somewhat more serious inquiry into Cubberley's text was initiated by educational "revisionist" historians who were in fact the actual targets of Diane Ravitch's traditionalist doctrinaire essay. David Tyack in *The One Best System*,[125] and with Elisabeth Hansot in *Managers of Virtue*,[126] opened the door of explanatory critique wider by signalling that more than Cubberley's race prejudices deserved mention: Cubberley's candid dismissal of democracy in his 1909 *Changing Conceptions of Education* makes his ideological, institutional and public policy efforts in constructing hierarchical bureaucracy, centralized authority, social and educational reorganization around differentiated races and socioeconomic classes, and his animated promotion of scientific efficiency look dangerously like fascism. David Nasaw, taking up this lead in *Schooled to Order*, devotes few words to Cubberley, but links Cubberley's 1909 description of society and his prescriptive policy statement to similar ones by others to establish what he sees as the anti-democratic ideological foundation undergirding twentieth century bureaucratic and authoritarian public school reorganization.[127]

Ellwood Cubberley, born 1868, and deceased in 1941, remains a potent ideological and directive force in educational historiography, in public school administration, and in just about every other nook and cranny of the state system of public school education. Perhaps one reason is because what he and like-minded social engineers in the educational and industrial establishment brought to pass in the ideological and structured bureaucratic reorganization of public school education in the early twentieth century is still very much with us today.

Merle Curti and Lawrence Cremin

The first edition of Merle Curti's *The Social Ideas of American Educators* appeared in 1935, one year after the second edition of Cubberley's *Public Education,* and was followed by a second edition in 1959. My copy of his text is the 1974 reprint by Littlefield, Adams, & Co.

In his chapter "New Conflicts And A New Solution, 1800-1860," Curti lays the ground work for his explication of the common school movement and its two principal leaders Horace Mann and Henry Barnard, followed by the selective education and training of women and the feminization of the teacher labor force. Curti takes pains in this chapter to identify the conflicting ideas and aims surrounding the formation and development of public school education, and to identify variances and conflicts between different geographical regions of the nation. In addition to identifying ideological and cultural movements, Curti congruently links these to specific empirical economic and political relations of this period. In one passage he writes,

> Much was also made of the necessity of educating the workingmen in particular, as well as people in general, in order to prevent labor uprisings. The manager of a Lowell mill testified that in times of agitation on account of some change in regulations or wages, he always looked to the most intelligent, best educated, and most moral for support, and seldom met disappointment. The ignorant and uneducated, on the other hand, were "generally found the most turbulent and troublesome, acting under the impulse of excited passion and jealousy." If attacks on property and security by "lewd fellows of the base sort" were to be put down, if the artful attempts of demagogues to array the poor against the rich were to be checked, then, argued B. P. Aydelott, correct schooling of the masses must be supported in order to refute in their minds the foolish and mischievous notion that there should be an "equality of condition."[128]

Curti demonstrates in this passage (1) the characterization of the uneducated, poor, unemployed, and labor generally as a dangerous, potentially revolutionary class by members of the governing classes; (2) the capitalist and workers oppose each other's interests; (3) the capitalist's primary concern is to protect his economic and political interests against the demands of the laboring poor; (4) the interests of capital are identical to the interests of the state, therefore if capital cannot conduct its affairs without the threat of revolt from labor, then the state itself is endangered; and (5) the connection between the control and suppression of labor, and the education of the masses is made directly. The main thesis communicated through the paragraph is educated workers acquiesce to lower wages and unequal social relations; that properly educated they will cooperate in their own subjugation without protest.

In this passage, too, Aydelott's insight into the power of education and its social and economic aims is critical to a fuller understanding of the common school system's agenda: the education of the masses is not meant to change their material conditions but to alter their minds, i.e., their consciousness and understanding of their social conditions.[129] If democratic ideology engenders notions that there must be equality among citizens, and such notions are dangerously wrong from the perspective of Aydelott, the factory manager, and Henry Barnard, then clearly it is through public education that they will be inculcated into a different ideology and culture compatible with unequal social relations generated by unequal material relations.

Granting the rich complexity of meaning Curti conveys through the speakers in this paragraph, the paragraph also reflects each subject's perception and understanding of social reality. Their class values, their position within existing social relations, and their expectations of public education are also apparent; what is not apparent, however, is the social reality in which these values, attitudes, positions and perceptions are formed. Unless these beliefs are metamorphosed into actions, they remain opinions. Their weight as historical evidence is partial until a correspondence between belief and action is identified. Historians and social scientists require knowledge of this hermeneutic domain, knowledge of what people think their social reality is, and what they understand the social relations they observe and participate in to be. Curti provides this window into the subjective empirical domain admirably, but this is only a piece of the social reality under study; it is valuable but insufficient. The representation of the subject's understanding, even through the subject's own words, is merely an aspect of the uppermost level of social reality. There remains the need to know the actual events out of which the subject's empirical understanding emerges. More than this, too, the identification of what generated the events in needed.

The advantage of limiting the object of study to "social ideas" is to clearly limit the inquiry and explanation to the domain of epistemology. The disadvantage of this limitation for readers, students, and other historians is there are no means by which to evaluate the truth or falsity of what's presented. Readers can accept on faith that the speaker believes what s/he is saying to be true, but before their statements can be accepted as true one must first find a congruent relation between the idea or statement and its empirical manifestation. Although the nature of events that condition the understanding of the Lowell mill manager and Aydelott can be surmised, it is necessary to excavate much more to discover if their beliefs about the common class of workers correspond with a truly dangerous class for the reasons given, and identify if these beliefs become motivations and actions leading to the construction of a repressive system of public education.

The propertied elite had reasons aplenty to fear the potential violence of the masses according to Curti's account. He demonstrates that suspicion and antagonism toward the laboring classes are voiced against the background of the French Revolution followed by Napoleon's adventures, the Dorr Rebellion, and the New York tenant wars.[130] In the cities and factory towns of the North the families of workers were massed together in abominable conditions. In spite of reform efforts these slum conditions persisted in New York City because they "were so profitable that a return of 100 per cent interest was not uncommon."[131] Workers were paid scanty wages and were forced in turn to pay excessive prices for necessary goods.[132] In 1825 not one town in Massachusetts reported less than an eleven hour work day for child laborers six to seventeen, and an 1833 survey of New England factories revealed that two-fifths of all those employed in factory work were children.[133] During periods of economic crisis, not only were a great many laborers unemployed, but the poor and unemployed were blamed for the circumstances in which they found themselves.[134] Slavery in the South engendered and sustained a stratified class and racial system in which the beneficiaries were plantation owners and merchants. In this social context public school education and the spread of literacy were viewed by those in power as certain to intensify class and racial tensions, and to foster revolution — a view that was widely shared in the North as well.[135]

These socioeconomic circumstances, the unequal distribution of resources and rights, and, in particular, those who benefited from the suffering of so many did not escape the attention of leaders among the working classes. Curti quotes Seth Luther, Thomas Skidmore, and Horace Greeley — each of whom challenges the validity of public school education and its promotional propaganda.[136] Any institution which is promised to correct economic and political injustices but which actually cannot provide the material needs of the people, nor transform the socioeconomic circumstances which generate these needs while failing to satisfy them, is not an institution which can be of any use to working people. Such an institution is created "for the purpose of diverting the people from the possession of [their] rights; that they may be held in bondage, even yet longer."[137]

The social construction of material conditions which caused hardship, and which were constructed to generate wealth through the exploitation of these hardships and of those upon whom these conditions were imposed, are also conditions which lend themselves to popular resentment and potential rebellion. More dangerous than mere conditions, however, was the emergence of radical democratic autodidacts who explained the causes of these material conditions, identified which class in society benefited from these conditions, and also proposed direct actions for the revolutionary transformation of society to achieve just and democratic economic and political relations. The fears, interests, and educational social aims prescribed by the Lawrence mill owner and Aydelott, among others cited by Curti, are thus given congruent economic and political substantiation.

Against this background of material, cultural, and ideological class struggle, and in the context of distinctive views by members of the governing classes as to the social aims of public education, Curti introduces Horace Mann. On page 104 of his text, and three pages into his characterization of Mann, he writes,

> A Puritan reformer, spotless in character and heroic in benevolence, Horace Mann was ready, after supplementing his college training by a little teaching and by legal study, to take the field in behalf of his convictions. Elected a member of the Massachusetts legislature from the town of Dedham, he made a notable defense of the principle of religious freedom. He also championed the cause of better treatment for the insane and was chiefly responsible for the establishment of the state hospital at Worcester. Desiring to help the drunken wretches exploited by the dram shops, he induced the legislature in 1836 to enact a law making it a crime to drink in public.[138]

In essence this is the portrait of Mann which dominates the educational establishment's construct of him and what he contributed to American society. As to its particulars, however, it requires translation. Prior to this passage Curti has written that Mann attended Brown University in 1816 by overcoming "the handicaps of poverty and slender schooling".[139] Mann or his second wife, Mary Peabody Mann, is the source for the story that his were humble beginnings. Mann's biographer Jonathan Messerli documents, to the contrary, that Mann was neither poor nor was his schooling significantly different from that of other young men from Franklin, Massachusetts, who had gone on to study at Brown. His family did well enough economically off their farm, which they owned, and home industry, supplying woven straw to hat manufacturers, that upon Thomas Mann's death each of the four living Mann children received an inheritance. Mann's sisters and his older brother Stanley used theirs to purchase part-ownership in a textile mill, and Mann used his to attend Brown.[140]

Was Mann "a Puritan reformer"? He wasn't a Puritan in any religious sense, although he is described on occasion as severe in demeanor, and he certainly was not reserved about meddling in other people's lives or passing judgement on their activities.[141] As a matter of fact, after abandoning Calvinism as a young man, he affiliated himself with Unitarianism for a time, but by the mid-1830s he was confirmed in his belief in Lord Brougham's Natural Theology.[142] Was he "spotless in character and heroic in benevolence"? He had the benefit of other people thinking highly of his character for honesty and hard work, but it is clear from his own writing that his activities were not driven by altruistic motives. Typical of other men of his class during this period, who occupied similar positions and enjoyed close relations to the wealthiest and most powerful men in Massachusetts, Mann had ambitions for "worldly distinction."[143] It should be said, however, that he exposes this ambition when writing that he renounces it upon accepting the position of Secretary to the Board.

As for Mann's benevolence, this is a trait open to serious dispute, for while it is true he labored strenuously to successfully engineer the common school system, it is also true that through this process he built a solid national reputation and a broad base of state-wide political support that elected him to several terms in state and federal government. We also know from Messerli's documentation that as a practicing lawyer in Dedham, Mann acted as a legal agent for Boston capitalists and other lawyers around the state to enforce collections of debt against local merchants and farmers, that, in addition to securing the demanded sums, he also acted as a money lender to the debtor—directly and through his connections with other lawyers. In this way he not only collected his fee from his clients, but he also collected interest upon the money lent. He also collected non-monetary capital in the form of good will or obligation from those for whom he collected and from those to whom he lent money. In this practical way he earned the money to join Stanley and his sisters in the owner-ship of two textile mills, City Manufacturing in Franklin, and the other, Eagle Manufacturing Company, in Wrentham, and with his non-monetary interest he secured election to the General Court, i.e., the lower house of the state con-gress, and later to the state senate.[144] I'm not sure Mann's behavior counts as benevolence, although it demonstrates considerable talent for making the most of his opportunities and resources.

Mann graduated from Brown, and he did teach there for two years. He also married Charlotte Messer, the daughter of the college's President. Mann's legal study was much more than Curti's treatment here implies. Part of its significance I have already addressed in the paragraphs above. Mann's study at Litchfield (which was a nationally famous school of law at the time) brought him into close contact with Edward G. Loring, another student there. When Mann reached the General Court in Boston, Loring "served as his social and political mentor." In addition, it is through Loring, a member of one of Boston's first families, that Mann becomes connected to Boston's economic and political elite, including Edmund Dwight, who "was amassing a fortune from [his family's] textile mills along the Connecticut River",[145] and Edward Everett, soon to be the governor of the state, an aristocratic capitalist, avid railroad promoter, capital investor, and promoter in western land speculation.[146] In short, the path to college, to the bar, and then into government was already a well travelled route to positions of wealth and power when Mann traversed it.

Mann's legislative record does include votes for "humanitarian" measures, but Curti's characterization is stilted. For example, on the matter of "religious freedom" the issue was whether or not the state had the authority to incorpo-rate a religious group as the "Trustees of the Ministerial Fund of Blandford," and "'confer on them and their successors in office forever, the powers and

privileges usually granted to similar corporations.'"[147] Mann argued that the
state had no such authority to incorporate any religious body, for it "was patently
wrong to grant something it could not rescind at a later date."[148] Messerli
reveals, too, that Mann's opposition to the sect's petition had less to do with
principle than with the fact that he had "little sympathy for orthodox clergy-
men."[149] Curti's characterization of the other items Mann voted for or actively
promoted is highly biased to color the reader's understanding, but this aside,
Curti is silent about the fact that as an "aristocratic Republican," and later a
Whig, Mann's voting record was indistinguishable from that of the capitalist
representatives from Suffolk County. So while Mann deserves credit for his
effort in behalf of the hospital and the insane, his promotion of temperance, on
the other hand, must be seen as a complex mix of personal values and class and
cultural prejudices which neatly coincided with the interests of the manufacturers in increased cheap production and regulation of the lives of workers outside
the mills and factories.

Curti's explication of Mann is not fully one sided. Curti does confront the
inconsistency of Mann's overt opposition to dogma and indoctrination that he
argued would result from allowing commentary on the Bible or active critical
debate in the classroom on foundational documents, republican practice and
political issues on one hand, and, on the other, his embedded program of indoctrination against violent resistance to capitalist social relations of exploitation
and to those oppressive laws which protected these relations. Curti writes,

> . . . Mann entirely approved of indoctrination. Like other educators and
> professional men of his time he not only denounced the violence which he
> saw in such affairs as the anti-rent war in New York, the anti-Irish mobs,
> and the Dorr rebellion, but he also insisted that school children should be
> indoctrinated against the use of rebellion to change "laws and rulers." Edu-
> cation, he argued, would and should prevent the masses from resorting to
> violence, and school children would be taught to despise the use of bullets
> for effecting social change. [. . .]

Mann's advocacy of indoctrination against the use of violence on the
part of the underdog is significant partly because he failed to see that vio-

lence on the part of the underprivileged might be due to sufferings and evils which made them desperate.[150]

Although he acknowledges Mann's duplicity, he explains it away. And too, Curti neglects to provide here what he does not shy away from elsewhere, e.g. his critique of Henry Barnard, the identification of Mann's position within the governing classes, his political position as President of the state senate, his ownership in two mills, his position of power and leadership in the Whig party, his connections to and sympathies with the railroad corporations, the factory and mill owners, the wealthy land owners, the land speculators, and his agency in their, and his own, behalf. And too, Curti does not specifically identify and explain here the capitalist relations of production and social mechanisms which generated and protected unequal social relations that forced dissenting laborers to violent reaction. For example, anti-Irish sentiment was fueled by religious intolerance, by competition between needy groups of workers for limited resources and jobs, and by capitalists pitting Anglo-American workers against Irish workers in an effective strategy to drive down wages.

The anti-rent war in New York was in fact a protracted struggle by thousands of tenant farmers to prevent their eviction by the Rensselaer family, "which ruled over about eighty thousand tenants and had accumulated a fortune of $41 Million."[151] In addition to fending off eviction during the prolonged depression that started early in the 1830s due to "over production of cotton" and low market demand, collapsed in 1837 due to N. Biddle's contraction of credit by the Bank of the United States in his attempt to turn public sentiment against President Jackson, and continued through 1844-45, the tenants were attempting to secure redress of grievances, and land reform legislation. The tenant farmers felt aggrieved that they were bound to pre-War of Independence contracts of perpetual economic obligation with no rights to the property. When they failed in the legislature and the courts, they resisted eviction by threat of arms. The standoff was put down when the governor sent in three hundred troops. Roughly eight of the strikers received sentences of life imprisonment on charges ranging from "high treason, rebellion against your government, and armed insurrection" to murder.[152] It is important to note that the election to state government of 14 of their members in 1845, and the election of a sympathetic governor in 1846, did not succeed in altering property relations. In the 1850s "court decisions began to limit the worst features of the manorial system, without changing the fundamentals of landlord-tenant relations."[153]

Finally, the Dorr rebellion in the early 1840s was instigated by the state of Rhode Island's refusal to grant the popular demand for universal democratic suffrage (which initially included all the people of the state regardless of property ownership, race, or sex.) The attempt by suffrage supporters to replace the sitting state government with a popularly elected body of representatives was put down by state violence. Covert resistance by the suffrage democrats was ultimately resolved by hegemonic compromise — the granting of pardon for those members in prison or exile, and suffrage for free white males only.[154]

To be clear about the significance of mentioning these three events without more elaboration, my point is: Curti is mystifying Mann's stand on indoctrination against violence. Indeed, he saves his elaboration of the Dorr War for his critique of Henry Barnard.[155] Once we have details of the events, and the real conditions which generated violence — in two of the cases it was armed violence by the state or its agents which brought on resistance by the people, and in all three cases it was the refusal of state government to redress legitimate grievances that necessitated civil disobedience — explaining or interpreting Mann's argument is no longer simple. Moreover, Curti engages in some highly questionable argumentation. Between the two statements I have quoted above, Curti quotes Mann on the need of educated intelligence as the preventative of violence when citizens cannot accomplish their object through the legislative process or the ballot. He follows this with the second of the two passages I quoted above, an apologia, a claim that Mann "failed to see" the reality of the conditions behind what he condemns. Yet, in the same source from which Curti extracts his quote of Mann, *The Twelfth Annual Report*, Mann makes it quite clear that he fully understands the unequal social relations generated by capitalism, and the extreme hardship imposed upon the working class by unrestrained appropriation, acquisition and oppressive exploitation. Curti is deliberately slanting his interpretation of Mann.

When events and the social structures which generate them are identified and established, it is possible to then identify the socioeconomic circumstances generating historically particular social relations. It becomes possible to answer such questions as: Who decides policy and law, and who resists or acquiesces, and what are the real consequences for each type of social action? Once the socioeconomic circumstances and mechanisms generating specific events have been identified, it is possible to explain the events themselves and establish an ontological measure by which to evaluate Mann's statements.

To look at it another way, were Mann truly concerned about the material conditions of the working class, and the governing classes' military, legislative and legal repression or minimal compromises in response to just demands by different groups among the lower classes, then wouldn't he attack the real economic and political structures that generate poverty, destitution, and desperation? In other words, Mann's program of indoctrination is aimed at the middle and working classes, while he labors to reinforce the structures that generate the unequal distribution of resources. Moreover, while one of the leading members of the Whig party in state government he was instrumental in promoting these very same structures and protecting them in behalf of the aggregate wealth of Massachusetts and the State.

Curti appears to anticipate this sort of critique of Mann, for on pages 114 and 115 he first explicates Mann's *Tenth Annual Report*, which he implies is indicative of Christian Socialism, (whereas Urban and Wagoner come straight out and say so,) and he follows this explication with a quotation to show us that Mann thought little enough of the evils of capitalism to attack it on the floor of the House of Representatives in 1852.[156] Commenting on the significance of the *Tenth*, Curti says that "this concept of the duties of property owners tended to qualify Mann's allegiance to industrial capitalism and to modify his individualist philosophy by the doctrine of social obligation."[157] In spite of what is said about the significance of Mann's emphasis on temporary stewardship of the land, however, the land was legally treated as private property, and it could be inherited by subsequent generations of descendants.

On its surface merits, Mann's argument is forceful, but beneath its rhetorical power, the truth of the matter is the *Tenth* is aimed at land owners, some of whom are old aristocracy or their descendants, who can well afford school taxes however much they might protest, but the great majority are yeoman farmers with small holdings, who since the 1780's were already hard pressed by a variety of taxes and economic pressures.[158] In addition, Mann has the responsibility to secure a state controlled tax for schools, which will place control of the schools in the hands of the propertied and capitalists and out of the hands of the poor, working class, and immigrants; and, on the other hand, Mann must continue to dissuade the skepticism of the working class.

In keeping with this latter objective, Mann's contention that property ownership is not an absolute right but is temporary stewardship mildly echoes Thomas Skidmore's radical critique of capitalist property relations in 1829. Significant among Skidmore's revolutionary proposals, however, is his insistence that children are not property, but young citizens who should be freed from the mills and educated at public expense from the age of 2 to 18, or through higher education for those capable and wanting such education. This element of Skidmore's argument is noticeably absent from Mann's, which suggests Mann's socialism was rather conservative.[159]

And, too, Mann's *Tenth*, as an indirect appeal for the working class's support of the common school system and for their political support of state taxation on property, is similar in political purpose to Orestes Brownson's "The Laboring Classes,"(1840).[160] Brownson reproduced Skidmore's critique of private property and the causes of unequal social relations — including the state and judicial mechanisms by which they were constructed, protected and reproduced—with the specific purpose of enticing working class votes for Democratic candidates.[161] Curti, however, constructs a different understanding of Mann. In particular he wants to distinguish Mann from the capitalists. He thus quotes from the 1852 speech by Mann on the floor of the U.S. Congress:

> The rich and strong live upon the poor and the weak, almost as much as in the waters on which they are situated, the great fishes eat up the little ones. When some one asked John Jacob Astor how so many men found business in the city of New York, his reply was: "They cheats one another, and they calls that business." The wealthy have more houses than they can live in, the costliest furniture, wardrobes, equipages, libraries, and all that art or nature can produce, while thousands of the children of the same Heavenly Father, around them, are houseless and shelterless, naked and hungry. Such is the type of civilization which our example proffers to Africa.[162]

As for these critical comments on the nature of capitalism they are similar to what Mann had to say about the evils of capitalism in the *Twelfth Annual*

Report. The significant difference is he does not cloak his criticism here by pretending his remarks pertain to England. It is conceivable that Mann had reached a point in his thinking where capitalist economic processes and social relations could not be reconciled with his concept of a moral society, but whatever his personal sentiments against the acquisitive behavior of the rich and well born, or the appropriation and accumulation of property and wealth by capitalists at the expense of the lower classes, Mann, in his various positions within the State, did not engage in practices or form policies contrary to the capitalist state or capitalist economic processes and relations of production.

If Mann's own words provide the sole basis for an interpretation of his motives and actions, then one might come to a conclusion more or less sympathetic with Curti's. If, on the other hand, Mann's positions and practices are used as the criteria for evaluating his reasons and actions, a rather different and more complex conclusion is called for about his engineering and promoting the common school system than the one encouraged by Curti.

I want to quote one passage from his treatment of Henry Barnard to demonstrate the contrast Curti constructs between the two men:

> In the midst of the depression of 1837, when palliative measures threatened vested interests, Barnard, now a member of the Connecticut legislature, fought every effort to weaken the power of the courts, which he frankly recognized as the guardians of property against the "frenzy of popular excitement."

> It was perhaps because of his own interests and associations that Barnard minced no words in painting, both in his private papers and published writings, what would now be called a class struggle. His eyes beheld with fear the sordid drudgery, misery, crime, and potential revolt which lurked about the crowded quarters of city districts. In a book of notes, presumably intended for a speech or lecture, he sounded a warning against the danger inherent in the volcanic mass of workers, who might not only usurp the judicial and executive power of society but through violent mobs destroy property itself. The working class was "a mighty power, and there is a physical strength slumbering in their arms in peaceful times and a greater and more terrible than mere strength of muscles in their uninformed intel-

lect and uninstructed heart, which is liable at any time to be called into exercise."

We may think, he continued, that in its blindness "we can with safety drive it [the working class] to grind at the mill for our pleasure and convenience—but we must take care how we sport with its awakened feelings lest the spirit of vengeance and of strength return upon it, and it bow itself mightily against the pillory of your unrighteous system and destroy the social structure, though itself perish." Alarmed at "all the elements of anarchy, revolution, and crime," which had been apparent, and which even as he wrote seemed to lie "weltering in the bosom of society" waiting to be let loose and scatter desolation, Barnard declared that it was time for awakened capitalists, patriots, and Christians to set the social house in order.[163]

Compare this passage to one written by the educational historian Clarence Karier regarding Mann's understanding of and reaction to the same class of citizens and social relations:

In a socially and politically stable society, poor educational conditions might have been overlooked; such, however, was not the case in Massachusetts. The Jacksonian Democrats, already successful at the national level of government, were threatening to take over the Massachusetts Statehouse. The rapid growth of the Jacksonian party combined with the swift rise of workingmen's parties gave men of property serious cause for concern. As early as 1834, Horace Mann, in a letter to Mary Peabody in Cuba, reported on a new Trades Union party which seemed to have sprung into existence. After watching their procession one evening, he concluded:

'The bond of association among these men is mutual support and defence against what they denominate aristocratic institutions and manners. This principle is rapidly extending itself in this country and if something be not done to check it, the advantages of possessing wealth will find what to me would be more than a counterpoise in the envy and dis-social feelings which it will occasion.'[164]

The words and the specific events may be different, but the sentiments are identical. Curti is performing a fancy rhetorical construction of yin and yang between his treatment of Mann on one hand and his treatment of Barnard on the other. Mann is the good guy republican, and Barnard is the bad guy capitalist. Or, to put it another way, Mann is used to communicate the humanitarian forces of democratic public education, and Barnard is used to communicate the forces of capital that want to and will take over the public school system for its own self-preservation, for its own economic and political ends.

But reading a larger sample of texts by Mann and Barnard, while revealing differences typical of any two individuals, also reveals very close, if not identical, similarities of class culture and political values; and, too, an examination and identification of their positions within the hierarchy of social relations reveals their similar political affiliations, friendships and associations with the powerful and wealthy capitalists of their respective states, and of their relations to the poor and working class. Indeed, both Mann and Barnard are Whig politicians, capitalists, and they each share the conviction that through education it is possible to check and suppress democratic ideology in the lower classes, and inculcate in its stead a republican Protestant/capitalist ideology. These concrete similarities are lost if only Curti's epistemological and hermeneutic representation of Horace Mann stands in contrast to his class analysis of Henry Barnard.

As important as Curti's book is to historians of education and to students of American intellectual history, it is out of print. But, too, even though he is heavily referenced and quoted, very little by Horace Mann is in print, which gives Lawrence A. Cremin's little book, *The Republic and The School: Horace Mann on the Education of Free Men*, special status. Cremin's heavily edited version of Mann's twelve annual reports is the only version still in print, thereby making it the one student teachers are most familiar with. What Cremin chooses to include or exclude of Mann's writings and what he has to say about Mann, the common school system, and Mann's legacy, therefore, is critical in shaping student teachers' understanding and knowledge. For example, Cremin excludes the text of the *Fifth Annual Report*, in which Mann speaks directly to manufacturers and laborers — telling manufacturers that educated workers are more productive and telling laborers that increasing their employer's wealth is a testimonial greater than any collection of college degrees — but he includes Mann's

Tenth Annual Report — the so-called Christian Socialist concept of property. Cremin's editing of Mann's reports, in other words, is meant to fit a highly ideological interpretation.

Cremin writes that

> For the more practical young idealist of 1819 there were two roads to success: law and the ministry. Mann chose the former.[165]

Linking "practical" and "idealist" is inventive, and suggestive. Cremin clearly colors how to "interpret" his meaning here. He has already informed the reader that Mann came from a environment "governed by poverty, hardship, and self-denial," that Mann was self-educated, and that it was at Brown University "that Mann's humanitarian propensities began to come into full bloom. Apparently the inclination toward service rather than wealth had appeared very early in his life."[166]   None of this is true, but in Cremin's text it is presented as true. Thus his sentence above is intended to convey the notion that Mann chose law as the most direct means to succeed in transforming an undemocratic and/or unjust society. Indeed, Cremin's final sentence in the paragraph, of which I have quoted the first, reads: "At thirty-one, the young reformer was well launched in his effort to do something 'for the benefit of mankind.'"[167]

Between the first and last sentence of the paragraph Cremin neglects to tell us how Mann built his law practice in Dedham as a collector of debts for merchant capitalists and as an agent for other lawyers, and as a lender to the debtors; he neglects to tell us that Mann joined his brother Stanley in the ownership of two mills; and he neglects to tell us that the National Republican party, under whose banner Mann was elected to the General Court, was the re-formed Hamiltonian Federalist party. More to the point, however, Cremin studiously avoids pointing out that in the tradition of the American economic and political elite, the path from university to the Bar to government was a well worn path, if only because controlling the State and the law was the quickest and surest route to advancing and protecting capitalist economic interests. Mann's career path, which parallels that of other elite men in the developing capitalist social order, raises uncomfortable questions about his behavior which challenge the motives and actions Cremin attributes to him in this text. Perhaps for this reason Cremin

excludes other routes to economic success available to young men with resources in this period: mercantile trading and manufacturing.

Turning to Mann's tenure in Massachusetts state government, Cremin writes:

> For Mann, principle was always uppermost, and his legislative career
> was marked from the first by service to humanitarian ideals. His reformist
> sympathies, however, were never of the more popular Jacksonian variety.
> He had come to the legislature as a National Republican, and his temper
> was far too conservatively moralistic to cater to the crowd.[168]

The record is more complicated, as revealed in part in my critique of Curti.
Cremin's emphasis on Mann as humanitarian social reformer depends on highly
manipulated treatment of Mann's attitudes and record as a legislator. For example, note that here it is Cremin, not Mann, who characterizes working class
voters as "the crowd" to explain Mann's political position and practice. It is
common knowledge that the Jacksonian Democrats came to political power
through their effective manipulation of labor's protest rhetoric, which led many
working men to believe the Jacksonians were going to equalize political power
between themselves and the monied aristocracy. And the Whigs, among whom
Mann was a leading power in the party, perceived Jackson as a demagogue
leading the working populace into political radicalism and social madness. Cremin
thus puts too nice of a spin on Mann's position. Mann had little sympathy for the
social protest and resistance of the lower classes, and their overwhelming support of the demagogue Jackson was proof of their incompetence as self-gov-
erning citizens. His conservative temper is in fact a sense of moral elitism and
superiority. In support of his contentions about Mann's "reformist sympathies,"
Cremin lists the usual items: the Worcester Hospital for the insane, prison reform, and temperance.

> From the beginning, Mann had displayed a vigorous interest in the tem-
> perance movement, and after his elevation to the state senate in 1834 he
> gave increasing attention to legislation regulating traffic in liquors.[169]

As Joel Spring, quoting the historian Daniel Walker Howe, points out however, not everyone perceived the temperance movement and the legislation it

spawned as humanitarian reform. In fact, it seems the common people viewed these activities of the governing classes as unwanted intrusions and undemocratic usurpation of their rights. According to Spring:

> Howe reports that many thought the Whigs' assumption of moral responsibility for others meddlesome. He tells the story of the burning of the church of Lyman Beecher, who was a Whig, temperance advocate, and minister.

> "When Lyman Beecher's church on Hanover Street burned down, the volunteer fire companies, who hated his temperance crusading, refused to fight the flames. Instead, it is reported, they watched and sang: 'While Beecher's church holds out to burn/ The vilest sinner may return'—a parody of a hymn."[170]

From the perspective of the working class, then, Mann's "humanitarian" agenda looks a lot like one class and culture imposing its will upon others through the powers of the State. As a matter of fact, Edward Everett will eventually lose his position as governor for having signed into law a temperance measure that forbid the sale of rum, whiskey, and gin in amounts of less than fifteen gallons.[171] Perhaps, however, a clearer insight into the nature of Mann's reformist humanitarianism can be had by looking at his vote on the Charles River Bridge and his support of railroad corporations.

In brief, the bridge is symbolic of the growing contest between the interests of the people and the interests of capital. Messerli tells us that "For years, the people of Charlestown had pressed for a free bridge. . . . To them, the tolls they paid on the old Charles River Bridge amounted to a tribute extracted by its owners who, by reason of an ancient charter, held a monopoly on what should have been the property of all." The stockholding owners of the bridge, who included "influential merchants and politicians," did not see it this way. From their point of view "a free bridge would make their holdings valueless, and they did everything in their power to prevent what they considered a confiscation of their property."[172] The people of Charlestown were repeatedly rebuffed, but finally, in 1828, they succeeded in getting their petition for a new bridge heard and voted on. They proposed that a temporary charter be granted to protect investors, that when their investment in the new bridge received a fair return of 5% profit, ownership of the bridge would pass to the people of Massachusetts, whose interests would be administered by the State. At the last minute before the governor signed the measure into law opponents submitted a "public protest" against granting a charter for the "free bridge." There were 65 signatures on the protest petition, one of whose was Horace Mann's. Messerli tells us that Mann stipulated that he opposed the free bridge on the grounds of propositions one and four of the protest petition: it was unnecessary, there being a bridge across the river already, and the legislature "had no right to obstruct a navigable river by an unnecessary bridge."[173] In short, where the interests of the people came into conflict with the economic and property interests of the capitalists, Mann sided with the capitalists. The Charles River Bridge is but one example; another would be his strong support of the railroad interests.

Mann became famous as the leading exponent of railroads in the Massachusetts legislature. He defended the railroads against yeoman farmers and small country merchants who protested that the railroads led to land speculation, which drove up the value of land and their taxes, that the railroads enabled disastrous competition from producers in other states and foreign countries in their small community markets, etc. It wasn't simply a matter of supporting the railroads as a matter of progress, rather the fact that corporations of businessmen and manufacturers in other states were developing railroads posed a problem of unequal competition between them and Massachusetts manufacturers. It was not coincidence that Mann joined "Edmund Dwight, Josiah Quincy and others who were pressing for state-supported railroad construction."[174] Economic competition with manufacturers of other states was a pressing motivation behind Mann's support of the railroads, but too, their operation would also benefit his mills by cheapening the cost of importing the raw materials and exporting the finished cloth. Nor was it coincidence that the railroads directly benefited his friends and associates.[175] The railroads, like the Charles River Bridge, served the interests of manufacturers, merchants, industrialists, and corporations with whom Mann was directly and indirectly associated at the expense of family farms, artisans, and shop keepers; and, too, railroad development and corresponding land speculation put the price of land beyond the reach of most young people, thus speeding up the process of their dislocation to the cities and towns, begun in 1780s and 1790s, and their transformation from farm-ers and apprentices into dependent wage laborers.[176] The ultimate irony, how-ever, was the two mills owned by Stanley, Lydia, and Mann were lost in the textile market crisis in the early to mid-1830s. Thus, by the time the first rail line was in operation in 1835, it was too late for Mann to benefit from the legislation he helped push through the state house and senate.[177]

Among Cremin's claims about Mann, one in particular must be addressed:

> Of the many causes dear to Mann's heart, none was closer than the education of the people. While his actual teaching experience had been brief, he had long displayed a keen interest in more general matters of school policy, an interest which was widely shared among his more reform-minded colleagues. Nineteenth-century Massachusetts could boast a proud heritage of public education dating all the way back to the "Old Deluder Satan" Act of 1647.[178]

Was "education of the people" the closest of all "dear causes" to Mann's heart? If true, we would expect Mann to give as much attention to the cause of educa-tion that he gave to prisons and the temperance movement. This is not the case however. Messerli documents that . . .

> Until 1837, the educational problems confronting school committees and parents had consumed a very small portion of Mann's time. In both the House and Senate, he had passed up appointments on the Committee on Education to take posts on the more influential Judiciary Committee. Nor had he been as active outside the General Court in working for better schools as he had been in the temperance cause. Some of his closest friends, including Samuel Gridley Howe and William B. Calhoun, had helped orga-nize the American Institute of Instruction, which hoped to spearhead the reform of the common schools; but Mann considered other humanitarian causes more promising.[179]

In the footnote accompanying this passage, Messerli tells us that "Mann was not listed as a member, officer, nor participant in any of the years from 1830 to 1836." He acknowledges, however, that Mann gave "one lecture on education, in 1832 before the local teachers organization in Dedham." In short, continues Messerli, Mann "paid lip service to education as an important reform, but at the moment, and in the immediate future, he would confine his interests to the Norfolk Association of Teachers at Dedham. . . ."[180] Interests, in other words, relevant to advancing his political ambitions.

Cremin seems to have exaggerated Mann's attachment to the cause of "education of the people." But he goes over the top. He is so enthusiastic a cheer leader that he makes Curti's positive treatment of Mann, and his apologetics for Mann's contradictions, look like a cutting attack. As I have tried to demonstrate in reference to both historians, however, it is dangerously inadequate to rely on the subject's own account of himself. Instead of a process of excavating history, we have instead a process of layering myth. Were this construction of the mythic hero merely innocent adulation, it might be forgiven, but it is neither innocent nor are the consequences harmless. It is not innocent because both historians know better, and the consequences are not harmless because student teachers, who do not know better, rely on these historians to identify and explain people, social relations, events, positions, and practices, etc., as they existed in a specific historical place and time. Instead of even a partial view of the governing classes' construction of schools as a centralized, socializing and indoctrinating institution of the capitalist State, students get ideological mystification of Mann and the genesis of the common school system.

For example, Cremin writes in a seemingly straight forward way the following:

> The key [to a public school system] apparently lay in the measure of centralization inherent in a vigorous policy of state support and concern for education. Sparked by Edmund Dwight, James G. Carter, Josiah Quincy, Jr., and the Reverend Charles Brooks, a reform movement arose dedicated to a similar policy for Massachusetts. An influx of reports on Prussian and French educational reform only quickened the imagination of these men.[181]

If Cremin explained that these men were Whigs, that three of the men were politicians in the Massachusetts state legislature, that Dwight, Mann's close friend and mentor, was one of the wealthiest and most powerful men in the State, that Quincy, Jr., was one of Mann's closest associates,[182] a railroad investor, a member of one of Boston's first families and son of the Mayor of Boston, that Carter had published a letter stridently attacking workers as "men of warm passion and little reason" and a revolutionary threat to property,[183] that Brooks was a dedicated promoter of the Prussian system of school indoctrination and socialization might readers think that the union of these men behind a centralized state system of education was motivated by concerns other than the welfare of those whom they intended to educate? Indeed, if knowledge of who these men are, their positions of power in the State, and their economic and political interests is revealed, readers might interpret the phrase "quickened the imagination of these men" as something other than humanitarian good will.

Cremin's partial truths are as dangerous as lies, for he completely distorts the history of the movement to establish the common school system, and he obscures the actual positions and practices of these men in the state, their actions within the system of unequal social relations, and their connections to Horace Mann, and, the corollary, Mann's connections to them and their agenda.

Cremin's rhetoric directs attention away from the causes of social crisis to which the common school system was a direct "preventative," as Mann explains in his *Twelfth Annual Report*. Cremin disregards the forces of class conflict at work in the streets, the factories, in the countryside, and which undergird the legislature's backing of a centralized state system of schooling for the middle class and the better off among the laboring classes.

In what appears to be a contradiction of his basic premise regarding Mann, Cremin writes,

> If ever a post called for *moral* leadership of the first order, it was this one, and it is to Dwight's lasting credit that he persuaded Horace Mann to accept it.[emphasis added][184]

After everything he has written to this point, readers might ask: If the education of the people was the cause closest to Mann's heart, if he "had long displayed a keen interest in more general matters of school policy," then why didn't Mann seek the position, and why was it necessary for Edmund Dwight to "persuade" him to accept the all important position of Secretary to the Board?

Cremin, apparently, does not find anything odd about this; but I do. Moreover, Messerli's research, recounted above, established that Mann did not belong to any of the associations, institutes, etc., promoting education prior to his taking up the position of Secretary. This is odd behavior indeed for someone whose most important cause according to Cremin was educating the people; odder still given the example of Mann's prolonged crusade to reform the social habits of the poor and working class, his active participation in temperance organizations and their frequent meetings, his active legislative efforts against the social drinking habits of the lower classes, and his untiring legislative labors in behalf of railroads and industry. Cremin's claims to the contrary, Mann's actions as a citizen, lawyer, and legislator do not substantiate a particular interest in education, but, rather, a fixed interest in regulating the productive and social life of the lower classes, and the increased prosperity of the merchant and manufacturing classes.

Curti and Cremin: Ideology and the Public School System

Until Messerli's minutely researched study of Horace Mann became available to educators and historians in 1963, Merle Curti's *Social Ideas* is perhaps the best known attempt to locate ideas about public education within the larger sphere of ideological warfare between democrats and republicans, between workers and capitalists, between Catholics and Protestants, and between those who opposed universal suffrage and those who championed it. And, too, his second chapter, "New Conflicts And A New Solution, 1800-1860," raises a provocative challenge to Cubberley's contention that the origins and evolution of public education were rooted in democratic ideals and the beneficent regard of the governing classes for the lower classes. In fact, Curti was determined to topple such notions.

At the risk of oversimplifying his argument, it goes something like this: While the common school movement was led by a coterie of religious and economic elite, the middle class and the lower classes wanted little to do with it. Under the crusading moral leadership of Horace Mann, a middle class "social reformer" and "poor boy" who made good, republican ideals and the social good became the guiding ethos of the common school movement. What Mann accomplished, however, was soon corrupted and exploited by capitalist society and its agents. Curti establishes the foundation of his argument in Chapter Two, uses Mann in Chapter Three, and consolidates it in Chapter Four:

> In other words, the chief causes of poverty were held to be extravagance, ungoverned passion, tardiness, and ignorance; under this last category was included "destitution resulting from a strike which was engaged in with a view of bettering their condition." The schoolmaster's duty [according to Barnard] was to instill correct virtues, impress youth with its duties, train them in right habits, and impart knowledge of proper social relationships.

> "As a *capitalist* he should so employ his capital as to produce that which society most wants in the greatest possible quantities, and at the smallest possible cost. He should select those laborers who can best help him in making his capital productive, those whose qualifications are the highest, who can produce most in proportion to the wages paid them. He should endeavor to turn their labor to the best account, availing himself of every aid that lies within his reach. In so doing, he will be the benefactory of society. . . . As his own special reward he will obtain large profits.
> "As a *laborer* he should endeavor to cultivate in himself those qualities, to attain that knowledge and skill which will make his services most acceptable to the capitalist. He should serve his employer faithfully, bringing all his intelligence to bear upon his work. He will then serve society by making capital upon which he is employed as productive as possible, and will earn for himself the reward of high wages. If his wages be lower than desirable, he should seek for the means of obtaining higher, taking care, at the same time, not to engage in strikes, or any other means, whose real tendency is the opposite of the one sought for. Should there be no means of immediately obtaining higher wages, he should endeavor to increase his productiveness as the only means of increasing the store out of which wages are paid, and of obtaining for himself a large share of that store."[185]

Barnard's editorial remarks which prefaced the second article suggest his willingness to indoctrinate schoolchildren and artisans in mechanic's institutes with definitely capitalist economics in order to prevent strikes and labor troubles.[186]

Ultimately, however, Curti backs away from the logical thrust of his argument. When public schools were an established fact instead of an idea, they embodied contradictory and exclusive expectations — expectations encouraged by Mann, Barnard, and other common school promoters:

> Above all, the privileged classes expected the free public school to increase wealth, secure their property, and prevent revolution, while the lower classes thought that popular education would break down class barriers, lift them into the ranks of the rich and bring about, in short, substantial equality. Could the schools do both? Could they leave the wealthy with all their economic power and privileges and at the same time enable the masses to enter the upper ranks without jeopardizing the position of those already on the top? Could all stand on the top of the pyramid?[187]

There are clearly different and contrary expectations of what public schools would achieve, and it is clear that as a practical matter the schools could not and cannot accommodate the expectations and objectives of both classes. Curti leaves us with a sense of on-going contested social relations with the schools at the center of the conflict. Lawrence Cremin's essay championing Mann and the common school system is a rebuttal to Curti's argument:

> Mann had won his victory, and it only presaged other great victories to come. The public school soon stood as one of the characteristic features of American life—a "wellspring of freedom" and a "ladder of opportunity" for millions. Yet, as with the battle for freedom itself, victories are never final, and somehow today's educators find themselves fighting the very same battle Mann was supposed to have won over a century ago. Popular apathy and dissatisfaction, rising private school enrollments, sectarianism, objections to school taxes, a shortage of qualified teachers, disagreements over what a good teacher is, calls for special attention to the "gifted," and cries for harsher discipline—all of these problems of Mann's time have been raised anew. The cry is that times have changed, that a different

America needs a different kind of school. Yet with all of the just claims of novelty, one cannot help but sense the continued timeliness of Mann's discussions. Areas of tension may change; for one generation it is religion, for the next it is race. Yet the idea of "commonness" at the heart of the public school remains ever pertinent. Similarly, while the specifics of the educational program may vary, teachers still must know what they are teaching as well as how to teach it.[188]

Class conflict as a central and determining cause of institutional problems does not exist in Cremin's account of Mann's victory or in his account of the reoccurrence in our own time of problems which Mann had supposedly laid to rest. These problems are not inherent to the public school system, Cremin argues, thus solutions to these external social pressures are to be found again in "Mann's discussions," and in the measures he enacted to resolve them a century ago. In Cremin's version of Horace Mann and the common school system a lone heroic crusader rescues the holy grail of education from the clutches of a multitude of selfish interest groups and returns it to its rightful place among a democratic free people. The selfish and greedy and narrow minded have not gone away, however, therefore it is the duty of educators to follow Mann's example and protect this cherished democratic institution from their schemes.

Messerli, Cremin, Urban and Wagoner: Ideology and Public Schools

The publication of Messerli's biography of Mann virtually eliminates Cremin's type of unembarrassed mythic hero worship on one hand and Curti's rhetorical manipulations on the other hand. The biography derives its critical power from Messerli's careful documentation of Mann's social ontology, his ideology, class and cultural biases, posturing, and intellectual contradictions, and then places these in relation to Mann's behavior and social position. In addition, and most significantly, Messerli does not explain Mann as an isolated individual but places him squarely within the complex social relations of his time.

Two rather typical treatments of the Prussian schools will serve to illuminate the extent to which Messerli has challenged the historiography of Mann
and the common school system. Lawrence Cremin writes:

> . . . there was talk that neighboring states like New York and foreign
> monarchies—yes, even monarchies!—like Prussia were outstripping Mas-
> sachusetts in the quality and vigor of their public schools. The key appar-
> ently lay in the measure of centralization inherent in a vigorous policy of
> state support and concern for education. Sparked by Edmund Dwight,
> James G. Carter, Josiah Quincy, Jr., and the Reverend Charles Brooks, a
> reform movement arose dedicated to a similar policy for Massachusetts.
> An influx of reports on Prussian and French educational reform only quick-
> ened the imagination of these men. Discussions, consultations, meetings
> and memorials gradually paved the way for legislative action, and no one
> was much surprised when Governor Edward Everett—later to be Presi-
> dent of Harvard—recommended to the legislative session of 1837 that a
> Board be created to further the cause of public education in the state.[189]

And Wayne Urban and Jennings Wagoner, Jr., write:

> Many of [Mann's] pedagogical ideas resulted from trips to Europe,
> where he studied schooling in Prussia and other countries. In Prussia, he
> admired the accomplishments of a centralized school system, which he sought
> to emulate in Massachusetts.[190]

Both are more or less accurate statements of fact; however, neither passage identifies and establishes what the Prussian school is. Cremin identifies
Prussia as a monarchy apparently surpassing Massachusetts in the quality of its
public school education. Urban and Wagoner's "centralized school system"
relies entirely on the reader's imagination to construct understanding.[191] What
the authors do write is not an explanation why so many Whig and Democrat
capitalists, politicians, and public school promoters found the Prussian model of
education so attractive. The failure of these and other commentators on Mann
and the common school system to identify and explain the conjunction between
the Prussian system of schools and social order, the American economic and

political elite, American public school education and Horace Mann is shoddy scholarship or deliberate ideological mystification. Messerli's thorough research and documentation of Mann's position within the social relations of his time, on the other hand, reveals the Prussian school system as the key to identifying and explaining the institutional State function of public education as understood by the governing classes and as Mann constructed it.[192]

Messerli's explanatory critique of Horace Mann, his social ontology, his position within the social relations of the period, and the seminal significance of the Prussian school system clears away much of the ideological mystification that has accumulated in educational historiography around Mann and the common school system. I do not mean that this ideological practice has been abandoned, after all Urban and Wagoner's history of American education was published in 1996, but Messerli's research ensures that where mystification occurs it will no longer be immune from exposure — something that was less likely in 1919 or 1934 when Cubberley published his *Public Education*, in 1935 when Curti's text first appeared, or in 1957 when Cremin's essay appeared.

Messerli's biography of Mann marks a critical division in the history of American public education in the antebellum period. First, Mann is removed from center stage in the most significant educational historiographic texts published after 1963 which deal with this period. His central social position and practices in both the construction of the elite and middle class Anglo-American Protestant consensus for tax supported state schools and the social construction of the common school system as an American version of the Prussian school system is thus muted and pushed under cover. Since Messerli's biography, Mann's usefulness as a vehicle for ideological mystification has been diminished. Thus, when Mann is treated as a distinct figure among the leaders of the common school "reform" movement objective details about him may be identified, but little attempt is made to explicate their meaning in relation to his position and practices, capitalist social relations, or the schools; e.g. seen in Urban and Wagoner's treatment of the Prussian school system above, or as will be demonstrated in the critique of Tyack and Hansot below. Second, post-Messerli educational historians tend to embrace the whole of the common school movement, usually with the purpose of arguing a wide spread consensus existed in support of the school system. Specifically, the claim is this consensus is rooted in and substantiates a dominant Protestant/capitalist ideology that was shared equally by all social classes. This claim, in Tyack and Hansot and in Kaestle, jettisons class conflict and the processes of constructing ideological hegemony from their explanation of antebellum social reality.

In a most interesting way, therefore, Horace Mann, by virtue of his uncritical representation or outright neglect and/or marginalization in the post-Messerli period, survives in the form of a constructed ideological icon.[193] That is, the traditional, ideological construction of Horace Mann in the pre-Messerli period of American education history stands unchallenged in the bulk of newer histories.

After Messerli

Messerli's research into the common school system and Horace Mann thus marks a definite point of division in educational history. Among the historians I identified as belonging to the post-1963 group, there is another distinction to be made between summary or synthetic histories of education, and those which I shall call historical critiques. Much of my critique is focused on the second category, but first a few words about the synthetic group that includes Urban and Wagoner, Button and Provenzo, and Joel Spring.

Button and Provenzo's chronicle of Mann and the common school system closely follows that of both Curti and Cremin. I have already remarked on the relativism of Urban and Wagoner's discussion. They do give considerable attention to Horace Mann and his "crusade" however.[194] Their explication of Mann and his contribution to the common school movement is consistent with Cubberley's and Cremin's celebratory myths, but it is ultimately remarkable for their claim that they have based their account of Mann on Messerli's biography.[195] Their claim is remarkable because Urban and Wagoner in fact restrict their borrowing to selective uncritical details of Mann's biography. Consistent with their explanation of the Prussian system, Urban and Wagoner are no more enlightening about Mann's social position and practices. Their explication of Horace Mann and the common school movement is significant, too, for being a rejection of Michael B. Katz's analysis of the relation between class conflict and public schools in *The Irony of Early School Reform*. By the conclusion of their fourth chapter, in which they explain Horace Mann and the formative development of public schools in the antebellum years, it is clear that Urban and Wagoner have joined Katz's critics, who "tend to see the common school, and public schools in the twentieth century, as imperfect institutions that nevertheless attempted to overcome, or mitigate, social divisions in American society and to help the members of the lower orders of that society to better themselves."[196]

Joel Spring's approach is simultaneously more complex than that of the other two texts, and more problematic. He has adopted a dialectical strategy as a means of introducing students to conflicting interpretations of the same historical periods of public school education. This strategy is in fact provocative, but rather than illuminate history it lends itself to increased attention to the historians and provokes investigation into their particular and contextual ideologies. There is justification for this skeptical critical work, and I am engaged in this enterprise myself here; but while my concern is to uncover a specific historical social reality, Spring lapses into a dangerous contextual relativism. For example: "As I discussed in Chapter 1, historians often reconstruct history from the perspective of the particular times in which they lived."

Writing during the politically peaceful times of the late 1970s and early 1980s, Kaestle [in *Pillars of the Republic*] found that the main concern of the post-Revolutionary period was to balance freedom and order: "Political theorists and policy makers were therefore concerned not only with protecting liberty, for which the Revolution had been fought, but also with maintaining order, without which all might be lost." The purpose of education, according to Kaestle, was to maintain the balance between order and freedom by producing virtuous, well-behaved citizens.

Writing in the radical economic and political climate of the 1930s, Curti states that Webster's spelling book contains a social philosophy "appropriate to a system which attached great value to acquiescence on the part of the poor in their poverty and at the same time promised ultimate success to those who would practice the virtues of frugality, industry, and submissiveness to moral teachings and to God's will."

Curti concludes from his review of the moral maxims in Webster's speller that they were designed primarily to protect the property of the wealthy and that "other half-truths, equally fitting to a society in which some had more and others less, were read and re-read by American youth who learned their letters from the old 'blue-back.'" In general, Curti finds that most post-Revolutionary educational practices and proposals continued, with only minor changes, the colonial class system of education.[197]

Spring provides minor editorial comment, but otherwise lets Kaestle's and Curti's arguments stand in counterpoint. He thus presents different versions of the same historical particulars, but identifies no criterion by which to judge the merits of one or the other. The only clear guide to interpretation that Spring makes explicit is: history is a context dependent, subjective reconstruction. Therefore, neither account is true, and neither account is false; or, to put it another way, both are false or true depending on one's historical time and perspective. On the basis of Spring's relativist premise, his own text is a context dependent fabrication which cannot be judged true or false. It is possible that this is not the conclusion Spring intends, but it is his ontological premise that no reality exists or can be known independent of context and subjective understanding. What began as a promising strategy ends in a relativist muddle. The ontological problem of Horace Mann and the common school system remains, because on one hand capitalist ideology continues to exert hegemonic dominance in the market place of textbooks, and, on the other hand, the relativist synthesis tells us a lot we need to know about one kind of historical discourse, but very little about the object of study itself.

Michael B. Katz: Public Education and the Capitalist Social Order

Michael Katz's *The Irony of Early School Reform*, is the first and perhaps most important historical critique to appear among the historical critiques belonging to the second category of post-1963 texts. Unlike the other educational histories I have engaged thus far, Katz is the first, after Messerli, to consider Horace Mann, the common school system, and common school promoters within the substantially more complex theoretical frame of social relations and cultural transformation as generated by capitalist conditions of economic production in nineteenth century.   One other characteristic distinguishes Katz's history from the others: he attempts to identify and establish degrees of congruence between the subjects' ideas and beliefs and their actions, and between class ideology and institution making.   Although empirical correspondence is a limited criterion within an open system and difficult to identify when poorly documented or anonymous individuals and/or groups are the focus of study, it tends to be much more identifiable when society and social relations are the object of study — i.e., the distribution of power and resources that results in the first place from structural change in the foundational conditions of economic production (from agrarian and artisan production to industrial mass production, from moderate self-sufficiency and local market economy to capitalism, etc.), and in the second place from all the subsequent social structural changes which emerge.   In other words, Horace Mann, other public school promoters, and the common school system cannot be adequately explained and critiqued outside of their positions and practices within the complex tensions that make up social relations in nineteenth-century American society.

To clarify what his social ontology and methodology entails Katz situates the life of Horace Mann within the empirical events of his historical period: rapid population growth; migration from the country to the cities; urban expansion and proliferating industrial centers; war and economic pressures; technological, production, transportation, and market innovations; mounting tension and confrontations between manufacturers, merchants and workers; immigration; racial, ethnic, and religious conflict; old culture-new culture tension and conflict; and, finally, patterns of social relations as determined by the unequal distribution of resources.[198]   Moreover, Katz makes clear that it was not only Horace Mann, or members of the governing classes, who confronted these dramatic events, the whole of American society was involved.   For example:

> For generations New England girls had remained with their families until marriage.   Now large numbers of farm girls left home to work in the mills of Lawrence, Lowell, and other places.   Whole families moved to manufacturing areas and worked in the mills in the southern part of the

state. Immigration changed this pattern. The immigrants swelled the labor force and fostered competition for jobs, and the consequent lowering of wages tended to discourage native girls from working in the factories. The supply of native girls was diminished further by the westward migration of entire farm families. Moreover, as large numbers of Irish entered the mills and factories, natives, who found the Irish repugnant, often left. By the 1860's the unskilled work in the new large industries was mainly the province of immigrants. In Horace Mann's lifetime Massachusetts had acquired a proletariat.[199]

The shortcoming of Katz's explication here in these broad strokes does not tell us why, for example, young girls and whole families moved from small farms in the country to manufacturing areas.[200] Identifying the structures generating events and social forces undergirding the movement from the farm to the factory is not as important to Katz, however, as identifying and establishing patterns of social behavior in response to these momentous changes in people's economic and political relations and cultural traditions.[201] Something of Katz's focus, however, is apparent in the above paragraph. Unspecified structural changes in the conditions of economic production set in motion the migration of people belonging to a particular stratum of society and changes in social relations. Then, "immigration changed this pattern." What follows this change in the social structure is the emergence of complex behavioral responses which, in turn, generate other social changes. The manufacturers exploit the desperation of the immigrants, who have swelled the size of the labor force, to create competition for limited numbers of jobs and thus drive down wages. When the wages are driven down to a level the native-born American girls will not tolerate, they seek other alternatives. Manipulated economic competition, language and cultural differences, and religious conflict are sufficient causes to alienate native workers from immigrant workers. All but the most destitute or incompetent among the native group of workers choose to leave the low wages and unskilled labor to the immigrants, who, by the 1860s, make up the unskilled and semi-skilled production forces.

Land speculation in the Western states had already increased the price of land, so only the more prosperous New Englanders had any expectation of successful resettlement. Single men could venture the risk of resettlement in undeveloped areas away from settlements and transportation routes.[202] By and large, however, displaced New Englanders who lacked sufficient resources or sense of adventure to risk their lives in frontier territories had to reorganize their society and construct new alternatives where they were.

It is Katz's conclusion that this social reorganization and construction of new alternatives by the displaced coincided with the governing classes' promotion of the common schools, but went beyond to the creation of the public high school.

> In every variety of work "rapid progress," commented the Brookline school committee in 1855, called for a "corresponding expansion . . . in education." "Modern commerce" required the "young merchant" to have "a more adequate knowledge of the great globe he dwells on than can be acquired from the pages of a Grammar School textbook"; the farmer could not "much longer dispense with some scientific knowledge of the soil he cultivates." Similarly, "the ships, the mills, and warehouses we need can no longer be built by the 'rule of thumb' of an ignorant mechanic." In short, "whole classes in our community who, not a generation ago, would have been content to earn their living by unskilled labor, are now thrust from that lower market, and forced to add knowledge and intelligence to the labor of their hands." The answer, to the committee, was "not to regret this state of things, but . . . to provide for it."   And provision to them meant a high school.[203]

One instance may be adequate to support his point, but it is Katz's purpose to clearly demonstrate the promotion and construction of public schools was neither the product of an "enlightened working class, led by idealistic and humanitarian intellectuals, triumphantly wresting free public education from a selfish, wealthy elite and from the bigoted proponents of orthodox religion," (a reference to Cubberley) or the product "of a consensus on fundamental principles."[204] Caught between the wealthy and manufacturers on one side and immigrant labor on the other, native New Englanders (the middle class in particular) needed to act if they were to preserve their status in a highly competitive and rapidly changing social order.

The Winchendon committee argued that the availability of foreigners to perform the "least desirable" sorts of work enabled "our sons to rise to other employments." To seize the new opportunities for its children a town required an advanced educational system, especially a high school; there was no other alternative if parents desired their children to rise on the economic and social scale. "Shall we," asked the committee, "stand still, and see our children outstripped in the race of life, by the children of those who are willing to pursue a liberal and far-sighted policy?" [. . .]

The argument that a high school would foster mobility probably appealed to parents of limited or moderate means, for they are the ones who would not be able to provide their sons with the capital or influence that might make a good education less necessary. It is likely that these arguments influenced many of the artisans and less wealthy businessmen who voted for the retention of Beverly High school. Similarly, it is likely that the affluent supporters were influenced by the appeal to communal wealth, since as owners of real estate and as investors they stood to gain the most from urban and industrial development. But would the arguments concerning mobility appeal to them? Had they an interest in paying taxes to develop competition for themselves and their children?[205]

Katz thus provides the articulated hermeneutic moment, that is, what the subjects themselves think their social reality is and what actions are required of them. Their understanding of society is clearly premised on a perception of competition; moreover, as a group they possess the economic and political resources to act in a way that will give their members an advantage. They may not be able to procure or grant ownership of the means of production, but through the provision of a high school education their children will easily outdistance the uneducated and unskilled class of immigrant labor. Their children will rise, in other words, to the level of skilled labor, clerks, managers, and, perhaps, the most gifted may join the ranks of the professions.

As I have already argued, the hermeneutic moment, the subject's own account of things, is necessary but insufficient to stand alone as evidence. Katz began by sketching in structural changes and events which generated dramatic changes in early to mid-nineteenth century society. He sketched in many of the changes in social relations and individual behaviors, and as shown in the passages quoted above, he renders his subjects' perceptions and thoughts about society and the actions they must take in response. What remains for him to do is to identify and establish congruence between structural change, events, perceptions and concrete responses — in this case institution making in the form of high schools. Simply showing a high school was built, however, is not enough in the context of the argument he has constructed. The two questions with which he concludes the quoted passage above indicate as much.

Higher education in this period is still the domain of the elite and the professional classes, and the common schools are available to any white child with time, economic means, and freedom from necessary labor to attend them.[206] The high schools, as conceptualized by the two school committees I have cited from Katz's text, are a middle level institution meant to provide a utilitarian education which will position its graduates closer to the upper classes without directly challenging them, and significantly ahead of the lower class of laboring immigrants. What is necessary to establish congruence, therefore, is a concretely detailed case study which clearly identifies not only the promotion of a high school, and its existence or defeat, but which also identifies a privileged distribution of resources that favors one group to the disadvantage of another.

Katz does precisely this in his critique of the promoters who campaigned for the high school, their social positions, their reasons and actions, and the voting results in the referendum over the Beverly High School. He reinforces his conclusions with shorter studies of Somerville High School, Groton Junction, and Ayer. Katz shows that the high schools were promoted most energetically by the professional and middle classes, and resisted most strenuously by the great majority of small farmers, self-employed workmen and striking wage laborers. In this way the class divisions in the social relations of the various communities are identified and established. Significantly, Katz finds little congruence between the universalist rhetoric of the school promoters and the actual performance of the high schools:

> Promoters had emphasized that the high school would promote social mobility, unify and civilize communities, awaken and sustain a community-wide interest in education, and raise the value of real estate. In reality, the

high school did none of these things: the statistical analysis, the facts of high school attendance, the developments in Beverly and Groton, and the complaints of schoolmen all make this clear. Only a minority of the children in a community, and those mainly from the more well-to-do sectors, attended the high school. The high school could not serve as a means of boosting many poor children up the economic ladder.[207]

The congruent correspondence he does uncover, however, establishes an uneven distribution of resources among different classes:

> The high school was, however, relevant to the mobility of middle-class children. For middle-class boys the high school probably served as both a means of status maintenance and an entree into the business world. Information in school registers has been found concerning thirteen boys who left Somerville High School between 1856 and 1860. Of these, eight became clerks, two entered business, and three became apprentices. For all but one of the apprentices the jobs represented an occupation different from that of their fathers, who with the exception of three businessmen were artisans and farmers. These seven, sons of artisans and farmers, very likely saw the high school as a way of helping to retain a middle-class status at a time when mechanization and other economic alterations made the future of their fathers' occupations less secure. They may have hoped, as well, that through business they could rise above the social level of their parents.
>
> The high school also had obvious uses for middle-class girls, and substantially more girls than boys attended. The high schools usually offered preparation for teaching; and teaching was undoubtedly the most attractive vocational goal for the middle-class girl who wanted to earn some money because all the other occupations populated by large numbers of females were manual, arduous, and decidedly lower-class. According to the state census of 1865, the largest number of employed females, 27,393, were domestics; next came operatives (meaning factory workers), 20,152; third came teachers, 6,050. Other groups of more than one thousand females were, in order of size, seamstresses, shoe workers, tailoresses, dressmakers, straw and palm leaf workers, milliners, laundresses, nurses, and clerks.

The middle-class girl who wanted to work at something respectable had little choice; teaching it almost had to be. For girls who had no intention of becoming gainfully employed the high school must have offered a relatively painless way of passing the time until they came of marrying age.[208]

Katz's contribution to defining the position of the common school system, particularly the public high school, within the context of nineteenth century social relations cannot be overestimated. Through his careful attention to the socioeconomic class and positions and practices of the promoters of school reform, and through his analysis of the opposition vote in the Beverly High School case study Katz identifies, establishes and explains the competition for control of resources, a competition that reveals class divisions constructed largely on the basis of ethnicity, religion, race and rural/urban cleavages. It is clear, in other words, that within nineteenth century competitive capitalist social relations the Protestant governing classes decide what issues will become policy on the basis of controlling the acquisition and distribution of resources, and it is largely the working class and immigrant laboring class which must — eventually if not immediately — acquiesce. Just as Messerli explodes the myth of Horace Mann the pure crusader, Katz exposes the myth that the public schools were promoted and created as the egalitarian democratic road to success for all children of all classes, and in the process he exposes the classless consensus myth. By doing so, however, he became the focus of a whole industry of texts by mainstream establishment scholars and hired mouthpieces who gamely attempted to reconstruct the old myths and patch up the achievement ideology of public schools by discrediting, dismissing, or diminishing Katz's explanatory critique of the class divisions inherent in public schools and the myths of social mobility and consensus engendered by the promoters.

Tyack and Hansot's *Managers of Virtue*, and Carl Kaestle's *Pillars of the Republic* are perhaps the two most significant attacks on Katz's revelations, and they are also the most subtle; for if students were not already familiar with Katz's demystifying historical excavations they would not recognize the submerged ideological reconstruction and mystification going on in these two widely used texts.

Tyack and Hansot: Protestant Ideology, Consensus, and Public School Leadership

Tyack and Hansot have chosen to focus on the leaders of public school reform from 1820 to 1980 as a means of tracing the development of the relationship between ideology, social theory, leadership, institutional policy and administration, and public school education. Although they do not appear to reproduce the traditional gallant crusader, social mobility, or the classless consensus myths, they do in fact give a new face to these myths. Their study resembles those that, as characterized by Urban and Wagoner, "tend to see the common school, and public schools in the twentieth century, as imperfect institutions that nevertheless attempted to overcome, or mitigate, social divisions in American society and to help the members of the lower orders of that society to better themselves."[209] Like Curti, Tyack and Hansot provide an introductory social overview to explain the context in which Protestant/capitalist ideology regarding public education and institution building in the nineteenth century are formed and become interactive. Unlike Curti's explication of class divisions and conflicting social values and attitudes, however, Tyack and Hansot tend to gloss over class conflict. For example, on the linkage between capitalism and public school education they write:

> Because the common school so rapidly became the mainstream of American education in the nineteenth century, it is tempting to assume that its hegemony was inevitable and hence to lose a sense of surprise at its triumph. But one can easily imagine a counterfactual history in which the divisions that marked education early in the nineteenth century persisted unabated, and schooling remained as separatist as Protestant churches.[210]

The first sentence is a masterful way of both identifying a critical event in the class motivation undergirding the governing classes' construction of the common school system and muting the revelation until it seems harmless. Hegemony, as explained by Sassoon, is both the domination by state power (as exercised through institutional positions and practices) over daily social relations, and "the organizing principle of a society in which one class rules over others not just through force but by maintaining the allegiance of the mass of the population. This allegiance is obtained both through reforms and compromises in which the interests of different groups are taken into account, and also through influencing the way people think."[211] In short, the Protestant Anglo-American capitalist governing classes triumphed over the white working class, immigrants, Catholics, Jews, Amerindians, Black-Americans, small farmers, and women. The nature of this triumph was the extension of Protestant/capitalist supremacist ideology from the economic and political spheres into the schools with the purpose of normalizing class, ethnic, religious, and racial inequality in the social consciousness of children. The hegemonic triumph of the common school system is nothing less than the suppression of democratic ideology and the legitimation of capitalist republicanism. The last sentence of their statement is especially important, for Tyack and Hansot's "counterfactual" history is one where social divisions and conflicts that typified public education early in the nineteenth century continued. In other words, the triumph of the common schools is also the ideological mystification of social divisions.[212] This implies an actual classless consensus regarding the common school system, but such a consensus did not exist as Katz demonstrated (and, ironically, as Cubberley revealed in his extended legitimation of the systemic reorganization of the twentieth century state system of public school education.) The only possible consensus regarding the schools that Tyack and Hansot, as well as Messerli and Katz, have identified and established is an Anglo-American Protestant/capitalist consensus among the governing classes. But the socioeconomic circumstances of competitive capitalism, and the middle class crisis triggered by industrialization and non-English immigration that energized this consensus remain vague in Tyack and Hansot's explanation.

Before the common-school crusade of the mid-nineteenth century, educational institutions had often reflected differences of class, ethnicity, and religion. To the crusaders themselves it was by no means a foregone conclusion that they would be able to attract rich and poor, Baptists and Unitarians, Germans and Yankees to the same common school. Free schools in cities had often been designed for the lower classes and carried a pauper taint.[213]

It is important to recall something of the historical specifics glossed over here. Emma Willard started her first Seminary for young women in Middlebury, Vermont, in 1807, as increasing numbers of young women were being displaced from farms and small home industries. At the behest of DeWitt Clinton, Willard relocated to New York, and in 1821 or 1822 opened the Troy Female Seminary. Her Seminary for the education and training of women as school teachers was financially aided by the city of Troy, and provided women with a respectable alternative to manual wage labor in the manufactories or prostitution. The education of native born Anglo-American young women of the middle and lower middle class provided communities with an inexpensive labor force of teachers who were culturally, racially, and religiously suited to fulfill the expectations of the common school promoters and the town and district school committees.[214] The displacement of some these young women, as well as the subjugation of women generally, and the governing classes' exploitation of this social phenomenon through domestic ideology in order to expand the labor force of teachers and, too, expand the common schools, did not, however, happen in a social vacuum.

Thomas Skidmore in the years 1828-30 was campaigning for a new revolution to realize the unfulfilled promises of the *Declaration of Independence*. He had identified inheritance and property monopolies as the cause of unequal social relations, and, therefore, the only way of correcting social inequities was to capture the State, remake the judiciary, and redistribute property among all citizens upon their reaching the age of majority.[215] Shortly after Shay's Rebellion the Federalists displaced democracy with capitalist republicanism through the constitutional convention of 1787. Market capitalism and the rapid development of industrial capitalism along with corresponding changes in banking, credit and forms of payment, and land-based property taxation in the early decades of the nineteenth century generated a wide spread economic and social crisis in the country side and in the cities. The children of small independent farmers left the struggling farms in increasing numbers for the growing cities, and the old order of small independent crafts people was rapidly coming undone. By the 1840s the American social order was in a turmoil, a crisis compounded by massive numbers of new immigrants.

Tyack and Hansot are minimizing this social crisis. As a matter of fact, by placing the common-school movement as a mid-century phenomenon, the earlier decades of middle class retrenchment and organizing against social and economic displacement are forgotten, as is the underlying class motivations for supporting the development of public schools. Indeed, as the next passage makes clear, the authors acknowledge the workings of capitalist ideology while simultaneously diminishing its social effects:

> Closely integrated with the religious and political case for the common school was the economic *folklore* of nineteenth century capitalism. Public education was designed to do more than produce moral citizens. By training children to be literate, temperate, frugal, hardworking, and good planners it also taught them to make their way in the small-scale capitalism idealized in the textbooks. The same virtues that made a young person a good employee could, with *appropriate modifications*, be translated into entrepreneurial assets. Long before economists developed their theories of "human capital" American citizens believed that investment in education paid off both in individual and collective economic benefits.[Emphasis added.][216]

The writing of this passage is ambiguous—are Tyack and Hansot paraphrasing the ideology of the middle class common school promoters or are they making a statement the reader is meant to accept as the reality of nineteenth century public education and its relation to actual economic and political circumstances? The last sentence suggests Tyack and Hansot believe the rhetoric of Mann and others among the promoters, and are themselves propagandizing, for they do not contradict these beliefs and pointedly make them universal. Their next paragraph redirects the historical perspective away from public school education as a developing system of social control and social reproduction to a democracy-building institution.

> Historians have analyzed the relationship between bureaucratic schooling and the new hierarchical social relationships of production in large-scale industrial and commercial capitalism. What is sometimes forgotten in such analyses is that during the mid-nineteenth century most schooling took place in one-room or small-town schools and that the economy was composed mostly of small-scale enterprises. In many parts of the nation the family

farm was the chief system of economic production, while in many industries old work techniques and shop cultures persisted. Thus in looking at the connection between capitalism and public schooling it is useful to focus on more than the new social relationships of production in large-scale industry. Capitalism not only entailed new and exploitative relations between employer and employee, important though these were; it also meant an unbound and mobile labor system, a complex system of markets, protection of private property, and a supportive ideology.[217]

This passage is also an implicit attack against Merle Curti's and Michael B. Katz's conclusions about the middle class and capitalist bias of public education in the nineteenth century. But this point aside, there is ample evidence that common people were vigorously contesting their loss of rights under the new capitalist regime before and during the period Tyack and Hansot have marked out. The contest over rights and against oppression, to cite one example, was central to Andrew Jackson's presidential campaign and election; and the fierce competition among the dominant political parties for the working men's protest vote in the 1830s is another. To get past Tyack and Hansot's euphemistic treatment of capitalism's praiseworthy accomplishments knowledge of the historical period is needed; for such knowledge makes it clear that (1) a mobile labor system meant unemployment, poverty, and grueling hardship for the common people of the time — that is why they were mobile — (2) and a complex system of (expanding) markets and post-War of Independence taxation were undermining the economic independence of small family enterprises, artisans, and farms, (3) and laws to protect property were legislated to attack worker organizations and strikers protesting the loss of autonomy, trades, low wages, oppressive exploitation and servile dependency, (4) and, finally, the "supportive ideology" legitimated the oppression and exploitation of wage laborers, Black Americans, women, and immigrants, and it undermined democracy.[218]

Finally, the hegemony of capitalist ideology as inculcated through the public schools is presented to us as a fact of life. Tyack and Hansot almost make a pastoral of it:

> It was through inculcating this ideology — and a related set of behavioral traits — that public education of the mid-nineteenth century probably

contributed most to American capitalism. By making the republican markets, by rationalizing wealth or poverty as the result of individual effort or
indolence, and by making the political economy seem to be not a matter of
choice but of providential design, the common school buttressed capitalism.
A large proportion of twentieth-century economic leaders—like the school
managers of that era—grew up in rural communities where they learned
the folklore of capitalism taught in textbooks like McGuffey's. It is perhaps
no accident that one of the industrialists who did most to change the organization of production, Henry Ford, so idealized the one-room school and
McGuffey that he enshrined them in a museum near Detroit.[219]

Tyack and Hansot do tell us that "the common school buttressed capitalism,"
but they do so without the particulars, without a detailed explanatory critique
that identifies what this means historically and specifically; for as much as they
reveal they could have as easily said "the madonna wrapped her infant in the
softest of swaddling clothes." They identify achievement ideology, and its centrality in the nineteenth century school lesson, but what they do not examine or
adequately explain is congruence between this ideology, the public school, and
actual socioeconomic circumstances. Did achievement ideology in the nineteenth century reflect actual circumstances, or is it a mystification of actual
circumstances? Thomas Skidmore, lacking Tyack and Hansot's appreciation of
capitalism and the ideology embedded in the promotion of common schools, did
not find so much to applaud about the promoters:

If they be sincere in their belief that such education is so very indis-
pensable as a previous step in this enjoyment [of food, clothing, material
comfort, and upward social mobility]; and that the people are not now sufficiently instructed, let me ask them how, under present circumstances, is it
ever *possible* to give it? Is a family, where both parents and children are
suffering daily, in their animal wants; where excessive toil is required to
obtain the little they enjoy; where the unkind and the unfriendly passions,
generated by such a wretched condition of things, reign with fell sway: is
such a family in a situation to receive instruction? . . . let all remember, that
those who undertake to *hold back* the people from their rights of property,
as shown in this work, until *education*, as they call it, can first be commu-

nicated . . . either do not understand themselves, or pursue the course they *are* pursuing, for the purpose of diverting the people from the possession of these rights; that they may be held in bondage, even yet longer.[220]

One could also turn to Seth Luther's 1832 *An Address To The Working-Men of New England* to identify how many tens-of-thousands of children labored in New England mills fourteen hours a day, six days a week, with only two 25 minute breaks during their shift to identify some of the historical particulars prompting Skidmore's complaint.[221] But the exploitation of working class parents and their children, and the socioeconomic circumstances which governed their daily existence, did not vanish because of the common school system or the development of high schools and land grant colleges — as Jacob Riis's written reports and photographs at the end of the nineteenth century attest, or as Lawrence Fell, chief factory inspector for the state of New Jersey, reported in the 1890s.[222] Capitalist processes of appropriation and accumulation of property opposed democracy, and the extreme inequities capitalism generated in society cannot be apologized away or quietly glossed over. To do so must be recognized as an act of ideological mystification and the perpetuation of capitalist hegemony.

The critical point made here is Tyack and Hansot's acceptance of the common school system as a correlative institution of capitalism is merely an acknowledgment of a social fact, for they do not answer the big "so what?" question. The common school system cannot "buttress capitalism" without also buttressing the unequal distribution of resources and rights and class divisions, i.e., reproducing stratified, unequal social relations while obscuring their cause. Although Tyack and Hansot tend to diminish rather than emphasize the logical conclusions of their argument, their explication of Pan-Protestant/capitalist ideology and the local and national linkages between promoters nonetheless makes it possible to read between the lines. Such a reading makes it apparent that the common school system as an ideological agency instituted to regulate mind and behavior (i.e., "character") to fit into an inequitable social order could not also promote upward social mobility, a more equitable and harmonious society, or achieve democratic ideals.

Tyack and Hansot's focused examination of Horace Mann is also problematic, if only because it is a descriptive rather than a critical study. They more or less adhere to the concrete details of Messerli's research, but their emphasis is stilted. Although they reference the Prussian school system twice, for example, once in connection with newly elected Democratic Governor Morgan's 1840 attempt to eliminate the Board of Education and its Secretary, and again in connection with Mann's fight with the Boston schoolmasters, they do not explain what the Prussian school system is, its importance to Mann as a model of ideological hegemony and social control, or that it was fundamental to Mann's blueprint for the common school system.[223]

Tyack and Hansot tell us that "Mann's career as an educational reformer started in 1837 after he had already established a promising reputation as a lawyer and Whig legislator in Massachusetts." They thus reference Mann's legal practice, but without providing specific details. They mention that he was a Whig politician, an Assemblyman and ultimately the President of the State Senate; but, again, they do not make it clear what this means within the historical context or in regard to his powerful position and practice within the context of contested and unequal social relations. They also tell us that he supported legislation which promoted humanitarian agencies as well as numerous capitalist ventures; that he believed the government had a responsibility to economically support private corporations in their development of roads, railroads, and industry; and, that he was aggressively opposed to the working class's social habits—i.e. visits to the local tavern. They conclude this itemized list with the sentence: "Like many other Whig politicians he believed it a virtue to mind other people's business."[224] Their description is a concisely understated description, suggestively detailed, but poorly elaborated and devoid of critical analysis.

Tyack and Hansot tend to attribute Mann's pronouncements on morality, his perceptions of society, and his actions in the economic and political spheres to his religious background — his struggle with and rejection of orthodox Calvinism and his conversion to Unitarianism. This is true as far as it goes, but they make no mention of Messerli's finding that Mann had embraced Lord Brougham's Natural Theology,

> which claimed that revelation and miracles had no place in true religion. The validity of religious teachings was better determined by scientific proof. Although Mann suspected most professing Christians would consider this a

"fatal heresy," he was prepared to go even further than Brougham and claim that "Natural Religion stands as preeminent over Revealed Religion as the deepest experience over the slightest hearsay," and he added that "the time is coming when the light of Natural Religion will be to that of Revealed, as the rising sun is to the star that preceded it."

According to Brougham and others, the human mind was nothing metaphysical but part of the natural and scientific world, subject to laws which could be discovered through inductive reasoning and investigation. Once these laws were learned, the clergyman, the educator, and the statesman could guide people to more virtuous lives. Mann could not have agreed more.[225]

Mann's beliefs were not merely inherited or typical as Tyack and Hansot seem to suggest. Mann was not exempt from the Protestant/capitalist zeitgeist of his society, but it is instructive to realize, contrary to all accounts but Messerli's, that unlike many of his contemporaries who were orthodox, liberal, or romantic Protestants, Mann embraced the scientific avant garde of his time. His scientific religion was consistent with his belief in George Combe's positivist science of the mind, Phrenology, and his belief in empirical causality. In other words, his believed that the mind was a faculty subject to corrective manipulation, reformation, and control. Society, likewise, could be causally constructed through social engineering; i.e., construct an institution which efficiently dominates what counts as right knowledge, and which then impresses this knowledge into the consciousness of pliant subjects, and one thus affects their social behavior, their character, and the stability of the existing social order. This is Mann's essential theory. The Prussian school system, and the conformity and order of Prussian society were Mann's empirical proof.

None of this is identified or explained by Tyack and Hansot. They reduce Mann to an "archetype of the mid-century school reformer."

Mann worried about signs of social disintegration: mob violence on the streets, bitter political partisanship, sectarian strife (especially between Catholics and Protestants), ill will and rivalry between the native-born [Anglo-Americans] and the immigrants flocking to . . . cities, and economic conflict between rich and poor, employers and employees. Mann told a friend that "as population increases, and especially as artificial wants multiply, and temptations increase, the guards and securities must increase also, or society will deteriorate." He believed that public education was equal to all these challenges, but that to win the support of all citizens it must not reflect or contribute to the fragmentation of the larger society. This meant that it must bypass all sectarian quarrels, all partisan issues in politics, and instead concentrate on just those moral and civic values that all Christian republicans could support.

Naturally most Catholics, some Protestant leaders, and a scattering of nonbelievers could not accept Mann's version of pan-Protestant teaching— reading the King James Bible and prayers without comment—as actually neutral. And in practice, as Ruth Elson has shown, the actual teaching of political and moral principles through common-school textbooks showed a marked conservative and often nativist bias. But in order to win public support for this presumed consensus, Mann was willing to ban controversy from the public school.[226]

Through the process of generalized description, as we see, they obscure Mann's dynamic position as a deliberate, politically astute, constructive agent. As I have already pointed out, Tyack and Hansot provided a general overview of the social context of the common school movement, but when they get to the system's "archetype," there is little connection between the triumph of hegemony in the common school system and Mann's monumental political accomplishment in bringing it about. At most Tyack and Hansot reference Mann's worrying about "signs of social disintegration" without sufficient explanation of the specifics, and none about structures and events which generated the observed social phenomena. They do not identify and explain the significant connections between class conflict, state repression and the common school system, or Mann's position and practice within these social relations. In this descriptive narrative Horace Mann appears as a man of his time, race, and class — full of complexities and faults — but in the end he emerges the heroic crusader. If the common school system does not foster upward social mobility and democracy . . . it is because someone else corrupted Mann's achievement:

Mann lacked an ability to put his values in perspective, to see the world with a sense of humor, to lose a few battles gracefully. But his extraordinary moral energy and commitment made him the great proselytizer for public education. When he looked back on his twelve years as secretary he could take pride in the founding of state normal schools to train teachers, on the creation of school libraries, on improved schoolhouses, on more regular school attendance, on enlarged public expenditures for education, on the beginning of graded classrooms in cities, on more responsible supervision by local committees. Above all, he could see about him a new sense of purpose, a stabilized ideology and a model of public schooling. Whether he would have approved of the ways in which these reforms became institutionalized in the decades to come is open to question. Whether his overselling of the benefits of education was to prove a boon or a bane is still debated. But he remains the archetype of the mid-century school reformer.[227]

There is more hidden than identified in Tyack and Hansot's description of the governing classes' Protestant/capitalist ideology and institution building. The specific details and the local and national linkages among members of the governing classes which Tyack and Hansot do identify must be used by the reader to construct his/her own valuable insights into historical continuities of cultural values and behaviors, and of positions and practices by the promoters and leaders of the educational establishment. For example, as already quoted, they wrote that Horace Mann "worried about signs of social disintegration. . . ." That, "Mann told a friend that 'as population increases, and especially as artificial wants multiply, and temptations increase, the guards and securities must increase also, or society will deteriorate.'"[228] If this is connected to their description of the progressive period at the end of the nineteenth century we see that Mann's identified causal relation between the production of "artificial wants" and increased "temptations" and the need for multiplied "guards and securities" remained a constant theme of the governing classes and its educational agents. Indeed, as demonstrated above in the critical explanation of *Public Education*, this theme is a continuous thread throughout Cubberley's text — a point Tyack and Hansot make themselves:

Members of [the] educational trust were acutely aware of how changes in the economy had transformed American Society. They were worried about the potential for class conflict and eager to use schooling to preserve—but improve—the existing social order. Ellwood P. Cubberley of Stanford, wrote in 1909 that the last decade had been "a period marked by the concentration of capital and business enterprise in all fields . . . 'trusts', combinations, and associations were formed in all lines of business; the specialization of labor and the introduction of labor-saving machinery took place to an extent before unknown." As urbanization accelerated, "a more cosmopolitan attitude began to pervade our whole life." Small-scale capitalism gave way "to large mercantile and industrial concerns. No longer can a man save up a thousand dollars and start in business for himself with much chance of success. The employee tends to remain an employee . . . the worker tends more and more to become a cog in the machine and to lose sight of his place in the industrial process." As a result of "the ever increasing subdivision and specialization of labor," he warned, "the danger from class subdivision is constantly increasing."

[. . .]

So concentrated was ownership of industry that by 1920 the top 5 percent of all industrial corporations earned 79 percent of total corporate income. The major beneficiaries of this were the wealthy; in 1910 the top 1 percent of the population received 33.9 percent of all personal income in the United States, while the bottom 20 percent earned only 8.3 percent. By very high rates of turnover, by absenteeism, strikes, and record-breaking votes for Socialist candidates in 1912 and 1920, industrial workers protested the degradation of work into mindless routines and the loss of control over the work process.[229]

Clearly the stratified and conflicted economic and political relations between the governing classes and laboring classes in Mann's time became only more extreme by Ellwood Cubberley's time. The tendencies (as identified by Curti and Katz, and, interestingly, by Cubberley himself) of the public schools to privilege the middle class by suppressing the educational and social opportunities of the working class without also challenging the elites correspond not only

with the historical specificities of the mid-nineteenth century, they also correspond to the social reality of the period between the late 1800s and the 1930s.
The common schools and the public high schools obviously did not contribute to
building a classless society, nor did they contribute to building a democratic
society. That the nineteenth century state system of public school education
was the product of widespread consensus, that it was a classless state institution, that it fostered a democratic society are great ideological myths, which
Katz demystified — and which Tyack and Hansot have not proved otherwise.

Carl Kaestle: Ideological Hegemony As Social Consensus

Carl Kaestle's history of the common school system, *Pillars of the Republic*, like Tyack and Hansot's, is primarily an interpretation of the dominant ideology of the Protestant Anglo-American governing classes. Whereas Katz exca-
vated the capitalist structures undergirding public schools and the schools' institutional social function of reproducing unequal social relations, Kaestle champions capitalism in his text and argues that Protestant/capitalist ideology (and by
implication the social relations which it supported and mystified) was embraced
and believed by all Americans except for a few powerless radicals. Like
Lawrence Cremin, Kaestle follows directly in the tradition of Horace Mann and
Ellwood Cubberley. Kaestle, like Mann and Cubberley, not only recasts the
past in the light of his ideological purpose, but he also advances a bold conception of public schools as republican engines of social reform, upward mobility,
and national progress.

Kaestle's history of nineteenth century public school education is by turns
exemplary scholarship and masterful mystification. Not least of his mystifications is the pretense of having no extra-scholarly motives in writing this historiographic text. Other than the paid traditionalist mouthpiece Diane Ravitch, and
the mainstream historian Marvin Vinovskis, with whom he is often a co-author,
Kaestle is Katz's most relentless critic. *Pillars of the Republic* has an explicit
argument and an agenda. The agenda is discrediting Katz's research and ex-

planations, and becomes a direct attack only late in Kaestle's text after lengthy preparation during which he attempts to jettison class conflict and persuade us that Protestant/capitalist ideology and support for the common school system were universal. The fact that Kaestle cloaks his ideology, and obscures his objective until late in the text undermines his credibility. As for his explicit argument, however, his explanatory summary of Protestant/capitalist ideology is both credible and concise, but the pro-capitalist interpretation in which it is embedded relies heavily on unsubstantiated assertions, rhetorical turns of phrase, half-truths and out-right deceptions.

In his preface Kaestle tells us that his two interrelated arguments are:

> I argue that the eventual acceptance of state common-school systems was encouraged by Americans' commitment to republican government, by the dominance of native Protestant culture, and by the development of capitalism. I argue that in translating republican, Protestant, and capitalist values into public policy leaders were guided by a particular ideology. The reform version of this ideology called for state-regulated common schools to integrate and assimilate a diverse population into the nation's political, economic, and cultural institutions.[230]

As I stated in regard to Curti, limiting one's study to "social ideas" or "ideology," as Kaestle does here, has distinct interpretive advantages in the sense that one need not attend too closely to the relation between subjects' empirical understanding of social reality and what is actually going on or what generated the observed events or behaviors.[231] By concentrating the study on ideology, this becomes the object of study; and the contradictions between ideological constructs of reality and actual social relations are shoved to the periphery and mystified. In other words, by marking out an object of study which is clearly epistemological and interpretive, the author is not obligated to establish a correspondence between his transitive understanding and an intransitive object of study; indeed, the object of study itself is made transitive. The only criterion imposed by the epistemological terrain Kaestle has marked out is that he construct a coherent interpretation of his assertions. He will attempt to fulfill this criterion, but as soon as one looks for a degree of congruence, the weakness of his interpretive ideological argument becomes apparent.

In the period "after 1830," "acceptance" of the common school system was conditioned by "Americans' commitment to republican government, by the dominance of native Protestant culture, and by the development of capitalism." If we are talking specifically about native-born Anglo-Americans this argument is, at best, only partially valid. First, Kaestle uses "republican government" as synonymous with democratic government. The two are not the same. Republican government was the embodiment of unequal rights, the institutionalization of rulers and the ruled, and the mechanism by which the elite among the governing classes promoted and protected their economic interests while repressing the demands of the lower classes. The elections of Jackson and Van Buren depended heavily on the antagonism of the lower classes against an elite dominated republican government. Support of Jackson, in particular, by the various Working Men's Associations was motivated in large measure by anticipation of Jackson's attack on the Bank of the United States, which was seen by the laboring classes and small merchants (as well as by excluded competitors) as the monopolistic foundation of "republican government" and the capitalist manufacturers and corporations.[232] And too, Dorr's War was a revolutionary democratic attempt by disfranchised citizens in Rhode Island to establish a popular people's government in opposition to the sitting republican government.

In Messerli's biography of Mann, there is an account of a crucial meeting in late 1837 between Mann and Franklin Dexter, "a prominent attorney and one of the leading men of Massachusetts." This account of the meeting follows:

> No sooner had Mann broached the subject of enlightening and elevating the common people than Dexter cut him off and gave his opinion of the undertaking in clear and unambiguous terms. To him it was plain for anyone to see who would not let himself be misled by all the nonsense about democracy and the wisdom of the majority. Society had been, was, and always would be sharply divided into two classes, commoners who were destined by nature to work and support themselves by the sweat of their brow and an aristocracy of birth and position who were obligated to guide and govern the less fortunate. Not only did Dexter invoke the spirit of a dead Federalist past, but he had the effrontery even to claim that the "British Government of Kings, Lords and Commons" was superior to American

constitutional government and that it was the duty of the American wealthy and well-born to prevent ingress into their ranks by those below. Only in such a way could a society maintain standards of morality, justice, and good taste. By implication, Dexter was placing a slur on Mann's own common origins and indirectly suggesting that he was a parvenu attempting to exploit a situation for his own advancement.[233]

The obvious question the above examples and this passage raise in regard to Kaestle's assertion of universal consensus is: which Americans does he have in mind? Drawing on Mann's journal, Messerli's account of Mann's reaction to his meeting with Dexter is illuminating and directly relevant:

> Once one granted Dexter's division of society, then the entire scheme of a comprehensive public system of education, which furnished avenues of upward mobility for all children, regardless of race, creed, or financial position, emerged as a foolish and even dangerous experiment. Perhaps Dexter would concede that even the lowliest needed a modicum of literacy if they were to know their place, remain law-abiding and docile, and show proper deference to those above them, but schooling which was the vehicle for a mobility that crossed class lines and challenged the established order was an American form of Jacobinism.[234]

Obviously, even within the domain of ideology and values, few among the governing classes favored democratic government, many suspected republican government, many more had grave reservations about suffrage, and still others rejected any state system of public school education that would alter the social hierarchy. And, Mann, "the archetype of mid-century" promoters, reminded rather bluntly of his class and position, adapted accordingly.

Secondly, Kaestle is on much stronger ground in asserting the "dominance of native Protestant culture," but the social reality is both different and more complex than his assertion implies. Indeed, native Protestant workers who were forced to compete against the steady influx of Irish Catholic immigrants, in particular, for employment, and were subsequently forced to accept lowered wages due to the competition, discovered they had more in common culturally and religiously with the Protestant/capitalist governing classes than with the foreigners who displaced them in the mills, factories, and "bastard" workshops. Largely because of this manipulated and exploited division of the working class along ethnic, religious and racial lines, the native Anglo-American workers were disposed to believe the rhetoric of promoters that the common school system would give them an advantage over the new comers — who clearly did not share the culture or ideology of the schools, nor, in a growing number of cases, the language of instruction and laws of the land.

Kaestle's third assertion is his strongest, and most misleading. Indeed, it was precisely because of the development of capitalism, the devastating social crises it generated, and the class warfare that erupted in reaction to its modes of production and resulting social relations that the governing classes accepted the necessity of public education as a means of bolstering the middle class, and socializing the lower classes and immigrants. And too, Horace Mann's masterful manipulation of class, ethnic, religious, and racial divisions served to create consensus among the governing classes for the common school system.[235] Katz, as well, established that the economic competition between classes set in motion by the rapid expansion of industrial capitalism and influx of immigrants proved a powerful stimuli to the native Anglo-American middle class to become directly involved in promoting and establishing public schools, especially the utilitarian high schools.

Kaestle's assertions, however, jettison a critique of class divisions over the issue of the common schools, and along with this critique he rejects the argument that the common schools were constituted to serve some segments of the citizenry more than others. In other words, he rejects Katz's findings. Whatever Kaestle thinks of Katz's historical excavations and the conclusions reached as a consequence, his assertions grossly distort the history of the period. According to Seth Luther in 1832, such assertions are humbug!

> . . . We have shown how great a mass of human misery is hidden in England, under the glare of National wealth, and the splendor of National glory. You have visited the thick and crowded manufacturing town,

> 'Where avarice plucks the staff away,
> Whereon the weary lean,

And vice reels o'er the midnight bowl,
With song, and jest, obscene.'

To hide existing, or anticipated and *inevitable* evils, of the like kind, resulting from like causes, our ears are constantly filled with the cry of National wealth, *National* glory, *American System*, and American industry. We are told that operatives are happy in our mills, and that they want no change in the regulation, and that they are getting great wages, saving 25 per cent over and above their living. This stuff is retailed by owners, and agents, and sold wholesale at the rate of eight dollars for a day's work of four hours in the capital at Washington. This cry is kept up by men who are endeavouring by all the means in their power to put down the wages of *our own people*, and who send agents to *Europe*, to induce *foreigners* to come here, to underwork *American* citizens, to support *American* industry, and the *American* system.

The whole concern, (as now conducted) is as great a humbug as ever deceived any people. We see the system of manufacturing lauded to the skies; senators, representatives, owners, and agents of cotton mills using all means to keep out of sight the evils growing up under it. Cotton mills where cruelties are practised, excessive labour required, education neglected, and vice, as a matter of course, on the increase, are denominated 'the principalities of the destitute, the palaces of the poor.'[236]

Perhaps Seth Luther is one of those Kaestle has in mind when he writes this conclusion to the summary explication of his two arguments:

This ideology and various aspects of the reform program were opposed by independent-minded local-control advocates, many Southern slaveholders, members of non-English and non-Protestant groups who favored cultural distinctiveness and independent schooling, blacks who had been left out of the new common-school systems, and a smattering of full-fledged radicals who opposed the whole religious and economic underpinning of the predominant ideology. These groups did not make common cause with each other, did not have the same goals, and did not succeed in preventing the creation of state common-school systems. They did, however, achieve various concessions and adjustments, thus contributing to the shape and content of American common schooling as it existed by 1860.[237]

Except for the exceptions he identifies, Protestant/capitalist ideology was pervasive and entrenched among New Englanders. The essence of Kaestle's argument is the depth of belief in this ideology by New Englanders, regardless of class or sex, undergirded their social consensus and unity of purpose and action. The institutions they built emerged naturally out of their homogeneous social, cultural and ideological cohesion, and did so with little or no opposition. To the very limited extent disagreement was voiced, this disagreement was either idiosyncratic — in which case ignored by all — or it was a question of *how* a thing was to be done rather than a question about *what* was being done, and in this case compromise usually settled the dispute.

This, then, is the explicit argument of Kaestle's thesis. The implicit argument, as I have already stated, is the common school system was not rooted in class stratification and conflict. Or, to put it another way, the common school system was not an institution established by the governing classes to protect their economic and political privileges by means of a dominant, hegemonic ideology imposed on the lower classes through a deliberate program aimed at industrializing their minds and behavior. Proving this implicit argument depends on proving the explicit argument that governing classes and working class believed in the same ideology without a prior hegemonic program of domination, that both classes supported the same institutions, i.e. the common school system and republican government, and were generally of one mind about the development of capitalism and its emergent social relations.

Before I continue with my critique, however, I should point out that as manifest in this particular text the strength of Kaestle's interpretation of public education in the period between 1780 and 1860 is his sympathy with and explication of Protestant/capitalist ideology and the successful establishment of its social hegemony through the public school system. Much of the rhetorical persuasiveness of his explicit argument derives from its apparent truth — as constructed through the lens of late twentieth century capitalist society. Two aspects of Kaestle's argument, as a matter of fact, are true — the "leaders" were bound together by a common Protestant/capitalist ideology, and their social practices and policies were determined by their ideological beliefs. In the distribution of resources they possessed the most and, moreover, they held control of both the resources and their distribution. It was in their intimate interest, therefore, that the masses perceive and accept this state of social relations as natural and just. Secondly, it is true that a sort of consensus coalesced among Anglo-American New Englanders in the antebellum period. But, though true, it is a half-truth. As I explained above, the ideological consensus was not inherent among all classes of New Englanders, it had to be socially constructed. The stimuli undergirding its construction was twofold: First, the rising power and opposition of the working class led by radical autodidacts the likes of Thomas Skidmore and Seth Luther, and their followers, in the period before 1840. And secondly, the influx of immigrants in the period after 1840, who were often enticed to come by American manufacturers for the singular purpose of swelling the ranks of labor, thus creating competition for employment, thus making it possible to decrease wages, and, most important, thus breaking apart the growing power of the organized Working Men's Associations. Squeezed, therefore, between the capitalists on one side and competitive immigrant labor on the other, the displaced native New Englanders acted pragmatically to protect their status in the social order by taking over positions in skilled trades, management, marketing, shop keeping, clerking, public schools, and the growing corporate and government bureaucracies, etc. All of these positions were dependant on the prosperity of the capitalist elite, and, therefore, the native lower and middle classes found themselves obliged to protect their interests by linking up with the capitalists in the social regulation of the fast expanding immigrant working class.

These socioeconomic circumstances are precisely what is obscured by Kaestle's half-truth. The process of constructing hegemonic consensus began in the late 1700s, gained enormous momentum in the period between 1820 and 1840, and was more or less complete by 1860, or soon thereafter, when the urban populations and the laboring class in the North and many Western industrial and mining areas were predominately composed of immigrants.[238] To the extent native white New Englanders (a gradually shrinking proportion of the population) did share a consensus based on Protestant/capitalist ideology, such a consensus among the different social classes was not genetic, was not inherent, but was, instead, socially constructed and propagandized by the dominant class and its surrogates. The critical flaw of Kaestle's interpretation, therefore, is his overt argument that this process of imposing ideological hegemony occurred without vigorous opposition, and his implication that it was never intended to privilege one class or cultural group and subjugate others. The critically important and relevant question, then, is the integrity of his explanation of the object of study; and integrity in this instance must be determined not by assertions alone, but by established congruence between what he has claimed about the object of study and the object itself — in other words, congruence between his explanation and economic and political relations in American society.

When established congruence is actively looked for in the text, however, it soon becomes apparent that Kaestle's characterization and explanation of the process of capitalism's domination of society through the positions and practices of capitalists, through constructed and propagandized ideology, through socializing institutions, is based, however, like his opening assertions, on half-truths, distortions, and overt mystification. And his rebuttal of Katz, as will be seen, is ideological mystification rather than historical explanation.

According to Kaestle,

> There is much evidence to support the view that school discipline was intended to inculcate habits leading to future work discipline. However, there is also much evidence to suggest that work discipline was not the central purpose of school discipline and is not a sufficient explanation for it. [. . .] Local school committees and other writers on education placed more emphasis on the prevention of crime and on the training of intelligent and acquiescent citizens than they did on behavior in the workplace.[239]

This is fairly representative of Kaestle's rhetorical method. He acknowledges a class based critique of the common school system, and then proceeds to dismiss it or discredit its validity in the manner demonstrated here. This passage also typifies the epistemological and ontological problem raised by much historiography, and which makes the identification and explanation of historical specificities so damned difficult. There is evidence, Kaestle argues, for both explanations of the object of study, and the evidence for one explanation contradicts the evidence of the other's explanation. It is obvious which explanation

Kaestle thinks is the correct one, the ideologically coherent one, but by what criterion is congruence established?

We know, for example, that Horace Mann made both sorts of arguments because he, and other members of the governing classes, made no distinction between a laborer's civic behavior or his productive behavior. (And on their side, laborers tended to make no distinction between capitalism, and its oppressive relations of production, and the State, upon whose powers of law and violence capitalists depended for expansion, appropriation and protection. As often as not the capitalist was also a sitting member of government and the courts.) Mann believed a disciplined, cooperative, productive worker was also obedient and acquiescent, hence an intelligent citizen. Moral discipline and responsiveness to authority, he argued in his 1841 and 1848 Reports, would be a product of the children's inculcation through common school education. The governing classes' strident attack on the taverns and laborers' drinking habits may have had a moral component, but it was also an effort to eradicate older artisan cultural habits that were incompatible with new industrial modes of production, e.g. "blue Mondays," and the flask or two of beer during mid-day break. It is likely, too, that E.P. Thompson's identification of the tavern as the meeting place where disgruntled workers in England planned and organized their resistance against the manufacturers[240] was also true of workers in New England, New York, and Pennsylvania; thus there was likely a stronger political and anti-laboring class stimuli underlying the temperance movement than any altruistic concern the governing classes might have had for the "moral" and economic well-being of workers.[241] Kaestle's distinction between the two arguments is a falsely constructed one, and rather than correctly identify social relations and practices, he mystifies and obscures them through his emphasis of one explanation and his rejection of the other — without establishing congruence or its absence in either case.

There is, as identified in Chapter Three and the above critiques, ample historical evidence of actual court cases and legislative actions to establish that during this historical period to strike was a crime; to drink in public was a crime; to purchase liquor in quantities less than fifteen gallons was a crime; to refuse work for the wage determined by the manufacturer was a crime; to organize for higher wages was a crime; to be poor was a crime. For a long time no white male could vote who did not own property. For a much longer time women could not own property or vote. For an even longer time Black-Americans were barred or segregated from all educational, civic and economic institutions. And, too, "acquiescent" citizens were as likely to accept the status quo of capitalist social relations as they were to be "acquiescent" workers.

In short, Kaestle selectively explicates Protestant/capitalist ideology. Franklin Dexter put it bluntly: there are rulers and there are the ruled. This differentiation is consistent with capitalist society, there are owners and there are wage dependent workers, there are landlords and there are tenants, there are masters and servants or slaves. Public schools, as Kaestle himself points out, embodied this ideology. Thus, as a formative institution of capitalist society, why wouldn't the public school system endeavor to address and secure structurally unequal social positions as a fundamental social aim . . . for one reinforces the other as Horace Mann well understood?! My problem with Kaestle's argument, therefore, is his jettison of one objective of capitalist hegemony while emphasizing its correlative, and furthermore, using this emphasis to refute the existence and practice of hegemony. Moveover, let me be precise about what it means in this historical period to be an intelligent citizen: one acquiesces to the governing policies, positions and practices of the rulers. One is productive for the owner, one doesn't strike for shorter working hours or for higher wages, and one knows better than to vote for the likes of Andrew Jackson!

The corollary of moral intelligence in common school ideology is moral discipline. Kaestle says,

> Promptness and industry were urged as the route to success not just for the manual worker but for the businessman and manager as well. Work discipline was not aimed uniquely at laborers. However, in general it did not pay off for them. Despite the claims of manufactures that educated men rose to be foremen, and despite the hard-earned savings set aside by some factory laborers, workers' frugality and industry were also widely rewarded by subsistence wages and discrimination. Still, many school people and social reformers believed that discipline would lead to self-help as well as stability, that imposed discipline would benefit the individual as well as the society. Their sincerity in this belief is not contradicted by the fact that it was a naive and inhumane view of the matter.[242]

Kaestle asks his readers to believe that Horace Mann and Henry Barnard, as well as Edward Everett, James Carter, and others of their position, did truly believe in the state system of public school education as preparatory training for social, economic, and political advancement by working class and immigrant children. Moreover, Kaestle insists, the fact that there is no pattern of congruence between achievement ideology and the children's social experiences is no reason to doubt the governing classes' sincerity. Perhaps it would be best to let Mann correct the misrepresentation:

> The Capitalist and his agents are looking for the greatest amount of labor, or the largest income in money from their investments; and they do not promote a dunce to a station where he will destroy raw material, or slacken industry. . . . The obscurest and humblest person has an open and fair field for competition. That he proves himself capable of earning more money for his employer is a testimonial better than a diploma from all the colleges.[243]

Kaestle either does not understand the tensions inherent in the unequal distribution of resources and contested social relations of the historical period he purports to explain, or he asks his readers to believe what is untrue. Indeed, the period between 1830 and 1845 was a prolonged series of crippling social and economic crises. It begins before Jackson's attack on the Bank of the United States and Biddle's counter-attack of contracting credit. This contest resulted in wide-spread business failures, and, among those businesses which remained, a severe reduction in wages prompted a wave of protest strikes.[244] The crisis peaked in the panic of 1837 and lasted through 1845 — and Kaestle makes no significant connection between this period of economic and political crises and the corresponding energized promotion of State controlled public school education. It is also important to remember that the great wave of Irish Catholic immigration started about 1840, right in the middle of the worst of things.

According to Mann's explanation of achievement ideology as inculcated through a common school education, the worker's achievement is determined by the increase of his employer's wealth through his intelligent, disciplined, industrious productivity. The worker, made valuable to his employer through his intelligent industry, thus benefited by continued employment. Within the context of widespread economic crisis and unemployment, Mann's message seems from the perspective of the twentieth century extremely effective in gaining manufacturers' support for the common school system on one hand, and on the other staying or overwhelming labor's rejection of the common school system. The manufacturer was desperate to get the most productive benefit from his factory, materials, and workers during this period of economic distress; and workers were desperate for any edge they could get for themselves and their children to secure employment and fend off the expanding competition for dwindling jobs. And too, given the fact that his report was widely circulated throughout the United States and abroad,[245] Mann expected workers would read it or hear of it and understand the importance of a common school education in a highly competitive labor market. And, as I illustrated above in quoting Messerli's summary of Mann's account of his meeting with Dexter, Mann harbored no misunderstanding about what the common school system would contribute to capitalist society.[246] Kaestle's rhetorical trick then is presenting the Protestant/ capitalist ideology surrounding the common school system as authentic, universal consensus rather than a deliberate mystification integral to the process of establishing hegemony and social domination. It is nonsense, as Dexter reminded Mann, to even suggest that the governing classes would provide the laboring classes with the education and resources required to depose the ruler's position of power and privilege in society.

Kaestle's problem here is the result of trying to refute Katz's history of the common school system as preparatory training for workers, and the public high school as utilitarian training for middle level positions in the period's stratified social relations. To do so he must persuasively argue that social outcomes were unintentional, and the dominant ideology undergirding the creation of a state school system was not governed by nor reflected unequal economic and political classes, positions and practices. In other words, although the schools were a public institution of a capitalist society their purpose and social aims were not determined by capitalist relations of production or the social and industrial needs of the State.

As schools became more graded and students more classified, the informal, chaotic, individualized instructional world of eighteenth-century classrooms gradually gave way to a well-defined, lock-step curriculum. Schools thus became in some respects like factories, but not necessarily because they were mimicking factories, or preparing children to work in factories. Rather, both the workplace and the schools, as well as other nineteenth-century institutions, were partaking of the same ethos of efficiency, manipulation, and mastery.

The second reason for encouraging childhood discipline is that most parents wanted children to behave in a deferential and obedient manner.[247]

David Nasaw starts off his own history of American public education with a number of outraged observers' accounts of American parents who treated their children with indulgence and encouraged their self-expression — even their resistance and questioning of authority.[248] Such free and independent behavior was fine for the children of the governing classes, but Nasaw finds that this tolerance did not extend to the behavior of poor and immigrant children. Indeed, Nasaw's study of the period literature reveals that the public outcry for moral education, the training of virtue, the inculcation of discipline, etc. were euphemistic expressions for the governing classes' determination to dominate and control the culture, thinking and behavior of the lower classes.[249] Kaestle's argument, then, is reductionist and inventive . . . for the change in attitudes regarding behavior that he describes here has two distinct origins: first, it came about after the emergence of capitalism and its pronounced inequalities in the control and distribution of resources, and the resistance it encountered among the working class and immigrants; and secondly, it reflects the continuation of the Puritan/British legacy of Anglo-Saxon supremacy.

More to the point, however, his attempt in the quoted passage is to direct attention away from the argument that the common schools were preparatory training for work by arguing that the factories and the schools — as well as other nineteenth century institutions — shared the same "ethos of efficiency, manipulation, and mastery." This is, however, exactly Katz's point! Each is a capitalist institution . . . and the schools prepared students to graduate from one to the next.

Several pages later, Kaestle approaches the problem from a slightly different perspective. In this instance he wants to demonstrate that Protestant/capitalist ideology transcended class divisions and thus bound the governing classes and the lower classes in a common regard for capitalism and its social institutions, in particular the common schools:

> Francis Wayland, perhaps the most influential political economist of the antebellum period, said that private property was responsible for "all progress in civilization." Theodore Sedgwick, another leading theorist, reminded readers that Christianity forbade the destruction of property and said that the uninhibited pursuit of property "explains the unexampled prosperity, riches and happiness" of the North. The key proposition was "that the labourers here are permitted to work for their own benefit, to work for profit."
>
> Antebellum Americans held varying opinions about property and the resulting class structure, reflecting different ideological leanings and different economic realities of the antebellum North. The Whigs and their Republican successors saw a land of small proprietors and small landholders, a land still full of opportunity and mobility. Northern Democrats and more radical critics saw a growing industrial proletariat and a growing capitalist class, and they emphasized the antagonism between those with property and those without. Nonetheless, even radicals felt compelled to deny that they were assaulting the sanctity of property. "Our object is as remote from that as the existing system of extortion is from justice," wrote Stephen Simpson in his Workingmen's Manual. School texts reinforced the sanctity and virtues of property and the folly of common ownership or redistribution of wealth.
>
> In this pro-capitalist native Protestant ideology, the availability of property and education combined to produce a system of fair opportunity.[250]

It is his argument to dismiss criticism of capitalist modes of production and social relations and his evidence to substantiate the dismissal that concerns me here. Wayland and Sedgwick are clearly prominent members of the governing classes, so we might expect their pronouncements on political economy to defend the sanctity of private property and the processes of capital appropriation and accumulation. But the use of Simpson as a working class "radical" is disingenuous. Indeed, Kaestle flies in the face of much labor history of the period inasmuch as Simpson contradicts other radicals of the period such as

Skidmore and Luther. But Kaestle's use of Simpson begs the argument rather than proves it. The reader has no way of knowing this from Kaestle's text, however; for the truth of the matter it is necessary to look elsewhere.

Joseph Dorfman, economic historian of American political economy, reveals that like its New York counterpart after the coup which ousted Skidmore and the Committee of Fifty, membership in the Philadelphia Working Men's Party "could hardly be said to be composed of mere laborers."[251] In particular, Dorfman has Stephen Simpson in mind. Simpson has been recognized as the Party's intellectual leader, and his admirers called him the "American Cobbett." So far there is nothing that sounds a clashing note with Kaestle's clever construction of pro-capitalist labor radicals. It is not until we get to Simpson's social background, and to his social positions and practices that it becomes clear that we cannot depend on Simpson as radical democratic labor's spokesman or archetype.

Dorfman writes,

> Simpson's father, George Simpson, had held the important position of cashier of the Bank of North America, the first Bank of the United States, and Girard's bank. The son, too, seemed embarked on a promising banking career as note clerk for the second Bank of the United States shortly after its establishment, but his job did not last long, and he returned to his earlier and precarious profession of journalist, which was, of course, tied up with office-seeking.[252]

Simpson deliberately courted the Working Men's Party in his campaign for congressional office in 1830 as a self-proclaimed Jackson supporter (under whom he served in the Battle of New Orleans) on the Pennsylvania "Federal Republican" ticket. The Working Men's Party supported Simpson solely on the basis of his positive stand on their demands for free and equal universal education. However, according to Dorfman, Simpson's "'new theory of political economy' for the workingmen, which he issued shortly after his defeat, turned out to be National Republican." Simpson's book, *The Working Man's Manual: A New Theory of Political Economy* (1831), is not what its title suggests; indeed, his central argument supports Alexander Hamilton's economic programs, which were based on permanent class divisions. In spite of his running as a Jacksonite,

Simpson actively opposed Jackson's attack on the Bank of the United States and supported Jackson's bitter rival, the president of the Bank, Nicholas Biddle.

Simpson's stand against usury laws perhaps best reveals his truer relation to the Working Men's Party: "Since it is labor that is in reality borrowed, the owner has the right to obtain the highest price; and, if unshackled by law, competition will prevent extortion because idle capitalists, being dependent for subsistence and luxuries on the labor of the borrower, will lend on reasonable terms."[253] And, on the point of education, Simpson argued that

> . . .if the laborers have an education, they will be stimulated to acquisition, to excel in whatever brings applause; and above all they will acquire polished manners. The lack of good breeding has been the chief cause of their inability to rise, for it prevents them from associating with the wealthy. The contempt of the wealthy and educated is not for the occupation of the poor, but for their ignorance. This is evidenced by the fact that when a vigorous intellect bursts the bonds of ignorance in the contemned class, it is immediately merged into the higher and cultivated class, and soon obtains respect.[254]

In August 1831, Simpson started the *Pennsylvania Whig*, an organ supporting the national bank against Jackson. The organ lasted only until the eve of the 1832 election, but it lasted long enough for "Jackson to list as evidence of corruption of the press by the bank, the bank's twenty-six subscriptions to the paper."[255]

Simpson's final relation to laborers came in the form of a "Savings Fund" bank that he established in partnership with Dr. Thomas W. Dyott in 1836. They solicited savings from workers, and guaranteed that deposits were protected by real-estate security up to an amount of $500,000 total. Simpson and Dyott issued bank notes which depositors could then use for exchange. Soon, however, when holders of the notes discovered the bank could not or would not redeem them, the bank was revealed as a fraud. Both Simpson and Dyott were convicted, but only Dyott was sentenced to a term of three years in jail while Simpson went free.[256]

Simpson next begged a job from his good friend and supporter of Jackson, Senator James Buchanan. He got the job, and "as Buchanan grew more powerful, Simpson's fortunes prospered."[257]

My point, then, is Kaestle's use of Simpson, obviously a middle class opportunistic capitalist, as the defining spokesman for the workers' position on capitalist property relations and property ideology leads to skewed conclusions and a highly distorted history of the period. Kaestle's interest seems to be the construction of an argument which erases the ideological and cultural antagonisms between labor and capital. By looking at Simpson's positions in relation to the Bank(s) and to political office, however, we have a clearer understanding of his true relation to labor, and the fact that he was not labor's spokesman. That he became so is due to the writing of historians seeking to ideologically mystify the vigorous class struggle and the vast social and material inequities that typified the reality of America's transformation under industrial capitalism.

Early in this critique I characterized Kaestle's history of the common school system as a masterful mix of exemplary scholarship and ideological mystification. The preceding deconstruction of his use of Simpson as representative of radical labor's beliefs demonstrated his practice of the latter, the following lengthy passage, however, reflects both characteristics:

> Several qualifications should be noted with regard to educators' pronouncements about equality of opportunity. First, and most important, the fair chance was open mainly to white native males. Even the most ringing statements about the equality of all men were not taken to include women or black people, and non-English immigrants faced various forms of discrimination. Samuel Goodrich, author of the popular Peter Parley stories, explained equality this way in a civics textbook: "Equality does not mean that a woman shall be equal to a man, but that all women, all children, all citizens, shall enjoy the same relative rights, privileges and immunities." Second, even for white males, occupational mobility through education was neither a central theme nor a central purpose of the antebellum public school reform movement. The overriding emphasis for all schoolchildren, and especially for children of the poor and the working class, was on morality, not mobility. Finally, educators frequently lapsed into an explicit expectation that most children would inherit their parents' station in life. *The Progressive Reader* (1834) counselled children that "everything ought to suit the

station in which we live, or are likely to live. . . . Make yourself contented and cheerful in your station, which you see is so much happier than that of many children." A Michigan education report of the 1840s lauded America's lack of hereditary privilege and abundance of opportunity but on the same page advised parents to educate children "in a manner suitable to their station and calling."

The theorists' rosy view of the American political economy found its support in English laissez-faire writings, in the democratic politics of antebellum America, and in the generally rising productivity of American industry and agriculture in the antebellum period. It was, however, a view of prosperity and opportunity that increasingly forced one to wear blinders in the 1840s and 1850s. Opportunity for advancement was almost nonexistent for blacks, almost irrelevant for women, and beyond the reach of many in an increasingly immigrant, urban work force. Although the American political economists created a description that was partial and quickly became dated, they provided many of the homilies of native Protestant ideology. And while its proponents were committed to the status quo of capitalism as they understood it, it was a status quo that they believed was freer and fairer than any the world had yet known.[258]

I may be overlooking something, but it seems to me that Kaestle has described a social reality of class stratification, ruling class domination, unequal social relations, unequal distribution of resources, and the governing classes' practice of ideological indoctrination of middle and lower class white male children through school inculcation and textbooks. Moreover, and most surprising to me, Kaestle concedes that the linkage between achievement ideology and real social mobility was nonexistent for the mass of the population. What he has not done, however, is indicate that this mass of subjugated population in any way rejected or resisted Protestant/capitalist ideology and the unequal social relations it supported. So, in spite of their rather obvious exploitation and oppression, the mass of the poor and working class population perceives no connection between their state of being, its cause, or the governing classes' practice of mystification. This implicit argument is consistent with his explicit argument. Kaestle thus identifies real structures of social stratification and subjugation, something of the process of imposing ideological hegemony over the lower classes, *and* he simultaneously avoids identification of class consciousness and overt class struggle against domination.

Kaestle does, however, eventually merge his implicit and explicit arguments:

> *In America, there was virtually no overt working-class resistance to middle-class reformers' proposals for state-sponsored schooling.* Working-class and middle-class educators shared the goals of morality, respectability, and self-improvement. Even if the concepts meant *somewhat* different things in the different class structures, many parents of both classes saw free common schools as desirable instruments of moral education. These shared commitments, sometimes reinforced by religious and ethnic identities that crossed class lines, produced an alliance in the 1820s and 1830s between American working-men's groups and middle-class reformers in favor of tax-supported common schooling. Because the workingmen's political parties were dominated by upper-status craftsmen and included merchants and professionals, there is even less reason to expect in their statements alienation from middle-class educational institutions and values.[emphasis added][259]

Contrary to what Kaestle argues here, it is a commonly known fact that while the Irish and German Catholic working classes lacked the political and economic resources to either halt or transform the common school system, many of them together with the Catholic church developed a parallel school system; or, in accommodation to some German groups, separate, publicly supported German language schools were established. In addition, as pointed out in my critique of Cubberley, there was protracted resistance by rural and small towns engaged in protecting their district schools against the State system. Clearly, then, the antebellum period was not characterized by widespread consensus as Kaestle states, but rather was deeply divided by class, cultural, ethnic, racial and religious conflicts. Clearly, too, there was working class opposition to the common school system. Consensus, therefore, existed only among certain groups, and the common school system, as a Protestant/Capitalist 'State' system, enjoyed no more acceptance or harmony from the working class than did the unequal production and economic relations of the factories or mills or tenant farms.

In short, Kaestle has much to say about the dominant ideology of the ante-bellum period, and of that of the promoters among the governing classes in particular, but his critique is limited by its ideological bias. Kaestle's explanation obscures the social reality of a common school system which was exploited by the Anglo-American Protestant elite and middle class and hegemonically imposed on the poor, working class, and immigrants. The common school system in the antebellum period was meant to secure, preserve and reproduce an inequitable social order. It was conceived and administered to be an institution of social inculcation, and never intended to provide the lower social classes with the knowledge or resources necessary to transform the material conditions of their lives let alone capitalist society's unequal economic, political, and cultural relations. And the emphasis on "morality" is clearly a euphemism for the protection of property, authority, and law and order.

And finally, by neglecting the specifics of working class life, e.g. the judiciary's protection of employer collectives and punishment of worker collectives, Kaestle is able to avoid a fuller critique of the different meaning "equal and general education" and "universal education" had for working people than the meaning such phrases had for the governing classes. Thus his reductionist "somewhat" to describe class differences over both the *how* and the *what* of public education can best be understood as serving a political agenda but not the identification and explanation of historical particulars.

The effect of reductionist tendencies throughout Kaestle's writing is the suppression of knowledge about (and the critical significance of) divergent and incommensurate ideologies rooted in unequal material relations, political rights, and contested social positions. Without such knowledge about the particulars of social history being made explicit we have only Kaestle's claims to go on. Kaestle's claims, however, cannot and do not explain if the largely absent children of working class families stayed away from the common schools and high schools for the same or similar reasons they avoided the earlier generation of charity schools; or if their absence from common schools might be caused (as Seth Luther and others showed) by socially generated poverty, by need driven conscription into factories (or as laborers in other sectors of the economy), and by harsh conditions and systemic exploitation — conditions and practices which were protected and enforced by the American system of law. These are two possible explanations for the general tendency of children from certain classes to be found working instead of learning in school, but the point is Kaestle's argument for common ideology and consensus on educational objectives cannot explain the empirical records available to us. Kaestle's claims have the appearance of knowledge, but this is because they are consistent with both the dominant ideology and the overwhelming speed with which the governing classes constructed and imposed the common school system and made the tax supported public school system an accomplished fact. That this happened is undeniable, but it is less proof of consensus ideology and common understanding than it is proof of cohesive dominant class interests and their domination of social resources; for excepting the expensive elite academies and the emerging Catholic schools, the working class had no viable public, secular or affordable alternative schooling for their children. In other words, by focusing on the emergent movement to establish common schools through the lens of dominant ideology it only *appears* that the working class and the governing classes shared the same ideology regarding the common school system.

Kaestle does not go this deep in his historical excavation and explanation, however, and so it is no surprise when he dismisses Katz's critique of the 1860 working class vote against the high school in Beverly, Massachusetts:

> A vote against public secondary schooling is, of course, not necessarily an indicator of working-class attitudes toward common elementary schooling, but it does indicate dissent against one particular reform at this point in Beverly's history. In a separate analysis of the same information, however, Maris Vinovskis has demonstrated that while the negative vote correlates with occupational and wealth status, the best predictor of how one voted on the Beverly high school issue was the voter's neighborhood. It appears that the Beverly vote depended to a great extent upon the fact that voters in outlying districts opposed the maintenance of this town-wide institution.[260]

Just as I thought Horace Mann could best rebut Kaestle's suggestion that the early promoters of achievement ideology did not know what they were about, Michael Katz's reply to Kaestle's (and Vinovskis') attack is illuminating:

The problem, as in the book he coauthored with Kaestle, is that despite his attention to the history of town politics, Vinovskis' account floats in a curious contextual vacuum. For it devotes little attention to the social and economic history of the town, and without a social and economic context, he is unable to explain his major findings in a coherent way, let alone reduce the influence of social class in antebellum American history.[261]

But to the central point of the argument:

Despite his multiple classification analysis, no one can deny that over 70 percent of voting farmers, mariners, and shoemakers and all the voting laborers (not broken out into a separate category by Vinovskis) cast their votes against the high school. Vinovskis attempts to mute the influence of working-class opposition to the high school by arguing that not all mariners, shoemakers, artisans, and farmers opposed it. However, most analysts consider a 70 or 80 percent vote by a group reasonable evidence of the attitude of its members.[262]

Katz meets Kaestle and Vinovskis on their own terms, and exposes their failure to adequately identify and establish economic and political relations that might have corrected his explanation. There is no argument, however, which can legitimate Kaestle's recognition of the unequal distribution of resources in the Beverly community and then arbitrarily ignore these social relations in order to argue that the vote against the high school was merely a matter of rural people against city people. And, even if the conflict could be so narrowed, Kastle's contentions still do not account for the conflict of economic and political interests between rural and urban communities which tend to support Katz in any case. Kaestle's argument is, in the best possible light, yet another attempt on his part to suppress knowledge of class opposition to the common school system. The darker interpretation of his argument is that Kaestle's text is capitalist propaganda meant to recast the old ideological myths which have served to obscure the intimate congruences between economic and political relations in American society and the common school system, and, by extension, American public education generally.

Finally, it is Kaestle himself who reveals what he spent so much effort to conceal:

> On the one hand, issues of control, centralization, and bureaucratization had an independent importance. On the other hand—and equally important—those who favored the centralized solutions were more often insiders, who had more power, while the groups who dissented were characteristically the outsiders. [. . .] The diversity of the opponents and their independent orientation spelled their defeat in the long run.[263]

So! There was opposition to the common school system among the non-governing class! Weak because diverse, fragmented, and localized, and thus more or less easily defeated by the steam-roller organization and domination of economic and political resources by the governing classes. But this rhetorical admission, necessitated by proper form, and soon dismissed by Kaestle, still stands in contradiction to his central claim that there was "virtually no overt working-class resistance." Clearly there was resistance, but like wage strikes and insurgent radical democratic movements throughout the nineteenth century, it was crushed. This little admission by Kaestle points to a radically different history of the period than that which he has constructed. Had Kaestle any real commitment to identifying and explaining the historical processes of the social imposition of Protestant/capitalist ideological hegemony in the nineteenth century, he might have seriously engaged and quoted Thomas Skidmore and Seth Luther, both self-educated working men, instead of Simpson — who was neither born into nor belonged to the working class. Or, and this is critical, were Kaestle really intent on identifying and explaining Protestant/capitalist ideology within the context of social relations and the conflict between democratic ideology and republican ideology he would have written a very different book which would have contributed greatly to our knowledge of class oppositions in society and the institutional and social function of public education.

ENDNOTES

¹   Ellwood Cubberley, *Public Education In The United States*, 2d ed. (Boston: Houghton Mifflin, 1934).
Lawrence Cremin, in his characterization of Cubberley's text, writes:

> When *Public Education in the United States* finally appeared — it was apparently in the making for at least two decades — it was an immediate success. Charles Judd of the University of Chicago called it "the first book which can in any proper sense be described as a history of American Schools," while Frank Herbert Palmer of *Education* pronounced it "a treasure house of inspiration and information." The book quickly captured the field . . . and it remains in use today as a textbook in educational history courses across the country.

Lawrence Cremin, *The Wonderful World of Ellwood Patterson Cubberley: An Essay on the Historiography of American Education* (New York: Bureau of Publications/ Teachers College, Columbia University, 1965), 4-5.

²   See: H. Warren Button and Eugene F. Provenzo, Jr., *History of Education & Culture in America* (Englewood Cliffs, NJ: Prentice-Hall, 1989), xiv, 227, 234; Joel Spring, *The American School: 1642-1993*, 3d ed. (New York: McGraw-Hill, 1994), 6, 45, 86-87, passim; Wayne Urban and Jennings Wagoner, Jr., *American Education: A History* (New York: McGraw-Hill, 1996), 14n, 203; Maris A. Vinovskis, *Education, Society, and Economic Opportunity* (New Haven: Yale University Press, 1995), 184.

³   Cremin, Wonderful, 5.

⁴   Bernard Bailyn, *Education in the Forming of American Society* (Chapel Hill: University of North Carolina Press, 1960; reprint New York: Norton, 1972), 12 (page references are to the reprint edition).

⁵   Cremin, *Wonderful*, 2.

⁶   Bailyn, 12.

⁷   Cremin, *Wonderful*, 2.

⁸   Cubberley emphasizes the singular importance of: Thorndike, Judd, Strayer, Terman, Flexner, Bobbitt, Freeman, Russell, Ayres. He quotes Harold Rugg's list, which adds Cubberley, Whippple and Gray to the leadership of new science movement. Among the nine educational histories published in the twentieth century which he identifies, four are his own, two are by F.P. Graves, and one is by his mentor at Teacher's College, Paul Monroe.

Cubberley also makes use of others outside the establishment circle, such as John Dewey. Cubberley transforms Dewey into a staunch supporter of Industrial education and stratified schools with differentiated curricula for different groups of children. If, however, one turns to the companion text, *Readings In Public Education* (Boston: Houghton Mifflin, 1934), and reads number 263, p.408-09, where Dewey is quoted at length, Dewey is not advocating Industrial education, but the education of children of the industrial working class, the largest class in society "upon whom the whole world depends for the supply of necessities. . . ." Dewey advocates an education ". . . that will as well give them enough control over their material environment to enable them to be economically independent." This is not one of Dewey's ideas which Cubberley entertains in his explanation of Dewey or public education.

Finally, there are few women educational leaders in Cubberley's history. He significantly ignores Ella Flagg Young, Superintendent of Chicago's public school system at the turn of the century, the first woman superintendent of schools in the country, and who, together with Margaret Haley, led a strong opposition movement against Cubberley and company, and their industrial friends. Cubberley has erased from his history Young and the unionized Chicago female teachers, and with them he has erased their determined resistance to centralized bureaucratic administration and their legal battles against no-tax corporations. He limits his comments to two brief remarks about Chicago schools before the Civil War, and he then writes as if Chicago vanished from the face of the earth — except for a passage valorizing Judd at the University of Chicago. (Cubberley, *Public Education*, 545n, 692n. 695, passim.)

[9]   See Bailyn for an excellent survey of the field.

[10]   Cubberley, *Public Education*, 619-631, passim.

[11]   Cubberley, v.

[12]   Cubberley, v, 692.

[13]   See, for example, Cubberley, 443: a substantial middle class is necessary to the establishment of a public school system; p. 483: formation of public school education was a nativist and class reaction to illiterate and poor Irish, German radicals, etc.; p. 495: upward social mobility is made possible by economic not educational means; p. 498: nineteenth century public school education was disciplinary for the purpose of inculcated docility; p. 502: public school education is determined by the nation's needs, not those of individuals; p. 504: nineteenth century public schools, especially the high schools, were for the well-to-do, and neglected the poor, immigrants, Blacks, and working class; and so on. Cubberley's argument at the end is new organization, new measures, new curricular programs are all necessary because of the exclusive and undemocratic character of the nineteenth century system of public school education.

[14]   Cubberley, 504, 516, 549, 556-57, passim.

[15]   Cubberley, 712.

[16]   Cubberley, 236-37, passim.

[17]   Cubberley, 480-560, 591, 732, passim.

[18]   Cubberley, 273.

[19]   Cubberley, 754.

[20]   "With the abolition of the rate-bill, which by 1860 had been done everywhere by the cities . . . this educational ladder [k through college] was finally open to all American children as their educational birthright. *The two requisites for the climb were money enough to obtain freedom from work in order to attend, and brains and perseverance enough to retain a place in the classes.*" [emphasis added] Cubberley, 273.

[21]   Cubberley, 760-61, 763, passim.

[22]   Cubberley, "CHAPTER XXIII," 750.

[23]   Cubberley has two standards regarding "democracy": when people are direct participants in self-government and self-determination, democracy is inefficient and chaotic and lends itself to corruption; on the other hand, under the modern system of centralized bureaucratic administration controlled by an appointed professional expert possessing appropriate authority, the inclusive school system, high school or factory is efficiently democratic. Clearly, both of Cubberley's standards are a perversion, the first by interpretation and the second by misrepresentation.
     Cubberley embraced Taylor's "scientific" efficiency model of industrial management, social order, economic and political relations and production. And, too, for Cubberley, like Taylor, workers had to be evaluated and differentiated in order to properly fit the required task, and workers had to willingly embrace their position and the task.

[24]   Cubberley, 202-03, passim. "Rate-bills" were a form of tuition charged by district schools to parents of school children. This tuition was primarily for the material support of the school and the school teacher. See: David Nasaw, 30, passim.

[25]   Cubberley, 219-221, 313-323, 732.

[26]   Cubberley, 230-40, passim. One does not have to read too carefully, however, to see that contradicting his "secularization" section title and his claims is Cubberley's elaboration of an established non-sectarian Protestant system of public instruction.

[27]   Cubberley, 273, 314, passim.

[28]   See, for example, Cubberley's commentaries on Pestalozzi, Froebel, the infant school, child labor laws, etc.

[29]   "The vocational high school is the most effective agency so far devised for the training of that 70 per cent of all our children who cannot or will not continue in the regular courses of the high school, and who have, at the rate of a million a year, been entering industries for which they have been but ill-fitted and in which they could have little hope of advancement or success." Cubberley, 647-648.
     See, too, his commentaries on Black-Americans (chp. XII), and on Eastern and Southern European immigrants, (chp. XIV).

30   Cubberley writes: "The people seldom have an opportunity to vote for a really good man for the office, as the best men usually cannot be induced to become candidates. [. . .]"

"In both county and state the demand today is for intelligent professional leadership . . . that the children in [the schools] may receive a better-directed education than they are now receiving. The important steps in the process of securing these results consist in . . . the reorganization and redirection of rural and village as well as city educational procedure; the abolition of the outgrown district system for a larger administrative unit; the elimination of politics and popular election in the selection of experts; and the concentration of larger authority in the hands of those whose business it is to guard the rights and advance the educational welfare of our children." (Cubberley, 731, 733.)

The tag-ending is an emotional appeal to distract from the non-democratic program he has just outlined.

Throughout these passages, however, Cubberley is studiously silent about the strenuous opposition of citizens and public school teachers to centralized bureaucratic administrative author-ity. (See, for example, Margaret Haley, *Battleground,* ed. Robert Reid (Urbana: University of Illinois Press, 1982).) And, too, he had nothing to say earlier in his commentary on the colonial period regarding the 1760 struggle by aristocrats and Tory merchant elite to capture control of Boston town government and to exclude the artisans and journeymen from direct participation. (See: Gary B. Nash, 23-27.) The idea of a supremely endowed, intelligent elite leadership is obviously not new to Cubberley.

For a persuasive challenge to Cubberley's interpretation of the district schools see: Hal S. Barron, "Teach No More His Neighbor: Localism and Rural Opposition to Educational Reform," *Mixed Harvest: The Second Great Transformation in the Rural North 1870-1930* (Chapel Hill: University of North Carolina Press, 1997) 43-77.

Barron illuminates the protracted ideological and political battle of rural people against the machinations of the capitalist governing classes and the promoters and bureaucrats of the central-ized, consolidated state educational system. According to Barron, rural Americans opposed — over a period of several generations — movements forced upon them from above and outside their communities to impose bureaucratic, centralized, impersonal, nonelective, and determining authoritarianism over their lives and their children. And, remarkably, rural opposition held its own — Barron reports — until after the Second World War — e.g., in Indiana until 1959. The locally administered district school remained a democratic fixture of the rural countryside well into the twentieth century, and gave way to consolidation and centralization of authority only after state and the Federal government largely equalized the tax burden between farmer and town/city dweller, heavily subsidized the cost of transportation, and, significantly, only after capitalist economic and political relations had become thoroughly insinuated into the culture and customs of rural America (which paralleled the depopulation of the farming country.)

31   Cubberley, 313, passim.

32   Except for selectively quoting dominant members of the economic and political elite on the need for a state system of public school education, and, except for casting several of these gentlemen in roles of humanitarian civic and educational leadership, Cubberley has little to say about the positions or occupants located at the pinnacle of what he describes as the social pyramid.

33   Cubberley, 64, 92, 106n, passim.

34   Cubberley, 222; see especially, 732.

³⁵   Cubberley, 233, 362.

³⁶   Cubberley, 228n, 229.

³⁷   Cubberley, 472.

³⁸   Where it serves his purpose, or does not obviously undermine it, Cubberley does include information which can be useful — such as the dates on which different state legislatures enacted laws establishing a state system of publicly funded schools, or when a state office of school superintendence was established. He occasionally also provides interesting details about particular individuals, such as DeWitt Clinton's petition to Emma Willard that she relocate her female seminary to New York State, and a cursory treatment of the financial arrangements which made this possible. In a different but related context Cubberley also reports that rather than establish an early system of normal schools, the New York legislature voted in 1827 to continue financial support of academies, of which Willard's was one, for the training of school teachers. See: Cubberley, 252n, 376.

³⁹   Cubberley, 527, passim. See: Frederick Winslow Taylor, *The Principles of Scientific Management*, reprint ed. (New York: W. W. Norton, 1967).

⁴⁰   See for example, Cubberley, 75: "We note again the rise of a distinctly American educational consciousness and the development of distinctly American schools once more begins." Cubberley repeats his homespun "all-American" claim frequently.
    What he actually identifies and establishes, however, is the institutional organization, teacher training, pedagogy, grade differentiation, and social aims of public school education all have their origin in Europe, particularly England in the early decades of American nationhood, and, by the 1820s, Prussia. See p.275n, for example, where Cubberley cites three city schools, each established on a different European model — Scottish, German, and English. The major influences on the development of American public education which he identifies are Lancaster, Cousin, Pestalozzi, Fellenberg, Froebel, Herbart, and Spencer. None of these men are American.
    Nineteenth-century American educational promoters — James G. Carter, Horace Mann, Henry Barnard, Calvin Stowe, John Pierce, Rev. Charles Brooks, Dr. Benjamin F. Smith, Henry E. Dwight, Wm. Russell — are distinguished within Cubberley's text for having popularized and adapted the Prussian (or German) system of social control and nationalism through public instruction to American circumstances. And, too, Cubberley consistently shows this system was (and is) the alternative preferred by humanitarian public men and educational leaders to the district school.
    Cubberley is disingenuous about these things. On page 273, figure 68, he renders the American democratic educational ladder, and on page 352, figure 99, he renders the "German State School systems Before 1914." Beneath the latter he has written: "Compare with Fig. 68 . . . and note the difference between a European two-class school system and the American democratic educational ladder." Cubberley's claims are consistent with his pictures, but not with his text. The "all-American" claims collapse under the weight of Cubberley's own text: first, American educational leaders are shown adapting the Prussian system and ideas to American circumstances; secondly, the claim of a democratic educational ladder is misleading because he deliberately ignores the elite private school system; and, thirdly, the two class system of the German system which he criticizes here is hardly distinguishable from the reorganized American state system of public school education he later promotes, rationalizes and justifies. The only schools after the colonial period which appear

to have a claim to being homespun American institutions are the district schools, but these have been repudiated by every educational leader (including himself) identified by Cubberley in his text.

41   Cubberley, 351.

42   Cubberley, 351.

43   Cubberley, 363. This is only one instance of Cubberley's sloppy scholarship. If Fellenberg's system was introduced in 1829, how does it come to serve as the basis for established schools before this date? If Cubberley knows, he does not tell.

44   Cubberley, 351.

45   Cubberley, 568-69, 702.

46   See: Sean Wilentz, *Chants Democratic*, 177-79. The notion of secluded or residential inculcation and socialization of children of the poor and working class apparently had considerable currency among both elite and middle class reformers and conservatives alike. Such sentiments can be found in the 1809 pronouncements of DeWitt Clinton on the Lancasterian schools, and were again expressed nearly three decades later by Henry Barnard:
> No one at all familiar with the deficient household arrangements and deranged machinery of domestic life, of the extreme poor and ignorant, to say nothing of the intemperate — of the examples of rude manners, impure and profane language and all the vicious habits of low-bred idleness, which abound in certain sections of all populous districts — can doubt that it is better for children to be removed as early and as long as possible from such scenes and such examples and placed in an infant or primary school.

From Barnard's *Sixth Annual Report*, quoted in David Nasaw, 35.

47   Cubberley, 365.

48   Cubberley will return to methods and schools for disciplining behavior later in his narrative (pp. 564-68), where he explains the institutional means adopted to insure the ideological and cultural purity of white children from middle-class and professional families against the bad influence of other classes of children. But he does not connect these twentieth century enlightened institutional measures to Fellenberg or the nineteenth century reform school movement. See especially: Cubberley, 567.

49   Cubberley, 517-21, 647-48, passim.

50   See: Cubberley, 148-50. Cubberley posits a coexistence of manufacturing, different classes, poverty, and increasing promotion of public school education. But the context of economic and political relations remains obscured behind vague generalizations.

Interestingly, Cubberley takes from each of his sources here the argument that socio-economic circumstances, social crisis, and human suffering are the product of ignorance arising from lack of education. *And*, the explicit charge that these conditions are largely the fault of the immigrants themselves. Clearly, then, public school education is the remedy. In addition, Cubberley advances the explanatory theory of breakdown: "The powerful restraining influences of the old home, with its strict moral code and religious atmosphere, seriously weakened."

The critical question that arises is: does relocation lead to cultural transformation of the family and individual? The answer herein is yes. At the same time, however, the eroding influence is said to be the city itself. This latter conception is clearly inconsistent with the conception of individual improvement. For if influences are embedded in the structural organization of urban and industrial society, they are not manifestations of individual choice. The rationale of individual improvement is, however, that it will lead to the improvement of society. But this begs such questions as: who determines the conditions and hours of labor, and wages, and who is responsible for building the "ugly tenements"? Why did families abandon their farms and lives in the country, or homeland, in exchange for wage-labor in the factories? In other words, did immigrants in the cities and factory towns create their own misery, or did they encounter and confront miserable conditions?

[51]   See: James D. Anderson, passim.

[52]   See: David Wallace Adams, *Education for Extinction: American Indians and the Boarding School Experience, 1875-1928* (Lawrence, KS: University Press of Kansas, l995).

[53]   Anderson, 36, 39, 44-45.

[54]   Cubberley, 744-45.

[55]   Equating Tuskegee with Hampton is problematic: although Washington promoted in public an enterprise at Tuskegee consistent with the subjugating program at Hampton, there are some indications that he may have been engaged in a radically different kind of education for Blacks. See, for example: W.E.B. DuBois, "The Talented Tenth," *The Negro Problem*, unidentified editor (New York: James Pott & Co., 1903; rpt. New York: Arno Press, 1969), 31-75; Kenneth James King, *Pan-Africanism And Education* (Oxford, U.K.: Clarendon Press, 1971).

[56]   See: Anderson, passim; Thomas Holt, "'Knowledge is Power': The Black Struggle for Literacy," in *The Right To Literacy*, eds. Andrea Lunsford, Helene Moglen, and James Slevin (New York: MLA, 1990), 91-102.

[57]   Cubberley, 464.

[58]   Cubberley, 462-469.

[59]   Cubberley, 439.

[60]   Ellwood P. Cubberley, *Readings In Public Education In The United States: A collection of Sources and Readings to Illustrate the History of Educational Practice and Progress in the United States* (Boston: Houghton Mifflin Co., 1934).

[61]   See Cubberley's acknowledgement on page 745, *Public Education*, that without federal expenditures and intervention such education as is available to Black-Americans benefits them little.

[62]   See: Anderson, 43, passim.

[63]   Anderson, 34-78.

[64]   See: James D. Anderson, "Secondary School History Textbooks and the Treatment of Black History," in *The State of Afro-American History, Past, Present and Future*, ed. Darlene Clark Hine (Baton Rouge, LA: Louisiana State University Press, 1986), 253-274.

[65]   Cubberley, *Public Education*, 666.

[66]   Cubberley, 667.

[67]   Cubberley, 667n.

[68]   Anderson, *The Education of Blacks In The South*, 1860-1935, 37, 48-49.

[69]   Cubberley, 668.

[70]   Cubberley, 431-432, 434-35, 591-92, 684-85.

[71]   Cubberley, 565-66, 647-48, passim.

[72]   Cubberley, 545, 545n.

[73]   Cubberley, 545, 692.

[74]   Cubberley's attitude toward and treatment of teachers in *Public Education* is inconsistent. He is certainly more generous with recognition and praise toward men (the Boston Masters excepted). When school teachers oppose the introduction of manual-labor subjects, Cubberley condemns them as narrow minded conservatives. But when teachers oppose the academic curriculum of the Committee of Ten, they are good counsel ignored. See: Cubberley, 505, 543, passim.

[75]   Cubberley has another use for Pestalozzi as well, which is to obscure the Prussian system of social control through public instruction behind Pestalozzi's dedication to children and his efforts to prepare them for the task of transforming society. In short, Cubberley uses what he describes as Pestalozzi's love and care for children to also describe the Prussian system.

[76]   Cubberley, 450.

[77]   Cubberley, 451.

[78]   Cubberley, 450.

[79]   Cubberley frequently equates "State" and "society," as in:

> . . . as our social and industrial life has become more extended, and as production has come to be more specialized and the possibility of change from one vocation to another more limited, we have come to see that both the nature and the extent of the education offered young people in preparation for life must both change and increase.
>
> [. . .] legislation has been enacted in the *interests of the State*, as well as in the interests of the child. [emphasis added] (Cubberley, 574.)

Cubberley uses similar constructions with regularity: "social and industrial life," "social and industrial whole," "social and industrial efficiency," "our social and industrial world," etc. His conflation and/or interchangeable use of "State" and "society" is not an understanding of society shared by me. Indeed, the State is not an autonomous entity. The role of the State in capitalist society has a tendency to be dominated by capitalist class fractions, thus when I talk about the role of the State I'm simply highlighting the role of the capitalist class through the mediation of the State. However, and importantly, I have synthesized the variations in form used by Cubberley to "the social and industrial needs of the State" as a means of clarifying and criticizing his argument and the socioeconomic and political aims of his policy proposals for the reorganization of public school education. See: Cubberley, 574-75, 689, 718, 734-35, 737, 750; and, Cubberley, *Changing Conceptions of Education*, (Boston: Houghton Mifflin Co., 1909), 20, passim.

[80]   Cubberley, *Public Education*, 451.

[81]   Cubberley, 504, 516, 549, 556-57, 591-92, 648n:1, 759-763, passim.

[82]   "Our city schools will soon be forced to give up the exceedingly democratic idea that all are equal, and that our society is devoid of classes . . . and to begin a specialization of education effort along many new lines in an attempt better to adapt the school to the needs of these many classes in the city life."

"The evils and shortcomings of democracy are many and call loudly for remedies and improvement." Cubberley, *Changing Conceptions of Education*, 56-57, 64.

[83]   For biological determinism and the argument that the public schools cannot create intelligence, see: Cubberley, *Public Education*, 700-02. For incapability of learning from books, see: ibid., 565-65.

[84]   See: Cubberley, "Editor's Introduction," *The Intelligence of School Children*, by Lewis M. Terman, ed. Ellwood P. Cubberley (Boston: Houghton Mifflin, 1919) ix-x. See: Terman, *Intelligence*, 55-56, 99, 111-34.

[85]   See: Cubberley, *The Principal and His School* (Boston: Houghton Mifflin, 1923), 508-09.

When Terman's IQ studies of immigrant children and his "scientific" findings are compared with Cubberley's text here, it is clear that vocational education prepares these low IQ groups for productive and useful lives as unskilled and semi-skilled laborers. One of the worst faults of the public school before the advent of science and efficient administration, according to Cubberley, was its tendency to inspire aspirations among certain groups of youths for positions of ownership, and of responsibility and/or decision making for which their IQs are clearly inadequate. Society could be spared much tumult, in other words, if Eastern or Southern European immigrant children or Black-American children were properly trained for occupations suited to their limited intelligence and thereby prevent frustration, resentment, and hostility.

[86]   Cubberley, *Public Education*, 565-66, 728, passim.

[87]   Cubberley, 451.

88   Ibid. Cubberley is also looking ahead to his explication of Spencer. Compare ". . . the right kind of knowledge, properly interpreted to the pupil so that clear ideas as to relationships might be formed," (p. 451) to: "help in the rearing and disciplining of offspring," and "maintaining one's political and social relations" (p. 470).

89   "Now, surely, nothing but Universal Education can counter-work this tendency to the domination of capital and the servility of labor. If one class possesses all the wealth and the education, while the residue of society is ignorant and poor . . . the latter, in fact and in truth, will be the servile dependents and subjects of the former. But if education be equably diffused, it will draw property after it, by the strongest of all attractions; for such a thing never did happen, and never can happen, as that an intelligent and practical body of men should be permanently poor. *Property and labor, in different classes, are essentially antagonistic; but property and labor, in the same class, are essentially fraternal.*" [emphasis added] Mann/Cremin, 84-87.

90   Cubberley, 452.

91   Cubberley, 452.
      See, too, Cubberley's use of John Dewey in this regard: "His work, both experimental and theoretical, has tended both to psychologize and socialize American education; to give to it a practical content, along scientific and industrial lines; and to interpret to the child the new social conditions of modern society connecting the activities of the school closely with those of real life. {R.260} . . . he has tried to change the work of the school so as to make it a miniature of society itself." Cubberley, 506, passim.
      Note the echo of Horace Mann (*12th Annual Report*) and of his own text in this characterization of Dewey's philosophy and educational pedagogy.

92   Cubberley, 453.

93   Ibid.

94   Cited authors and texts are referenced by Cubberley, 454. He provides no bibliographic data beyond what he has cited in his text however, but he does add the following entry in his end of chapter "Selected References" (478): "De Garmo, Charles. *Herbart and the Herbartians.* 268 pp. New York, 1895."

96   For Cubberley's explicit argument see the last chapters of Public Education, and especially see: Cubberley, *School Organization and Administration* (Yonkers-On-Hudson, NY: World Book Co., 1923).

97   Cubberley, *Public Education*, 470.

98   Cubberley, see: p. 504: "the danger from class subdivision has been constantly increasing". See, too: p. 575: "general legislation to protect youths from exploitation and the State from danger".

99   Cubberley, Fig.136 between pages 548 and 549. Regarding industrial society in the late 1920s, Russell describes under the heading of "Employment": "All of the workers idle some of the time. Some of the workers idle all of the time. Because of (a) Increasing technological unemployment, (b) Mergers, (c) Emphasis on the younger worker, (d) Closed frontier." And under the heading of

"Tempo": "Quick Tempo/ Short Hours—High Productivity/ Periodic Shutdowns/ Much Idleness or Leisure/ When is a vacation unemployment?" And under "Control": "Increasing Government Control By/ Information/ Advice/ Direction."

And, perhaps because of socioeconomic circumstances generated by the Great Depression, Russell includes under "Possible Implications For The Schoolmaster" the caution to give "Much attention to problems of the use of leisure."

[100]   Cubberley, 590.

[101]   See: Jackson Lears, *Fables Of Abundance* (New York: Basic Books, 1994.)

[102]   See: David Nasaw, *Going Out* (New York: Basic Books, 1993); and, Paul Violas, passim.

[103]   In addition to Cubberley's text along these lines, see Terman's text cited above. See, too: Edward A. Ross, *Civic Sociology: A Textbook In Social And Civic Problems For Young Americans*, rev. ed. (Yonkers-on-Hudson, NY: World Book Co., 1935.)

For a scientist's critique, see: Stephen J. Gould, *The Mismeasure of Man* (New York: Norton, 1981) 174-191, passim. For an historical critique and explanation, see: David R. Roediger, *The Wages of Whiteness*; and, George M. Frederickson, *White Supremacy*.

[104]   See, for example: Leonard Covello (with Guido D'Agostino), *The Heart Is The Teacher* (New York: McGraw-Hill, 1958), 144. See, too: Seth Luther, passim; and Gutman's quotations of Lawrence Fell, *Power and Culture*, 109-10.

[105]   Cubberley, 225, 259, 316, 327, 365, 718.

[106]   Cubberley, 471.

[107]   "Brought in from Africa by former slaves, the disease [hookworms] had been passed on to the whites, who suffered more seriously from it, with the result that men of English, Scotch, and Irish stock, who elsewhere in America had built up our civilization and been leaders in church, and school, and State, in the South had become the so-called "poor white-trash" and were headed downward toward degeneracy and extinction." Cubberley, 677.

[108]   See the quotation from *Changing Conceptions of Education* cited above, and in *Public Education*, see p.745.

[109]   Cubberley, *Public Education*, 496-97, 700n3, 718, 729, 732. And, for what is wanted and needed in place of citizen democracy, see p. 733.

[110]   Cubberley, 489.

[111]   Cubberley, 496-97.

[112]   Cubberley, 504.

[113]   See, for example: Cubberley, 574. And in *Changing Conceptions of Education* (1909: 56-57) we find the statement: "some way must be found to awaken a social consciousness as opposed to class consciousness. . . ."

[114]   Cubberley, *Public Education*, 760.

[115]   Cubberley does not name fascism. He may well have been strongly attracted by what he perceived and understood as the efficiency, the scientism, and bureaucratic administration of society projected by the fascist countries he explicitly names without necessarily wanting to reproduce a fascist government. The problem, however, is one cannot energize fascist ideology and its mechanisms of social efficiency without also energizing those structures inherent to fascist economic and political relations. In other words, one cannot separate the cake from its ingredients. It is for this reason that I have not shied away from making explicit what Cubberley is in fact constructing and proposing in his text by repeatedly holding up first the Prussian social order and then the fascist social order as superior models of society that the United States might well emulate in its pursuit of greater social and industrial efficiency and order.

[116]   Bailyn, 3-4, 9-11, 12-15, 56, 58-59, passim.

[117]   Bailyn, 12-13.

[118]   Cremin, *Wonderful World*, 42-52, 75.

[119]   Cremin, *Wonderful*, 1-5, 52, passim.

[120]   Cremin, *Wonderful*, 2, 5, 45, 73n74.

[121]   Diane Ravitch, *The Revisionists Revised: A Critique of the Radical Attack on the Schools* (New York: Basic Books, 1978), 28.

[122]   R. Freeman Butts, "Public Education and Political Community," *History of Education Quarterly*, Vol. 14, No. 2 (Summer 1974): 165-183; cited by Ravitch, 27.

[123]   As I have attempted to establish and demonstrate in my critique of the ideological construction of his text, Cubberley does in fact address the complex relation of the state system of public school education to the "social and industrial needs of the State," or, to put it accurately, Cubberley's guiding premise in *Public Education* is the efficient relation and integration of public school education in capitalist society. To declare otherwise, as does Ravitch, is to mystify this aspect of Cubberley's text and the purpose for which it was written.

[124]   See: Bailyn, 45, 47-49 (Bailyn does not ever endorse Cubberley, but rather posits the ideology of education as the engine of progress. But, too, his pluralist liberal rejection of class structures in American society is intimately compatible with Cubberley's ideological mystification of the relation of public school education and capitalist society.); Cremin, *Wonderful*, 2, 73n74, passim; Ravitch, 78-98, 99, passim.

[125]   David Tyack, *The One Best System: A History of American Urban Education* (Cambridge, Mass.: Harvard University Press, 1974), 264-265.

[126]   Tyack and Hansot, *Managers of Virtue*, 103, 109.

[127]   David Nasaw, *Schooled to Order*, 130-33.

[128]   "Education in Its Relation to Health, Insanity, Labor, Pauperism and Crime," in *Educational Tracts*, Vol. II (prepared by Henry Barnard, n.p., n.d.); and B.P. Aydelott, *Our Country's Evils and Their Remedy* (Cincinnati, 1843), pp.12-13, quoted in Curti, 82-83.
   Compare Curti's summation of Aydelott's argument to Cubberley's statement in *Changing Conceptions of Education* (1909: 56-57): "Our city schools will soon be forced to give up the exceedingly democratic idea that all are equal, and that our society is devoid of classes . . . and to begin a specialization of education effort along many new lines in an attempt better to adapt the school to the needs of these many classes in the city life."

[129]   See in particular DeWitt Clinton's 1809 celebratory statement about the New York Free School Society's adoption of the Lancasterian Monitorial School plan, found in: "DeWitt Clinton Champions the Lancasterian Plan," *Theories of Education in Early America 1655-1819*, ed. Wilson Smith (Indianapolis: Bobbs-Merrill, 1973), 345-360.
   For Clinton, too, public education was not to transform the material conditions of the laboring poor, but to inculcate their children into the ideology and culture of the dominant economic and political class: "In New England, the greatest attention has been invariably given to this important object. In Connecticut, particularly, the schools are supported, at least three fourths of the year, by the interest of a very large fund created for that purpose, and a small tax on the people; the whole amounting to seventy-eight thousand dollars per annum. The result of this beneficial arrangement is obvious and striking. Our Eastern brethren are a well-informed and moral people. In those States it is as uncommon to find a poor man who cannot read and write, as it is rare to see one in Europe who can." And where education of the laboring poor is neglected there is "moral debasement," and government and private property are exceedingly insecure.

[130]   Curti, 81.

[131]   Curti, 97.

[132]   Curti, 97-98.

[133]   Curti, 98.

[134]   Curti, 78-79, 83-84.

[135]   Curti, 72-75, 87-88. Curti does not address slavery in the North, but slavery and indentured servitude in the so-called free states contributed substantially to the reluctance of the elite to grant suffrage. And when suffrage was granted, it was limited to free white males.

[136]   Curti, 89-92. Curti also cites Stephen Simpson, Robert Dale Owen, and Robert Rantoul, Jr. But he also casts doubt on their sincerity and the validity of their arguments: "It is clear that friends of labor exaggerated the benefits education would bring to the wage earner."

[137]   Thomas Skidmore, *The Rights of Man to Property! Being a Proposition to Make it Equal Among the Adults of the Present Generation* (New York, 1829), p.369; quoted in Curti, 91.

[138]   Curti, 104.

[139]   Curti, 103.

[140]   Messerli, 5-7, 12-18, 23-27.

[141]   Tyack and Hansot, 12; Messerli, 256-7.

[142]   Messerli, 243-244. See: Curti, 84, 94n.

[143]   Mann, quoted in Messerli, 232.

[144]   Messerli, 74-91.

[145]   Messerli, 96.

[146]   Curti, 69; Sol Cohen, II:1070; and Dorfman, I:391-92, II:596, 633, 648.

[147]   For full details see: Messerli, 97-98, 99n.

[148]   Messerli, 100.

[149]   Messerli, 99.

[150]   Curti, 128, 129.

[151]   Zinn, 208.

[152]   Ibid.

[153]   Ibid.

[154]   Zinn, 209-211.

[155]   Curti, 165.

[156]   Urban and Wagoner, 103-104.

[157]   Curti, 115.

[158]   See my elaboration of the unequal distribution of taxation and Shays' Rebellion in Chapter Three, above.

[159]   Thomas Skidmore, passim. For additional information on the "free soil" movement in the late 1830s and 1840s see: Gutman, et al., *Who Built America?*, 351-354.

[160]   See: Craven, et al., 349-350.

[161]   Dorfman, II:661-67.

[162]   Horace Mann, quoted in Curti, 115.

[163]   Curti, 145-146.

[164]   Clarence J. Karier, *The Individual, Society, And Education: A History of American Educational Ideas* (Urbana: University of Illinois Press, 1967), 59.

[165]   Cremin, "Horace Mann's Legacy," introduction to *The Republic and the School*, 5.

[166]   Cremin, 4.

[167]   Cremin, 5.

[168]   Ibid.

[169]   Ibid.

[170]   Daniel Walker Howe, *The Political Culture of the American Whigs* (Chicago: University of Chicago Press, 1979), pp.34-35, quoted by Joel Spring, *The American School*, 79.

[171]   Messerli, 327-328.

[172]   Messerli, 94.

[173]   Messerli, 94, 102.

[174]   Messerli, 103.

[175]   On Josiah Quincy, Jr., one of Mann's "closest associates," see: Messerli, 103, 207-208, 364.

[176]   See: Szatmary, passim; and, Paul W. Gates, *Landlords and Tenants on the Prairie Frontier: Studies in American Land Policy* (Ithaca, NY: Cornell University Press, 1973).

[177]   According to Freeman Hunt, *Lives of American Merchants* (New York, 1856), and cited in Craven, et al., 304-5, Patrick Tracy Jackson, together with Lowell and others, completed construction of the first Massachusetts railroad for power locomotives between Boston and Lowell in 1835.

[178]   Cremin, 6.

[179]   Messerli, 223-224.

[180]   Messerli, 224n.

[181]   Cremin, 6.

[182]   Messerli, 364.

[183]   Curti, 78-80.

[184]   Cremin, 7.

[185]   Henry Barnard, *Object Teaching*, 129-30; quoted in Curti, 156.

[186]   Curti, 156-57. Note that Mann promoted the same sort of indoctrination through the common schools for the same reasons Barnard gives: to construct social hegemony for the prevention of violent labor resistance against capitalist industry and the state. In Mann's case, however, Curti tells us he did not know or understand the real causes and state protection of the economic conditions of production which made social violence by the lower classes their only remaining course of resistance. Treating Mann so differently from his treatment of Barnard is rhetorical manipulation and ideological mystification by Curti. Curti's deliberate manipulation of his explanation of Mann seems based on two reasons: 1) to protect his argument that the common school system was humanitarian and democratic until it was corrupted by capitalists such as Barnard; and, 2) it is ideologically necessary to distinguish between Mann's pronouncements (those which Curti finds sympathetic to his argument) and Mann's contradictory positions and practices.

[187]   Curti, 199. Note, too, how closely this resembles Katz's conclusions about the social organization and aims of nineteenth century high schools in *The Irony of Early School Reform*, 92, 112.

[188]   Cremin, 27.

[189]   Cremin, "Horace Mann's Legacy", 6.

[190]   Urban and Wagoner, 106.

[191]   Indeed, when it comes to explaining the actuality of the Prussian system of public instruction, its organization of public schools for this purpose, and the particular attraction it has for those Americans busy constructing and implementing public policy, Cubberley, too, does a dodge. He resorts to hiding the Prussian system behind Pestalozzi. Ultimately, however, Cubberley explicitly identifies the attraction of the Prussian system for some Americans in the passage quoted above in which he details the sort of society Germany had created before 1914. See: Cubberley, *Public Education*, 760.

[192]   See: Messerli's depiction of Prussia, quoted in Chapter Three, and found in Messerli, 392.

[193]   David Nasaw's treatment of Mann in *Schooled to Order* is an exception to this passive treatment of Mann. Although Nasaw relies heavily on Messerli's research and documentation, his study is one of the few in addition to Katz's to make significant use of it.

[194]   Urban and Wagoner, "Chapter 4, The Common Man and the Common School 1820-1860," 93-117.

[195]   Urban and Wagoner, 99n.

[196]   Urban and Wagoner, 113, 116-17.

[197]   Spring, 56-57.

[198]   Katz, *Irony*, 5-9.

[199]   Katz, *Irony*, 7.

[200]   Failure to consider the prevalence and continuity of child labor in nineteenth century New England, and its influence on educational legislation in Massachusetts, specifically, constitutes a glaring void in Katz's historical explanation of the common school movement generally and the emergence of the high school in particular. This fault, however, is counterbalanced by Katz's elaborated study, "The Urban Delinquent," *Irony*, 162-211, in which he provides an historical explanation of the reform school and its relation to society and the state system of public school education.

[201]   Katz, *Irony*, 14.

[202]   See: Szatmary, passim; and Gates, passim.

[203]   Brookline report abstracted in "Eighteenth Report," p.205; quoted in Katz, *Irony*, 29.

[204]   Katz, *Irony*, 1.

[205]   *Winchendon*, 1852-53, 15; quoted in Katz, *Irony*, 30-31.

[206]   See, for example: essays by Allmendinger, Story, and Troen in Part II of *The Social History of American Education*, eds. R. Edward McClellan and William J. Reese (Urbana: University of Illinois Press, 1988), 65-72, 73-90, 119-136.

[207]   Katz, *Irony,* 90.

[208]   Katz, *Irony*, 91, 302n135.

[209]   Urban and Wagoner, 113.

[210]   Tyack and Hansot, 23.

[211]   Anne Showstack Sassoon, "Hegemony," *Twentieth-Century Social Thought*, eds. William Outhwaite and Tom Bottomore, et al. (Oxford, U.K.: Blackwell, 1994), 255.

²¹² The triumph of the common school was not a triumph over the privileged academies. Contrary to the claim of Tyack and Hansot, therefore, the dual system of schooling divided between the elite and common classes of American society continued. What is significant about the establishment of the common schools, in other words, is it signalled the class consciousness of an energized and assertive middle-class in nineteenth century American society.

²¹³ Tyack and Hansot, 23.

²¹⁴ See: Scott, "The Ever-Widening Circle . . .," in *Social History*, 137-159. See, too: Cubberley, *Public Education*, 252n, 274n, 705n.

²¹⁵ See: Gutman, et al., *Who Built America?*, I:326-7.

²¹⁶ Tyack and Hansot, 23.

²¹⁷ Tyack and Hansot, 24.

²¹⁸ (1) Thomas J. Sugrue, "The Structures of Urban Poverty," in *The Underclass Debate*, ed. Michael B. Katz (Princeton, NJ: Princeton University Press, 1993), 87.

(2) See Szatmary, passim; and William H. Mulligan, Jr., "From Artisan to Proletarian: The Family and the Vocational Education of Shoemakers in the Handicraft Era," in *Life and Labor*, eds. Charles Stephenson and Robert Asher (Albany, NY: SUNY Press, 1986), 22-36.

(3) William Cullen Bryant, "The Right of Workingmen To Strike," in *A Documentary History of the American People*, eds. Craven, Johnson, and Dunn (Boston: Ginn & Co., 1951), 312. Also see: Christopher L. Tomlins, "Prologue: two moments of the republic," *Law, Labor, and Ideology*, 1-16; and, Gutman, et al., *Who Built America?*, passim, and Gutman, *Power and Culture*, passim.

(4) Dorfman, II:532:

> It may be said, [Thomas Cooper, political economist and close presidential advisor,] wrote Jefferson, that if manufacture is introduced, "you introduce capitalists who live by the life blood of the starving poor whom they employ," and that the mass are "systematically kept in abject poverty and to all real purposes and interests enslaved." But the great increase in national power and wealth might overbalance the evils. For instance, how can armies be obtained for defending the country, when by a kind of idle labor a man in four or five days a week can earn enough for subsistence and in addition enough whisky for intoxication?

²¹⁹ Tyack and Hansot, 24-25.

²²⁰ Thomas Skidmore, *The Rights of Man to Property!* (New York, 1829), 369; quoted in Curti, 91.

²²¹ Seth Luther, passim.

²²² Jacob Riis, *How The Other Half Lives*, ed. Francesco Cordasco (New York: Dover, 1971). For Lawrence Fell, see: Herbert G. Gutman, *Power and Culture*, 108-110.

For additional evidence of the historical continuity of the economic and political relations and socioeconomic circumstances which outraged Skidmore and Luther, see: Henry F. Bedford, ed., *Their Lives and Numbers*.

223   Tyack and Hansot, 60, 62.

224   Tyack and Hansot, 58.

225   Messerli, 244.
More than Lord Brougham's Natural Theology may have attracted Mann to him. The following is from Curti's text:

> Lord Brougham, prominent English Whig who took the leading role in promoting education for "the people" of his country, clearly saw the conservative potentialities of popular education. "The interest of both [working classes and their superiors] are deeply concerned in sounder views being taught them; I can hardly imagine, for example, a greater service being rendered to the men, than expounding to them the true principles and mutual relations of population and wages; and both they and their masters will assuredly experience the effects of the prevailing ignorance upon such question, as soon as any interruption shall happen in the commercial prosperity of the country, if indeed the present course of things, daily tending to lower wages as well as profits, and set the two classes in opposition to each other, shall not of itself bring on a crisis."

Henry Lord Brougham, "Practical Observations upon the Education of the People, 1825," in *Sketches of Public Characters* (Philadelphia, 1839), Vol. II, pp.45-46; quoted in Curti, 84. See: Ibid., 94n.

226   Tyack and Hansot, 61.

227   Tyack and Hansot, 62-63.

228   Tyack and Hansot, 61.

229   Tyack and Hansot, 109.

230   Carl F. Kaestle, *Pillars of the Republic: Common Schools and American Society, 1780-1860* (New York: Hill and Wang, 1983), x..

231   Treating ideology as if it is reality also has enormous pitfalls — the least of which is not perceiving critical distinctions in meanings intended by different speakers.
See: Sean Wilentz's historical reconstruction of the period 1837-1849 in New York City (*Chants Democratic*, 297, passim.) in which it becomes apparent that the relation between rhetoric and ideology is hardly simple.
Although a class based language was certainly emerging in the General Trade Union, it was limited to social critique. My observation is not meant to detract from its educative and critical power, but to underscore a crucial weakness in the unionist movement. The GTU radicals (by rejecting Skidmore's revolutionary democratic program, for instance), were forced to adapt republican ideology and language to their cause. Such a strategy initially appeared effective . . . but, in the long run, it proved fatal. The same ideology/language, even though it is used by opposing social classes to convey very different meanings, cannot be perceived by outsiders as anything but the same. And, too, even for insiders the task of distinguishing meaning between one speaker and

another is inherently daunting. In short, this strategy works against the unionists and for the capitalist class. Without a distinct, coherent ideology and program of hegemony of their own — a viable alternative society does not become visible and obtainable!

Without looking deeper than language, in other words, identifying and establishing actual differences in meaning and social aims becomes extraordinarily difficult if not altogether impossible, and one might easily conclude, as Kaestle has, that a consensus crossing class lines exists.

[232]   Philip Foner, in *History of Labor*, I:143-166, argues that the working men weren't dupes in this contest between Democrats and Whigs over the Bank. They understood that where the Whigs benefited from their control of the Bank, the Democrats would benefit equally from its demise and the shift of credit to the control of state and corporate banks. The workers lacked the economic and political resources of the two dominant parties —because of wage dependency they were vulnerable to employment and market crises, black listing, and legal and physical repression — they thus did the best they could by playing one party against the other, and used their votes in an attempt to gain legislation favorable to their human and social needs. This was an imperfect and unsatisfactory practice, however, for their candidates often exploited and then betrayed them, economic events destroyed their membership and organization, corporations outlived their leadership or sympathetic legislators, and, internal disputes and power struggles also worked against them. See, too: Gutman, "Joseph P. McDonnell and the Workers' Struggle in Paterson, New Jersey," *Power and Culture,* 70-92.

[233]   Messerli, 271.

[234]   Messerli, 271-72.

[235]   Messerli, 281, 334-341.

[236]   Seth Luther, quoted in Craven, et al., 306-307.

[237]   Kaestle, x.

[238]   See: Gutman and Berlin, "Class Composition and the Development of the American Working Class, 1840-1890," *Power and Culture*, 380-394.

[239]   Kaestle, 67.

[240]   See: E.P. Thompson, passim.

[241]   See: Sean Wilentz, *Chants Democratic*, 306, passim, for a revealing instance of ideological, class and cultural conflict in which relatively successful workingmen's temperance unions were vigorously attacked by elite and middle class temperance leaders for failing to properly socialize and inculcate participating laborers.

[242]   Kaestle, 68.

[243]   Mann, "Report for 1841," quoted in *The American Mind*, 2 vols., eds. Warfel, Gabriel, and Williams (New York: American Book Company, 1937), I:431.

[244] Howard Zinn claims there were 140 strikes in the eastern part of the nation during 1835-36. Zinn, *People's History*, 225.

[245] Curti, 113.

[246] For additional textual evidence, see Mann's *Fifth Annual Report*, (Washington, D.C.).

[247] Kaestle, 69.

[248] David Nasaw, 9-10.

[249] Ibid., 10-28.

[250] Kaestle, 90-91.

[251] Dorfman, II:645-648.

[252] Dorfman, II:645.

[253] Dorfman, II:647.

[254] Dorfman, II:647.

[255] Ibid.

[256] Dorfman, II:648.

[257] Ibid.

[258] Kaestle, 91-92.

[259] Kaestle, 141.

[260] Kaestle, 146.

[261] Katz, *Reconstructing American Education*, (Cambridge, MA: Harvard University Press, 1987), 143.

[262] Katz, *Reconstructing*, 142; see pp. 136-144 for full response.

[263] Kaestle, 148.

CHAPTER SIX

Conclusion: A Critical Summary Of The Relation
Between Public School Education, Capitalism,
Ideological Conflict, And The Social Forces
Driving The Construction And Imposition
Of Hegemony

In the first half of the nineteenth century democracy was considered a dangerous, revolutionary ideology by the governing classes in the United States. It was believed to be dangerous and revolutionary because its primary tenets of freedom and equality inspired large numbers of women, artisans, craftsmen, black slaves and freemen, tenant farmers, yeoman farmers, and laborers to actively protest and resist the expansion of government powers of appropriation on one hand, and the expanding domination of exploiting and appropriating wealthy landowners, merchants, bankers, emerging industrialists and their surrogates on the other.[1] The contradiction between the promise of the Declaration of Independence and society dominated by the elite revealed to large numbers of "equal" men and women the contradiction between the language of republicanism and the fact of concentrated economic and political resources and powers. The merchant elite, the manufacturers, and the landlords were a dominant and controlling presence in all levels of government, in the economy, and the courts. As a consequence of this clear structural division between social classes, resistance or insurgency by large segments of the laboring classes against members or groups of the elite frequently translated into resistance and insurgency against the State. The understanding fostered by democratic ideology that the elite and the State were an integrated entity was empirically reinforced by the reaction of the elite to protesting workers, tenant farmers, small free-hold farmers, or the poor entailing a corresponding reaction of the State, or, as in cases where members of the elite class employed private armies to suppress resistance, its studied inaction.[2] Although full blown competitive party politics beginning with Andrew Jackson's campaign and election went a long way toward constructing the appearance of a separation of private property with its fundamental conditions and relations of economic production from politics and government, political participation of free white laborers did not do away with their belief in democratic ideology.[3] Nor did partial inclusion of the citizenry in political contests between factions of the elite deplete the power of democratic ideology to define social inequities and their structural causes, or to express an as yet unrealized society of free and equal citizens.

Under the leadership of Horace Mann, the "Father" of American public education, schools in the mid-nineteenth century were conceived as the State's primary institution of inculcation and indoctrination. The capitalist ideology of private property, appropriation, accumulation, and productivity was substituted for democratic ideology in the classroom, in textbooks, and in establishment journals and newspapers; and American government was clearly constituted in public rhetoric and school textbooks as a republic governed by law — and not by the will of the people.[4] Indeed, in Mann's last and most famous *Report* on the status and goals of public schools in the State of Massachusetts, he never mentions "democracy." Democratic ideology, however, was tenacious; waves of new immigrants seeking freedom and economic opportunities, Black Americans seeking freedom and citizen rights, women seeking full equality, small farmers seeking an end to debilitating taxation, the poor and workers seeking an end to exploitation, and small-time capitalists seeking an end to exclusive contract corporations all contributed to keeping democratic ideology alive. By the turn of the twentieth century some educators, like Margaret Haley, a school teacher and agent of the Chicago Teachers Federation, argued that democracy remained an idea and social vision to struggle for; but others, such as Ellwood Cubberley, argued that society had progressed beyond such a dangerous and out-of-date idea. Whatever their opposing visions of society might be, it is clear that neither the advocates or opponents of democratic ideology believed American society was democratic.[5]

Unlike Mann's powerful and privileged position within the economic and political elite of mid-nineteenth Century New England, Cubberley's linkage to the national political structure and his power stemmed from his elite position in the education establishment as Dean of the School of Education at Stanford University — one of the first such schools other than Teachers College at Columbia to train principals and superintendents as professional administrative bureaucrats, — his role in constructing a powerful and influential network of public school superintendents, administrators and principals, his central role in forming the governing "Superintendents" committee within the NEA, his profound influence on the construction and orchestration of centralized bureaucratic school administration, his national renown among industrialists, business leaders, educators, state boards of education, and local school districts, and his seminal contribution to the constructed ideology of the state system of public school education through his own texts and those which he edited. In addition, Cubberley himself was a firm capitalist, an educational entrepreneur, and, though he came from a modest midwest small town background (similar in a way to Mann's New England background), he accumulated a considerable fortune of which he gave $772,332.03 to Stanford University for the purpose of erecting a school of education building.[6] Ellwood Cubberley, in short, was in his time one of the most powerful and influential leaders in public education. Although he has not been mythologized in popular culture as Mann has been, his direct influence on the development and transformation of public school education is still with us. He wrote in 1909 that it was time for schools to

> give up the exceedingly democratic idea that all are equal, and that our society is devoid of classes. . . . Increasing specialization . . . has divided the people into dozens of more or less clearly defined classes, and the increasing centralization of trade and industry has concentrated business in the hands of a relatively small number.[7]

The contradiction between the achievement ideology of capitalism, that Mann and his followers had made the foundation of the state system of public school education, and the reality of American society had become increasingly difficult for the public schools to hide or explain away. The public schools were an institutional adjunct of the State, and their inculcating/socializing function was being eroded by the reality of social relations over which the schools, its leaders claimed, had no direct control. Cubberley thus argued for a non-academic, industrial and utilitarian curriculum, especially in those secondary schools for the education of the immigrant and Black working class, as a means of damping down the jolt of the contradiction. It was necessary to bring the schools in line with social reality, but this is not the same thing as making apparent and understandable to the students attending public schools how unequal social relations come about, or why certain groups in society believed these relations were necessary and normal. On the contrary, Cubberley believed the public educational establishment needed to be more closely integrated into the actual economic and political relations of the State and closely tuned to relations of production and the needs of industrial society. And, too, he believed that school curriculum and administration also needed restructuring to efficiently obscure its necessary processes of social engineering. Cubberley believed this program was of such importance that he quotes what he wrote in 1909 again in 1919, and again in 1934:

> The modern city is essentially a center of trade and industry, and home life and home conditions must inevitably be determined and conditioned by this fact. The increasing specialization in all fields of labor has divided the people into dozens of more or less clearly defined classes, and the increasing centralization of trade and industry has concentrated business in the hands of a relatively small number of people. All standards of business efficiency indicate that this should be the case, but as a result of it the small merchant and employer are fast giving way to large mercantile and commercial concerns. No longer can a man save up a few thousand dollars and start in business for himself with much chance of success. The employee tends to remain an employee; the wage-earner tends to remain a wage-earner. New discoveries and improved machinery and methods have greatly

increased the complexity of the industrial process in all lines of work, and the worker in every field of trade and industry tends more and more to become a cog in the machine, and to lose sight of his part in the industrial processes and his place in our industrial and civic and national life.[8]

The problem of democratic ideals, public education, social relations, and the State was central to Cubberley's thinking about American society. In 1909 he was primarily concerned about the contradictions and mounting tensions between school ideology and the reality of unequal social relations, but by 1919, and again in 1934, he felt compelled to include among his concerns the effects he believed waves of Italian and East European immigrants were having on the social order:

Practically no Italians came to us before 1870, but by 1890 they were coming at the rate of twenty thousand a year, and during the five-year period 1906-10 as many as 1,186,100 arrived. After 1880, in addition, people from all parts of that medley of races which formerly constituted the Austro-Hungarian Empire . . . also came in shiploads to our shores. French Canadians also have crossed the border in large numbers and crowded into the milltowns of New England. As a result we had, in 1930, almost thirteen and a half millions of foreign-born people in our population, of whom practically forty-five per cent had come from the South and East of Europe. Of the immigration since 1900 almost eighty per cent has come from there. In addition to these thirteen and a half millions of foreign-born, an additional nine and a half million were native-born but the children of foreign parents, and of another six million one parent was foreign born.

These Southern and Eastern Europeans were of a very different type from the North and West Europeans who preceded them. Largely illiterate, docile, often lacking in initiative, and almost wholly without the Anglo-Saxon conceptions of righteousness, liberty, law, order, public decency, and government, their coming has served to dilute tremendously our national stock and to weaken and corrupt our political life. Settling largely in the cities of the North, the agricultural regions of the Middle and the Far West, and the mining districts of the mountain regions, they have created serious problems in housing and living, moral and sanitary conditions, and honest and decent government, while popular education has everywhere been made more difficult by their presence. The result has been that in many sections of our country foreign manners, customs, observances, and language have tended to supplant native ways and the English speech, while the so-called "melting-pot" has had more than it could handle. The new peoples, and especially those from the South and East of Europe, have come so fast that we have been unable to absorb and assimilate them, and our national life, for the past quarter of a century, has been afflicted with a serious case of racial indigestion.[9]

From the conclusion of the War of Independence to the Second World War, democratic ideology was central to the struggle between the poor, workers, and immigrants on one side and members of the governing classes on the other. In the nineteenth century Horace Mann sought to suppress democratic social forces by inculcating children in capitalist ideology through public schools, and thus assimilate them into capitalist culture and inure them to the existing order of social relations. And over half a century later, we find Cubberley busy arguing in his books on American public school education and administration that notions about democracy, upward social mobility and/or equality among citizens should be jettisoned. The real problem before educators and the State, according to Cubberley, is how best to contain, assimilate and govern the working class and immigrants in a highly differentiated and stratified society. Cubberley's proposed solution is a systemic reorganization of public school education, and, for the lower 70 percent of all children, the implementation of an industrial or vocational curriculum that will prepare these children of the working class and immigrants to look no further than their limited opportunities within society on one hand, and to act as moral, intelligent, and efficient citizens of society on the other.

The above summary is just that—a summary. It is, as well, incomplete; for I have glossed the perceptions and resistance of the lower classes, choosing instead to emphasize the perception and actions of two central agents of the capitalist class, who are also the most powerful social engineers in the construction of the institution of public schools. Although I present the case in the above summary from the view of the governing classes, I have tried throughout this essay to demonstrate through an examination of class, positions and practices, within the broad spectrum of class fractions and economic and political relations that ideological hegemony was not achieved through popular consensus but was in fact constructed and imposed by the ruling elite and its surrogates. That this process of establishing their hegemony over the population took on enormous urgency in the 1830s was not simple coincidence or a historical accident. The governing classes were reacting to increasingly powerful democratic forces in society led by radical autodidacts vigorously opposed to capitalist processes of appropriation and accumulation of wealth; and to the capitalists' subjugation, oppression, and exploitation of men, women, and children, and to their dominant control of society's resources — including the judiciary and the government. Thus, when Protestant/capitalist ideology is examined within the historical context of economic and political relations and their identifiable particularities, and when the architects of its hegemonic imposition are examined on the basis of their social positions and practices a much more complex and accurate explanation of the historically specific social reality surrounding the formation and development of the state system of public school education emerges.

Indeed, as Marx, the great social scientist of capitalist society, Michael Katz, the educational historian, Michael Parenti, a political scientist, and Jay MacLeod, a sociologist, have each demonstrated in their respective research and writings,[10] an adequate explanation of an historical period's social reality requires a complex excavation of its particular cultural, economic and political relations, and an identification and explanation of the social structures which determine the actual composition of these relations, as well as an accounting of what the participants think about their social experiences and actions. When the study of society is pursued as a stratified and interdisciplinary activity it is possible to identify people, their positions and practices within the context of social relations, their ideology, and, perhaps, their reasons as well. By seeking and identifying points of congruence, our explanations of people, events and historical movements are more complete, more complex, and more valid — and less susceptible to epistemic fallacy (i.e., mistaking ideology for what is actual.)

Central to this critique of educational historiographic texts is my argument that public and educational policy, and people's actions, are generated from what folks believe. Controlling what people can know through the ideological construction of the history of American society and its institutions is therefore highly political. Hegemonic control of what constitutes reality is a political necessity because it conditions and privileges what counts ideologically as proper knowledge, e.g. people are poor because they are lazy, governed by their passions, or biologically unequal;[11] the working class is a dangerous revolutionary class unless indoctrinated through moral object education; capitalism and democracy are the same thing; "ending welfare as we know it" will make the poor moral, industrious and productive; educating public school children for today's social relations and job market is the best possible education society can provide; etc.

It seems significant to me, therefore, that all but the one most recent of Katz's relational class critiques of educational history are out-of-print, while Kaestle's pro-capitalist tract remains in print.[12] It is significant because the twelve or sixteen week sessions into which teacher education courses are packaged forces educators of historical foundations to rely on textbooks to cover 250 years of American social history. Engendering critical inquiry and reflective thinking through public school education and teacher education thus becomes a problematic exercise when some kinds of ideological history remain in print, become part of the dominant ideological canon in educational and American history, are widely promoted and cited, are treated as authentic explanations of "reality," while counter-hegemonic explanatory critiques of historical phenomena, although published, are allowed to go out of print.

It can be argued that all of the educational historiographic texts critiqued here possess greater or lesser degrees of coherent interpretation, and, therefore, most (perhaps, from an interpretivist perspective, all) are legitimate textbooks for classroom use and teacher education. It is, after all, the professor's responsibility to "illuminate" the text and draw attention to other "interpretations." I hope I have demonstrated why such an argument (assuming it is a valid one as reflected by the existence of the more relativist texts and their sales) has its basis in capitalist ideology and has nothing to do with legitimate scholarship or the practice of identifying, establishing, and explaining the historical object of study. Indeed, what this exegetic, interdisciplinary critique reveals is the on-going process of ideological hegemony first established successfully by Horace Mann and other promoters in the antebellum period.

The fact that so much relativist interpretivism parades as historical explanation is not simply political, it is a form or intellectual eugenics. In the place of knowledge about society and its history, relativist interpretations mystify the actual social causes of human misery and construct lies which legitimate and help reproduce those processes and mechanisms of oppression and exploitation which depend for their continuance on ideological hegemony. Congruent historical knowledge, on the other hand, would guide us toward emancipatory democratic projects.

Final Comments

I actually began research for this essay from a position and attitude very different from the one my argument and critique may suggest. I read an essay by two highly regarded educational scholars which they claimed would explain the different educational experiences of different immigrant groups. Their explanation and conclusions were interesting — because, as a member of one of the groups included for elaborate study, their findings and arguments contradicted my life experience and that of other Italian-Americans I know. The contention that Italian-American family culture and customs stood in opposition to public school education and/or academic success in school had no basis in my working class family or community. Motivated by this moment of critical incongruity I set about the task of clearly establishing the importance of education to Italian-Americans and the social forces which directly influenced their experiences, opportunities and choices. My appointed task, in other words, was to establish the positive attitudes and expectations Italian parents had of public school education, and the hope they invested in it as the most important second step (the first being the Church) of their children achieving a life free of back-breaking labor and insecure economic dependence.

In a study such as this, interesting or distressing revelations happen. Quite aside from all that I have written so far, what I discovered (noting the rare exceptions) is an unbroken, continuous stream of denigration, distrust, hostility, and antagonism spewed over the poor, the working class, Black-Americans, and immigrants by many of America's elite, its politicians, its bosses, its corporate executives, and, significantly, its educational promoters and school establishment men. What I also found, and what in fact became the focus of this essay, is a tradition of glossing, cover-up, mystification, misdirection, misinformation, and casting children as villains. Perhaps the most startling of these several revelations is the extent to which the military strategy of divide, isolate, and conquer is inherent in the social ontology, theory and practice embedded in public school education by so many of the school promoters and practitioners.

Speaking to an audience in commemoration of the opening of a new school building in 1809, DeWitt Clinton had this to say:

> A number of benevolent persons had seen, with concern, the increasing vices of the city, arising, in a great degree, from the neglected education of the poor. Great cities are, at all times, the nurseries and hot-beds of crimes. And the dreadful examples of vice which are presented to youth, and the alluring forms in which it is arrayed, connected with a spirit of extravagance and luxury, the never-failing attendant of great wealth and extensive business, cannot fail of augmenting the mass of moral depravity. The mendicant parent bequeaths his squalid poverty to his offspring, and the hardened thief transmits a legacy of infamy to his unfortunate and depraved descendants.[13]

DeWitt Clinton was for much of his adult professional life the President of the New York Free School Society, a non-sectarian Protestant organization made up New York's leading citizens and dedicated to transforming (i.e., moralizing) the working poor. He was, in addition, Mayor of New York City, Governor of New York State, and an investor and leading proponent of the Erie Canal. According to Clinton, then, the city attracts people by virtue of the economic activities concentrated there. The result of this concentration of population is the rich and the poor are brought into close proximity of one another. Thus crowded together, the ostentatious show of wealth and extravagance by the rich acts upon the poor to drive them to acts of moral depravity (i.e., they exhibit antagonism for the rich, have a tendency to attack or confiscate property, and exhibit a deplorable disregard for law and order through food riots and strikes against employers.)

Vice and moral depravity, according to Clinton's depiction, are characteristic of poor people living in the same town or city with the wealthy. That the poor behave as they do amongst themselves and toward the rich results from their lack of education. Clinton's remedy is not directed at the adult working or unemployed poor, but at the children of these adults. It is public education, and not the community, church or family, which will alter the young of the criminal or depraved uneducated poor — and thereby transform the very nature of the economic and political relations he has described. Public education is not presented in Clinton's speech as a remedy to poverty. Yet, in pointing to what mendicant and/or criminal parents leave their children, Clinton suggests public education will break the cycle of poverty and crime. Educated children of the poor will be unlike their parents, and will have more to bestow upon their descendants than poverty and/or infamy. That Clinton posits an eventual material distinction between the educated child and his parent(s), as well as a moral distinction, certainly suggests an undergirding achievement ideology. In the introduction of his speech, however, Clinton makes it clear that one can be educated, can be literate and informed, and yet still be poor.[14]

What we have in Clinton's address, therefore, is a rational plan for stratified levels and kinds of education organized along the lines of wealth-holding and property ownership on one hand and poverty on the other. Hence tutors, academies, and colleges for the education of gentlemen. Hence the designation of academies for the selection and training of teachers for the poor schools. Education of the poor, such as Clinton outlines it, is not meant to facilitate the upward mobility of the poor in society, but to separate the child from his parents and community. By separating the child from the family and community the argument is the child can then be reformed and reshaped. Separation from family and community is meant to make possible the transformation of the child's consciousness that he (and it is a "he") will no longer resent his poverty in the face of extravagant shows of wealth — that he will not be antagonistic toward the rich nor rebellious toward his employer or the government (which is controlled by the wealthy,) that he will in the end reject the habits, beliefs, and culture of his family. The educated poor man will be virtuous, intelligent, and industrious. In short, a happy worker content to be poor.[15]

It is Clinton's characterization of the working poor family and his explicit plan for public school education to ideologically and culturally separate the child from the family that I want to draw attention to. Some decades later, Henry

Barnard wrote in his *Sixth Annual Report* to the Connecticut General Assembly:

> No one at all familiar with the deficient household arrangements and deranged machinery of domestic life, of the extreme poor and ignorant, to say nothing of the intemperate—of the example of rude manners, impure and profane language and all the vicious habits of low-bred idleness, which abound in certain sections of all populous districts—can doubt that it is better for children to be removed as early and as long as possible from such scenes and such examples and placed in an infant or primary school.[16]

Barnard is writing years after Clinton's death, he is in a different state and addressing a different audience, yet his depiction of the working poor family, and his plan to physically separate the child from his/her family, to inculcate the child in a radically different ideology and culture, corresponds with Clinton's. Almost a full century later, Cubberley writes in *Public Education*:

> These Southern and Eastern Europeans were of a very different type from the North and West Europeans who preceded them. Largely illiterate, docile, often lacking in initiative, and almost wholly without the Anglo-Saxon conceptions of righteousness, liberty, law, order, public decency, and government, their coming has served to dilute tremendously our national stock and to weaken and corrupt our political life. Settling largely in the cities of the North, the agricultural regions of the Middle and the Far West, and the mining districts of the mountain regions, they have created serious problems in housing and living, moral and sanitary conditions, and honest and decent government, while popular education has everywhere been made more difficult by their presence.[17]

Over the period of the intervening century it appears some important new elements have been added to the strategy of separate, isolate, and conquer — although the denigration and criminalization of the family remains a constant characterization. The new elements are (1) an argument that the state system of public school education as it exists in the early years of the twentieth century is inadequate to "educate" these "new" masses of working poor, and (2) because of these inadequacies a reorganization of the school system on a national scale is both necessary and justified. The program advocated by Cubberley in *Public Education* is not a radical departure from that proposed by Clinton, by Barnard, or by Horace Mann. Rather it is an adaptation of rhetoric and organizational structure to contemporary socioeconomic circumstances. It carries the strategy of conquest and domination into the present of the twentieth century and remodels the state system of public school education into a form which, instead of transforming a few hundreds or thousands of children, can accomplish the same social aim with millions of children.

Where Clinton and Barnard could depend as members of the elite on a common race, religion, ideology, and culture with their specific audiences to legitimate their plans for the children of the working poor, Cubberley and company in the early twentieth century did not enjoy such a luxury — or at least Cubberley suggests that socioeconomic circumstances in America did not readily lend themselves to direct and overt programs of class domination. But whatever the reasons, Cubberley, Terman, Thorndike and others turned to science to legitimate a revamped strategy of class conquest:

> From the use of these tests we now know that the school cannot create intelligence; it can only train and develop and make useful the intelligence which the child brings with him to school. While environment is undoubtedly a factor in *mental development*, it is a factor largely limited in turn by native mental capacity, and this is *a matter of the pupil's racial and family inheritance*, and nothing within the gift of the schools or our democratic form of government.[emphasis added][18]

Having scientifically established a biological basis for economic and political inequities, it serves as well to establish the intellectual inferiority of particular groups of children in American society. And, acknowledging that the benefits of an academic or intellectual education can do nothing for the 70 percent of children who just happen to come from immigrant and Black-American working class and/or poor families, we must also acknowledge the need for an appropriate education which can aid these children in making the most of their limited capabilities. Hence the beneficent provision of schools which train students for useful occupations as store clerk, laundry, sewing, typing, barbering, and factory or construction work. Make no mistake, however, these new types of schools still carry on the traditionally important and necessary burden of socializing and assimilating children into the ways, means and advantages of our "democratic" institutions and social life.

If the strategy of divide, isolate, and conquer depended in the nineteenth century on a program of ideological and cultural inculcation, in the twentieth century it is clearly premised on mass sorting and the inculcation of ignorance. The strategy, and the various programs generated to carry it out, has been successful with catastrophic consequences.

From the time of DeWitt Clinton to Horace Mann and Henry Barnard to Ellwood Cubberley policy makers have blamed the working class family (white, Black, or immigrant) for social conditions which they did not create or possess the requisite resources to transform. These policy makers have criminalized those among the working class for resistance and protest against unequal economic and political relations. The strategy of dividing the child against his or her family has produced isolated individuals and consumers, yes, but also individuals who have little sense of being connected to others around them or a sense of social responsibility and obligation. Families send their children off for a public school education, and then see them depart for a life in the streets or to work in some distant corner of the nation. We have secured social stratification through a policy of social fragmentation — and, unbeknownst to most of us, the state system of public school education has been a key agency in reinforcing these social conditions.

Former First Lady Hilary Clinton's popularization of 'it takes a community (village) to raise a child' is perhaps well intended and sincere, but it is ultimately misleading; for it ignores the insidious strategy of inculcating children against their family and community which is embedded (and hence invisible) in our theory and practice of public school education. The class stratification of capitalist society is sustained by social fragmentation and inculcated ignorance of society, for fragmentation and ignorance work against cohesive emancipatory movements of the working class and poor. Capitalist society is sustained, in short, by an impotent mass of wage dependent laborers, and by insensitive bureaucrats, technocrats, lawyers, and police, and by such institutions as mass media, courts, banks, factories, office towers, schools, and prisons. Such a society is incapable of raising healthy well-adjusted children.

Not only does it take a community to raise a healthy child, but it takes healthy children to sustain and reproduce a healthy community. For this to happen, there must be a sense and a reality of belonging; and, too, there must be life-sustaining opportunities in the community for children to become producers of life-sustaining necessities. There must also be knowledge of society and its composite of associated relations, knowledge of what actually constitutes its complex and stratified reality, and knowledge of how it works or does not work for all citizens, and why.

Leonard Covello and his East Harlem community of mostly Italian and Irish Americans fought a hard political battle to secure a high school for the children there. They fought a much tougher battle against the industrial school the State wanted to impose upon them. Once a comprehensive academic high school was won it was quickly transformed into a community center. Covello consciously recognized and rejected the strategy of divide and conquer, and, instead, proceeded to use the school for the education (in its broadest conception) of the community, the families, and the children. The curriculum and pedagogy at Benjamin Franklin High School did not follow Cubberley's prescription for training children to take their place in the social pyramid as efficient cogs; Fellenberg, Herbart, and Spencer were ignored, as was Terman. Both ambitions and social responsibility were fostered through an education which generated the knowledge needed to confront and respond to actual social needs and relations, that fed the minds and spirits of the young students there and their families, that made students responsible for themselves and their community, and that, most importantly, cherished them as human beings.[19]

The students of Benjamin Franklin High School who became teachers, dentists, doctors, nurses, lawyers, artists, judges, state and federal representatives, government employees, and contributors to their East Harlem community make up a long list. Their achievements are no less impressive. Benjamin Franklin High School should have been the beginning of a revolutionary transformation of the state system of public school education. Shame on us that we did not follow its beginning. Shame on us that it is the military which promises to help our children to become the best they can be.

It is past time to reject the insidious tradition of divide and conquer. It is past time to reject educating children that they can be offered up to satisfy the social and industrial needs of the State. Nineteenth-century working class autodidacts Thomas Skidmore and David Walker are still correct, children are not property that we can decide how best to exploit and dispose of. It is time that public school education become a democratic cornucopia in which each and every child may take all of whatever they need to develop into healthy adults prepared to produce and reproduce a healthy democratic community. It is time for more schools like Covello's Benjamin Franklin.

ENDNOTES

[1]   See: Zinn; Szatmary; Gutman, *Power and Culture*; and William Manning.

[2]   For details of Shays' Rebellion see: Szatmary, passim. For details of Dorr's rebellion see: Zinn, 209-11; and, Marvin E. Gettleman, *The Dorr Rebellion: A Study in American Radicalism 1833-1849* (New York: Random House, 1973.) For details on the Working Men's Associations see: Gutman, et al., *Who Built America?* Vol.1, 319-364, passim; and, Sean Wilentz, *Chants Democratic*, passim.
        And, see: Thomas Skidmore, *The Rights of Man to Property!* (New York, 1829), in *Socialism In America From the Shakers to the Third International: A Documentary History*, ed. Albert Fried (Garden City, NY: Doubleday Anchor, 1970), 124-132; and, in: Joseph Blau, ed., *Social Theories of Jacksonian Democracy* (Indianapolis: Bobbs-Merrill, 1954), 355-364.

[3]   Dorfman, vols. I & II, passim. See, as well: Gutman, et al., *Who Built America?*, vol. I, passim.

[4]   See: Ruth Miller Elson, passim; Sean Wilentz, *Chants Democratic*, passim; and, Tomlins, passim.

[5]   Margaret Haley, Battleground: The Autobiography of Margaret A. Haley; and, Haley, "Why Teachers Should Organize," NEA *Journal of Proceedings and Addresses of the 43rd Annual Meeting* (Winona, MN: NEA, 1904), 145-152. Cubberley, *Changing Conceptions of Education*, 56-57.

[6]   Tyack and Hansot, *Managers of Virtue*, 127.

[7]   Ellwood Cubberley, *Changing Conceptions of Education*, 56.

[8]   Ellwood Cubberley, *Public Education*, 496-497.

[9]   Cubberley, *Public Education*, 484-486.

[10]   Michael Parenti, "Power And Pluralism: A View From The Bottom," *Journal of Politics*, Vol.32, August, 1970: 501-530; Jay MacLeod, *Ain't No Makin' It*, 2nd ed. (Boulder, CO: Westview Press, 1995).

[11]   See: Richard J. Herrnstein and Charles Murray, *The Bell Curve: Intelligence and Class Structure in American Life* (New York: Free Press, 1994).

[12]   Katz, *Reconstructing American Education*. Not very long after *Social Hegemony* was published, Michael Katz's *The Irony of Early School Reform* was reprinted: NY: Teacher's College Press, 2001.

[13]   From DeWitt Clinton, "Address on the Opening of a New School Building," December 11, 1809; quoted Sol Cohen, "DEWITT CLINTON ON THE LANCASTER SYSTEM (1809)," II:986.

[14]   See: footnote 129, Chapter Five, above: "Our Eastern brethren are a well-informed and moral people. In those States it is as uncommon to find a poor man who cannot read and write, as it is rare to see one in Europe who can."

[15]   Raymond A. Mohl reveals a New York Free School Society rather different from that gloriously portrayed by Ellwood Cubberley:

"An 1822 petition to the common council typified the society's position:

If we would lessen taxes by preventing pauperism; if we would lessen public burdens by diminishing crimes and offenses; if we would render the City more wealthy by increasing individual exertion and enterprize; if we would give greater peace and security to our citizens and render property more sacred; if we would give a broader basis and render firmer the foundations of our political and civil institutions — we shall encourage early education among the poor, inculcate virtuous maxims in the young mind as its powers are unfolded, and teach the principles of self-respect — industry, sobriety, enterprize and usefulness will follow.

[. . .]
"Throughout the preindustrial period the Free School Society remained one of the most important 'engines' of moral reform in New York. The society's schools used moral coercion and religious proselytizing to achieve social order in the urban community. Much of the curriculum centered on religious and moral themes. Bible readings opened a school day filled with scripture lessons and recitations from a nonsectarian catechism. School children also pored over a number of secular schoolbooks which elaborated and reinforced 'the great and generally acknowledged principles of Christianity.' For a time students even memorized passages from temperance tracts. [. . .]
"The New York free schools also adopted unique discipline methods to exact submission and proper conduct. With standard corporal punishment disallowed, Lancasterian schoolmasters used a variety of unusual techniques: six-pound logs, which, when placed on the shoulders of an offending child, bound him to his seat; arm shackles, which locked students at their desks; leg shackles, which made walking almost impossible; a small closet with barred windows for solitary detention; a cagelike arrangement, in which serious transgressors were suspended from the ceiling in full view of jeering classmates. By contrast, masters rewarded good behavior with prizes and honors. Such

methods of punishment and reward forced or induced children to conformity, subordination, and submission to authority. Free-school discipline, in other words, reinforced the moral indoctrination of classroom lessons. Both discipline and lessons consciously fostered social control."

Raymond A. Mohl, *Poverty in New York, 1783-1825* (New York: Oxford University Press, 1971), 183-84.

[16] Henry Barnard, *Sixth Annual Report* (1851), quoted David Nasaw, 35.

[17] Cubberley, *Public Education*, 485.

[18] Cubberley, *Public Education*, 700.

[19] Leonard Covello, *The Heart Is The Teacher*, passim.

SELECTED BIBLIOGRAPHY

Abbott, Edith. *Immigration: Select Documents and Case Records.* Chicago: University of Chicago Press, 1924.

———. *Historical Aspects of the Immigration Problem.* Chicago: University of Chicago Press, 1926. Reprint, New York: Arno Press, 1969.

Adams, David Wallace. *Education for Extinction: American Indians and the Boarding School Experience, 1875-1928.* Lawrence: University Press of Kansas, 1995.

Allmendinger, Jr., David F. "New England Students and the Revolution in Higher Education, 1800-1900." In *The Social History of American Education,* edited by B. Edward McClellan and William J. Reese, 65-72. Urbana: University of Illinois Press, 1988.

Altenbaugh, Richard J., ed. *The Teacher's Voice: A Social History of Teaching in Twentieth Century America.* Washington, DC: The Falmer Press, 1992.

Anderson, Charles H. *The Political Economy of Social Class.* Englewood Cliffs, NJ: Prentice-Hall, 1974.

Anderson, James D. "Secondary School History Textbooks and the Treatment of Black History." In *The State of Afro-American History, Past, Present and Future,* edited by Darlene Clark Hine, 253-274. Baton Rouge: Louisiana State University Press, 1986).

———. *The Education of Blacks in the South, 1860-1935.* Chapel Hill: University of North Carolina, 1988.

———. "Northern Foundations and the Shaping of Southern Black Rural Education, 1902-1935." In *The Social History of American Education,* edited by B. Edward McClellan and William J. Reese, 287-312. Urbana: University of Illinois Press, 1988.

Anyon, Jean. "Workers, Labor and Economic History, and Textbook Content." In *Ideology and Practice in Schooling*, edited by Michael W. Apple and Lois Weis, 37-60. Philadelphia: Temple University Press, 1983.

Aronowitz, Stanley and William DiFazio. *The Jobless Future:Sci-Tech and the Dogma of Work*. Minneapolis: University of Minneapolis Press, 1994.

Ashworth, John. *Slavery, Capitalism and Politics in the Antebellum Republic*. Vol. I. New York: Cambridge University Press, 1995.

Aston, T.H. and C.H.E. Philpin, eds. *The Brenner Debate: Agrarian Class Structure and Economic Development in Pre-Industrial Europe*. Cambridge, U.K.: Cambridge University Press, 1985.

Bagley, William C. *Education, Crime, and Social Progress*. New York: Macmillan Co., 1931.

Bailyn, Bernard. *Education in the Forming of American Society*. Chapel Hill: University of North Carolina Press, 1960. Reprint, New York: Norton, 1972.

Barolini, Helen. "The Historical and Social Context of Silence." In *The Dream Book: An Anthology of Writings by Italian American Women*, edited by Helen Barolini, 1-56. New York: Schocken Books, 1985.

Barron, Hal S. "Teach No More His Neighbor: Localism and Rural Opposition to Educational Reform." In *Mixed Harvest: The Second Great Transformation in the Rural North 1870-1930*, 43-77. Chapel Hill: University of North Carolina Press, 1997.

Beale, Howard K. *Are American Teachers Free?*. New York: Scribners, 1936. Reprint, New York: Octagon Books, 1972.

Beard, Charles A. *The Economic Interpretation of the Constitution of the United States*. New York: The Free Press, 1986.

Bedford, Henry F., ed. *Their Lives and Numbers: The Condition of Working People in Massachusetts, 1870-1900*. Ithaca, NY: Cornell University Press, 1995.

Bennett, William J. *The De-Valuing of America: The Fight for Our Culture and Our Children.* New York: Summit Books, 1992.

Betti, Emilio. "The Epistemological Problem of Understanding as an Aspect of the General Problem of Knowing." Translation by Susan Noakes. In *Hermeneutics: Questions and Prospects*, edited by Gary Shapiro and Alan Sica, 25-53. Amherst: The University of Massachusetts Press, 1984.

Bhaskar, Roy. *Scientific Realism and Human Emancipation.* London/New York: Verso, 1987.

_____. *Reclaiming Reality.* London/New York: Verso, 1989.

Binder, Frederick M. and David M. Reimers, eds. *The Way We Lived: Essays and Documents in American Social History.* Vol. I: 1607-1877. Lexington, MA: D.C. Heath, 1988.

Blau, Joseph, ed. *Social Theories of Jacksonian Democracy: Representative Writings, 1825-1850.* Indianapolis: Bobbs-Merrill, 1954.

Bledstein, Burton J. *The Culture of Professionalism: The Middle Class and the Development of Higher Education in America.* New York: Norton, 1978.

Bodnar, John, Roger Simon, and Michael P. Weber. *Lives of Their Own: Blacks, Italians, and Poles in Pittsburgh, 1900-1960.* Urbana: University of Illinois Press, 1983.

Bond, Horace Mann. *The Education of the Negro in the American Social Order.* New York: Prentice-Hall, 1934.

Bottomore, Tom, Laurence Harris, V.G. Kiernana and Ralph Miliband, eds. A *Dictionary of Marxist Thought.* 2d ed. Oxford, U.K.: Blackwell, 1991.

Bourne, Randolph S. *The Gary Schools.* Edited by Adeline and Murray Levine. Cambridge, MA: M.I.T. Press, 1970.

Bowden, Henry Warner. *American Indians and Christian Missions: Studies in Cultural Conflict.* Chicago: University of Chicago Press, 1985.

Bowles, Samuel and Herbert Gintis. *Schooling in Capitalist America: Educational Reform and the Contradictions of Economic Life.* New York: Basic Books, 1976.

Bradley, Ann Kathleen. *History of the Irish in America.* Secaucus, NJ: Chartwell Books, 1986.

Brantlinger, Patrick. "Victorians and Africans: The Genealogy of the Myth of the Dark Continent." *Critical Inquiry* 12 (Autumn 1985): 166-203.

Briggs, John W. *An Italian Passage: Immigrants to Three American Cities, 1890-1930.* New Haven: Yale University Press, 1978.

Bryman, Alan. "The Debate about Quantitative and Qualitative Research: A Question of Method or Epistemology?" *The British Journal of Sociology* 35, no. 1 (1984): 75-92.

Buhle, Paul and Alan Dawley, eds. *Working for Democracy: American Workers from the Revolution to the Present.* Urbana: University of Illinois Press, 1985.

Burns, James MacGregor and Stewart Burns. *A People's Charter: The Pursuit of Rights in America.* New York: Knopf, 1991.

Button, H. Warren and Eugene F. Provenzo, Jr. *History of Education and Culture in America.* Englewood Cliffs, NJ: Prentice-Hall, 1983.

Calhoun, John C. "Speech on the Tariff Bill (1816)," and "Exposition and Protest (1828)." *Union and Liberty: The Political Philosophy of John C. Calhoun,* 299-309, 311-365. Indianapolis: Liberty Fund, 1992.

Churchill, Charles W. *The Italians of Newark: A Community Study.* n.p. Reprint, New York: Arno Press, 1975.

Clifford, James and George E. Marcus, eds. *Writing Culture: The Poetics and Politics of Ethnography.* Berkeley: University of California Press, 1986.

Clinton, DeWitt. "DeWitt Clinton Champions the Lancasterian Plan." In *Theories of Education in Early America 1655-1819,* edited by Wilson Smith, 345-360. Indianapolis: Bobbs-Merrill, 1973.

Cohen, Ronald D. *Children of the Mill: Schooling and Society in Gary, Indiana, 1906-1960.* Bloomington: Indiana University Press, 1990.

Cohen, Sol, ed. *Education in the United States: A Documentary History.* 5 vols. New York: Random House, 1974.

Collier, Andrew. *Critical Realism: An Introduction to Roy Bhaskar's Philosophy.* London: Verso, 1994.

Commager, Henry Steele. "Schoolmaster to America," an introduction to *American Spelling Book*, by Noah Webster. New York: Teachers College/ Columbia University, 1962.

Commager, Henry Steele. *Documents of American History.* New York: Appleton-Century-Crofts, Inc., 1934.

Commons, John R., ed. *A Documentary History of American Industrial Society.* 10 Vols. Cleveland, OH: Arthur H. Clark, 1910.

Condon, Edward O'Meagher. *The Irish Race in America.* Reprint, Spring Valley, NY: Ogham House, 1976.

Cordasco, Francesco, ed. *Immigrant Children in American Schools.* Fairfield, NJ: Augustus M. Kelley, 1976.

Cordasco, Francesco and Eugene Bucchioni, eds. *The Italians: Social Backgrounds of an American Group.* Clifton, NJ: Augustus M. Kelley, 1974.

Countryman, Edward. "'Out of the Bounds of the Law': Northern Land Rioters in the Eighteenth Century." In *The American Revolution: Explorations in the History of American Radicalism*, edited by Alfred F. Young, 37-69. Dekalb: Northern Illinois University Press, 1976.

Covello, Leonard. *The Social Background of the Italo-American School Child.* Edited and introduction by Francesco Cordasco. Leiden, Netherlands: E.J.Brill, 1967.

_____. (with Guido D'Agostino). *The Heart is the Teacher.* New York: McGraw-Hill, 1958.

Craven, Avery, Walter Johnson, and F. Roger Dunn, eds. *A Documentary History of the American People.* Boston: Ginn & Co., 1951.

Cremin, Lawrence A. "Horace Mann's Legacy," an introduction to *The Republic and the School: Horace Mann on the Education of Free Men*, by Horace Mann, edited by Lawrence A. Cremin, 3-28. New York: Teachers College/Columbia University Press, 1957.

_____. *The Wonderful World of Ellwood Patterson Cubberley: An Essay on the Historiography of American Education.* New York: Teachers College/Columbia University Press, 1965.

_____. "The Outcasts." *American Education: The National Experience 1783-1876*, 218-248. New York: Harper & Row, 1980.

Cubberley, Ellwood P. *Changing Conceptions of Education.* Introduction by Henry Suzzallo. Boston: Houghton Mifflin Co., 1909.

_____. *Public School Administration.* Boston: Houghton Mifflin Co., 1916.

_____. *Public Education in the United States.* 2d ed. Boston: Houghton Mifflin Co., 1934.

_____. *The Principal and His School.* Boston: Houghton Mifflin Co., 1923.

_____. *School Organization and Administration.* Yonkers-on-Hudson, NY: World Book Company, 1923.

Curti, Merle. *The Social Ideas of American Educators.* New York: Scribners & Sons, 1935. Reprint, Totowa, NJ: Littlefield, Adams, 1960.

_____. *The Growth of American Thought.* 3d ed. New Brunswick, NJ: Transaction Publishers, 1995.

Dahl, Robert A. *Who Governs?: Democracy and Power in an American City*. New Haven, CT: Yale University Press, 1961.

Dewey, John. *How We Think*. D.C. Heath, 1910. Reprint, Buffalo, NY: Prometheus Books, 1991.

DiMaggio, Paul. "Cultural Capital and School Success: The Impact of Status Culture Participation on the Grades of U.S. High School Students." *American Sociological Review* 47 (April, 1982): 189-201.

DiMaggio, Paul and John Mohr. "Cultural Capital, Educational Attainment, and Marital Selection." *American Journal of Sociology* 90, no. 6 (1985): 1231-1261.

DiMaggio, Paul and Michael Useem. "Cultural Property and Public Policy: Emerging Tensions in Government Support for the Arts." *Social Research* 45, no.2 (Summer 1978): 356-387.

Domhoff, G. William. *The Power Elite and the State: How Policy is Made in America*. New York: Aldine De Gruyter, 1990.

Dorfman, Joseph. *The Economic Mind in American Civilization 1606-1865*. 3 Vols. New York: The Viking Press, 1946.

Douglass, Frederick. *Narrative of the Life of Frederick Douglass, an American Slave*. New York: Penguin, 1986.

Dublin, Thomas. *Women at Work: The Transformation of Work and Community in Lowell, Massachusetts, 1826-1860*. New York: Columbia University Press, 1979.

DuBois, W.E.B. *Black Reconstruction*. Millwood, NY: Kraus-Thomson Organization, 1976.

_____. *The Souls of Black Folk*. New York: Vintage/The Library of America, 1990.

Dunwell, Steve. *The Run of the Mill*. Boston: David R. Godine, 1978.

Durey, Michael. *Transatlantic Radicals and the Early American Republic*. Lawrence: University of Kansas Press, 1997.

Elson, Ruth Miller. *Guardians of Tradition: American Schoolbooks of the Nineteenth Century*. Lincoln: University of Nebraska Press, 1964.

Enzensberger, Hans Magnus. "The Industrialization of the Mind." *The Consciousness Industry*, 3-15. Edited by Michael Roloff. New York: Seabury Press, 1974.

Ernst, Joseph. "'Ideology' and an Economic Interpretation of the Revolution." In *The American Revolution: Explorations in the History of American Radicalism*, edited by Alfred F. Young, 159-185. Dekalb: Northern Illinois University Press, 1976.

Ewen, Elizabeth. *Immigrant Women in the Land of Dollars*. New York: Monthly Review Press, 1985.

Ferber, Nat J. *A New American: Justice Salvatore A. Cotillo*. New York: Farrar & Rinehart, 1938.

Finkelstein, Barbara. *Governing the Young*. New York: The Falmer Press, 1989.

Finkelstein, Barbara. "Education Historians as Mythmakers." In *Review of Research in Education 18*, edited by Gerald Grant, 255-297. Washington, DC: American Educational Research Association, 1992.

Finn, Chester E., Jr. *We Must Take Charge: Our Schools and Our Future*. New York: Free Press, 1991.

FitzGerald, Frances. *American Revised*. Boston: Little, Brown and Company, 1979.

Foner, Eric. "Tom Paine's Republic: Radical Ideology and Social Change." In *The American Revolution: Explorations in the History of American Radicalism*, edited by Alfred F. Young, 187-232. DeKalb: Northern Illinois Press, 1976.

Foner, Philip. *History of the Labor Movement in the United States, Vol. One: From Colonial Times to the Founding of the American Federation of Labor*. New York: International Publishers, 1947.

Franklin, Benjamin. "Benjamin Franklin: Worldly Wisdom and The Academy." In *Theory and Practice in the History of American Education: A Book of Readings*, edited by J. W. Hillesheim and G. D. Merrill, 94-122. Washington, DC: University Press of America, 1980.

Franklin, John Hope. *Race and History: Selected Essays 1938-1988*. Baton Rouge: Louisiana State University Press, 1989.

Frazier, Thomas R., ed. *The Underside of American History*. Vol. I *To 1877*. New York: Harcourt, Brace, Jovanovich, 1971.

Frazier, Thomas R., ed. *The Underside of American History*. Vol. I *To 1877*. 5th ed. New York: Harcourt, Brace and Jovanovich, 1987.

Fredrickson, George M. *White Supremacy*. Oxford, U.K.: Oxford University Press, 1982.

Fried, Albert, ed. *Socialism in America: From the Shakers to the Third International—A Documentary History*. Garden City, NY: Anchor Books, 1970.

Gage, N. L. "The Paradigm Wars and Their Aftermath: A 'Historical' Sketch of Research on Teaching Since 1989." *Educational Researcher* 18 (October, 1989): 4-10.

Galbraith, John Kenneth. *The Age of Uncertainty: A History of Economic Ideas and Their Consequences*. Boston: Houghton Mifflin Company, 1977.

Galenson, David. *White Servitude in Colonial America: An Economic Analysis*. New York: Cambridge University Press, 1981.

Gambino, Richard. *Blood of My Blood*. Garden City, NY: Anchor Books, 1975.

Gans, Herbert J. *The Urban Villagers: Group and Class in the Life of Italian-Americans*. Rev. ed. New York: Free Press, 1982.

Garrison, James W. "Some Principles of Postpositivistic Philosophy of Science." *Educational Researcher* 15 (November, 1986): 12-18.

Gates, Paul W. *Landlords And Tenants on the Prairie Frontier*. Ithaca, NY: Cornell University Press, 1973.

Geertz, Clifford. "Deep Play: Notes on the Balinese Cockfight." In *The Interpretation of Cultures: Selected Essays*, 412-54. New York: Basic Books, 1973.

Gilbert, Amos. *The Life of Thomas Skidmore*. Chicago: Charles H. Kerr, 1984.

Gilkeson, John S., Jr. *Middle-Class Providence, 1820-1940*. Princeton, NJ: Princeton University Press, 1986.

Gitelman, Howard M. *Workingmen of Waltham: Mobility in American Urban Industrial Development 1850-1890*. Baltimore: Johns Hopkins University Press, 1974.

Gove, Aaron. "Limitations of the Superintendents' Authority and of the Teacher's Independence." In *NEA Journal of Proceedings and Addresses of the 43rd Annual Meeting*, 152-53. Winona, MN: NEA, 1904.

Gramsci, Antonio. *An Antonio Gramsci Reader*. Edited by David Forgacs. New York: Schocken Books, 1988.

Greene, Jack P., ed. *Colonies to Nation 1763-1789: A Documentary History of the American Revolution*. New York: W.W. Norton, 1975.

Greer, Colin. *The Great School Legend*. New York: Basic Books, 1972.

Griffin, William D. *The Book of Irish Americans*. New York: Random House, 1990.

Guba, Egon G. and Yvonna S. Lincoln. "Competing Paradigms in Qualitative Research." In *Handbook of Qualitative Research*, edited by Norman K. Denzin and Yvonna S. Lincoln, 105-117. Thousand Oaks: Sage, 1994.

Gutman, Herbert G. *Power and Culture: Essays on the American Working Class*. Edited and introduction by Ira Berlin. New York: The New Press, 1987.

_____. "A Note on Immigration History, 'Breakdown Models,' and the Re-writing of the History of Immigrant Working-Class Peoples." In *Power and Culture: Essays on the American Working Class*, 255-59. New York: The New Press, 1987.

_____. "Schools for Freedom: The Post-Emancipation Origins of Afro-American Education." In *Power and Culture: Essays on the American Working Class*, 260-97. New York: The New Press, 1987.

Gutman, Herbert G. and Ira Berlin. "Class Composition and the Development of the American Working Class, 1840-1890." In *Power and Culture: Essays on the American Working Class*, by Herbert G. Gutman, 380-94. New York: The New Press, 1987.

_____. *Work, Culture and Society in Industrializing America*. New York: Vintage Books, 1966.

Gutman, Herbert G. and Gregory S. Kealey, eds. *Many Pasts: Readings in American Social History, 1865-the Present*. 2 vols. Englewood Cliffs, NJ: Prentice-Hall, 1973.

Gutman, Herbert G., Bruce Levine, Stephen Brier, David Brundage, Edward Countryman, Dorothy Fennell, Marcus Rediker. *Who Built America?: Working People and the Nation's Economy, Politics, Culture, and Society*. 2 vols. New York: Pantheon Books, 1989.

Haley, Margaret A. "Why Teachers Should Organize." In *NEA Journal of Proceedings and Addresses of the 43rd Annual Meeting*, 145-152. Winona, MN: NEA, 1904.

_____. *Battleground: The Autobiography of Margaret A. Haley*. Edited by Robert L. Reid. Urbana: University of Illinois Press, 1982.

Harley, Sharon. *The Timetables of African-American History*. New York: Touchstone, 1995.

Harrison, Barbara Grizzuti. *Foreign Bodies*. Garden City, NY: Doubleday, 1984.

Hausman, Daniel M., ed. *The Philosophy of Economics: An Anthology.* New York: Cambridge University Press, 1984.

Hendin, Josephine Gattuso. *The Right Thing To Do.* Boston: David R. Godine, 1988.

Herrnstein, Richard J. and Charles Murray. *The Bell Curve: Intelligence and Class Structure in American Life.* New York: Free Press, 1994.

Hiley, David R., James F. Bohman, and Richard Shusterman, eds. *The Interpretive Turn: Philosophy, Science, Culture.* Ithaca, NY: Cornell University Press, 1991.

Hobsbawm, Eric and Terence Ranger, eds. *The Invention of Tradition.* Cambridge, U.K.: Canto/Cambridge University Press, 1992.

Hoerder, Dirk. "Boston Leaders and Boston Crowds, 1765-1776." In *The American Revolution: Explorations in the History of American Radicalism*, edited by Alfred F. Young, 233-271. DeKalb: Northern Illinois University Press, 1976.

Hollinger, David A. and Charles Capper, eds. *The American Intellectual Tradition.* 2 vols. New York: Oxford University Press, 1997.

Holt, Thomas. "'Knowledge is Power': The Black Struggle for Literacy." In *The Right to Literacy*, edited by Andrea Lunsford, Helene Moglen, and James Slevin, 91-102. New York: MLA, 1990.

House, Ernest R. "Realism in Research." *Educational Researcher* 20, no. 6 (August-September 1991): 2-25.

Hughes, Jonathan. *American Economic History.* 3d ed. New York: HarperCollins, 1990.

Hunter, Jane. *The Gospel of Gentility: American Women Missionaries in Turn-of-the-Century China.* New Haven, CT: Yale University Press, 1984.

Hyneman, Charles S. and Donald S. Lutz, eds. *American Political Writing during the Founding Era: 1760-1805.* Indianapolis: Liberty Press, 1983.

Iorizzo, Luciano J. and Salvatore Mondello. *The Italian Americans.* Boston: Twayne Publishers, 1980.

Jefferson, Thomas. *Crusade against Ignorance.* Edited by Gordon C. Lee. New York: Teachers College/Columbia University Press, 1961.

_____. "Report of the Commissioners for the University of Virginia, 1818." *Public and Private Papers*, 132-47. New York: Vintage/The Library of America, 1990.

Jordan, Winthrop D. *White over Black: American Attitudes toward the Negro, 1550-1812.* Chapel Hill: University of North Carolina Press, 1968. Reprint, New York: W. W. Norton, 1977.

Kaestle, Carl F. *The Evolution of an Urban School System: New York City, 1750-1850.* Cambridge, MA: Harvard University Press, 1973.

_____. *Pillars of the Republic: Common Schools and American Society, 1780-1860.* New York: Hill and Wang, 1983.

Kaestle, Carl F. and Maris A. Vinovskis. *Education and Social Change in Nineteenth-Century Massachusetts.* Cambridge, U.K.: Cambridge University Press, 1980.

Karier, Clarence J. *The Individual, Society, and Education: A History of American Educational Ideas.* Urbana: University of Illinois Press, 1967.

Kasson, John F. *Civilizing the Machine: Technology and Republican Values in America, 1776-1900.* New York: Grossman, 1976.

Katz, Michael B. *The Irony of Early School Reform.* Cambridge, MA: Harvard University Press, 1968.

_____. *Class, Bureaucracy, and Schools: The Illusion of Educational Change in America.* New York: Praeger, 1971.

_____. *Reconstructing American Education*. Cambridge, MA: Harvard University Press, 1987.

_____. "The Origins of Public Education: A Reassessment." In *Social History of American Education*, edited by B. Edward McClellan and William J. Reese, 91-117. Urbana, IL: University of Illinois Press, 1988.

_____. "The Urban 'Underclass' as a Metaphor of Social Transformation." In *The "Underclass" Debate: Views from History*, edited by Michael B. Katz, 3-26. Princeton: Princeton University Press, 1993.

Kay, Marvin L. Michael. "The North Carolina Regulation, 1766-1776: A Class Conflict." In *The American Revolution: Explorations in the History of American Radicalism*, edited by Alfred F. Young, 71-123. DeKalb: Northern Illinois Press, 1976.

Kent, Noel J. *Hawaii: Islands under the Influence*. Honolulu: University of Hawaii Press, 1993.

King, Kenneth James. *Pan-Africanism and Education*. Oxford, U.K.: Clarendon Press, 1971.

Kliebard, Herbert M. *Forging the American Curriculum*. New York: Routledge, 1992.

Kozol, Jonathan. *Savage Inequalities*. New York: Crown, 1991.

Kohl, Herbert. *I Won't Learn from You!*. Minneapolis: Milkweed Editions, 1991.

Kuhn, Thomas S. *The Structure of Scientific Revolutions*. Chicago: University of Chicago Press, 1962.

_____. *The Essential Tension*. Chicago: University of Chicago Press, 1977.

Kulikoff, Allan. *The Agrarian Origins of American Capitalism*. Charlottesville: University Press of Virginia, 1992.

Jaher, Frederic Cople. *The Urban Establishment*. Urbana, IL: University of Illinois Press, 1982.

Joyce, Patrick, ed. *Class*. New York: Oxford University Press, 1995.

Lause, Mark A. "The Hard-Earned Obscurity of Thomas Skidmore," an introduction to *The Life Of Thomas Skidmore*, by Amos Gilbert. Chicago: Charles H. Kerr, 1984.

Lazerson, Marvin. "Urban Reform and the Schools: Kindergartens in Massachusetts, 1870-1915." *History of Education Quarterly* 11, no.2 (Summer 1971): 115-42.

Lears, Jackson. *Fables of Abundance*. New York: Basic Books, 1994.

Lerner, Gerda, ed. *Black Women in White America: A Documentary History*. New York: Vintage, 1992.

Levy, Leonard W. *Jefferson and Civil Liberties: The Darker Side*. Chicago: Ivan R. Dee, 1989.

Levy, Michael B., ed. *Political Thought in America: An Anthology*. Prospect Heights, IL: Waveland Press, 1992.

Licht, Walter. *Getting Work: Philadelphia, 1840-1950*. Cambridge, MA: Harvard University Press, 1992.

Luther, Seth. "An Address to the Working-Men of New-England.(1832)" In *Religion, Reform, and Revolution: Labor Panaceas in the Nineteenth Century*, edited by Leon Stein and Philip Taft. New York: Arno Press, 1969.

MacLeod, Jay. *Ain't No Makin' It: Aspirations and Attainment in a Low-Income Neighborhood*. 2d ed. Boulder, CO: Westview Press, 1995.

Mangione, Jerre and Ben Morreale. *La Storia: Five Centuries of the Italian American Experience*. New York: HarperCollins, 1992.

Mann, Horace. *Annual Reports*. 12 vols. Washington, DC: NEA/Horace Mann League, 1947.

_____. "Twelfth Annual Report (1848)." In *The Republic and the School: Horace Mann on the Education of Free Men*, edited by Lawrence A. Cremin, 79-112. New York: Teachers College/Columbia University Press, 1957.

_____. "From Report for 1841 'Pecuniary Value of Education." *The American Mind*, edited by Harry R. Warfel, Ralph H. Gabriel, and Stanley T. Williams, I: 430-31. New York: American Book Company, 1937.

Manning, William. *The Key of Liberty: The Life and Democratic Writings of William Manning, "a Laborer," 1747-1814*. Edited and introduction by Michael Merrill and Sean Wilentz. Cambridge, MA: Harvard University Press, 1993.

Markowitz, Ruth Jacknow. *My Daughter, the Teacher: Jewish Teachers in the New York City Schools*. New Brunswick, NJ: Rutgers University Press, 1993.

Marx, Karl. "*The Communist Manifesto*." In *Karl Marx: Selected Writings*, edited by David McLellan. New York: Oxford University Press, 1977.

_____. *A Contribution to the Critique of Political Economy*. Translation by S.W. Ryazanskaya, and edited by Maurice Dobb. New York: International Publishers, 1970.

_____. *Value, Price and Profit*. Translated and edited by Eleanor Marx Aveling and Edward Aveling. Chicago: Charles H. Kerr & Company Co-operative, n.d.

_____. *Grundrisse*. Foreword and translation by Martin Nicolaus. London: Penguin Books, 1973.

_____. *Marx on Economics*. Edited by Robert Freedman. New York: Harvest Books, 1961.

_____. *Marxist Social Thought*. Edited by Robert Freedman. New York: Harvest Books, 1968.

Matthews, Sr. Mary Fabian. "The Role of the Public School in the Assimilation of the Italian Immigrant Child in the New York City, 1900-1914." In

The Italian Experience in the United States, edited by Silvano M. Tomasi and Madeline H. Engel, 125-141. Staten Island, NY: Center For Migration Studies, 1970.

McClellan, B. Edward and William J. Reese, eds. *The Social History of American Education*. Urbana: University of Illinois Press, 1988.

McCulloch, Hugh. *Men and Measures of Half a Century*. New York: Charles Scribner's Sons, 1888. Reprint, New York: DaCapo Press, 1970.

Merrill, Michael and Sean Wilentz. "William Manning and the Invention of American Politics," an introduction to *The Key of Liberty*, by William Manning, 1-88. Cambridge, MA: Harvard University Press, 1993.

Messerli, Jonathan. *Horace Mann: A Biography*. New York: Knopf, 1971.

Meszaros, Istvan. *The Power of Ideology*. Washington Square, NY: New York University Press, 1989.

Meyer, Adolphe E. *An Educational History of the American People*. New York: McGraw-Hill, 1957.

Meyers, Marvin. *The Jacksonian Persuasion: Politics and Belief*. Stanford, CA: Stanford University Press, 1957.

Mohl, Raymond A. *Poverty in New York: 1783-1825*. New York: Oxford University Press, 1971.

Mooney, Patrick H. and Theo J. Majka. *Farmers' and Farm Workers' Movements: Social Protest in American Agriculture*. New York: Twayne, 1995.

Mulligan, William. "From Artisan to Proletarian: The Family and the Vocational Education of the Shoemaker in the Handicraft Era." In *Life and Labor: Dimensions of American Working-Class History*, edited by Charles Stephenson and Robert Asher, 22-36. Albany: State University of New York Press, 1986.

Murphy, Marjorie. *Blackboard Unions: The AFT & the NEA, 1900-1980*. Ithaca, NY: Cornell University Press, 1992.

Nasaw, David. *Schooled to Order: A Social History of Public Schooling in the United States*. New York: Oxford University Press, 1979.

Nash, Gary B. "Social Change and the Growth of Prerevolutionary Urban Radicalism." In *The American Revolution: Explorations in the History of American Radicalism*, edited by Alfred F. Young, 3-36. DeKalb: Northern Illinois University Press, 1976.

Nelli, Humbert S. "Italians in Urban America." In *The Italian Experience in the United States*, edited by Silvano M. Tomasi and Madeline H. Engel, 77-107. New York: Center for Migration Studies, 1970.

_____. *Italians in Chicago, 1880-1930: A Study in Ethnic Mobility*. New York: Oxford University Press, 1970.

_____. *From Immigrants to Ethnics: The Italian Americans*. New York: Oxford University Press, 1983.

O'Connor, Thomas H. *The Boston Irish: A Political History*. Boston: Northeastern University Press, 1995.

Olneck, Michael R. and Marvin Lazerson. "The School   Achievement of Immigrant Children: 1900-1930." In *The Social History of American Education*, edited by B. Edward McClellan and William J. Reese, 257-286. Urbana: University of Illinois Press, 1988.

Pessen, Edward. *Most Uncommon Jacksonians: The Radical Leaders of the Early Labor Movement*. Albany: State University of New York Press, 1967.

_____. *Riches, Class, and Power*. New Brunswick, NJ: Transaction, 1990.

Quarles, Benjamin. "The Revolutionary War as a Black Declaration of Independence." In *Slavery and Freedom in the Age of the American Revolution*, edited by Ira Berlin and Ronald Hoffman, 283-301. Urbana: University of Illinois Press, 1986.

Ravitch, Diane. *The Revisionists Revised: A Critique of the Radical Attack on the Schools*. New York: Basic Books, 1978.

Reese, William J. *Power and the Promise of School Reform: Grass-roots Movements During the Progressive Era*. Boston: Routledge & Kegan Paul, 1986.

Riis, Jacob. *Jacob Riis Revisited: Poverty and the Slum in Another Era*. Edited and introduction by Francesco Cordasco. Garden City, NY: Doubleday Anchor, 1968.

Roediger, David R. *The Wages of Whiteness: Race and the Making of the American Working Class*. London/New York: Verso, 1991.

Roll, Eric. *A History of Economic Thought*. Rev. ed. London: Faber & Faber, 1992.

Ross, Edward A. *Civic Sociology: A Textbook in Social and Civic Problems for Young Americans*. 2d ed. Yonkers-on-Hudson, NY: World Book Co., 1935.

Ross, Steven J. *Workers on the Edge: Work, Leisure, and Politics in Industrializing Cincinnati, 1788-1890*. New York: Columbia University Press, 1985.

Rozwenc, Edwin C., ed. *Ideology and Power in the Age of Jackson*. Garden City, NY: Anchor Books, 1964.

Rude, George. *Ideology and Popular Protest*. Chapel Hill: University of North Carolina Press, 1995.

Rush, Benjamin. *The Selected Writings of Benjamin Rush*. Edited by Dagobert D. Runes. New York: Philosophical Library, 1947.

_____. "Plan for the Establishment of Public Schools." In *Essays on Education in the Early Republic*, edited by Frederick Rudolph, 3-23. Cambridge, MA: Harvard University Press, 1965.

Sayer, Andrew. *Method in Social Science: A Realist Approach*. 2d ed. New York: Routledge, 1994.

Schnapper, M. B. *American Labor*. Washington, DC: Public Affairs Press, 1972.

Scott, Anne Firor. "The Ever-Widening Circle: The Diffusion of Feminist Values from the Troy Female Seminary, 1822-1872." In *Social History of American Education*, edited by B. Edward McClellan and William J. Reese, 137-159. Urbana: University of Illinois Press, 1988.

Shively, W. Phillips. *Power and Choice: An Introduction to Political Science*. 4th ed. New York: McGraw-Hill, 1995.

Skidmore, Thomas. "The Rights of Man to Property!." In *Socialism in America from the Shakers to the Third International: A Documentary History*, edited by Albert Fried, 124-132. Garden City, NY: Doubleday Anchor, 1970; and in *Social Theories of Jacksonian Democracy*, edited by Joseph Blau, 355-364. Indianapolis: Bobbs-Merrill, 1954.

Smith, Billy G. *The "Lower Sort": Philadelphia's Laboring People, 1750-1800*. Ithaca, NY: Cornell University Press, 1990.

Smith, John K. "Quantitative Versus Interpretive: The Problem of Conducting Social Inquiry." *In Philosophy of Evaluation*, edited by Ernest R. House, 27-51. San Francisco: Jossey-Bass Inc., 1983.

Sowell, Thomas. *Ethnic America*. New York: Basic Books, 1981.

Speranza, Gino C. "Forced Labor in West Virginia." In *A Documentary History of the Italian Americans*, edited by Wayne Moquin and Charles Van Doren, 117-121. New York: Praeger, 1974.

Spring, Joel. *The American School: 1642-1993*. 3d ed. New York: McGraw-Hill, 1994.

Staff, Social Sciences, University of Chicago. *The People Shall Judge: Readings in the Formation of American Policy*. 2 vols. Chicago: University of Chicago Press, 1949.

Steinberg, Stephen. *The Ethnic Myth: Race, Ethnicity, and Class in America*. 2d ed. Boston: Beacon Press, 1989.

Steinfeld, Robert J. *The Invention of Free Labor*. Chapel Hill: University of North Carolina Press, 1991.

Stockham, Peter, ed. *Old-Time Crafts and Trades.* Part II. Whitehall (Phila-delphia) and Richmond: Jacob Johnson, 1807. Reprint, New York: Do-ver, 1992.

_____. *Early Nineteenth-Century Crafts and Trades.* Part III. Whitehall (Philadelphia) and Richmond: Jacob Johnson, 1807. Reprint, New York: Dover, 1992.

Story, Ronald. "Harvard Students, the Boston Elite, and the New England Pre-paratory System." In *The Social History of American Education,* edited by B. Edward McClellan and William J. Reese, 73-90. Urbana: University of Illinois Press, 1988.

Sugrue, Thomas J. "The Structures of Urban Poverty: The Reorganization of Space and Work in Three Periods of American History." In *The "Underclass" Debate: Views from History,* edited by Michael B. Katz, 118-160. Princeton, NJ: Princeton University Press, 1993.

Suzzallo, Henry. "Editor's Introduction," to *Changing Conceptions of Edu-cation,* by Ellwood P. Cubberley. Boston: Houghton Mifflin Co., 1909.

Szatmary, David P. *Shays' Rebellion: The Making of an Agrarian Insur-rection.* Amherst: The University of Massachusetts Press, 1980.

Taylor, Charles. *Philosophy and the Human Sciences: Philosophical Pa-pers.* 2 vols. Cambridge, U.K.: Cambridge University Press, 1985.

Taylor, Frederick Winslow. *The Principles of Scientific Management.* Re-print ed. New York: W. W. Norton, 1967.

Thernstrom, Stephan and Richard Sennett, eds. *Nineteenth-Century Cities: Essays in the New Urban History.* New Haven, CT: Yale University Press, 1969.

Thompson, E.P. *The Making of the English Working Class.* New York: Vintage Press, 1966.

Thorndike, Edward L. "The Elimination of Pupils from School (1907)." In *Immigrant Children in American Schools,* edited by Francesco Cordasco, 217-280. Fairfield, NJ: Augustus M. Kelley, 1976.

Tindall, George Brown and David E. Shi. *America: A Narrative History*. 4th ed. New York: W.W. Norton, 1996.

Tomasi, S.M. and M.H. Engel, eds. *The Italian Experience in the United States*. Staten Island, NY: Center for Migration Studies, 1970.

Tomlins, Christopher L. *Law, Labor, and Ideology in the Early American Republic*. New York: Cambridge University Press, 1993.

Troen, Selwyn K. "Popular Education in Nineteenth-Century St. Louis." In *Social History of American Education*, edited by B. Edward McClellan and William J. Reese, 119-136. Urbana, IL: University of Illinois Press, 1988.

Tyack, David. *The One Best System: A History of American Urban Education*. Cambridge, MA: Harvard University Press, 1974.

Tyack, David and Elisabeth Hansot. *Managers of Virtue: Public School Leadership in America, 1820-1980*. New York: Basic Books, 1982.

Ulin, Richard Otis. *The Italo-American Student in the American Public School*. New York: Arno Press, 1975.

Urban, Wayne and Jennings Wagoner, Jr. *American Education: A History*. New York: McGraw-Hill, 1996.

Vidal, Gore. "The Day the American Empire Ran Out of Gas." *At Home: Essays 1982-1988*, 105-114. New York: Vintage, 1990.

Violas, Paul. *The Training of the Urban Working Class: A History of Twentieth Century American Education*. Chicago: Rand McNally College Publishing Co., 1978.

Walker, David. *To the Coloured Citizens of the World, but in particular, and very expressly, to those of the United States of America*. Edited and introduction by Sean Wilentz. Boston: by the author, 1829, 1830. Reprint, New York: Hill and Wang, 1995.

Warfel, Harry R., Ralph H. Gabriel, and Stanley T. Williams, eds. *The American Mind*. 2 vols. New York: American Book Company, 1937.

Wayland, Francis. *The Elements of Political Economy*. Rev. ed. Boston: Gould and Lincoln, 1860.

Webster, Noah. "On the Education of Youth in America." In *Essays on Education in the Early Republic*, edited by Frederick Rudolph, 41-77. Cambridge, MA: Harvard University Press, 1965.

Weiss, Bernard J., ed. *American Education and the European Immigrant, 1840-1940*. Urbana: University of Illinois Press, 1982.

Welter, Rush. *The Mind of America 1820-1860*. New York: Columbia University Press, 1975.

_____. *American Writings on Popular Education: The Nineteenth Century*. Indianapolis: The Bobbs-Merrill Co., n.d.

Whittemore, Robert C. *Makers of the American Mind*. New York: William Morrow & Co., 1964.

Whyte, William Foote. *Street Corner Society: The Social Structure of an Italian Slum*. 2d ed. Chicago: University of Chicago Press, 1993.

Wilentz, Sean. *Chants Democratic: New York City & the Rise of the American Working Class, 1788-1850*. New York: Oxford University Press, 1986.

_____. "Society, Politics, and the Market Revolution, 1815-1848." In *The New American History*, edited by Eric Foner, 61-84. Rev. ed. Philadelphia: Temple University Press, 1997.

_____. "The Rise of the American Working Class, 1776-1877." In *Perspectives on American Labor History*, edited by J. Carroll Moody and Alice Kessler-Harris, 81-151. DeKalb: Northern Illinois University Press, 1990.

Wood, Ellen Meiksins. *Democracy Against Capitalism: Renewing Historical Materialism*. Cambridge, U.K.: Cambridge University Press, 1995.

Woodson, Carter G. *The Education of the Negro Prior to 1861*. New York: Arno Press, 1968.

Wright, Carroll D. *Industrial Depressions: The First Annual Report of the United States Commissioner of Labor.* New York: Augustus M. Kelley, 1968.

Young, Alfred F. "George Robert Twelves Hewes (1742-1840): A Boston Shoemaker and the Memory of the American Revolution." In *The New England Working Class and the New Labor History*, edited by Herbert G. Gutman and Donald H. Bell, 3-71. Urbana: University of Illinois Press, 1987.

Young, Alfred F., ed. *The American Revolution: Explorations in the History of American Radicalism.* DeKalb: Northern Illinois University Press, 1976.

Zinn, Howard. *A People's History of the United States.* New York: Perennial Library, 1980.

Zonderman, David A. *Aspirations and Anxieties: New England Workers and the Mechanized Factory System 1815-1850.* New York: Oxford University Press, 1992.

ACKNOWLEDGMENTS

I want to acknowledge the following persons who helped along the way: Francesco Cordasco, Stuart McAninch, Dianne Smith, Morteza Ardebili, Jeffrey Longhofer, Vincenzo Milione, James Sturgeon, Ralph Parish, Henry Auster, Caesar Blake, Joe and Charlotte Stornello, and my children, Michael and Lorenza. I also want to thank Dean Anthony J. Tamburri, Itala Pelizzoli, Carmine Pizzirusso, Sian Gibby, and Lisa Cicchetti of the Calandra Institute staff who made this second edition possible.

This essay first appeared as my dissertation, submitted to and accepted by the University of Missouri in Kansas City in July of 1998. Portions of chapters 4 and 5 appear in altered form as "Teacher Education, Knowledge Most Worth, and Ellwood P. Cubberley," in *Advances in Teacher Education, Volume 5: What Counts as Knowledge in Teacher Education?*, eds. James D. Raths and Amy C. McAninch (Stamford CT: Ablex, 1999).

CONTRIBUTORS

Joe A. Stornello is an Italian American born 1951 in the former industrial city of Flint, Michigan. He graduated from Northwestern High School in 1969, and has degrees from Michigan State University, the University of Toronto and the University of Missouri at Kansas City (UMKC, Ph.D., 1998). Stornello's doctoral studies encompassed Urban Leadership and Policy Studies in Education, Curriculum and Instruction, and Economics, Political Science, and Sociology. In addition to numerous other scholastic awards, he was twice a Chancellor's Interdisciplinary Doctoral Fellow, UMKC's highest academic distinction. Stornello is proud of having been employed as a dishwasher, house painter, factory worker, photographer, high school teacher and university instructor. His interdisciplinary research has focused on literacy and learning, schools and society, ethnicity and class, and democratic community development. For several years he has been using a camera to document what he describes as concentrated moments of social history.

Vincenzo Milione is the Director of Demographic Studies at the John D. Calandra Italian American Institute of the City University of New York. Dr. Milione is responsible for social science research on Italian Americans as well as conducting institutional research on CUNY faculty, administrative staff, and students for civil rights and affirmative action purposes. His research has included: the educational and occupational achievement of Italian Americans; Italian language studies at the elementary and secondary levels; high school non-completion rates; negative media portrayals of ethnic populations; and Italy/U.S. student exchange programs. Milione is a technical civil rights expert designated by Federal Judge Constance Baker Motley for affirmative action. He received his Ph.D. from SUNY Buffalo in Civil Engineering, specializing in socioengineering systems. He earned his B.S. in Physics and M.S. in Earth and Space Sciences from SUNY Stony Brook. Milione has received four honorary doctorates and five honorary professorships. He is a Board Director of the Association of Italian American Educators and the Council of Latin American Educators.

INDEX

achievement ideology, xiii, xiv, 1, 10, 35–117

Adams, Sam, 46

American immigrant groups, xiii

American society, xiii, xiv

Anderson, James D., 32, 99n37

antebellum period, 5, 9, 29

Ardebili, Morteza, 299

Armstrong, Samuel, 142

atomistic theory, 3, 4

Auster, Henry, 299

autodidact laborers, 14, 15, 29

Aydelott, B.P., 163, 248n128

Bailyn, Bernard, 128

Barlett, H., 115n158

Barnard, Henry, 128

Berlin, Ira, 110n102

Berlin, James, 19n19

Bhaskar, Roy, 18n16, 19n20, 36

Biddle, Nicholas, 71

Black Americans, 2, 39, 101n54, 103n70

Blake, Caesar, 299

Blatchly, Dr. Cornelius, 106n88

Bourdoin, James, 46

British colonial order, 14

Brooks, Rev. Charles, 204n40

Brownson, Orestes, 68

Bryant, William Cullen, 105n79

Butts, R. Freeman, 161

Byllesby, Landon, 106n88

Calhoun, William B., 181

capitalism, 3, 17n11

Carlyle, Thomas, 85

Carter, James, 72

children, xiii, xvii, 14, 15, 30, 93, 148

class fractions, 8, 18n15

Clinton, DeWitt, 240n38

Collier, Andrew, 19n21, 36

colonial period, 9

colonies, xiv

Combe, George, 84

congruence, 124n2

Cook, Noah, 61

Cooper, Thomas, 57

Cordasco, Francesco, 299

Covello, Leonardo, 246n104, 271

covenants and residential segregation, xiv, xv

Cremin, Lawrence, 2, 12, 21, 163, 184

Cubberley, Ellwood P., xxi, 116n160, 116n162, 127

culture, xiii, 1–20, 16n9, 18n17

Curti, Merle, 33n14, 163, 184

definition of truth/criterion of truth, 10, 19n21

DeGamo, Charles, 152

Democratic ideology, 258

Democratic Party, 61

Democratic radicalism, xiv, 13, 14

Democratic society, xiv, 35–117

Dewey, John, 36, 95n3

Dexter, Franklin, 214–15

Dickens, Charles, 85

disciplinary institution, 14

dominant ideological paradigm, 21

Dorfman, Joseph, 3, 58

D'Souza, Dinesh, 2

Duane, William, 108–09n99

DuBois, W.E.B., 141

Dwight, Edmund, 76

Dwight, Henry E., 204n40

economic conditions of production, i

educational history texts, xvii–xx

English common law, 14, 35–117

Enzensberger, Hans Magnus, 93

epistemic fallacy, 10, 19n20

ethnic culture, 2

Evans, George Henry, 68

Everett, Edward, 70, 76

www.ingramcontent.com/pod-product-compliance
Lightning Source LLC
Chambersburg PA
CBHW080129270326
41926CB00021B/4409